IN DOUBT

IN DOUBT

The Psychology of the
Criminal Justice Process

DAN SIMON

Harvard University Press

Cambridge, Massachusetts

London, England

2012

Library of Congress Cataloging-in-Publication Data

Simon, Dan, 1955–
In doubt : the psychology of the criminal justice process / Dan Simon.
    p.   cm.
Includes bibliographical references and index.
ISBN 978-0-674-04615-3 (alk. paper)
1. Criminal justice, Administration of—Psychological aspects.
2. Criminal investigations—Psychological aspects.
3. Judicial process—Psychological aspects.   I. Title.
HV7419.S57   2012
364.01'9—dc23   2011038133

This book is dedicated to
my parents, Myra and Smoky, for their
boundless support,
and to Anne for the superb partnership.

CONTENTS

IN DOUBT

1

INTRODUCTION

Criminal punishment is the most palpable and ubiquitous means by which the state maintains social order. However, before it unleashes its punitive powers, the state must determine with high certitude which human behaviors amounted to criminal events, and who perpetrated them. This feat requires compliance with an intricate legal regime that constitutes the criminal justice process. The workings of this process and the accuracy of the verdicts it produces are the subject of this book.

The following three cases offer a glimpse into the operation of the criminal justice process. Peter Rose, a California man, was charged with the rape of a thirteen-year-old girl. On the stand, the victim stated that she was 100 percent certain that Rose was her assailant, and a bystander witness stated that the perpetrator was either Rose "or his twin brother."[1] Bruce Godschalk of Pennsylvania was charged with two counts of burglary and forcible rape. The case against Godschalk was replete with incriminating evidence: one of the victims identified him; a jailhouse informant testified that he made inculpatory statements; and a forensic expert provided a blood-typing match. Critically, the prosecution presented a thirty-three-minute tape recording in which Godschalk confessed to the crimes, providing specific details that could not have been known to the public.[2] In his confession, Godschalk blamed his crime on his drinking problem, and added, "I'm very sorry for what I've done to these two nice women."[3] Kirk Bloodsworth was charged with the capital offense of raping and murdering a nine-year-old Maryland girl. At trial, Bloodsworth was identified by five eyewitnesses. The prosecution also provided testimony of statements he made about the rock that was used as the murder weapon, and a forensic investigator testified that the murderer's shoe print matched Bloodsworth's shoes.[4]

In all three cases, the evidence of guilt was indeed compelling, and the men were found guilty beyond a reasonable doubt. Rose was sentenced to twenty-seven years in prison, Godschalk was sentenced to 10–20 years, and Bloodsworth was given a death sentence. For years, nothing seemed out of the ordinary with these convictions, until DNA testing showed that none of these men had actually perpetrated the crime for which he was being punished. The witnesses who testified in these cases were mostly wrong, especially on the crucial aspect concerning the identity of the men who committed the crimes. By the time Rose was released, he had served eight years in prison, Godschalk had served fourteen and a half, and Bloodsworth had served eight years, two of which were on death row.

These cases raise a series of difficult questions pertaining to the functioning of both the investigative and adjudicative phases of the criminal justice processes: What caused the witnesses to provide mistaken testimony? Why did the police investigators, prosecutors, and jurors believe the witnesses? Could the mistakes have been caught? Most importantly, what can be done to prevent such occurrences in the future?

The View from Experimental Psychology

One of the obvious features of the criminal justice process is that it is operationalized mostly through people: witnesses, detectives, suspects, lawyers, judges, and jurors. The wheels of the system are turned by the mental operations of these actors: memories, recognitions, assessments, inferences, social influence, and decisions, all tied in with moral judgments, emotions, and motivations. Criminal verdicts can be no better than the combined result of the mental operations of the people involved in the process. It thus seems sensible to examine the workings of the criminal justice process from a psychological perspective. Fortunately, a large body of experimental psychological research is at our disposal. For some decades now, legal psychologists have been earnestly studying the conditions under which people tend to succeed or fail in fulfilling their designated roles in the operation of the criminal justice process. Likewise, research in a range of related fields—notably cognitive psychology, social psychology, and decision making—has accumulated a wealth of knowledge about the mental processing that is inevitably implicated in the workings of the process.

The principal endeavor undertaken in this book is to apply a part of this vast and dispersed body of experimental psychology toward a better understanding of the operation of the criminal justice process. The overall observation that emanates from this research is that human performance on the tasks involved in the process can be exceedingly complicated and nuanced. Tasks that are generally taken for granted—such as identifying a stranger, remembering a specific detail from an event, and ascertaining the accuracy of such testimonies—are not as straightforward as they seem. The accuracy of these tasks is contingent on multitudes of factors, many of which are unknown, underappreciated, and easily overwhelmed by the harsh reality of crime investigations and the contentious legal process that ensues.

This observation leads to the twofold claim that lies at the heart of this book: first, in nontrivial criminal cases, the evidence produced at the investigative phase—in particular, human testimony—comprises an unknown mix of accurate and erroneous testimony, and is thus not always indicative of the defendant's guilt. The following four chapters are devoted to providing insight into the prospect of error in criminal investigations. Chapter 2 explores the work of police investigators, focusing on the conditions that can facilitate and even stoke mistaken investigative conclusions. Chapter 3 deals with the topic of identification of perpetrators by eyewitnesses. Chapter 4 examines witnesses' memory of the criminal event. Chapter 5 deals with the interrogation of suspects.

The second key claim is that the ensuing adjudicatory phase is not well suited to ascertain the accuracy of the evidence, and thus cannot distinguish reliably between guilty and innocent defendants. The limited diagnostic capabilities of the adjudicatory process are the subject of the two subsequent chapters. Chapter 6 explores problems that fact finders encounter in determining the truth from the evidence presented at trial. Chapter 7 examines the efficacy of the legal mechanisms that are designed to support the fact finders in performing that task.

In sum, the research will indicate that criminal investigations are prone to produce evidence that contains substantial errors, which the adjudicatory process is generally incapable of correcting. The compounded problems with the accuracy of the investigative phase and the diagnosticity of the adjudicatory phase lead to the conclusion that the criminal justice process falls short of meeting the level of certitude that befits its solemn nature.[5] This shortfall is generally overlooked or denied by the people entrusted with designing and governing the system—notably, police personnel, prosecutors, judges, and law makers—and it is not adequately recognized in the scholarly and public debates. Chapter 8 examines the implications of this state of affairs and explores some systemic ways to promote the accuracy of the process.

Process Breakdowns

Criminal cases can break down in two ways. A person who perpetrated a crime might escape punishment, or an innocent person might be convicted and punished for a crime he did not commit.[6] The failure to convict guilty people—which can be loosely labeled *false acquittals* (even though most such cases do not make it to a formal acquittal at trial)—is a grave problem for an ordered society. Fewer than one-half of felony crimes are ever reported to the police,[7] and only one of every five reported felonies is cleared by an arrest.[8] Crimes are unlikely to be cleared, for example, when they are not witnessed, when the witnesses refuse to cooperate with the police, or when the witnesses cannot provide the necessary information to solve the case.[9] In these instances, the criminal justice process fails because it lacks the requisite evidence to attain a conviction. The psychological research is best suited to provide insight into cases in which evidence *is* present, particularly by identifying the conditions that make that evidence more or less likely to sustain an accurate conviction. Thus, this book will focus mostly, though not exclusively, on false convictions. It is important to note that some key recommendations proposed in this book are designed to enhance the accuracy of the evidence overall and thus stand also to reduce the incidence of false acquittals.

The steady flow of exonerations in recent years has turned a spotlight onto the accuracy of the criminal justice process.[10] Many of these exonerations have resulted from the work of the Innocence Project, co-founded by Barry Scheck and Peter Neufeld. Some critics of the system describe the recent revelations of false convictions as a momentous, even revolutionary, event.[11] In contrast, proponents of the system steadfastly trivialize their import and dismiss them as "an insignificant minimum."[12] According to a data set maintained by the Innocence Project, 281 convicted inmates have been exonerated on the basis of DNA testing as of the beginning of December 2011,[13] and many more have been exonerated by other types of evidence.[14] The true number of false convictions is unknown and frustratingly unknowable. Based on exoneration data in two categories of capital homicide, the rate of error is estimated at about 3–4 percent, with a possible upper boundary of 5 percent.[15] The rate of false convictions is most likely considerably higher. Given the difficult, even tortuous, legal hurdles that stand in the way of exposing false convictions, there is no doubt that a large number of falsely convicted persons have not been, and will never be, exonerated. While a detailed argument on the incidence of false convictions is beyond the scope of this book, it is worth noting that an innocent defendant stands a chance of exoneration if he was convicted for murder or rape;[16] did not accept a plea bargain;[17] was sentenced to a lengthy prison term;[18] and was able to secure good legal representation and investigation in the post-conviction phases. It is essential also that the case centered upon the identity of the perpetrator;[19] physical or otherwise strongly exculpating evidence was present;[20] and that the exculpating evidence was collected,[21] properly preserved,[22] and made available to the defendant.[23] A healthy dose of luck can be very helpful,[24] and in the absence of DNA evidence, it is all but essential.[25] Innocent people for whom any of these conditions do not obtain are unlikely to be exonerated, because the errors underlying their convictions will rarely be detected.

False convictions are the joint product of breakdowns in both the investigative and adjudicative phases of the criminal process. These breakdowns call for a closer look at the system's methods of sorting out criminal responsibility in each of the respective phases.

Investigation breakdowns. An investigative process that results in a false conviction involves a combination of failures. First, the investigation failed to discover the truth, as manifested by the simple fact that the true perpetrator got away. Second, the investigation failed to discern the faulty nature of the evidence it collected, as manifested by the fact that the investigators cleared the case and recommended it for prosecution. The least familiar, though most dire, failure is that in many instances the investigation itself contributed to the mistaken conclusion.

To better understand how mistaken testimony comes about, it would be useful to propose a distinction between two types of error. First, some errors are caused by random cognitive failures that are inherent to human cognition. This category of *spontaneous error* pertains to occasional failures in human performance that cannot be attributed to any obvious external cause. Errors are taken to be spontaneous, for example, when an honest eyewitness mistakenly confuses an innocent person with the perpetrator or when he misremembers a particular detail from the crime scene. Spontaneous errors do not have a directional tendency; they are as likely to inculpate an innocent defendant as they are to exculpate a guilty one. A number of innocent people were spontaneously misidentified by witnesses while walking down the street, shopping in a store, or riding in an elevator.[26]

However serious, these cases do not begin to capture the intricate relationship between the investigative process and the occurrence of error.

Errors can also be caused or exacerbated by situational factors. In the context of the criminal justice process, such situational factors follow from the investigative procedures or from interactions with criminal justice officials and lawyers. Such is the case when a witness picks an innocent person from a skewed lineup or reports an erroneous memory as a result of a suggestive question posed by a detective. These instances represent a second type of error, which can be labeled *induced error*.[27] Induced errors have a directional tendency to coincide with their inducing influences. As discussed in the following chapters, these influences tend more often to pull the case toward conclusions of guilt.

Although law enforcement officials tend to view false convictions as caused by spontaneous errors,[28] induced errors figure more prominently in the studied DNA exoneration cases. In the three abovementioned cases, for example, we see a transformation of the witnesses' statements toward conformity with the police's case against the suspect. The evidence presented in court was considerably different from—and indeed, more incriminating than—the witnesses' initial statements given to the police. Notwithstanding her certain identification of Peter Rose in the courtroom, the victim was initially adamant that she did not see the face of the man who dragged her into an alley, raped her from behind, and fled. When presented with a photograph lineup that contained Rose's photo, she could not pick anyone out. At the lineup, the bystander witness, who later testified that Rose was either the perpetrator or his twin brother, had actually selected a photo of an innocent filler.[29] At first, Bruce Godschalk denied his involvement in the crime, and he could not provide any details about it. By the end of the interrogation, however, he confessed to horrible deeds that he had not perpetrated, and provided intricate corroborating details that he could not possibly have known.[30] Four of the five witnesses who testified against Kirk Bloodsworth had provided the police with inconsistent and unreliable statements. One witness had previously tipped the police that the suspect matched a different person whom she knew, and a second witness had initially told investigators that she did not see the face of the perpetrator. At the lineup, one of the two child witnesses picked an innocent filler and the other failed to choose anyone.[31] Similar transformations of evidence were observed in the cases of Walter Snyder,[32] Edward Honaker,[33] Darryl Hunt,[34] William O'Dell Harris,[35] Ronald Cotton (discussed in Chapters 2 and 3), and numerous others.[36]

These cases illustrate that criminal investigations can overwhelm the often weak and vague remnants of the truth, and thus shape the testimony to substantiate a prosecution.

Another observation that has come to light from the studied exoneration cases is that the inculpating evidence presented at trial often hinged not just on a single mistaken evidence item. Rather, as seen in the cases of Rose, Godschalk, and Bloodsworth, prosecutions are typically based on an array of seemingly independent pieces of evidence, all of which connect the defendant to the crime.[37] An analysis of DNA exoneration cases shows that 71 percent of the cases involved mistaken identification, 63 percent involved forensic science errors, 27 percent involved false or misleading testimony by forensic scientists, 19 percent involved dishonest informants, 17 percent involved false testimony by lay witnesses, and 17 percent involved false confessions.[38] These evidentiary causes sum to 214 percent of the cases, which means that on average, each case was afflicted by more than two types of bad evidence.[39] In reality, the number of mistaken evidence items is much greater. For example, many misidentification cases contain erroneous testimony from multiple witnesses, and each mistaken identification typically includes numerous additional incorrect corroborating statements.

Given that these convicted persons were ultimately found to have not perpetrated the crimes, it follows that the bulk of the evidence used to convict them, if not all of it, was wrong. While it is theoretically possible that all the errors just happened to coincide, there is strong reason to suspect that they were induced by the investigative process. As discussed in Chapter 2, due to the dynamic nature of police investigations, errors can beget more errors. By way of illustration, a mistaken fact suggested by one witness can lead the detective toward a mistaken conclusion, which can then induce the forensic examiner to confirm the hypothesis, and so on. This *escalation of error* can transform even a flimsy mistake into a full-blown case replete with overwhelming evidence strong enough to support the conviction of an actually innocent person.

Adjudication breakdowns. Mistaken verdicts also entail a breakdown of the adjudicative phase. The failure to distinguish between guilty and innocent defendants typically follows from the failure to tell apart accurate and erroneous testimony. Virtually every exoneration follows a conviction by a jury or judge who believed that the faulty evidence was true beyond a reasonable doubt. Some prosecutions of innocent defendants failed to raise even the slightest suspicion from the fact finder. One jury, for example, took no more than seven minutes to convict an innocent man for a crime that resulted in a life sentence.[40] By the same token, the limited diagnosticity of the adjudicative process can also lead to false acquittals. Indeed, some juries have refused to convict defendants in the face of compelling evidence of guilt.[41] Hence jury verdicts are often perceived to be unpredictable, even by professionals who sit through the whole trial and see all the evidence.[42]

Case Typologies

Easy and difficult cases.   Not all criminal events are born equal, nor are the ensuing investigations. Police studies show that the majority of serious criminal events that get cleared are solved quite easily. In fact, most of them are solved at the first encounter with the responding patrol officer, that is, without any investigatory effort by detective units.[43] For example, crimes are solved easily when a witness identifies the perpetrator by his name, address, vehicle, or place of employment. Solving cases is also relatively straightforward when the perpetrator is caught in the act, in possession of the contraband, or singled out by means of forensic tests, surveillance cameras, or telecommunication records. This category of *easy cases* accounts for a large majority of the people sitting in prisons, but it tends to account for only a small fraction of the investigative and adjudicative resources expended. Habitually, these cases are disposed through plea bargaining, and when they do go to trial, they hardly challenge the adjudicative process. At the other extreme, there is a large category of crimes that are exceedingly difficult to solve because of a dearth of evidence, lack of resources, or noncooperation by victims and witnesses. Although some of these cases consume heavy investigative resources, most are readily abandoned. Either way, these cases tend not to be cleared, and thus do not evolve into prosecutions, not to mention convictions.

The criminal justice process is brought to bear mostly in the middle category of *difficult cases,* where solving the case is neither easy nor impossible. In these instances, the initial information made available to the responding officer falls short of enabling her to clear the crime or to single out the perpetrator. The investigative effort required to overcome this evidentiary shortfall is what makes these cases difficult. This relatively narrow category of cases consumes the bulk of the investigatory and adjudicatory resources, and it also puts the criminal justice process to the test. This category of cases is the focal point of this book.

Identity cases and culpability cases. At the most general level, criminal cases center upon two types of questions. Some cases are concerned primarily with figuring out who committed the crime, the *whodunit* question. These can be labeled *identity cases.* Accurate verdicts in this category mean that the true culprit was convicted, whereas false convictions typically mean that an innocent person was found guilty. *Culpability cases* center upon determining the criminality of a suspect whose identity is not in question. Accurate verdicts in these cases mean that the perpetrator was appropriately convicted for his criminal actions. False convictions in this category mean that the defendant's innocent behavior was mistakenly taken to be guilty, or that he was convicted on a charge that was more severe than warranted by his conduct.

This book is concerned primarily with the factual accuracy of verdicts, and thus focuses on case outcomes that can, in principle, be determined as being correct or incorrect. As such, the book pertains straightforwardly to almost all identity cases, which can be resolved by showing that the defendant was or was not the person who committed the crime. The vast majority of exonerations stem from identity cases, where subsequent evidence demonstrated that the inmate did not perpetrate the crime for which he was convicted. The book does not apply directly to questions of culpability that hinge on value judgments, such as the morality of a behavior, the reasonableness of an act, or the fairness of the law. It does, however, apply to culpability cases that revolve around determinations of factual questions such as the defendant's actions and mental states. It should be noted that culpability cases rarely result in exonerations. Culpability questions tend to hinge on subtle and elusive aspects of the criminal event, and thus are not readily subject to objective confirmation or refutation. It follows that mistaken determinations of the defendant's culpability are rarely traceable. The dearth of culpability cases among the exoneration cases should not be taken to suggest that these mistakes do not occur.

Some Caveats and Qualifications

It is imperative to keep this book's claims and objectives in perspective. While the book attempts to provide a relatively broad application of legal psychology to the criminal justice process, it necessarily leaves out some important aspects of the research. For one, it does not examine differences in performance among people, which are bound to influence verdicts under some conditions.[44] Rather, it seeks to capture broader phenomena entailed in legal procedures and practices, and thus focuses on the overall performance of legal actors. Nor does the book deal with the performance of special populations, such as children, the elderly, and people affected by mental disease, retardation, drug dependence, and the like. By concentrating on healthy adults, the book examines the performance of the criminal justice process as it is operationalized by well-functioning actors.

The book does not offer an examination of the ubiquitous practice of plea bargaining, the process by which some 95 percent of felony convictions are obtained.[45] Plea bargaining is one of the most obscure and troubling aspects of the criminal justice system,[46] but it does not readily lend itself to psychological experimentation. Still, it warrants noting that the problems with the integrity of the evidence discussed in the following chapters are bound to affect plea negotiations no less—and, probably, even more—than they do criminal trials. Effectively, defendants' decisions to plead guilty are based on sparse, uncertain, and questionable evidence that will rarely be subjected to any meaningful scrutiny.

A substantial number of known mistaken verdicts have been caused at least in part by conscious and deliberate efforts to distort the truth. The culprits in these transgressions have been people with a stake in the outcome, such as codefendants, and overreaching or corrupt detectives, prosecutors, and forensic examiners.[47] Numerous convictions that resulted in DNA exonerations were driven by police misconduct,[48] prosecutorial misconduct,[49] and misleading or fraudulent forensic testimony.[50] Deliberate distortions are the most egregious type of miscarriage of justice, especially when perpetrated by state officials. This book, however, focuses primarily on the working of the process when all the actors seek to fulfill their roles honestly and dutifully.

The book should not be taken to stand for the proposition that the legal system is entirely insensitive to any psychological aspects involved in the production of criminal verdicts. Indeed, the criminal justice system embodies a considerable amount of psychological insight. For example, the law recognizes the possible effects of leading questions, coercion in the interrogation room, and prejudicial evidence.[51] Still, law's psychological sensibilities are mostly frozen at the state of the pre-experimental psychological knowledge that prevailed at the time these common-law rules were forged. Law's intuitions tend to overestimate the strengths of human cognition and to underappreciate its limitations. There is good reason to update the system with more reliable and nuanced knowledge of this complex matter.

The book's focus on psychological causes of mistaken verdicts should not obscure the fact that the criminal justice process is plagued by a host of other factors, which have not been the subject of substantial psychological experimentation and are thus not discussed here in any detail. The late William Stuntz repudiated the system for the excessive discretion awarded to prosecutors, inconsistent policing, the infrequency of jury trials, and the inordinate reliance on plea bargaining.[52] Other factors include insufficient access to appropriate legal representation and investigation,[53] inadequate training and lack of discipline of law enforcement personnel, improper forensic procedures, and the frequent reliance on unreliable evidence such as informants.[54]

Methodological Concerns

It must be acknowledged that the research that underlies this project is naturally susceptible to methodological concerns. No single study, body of research, or experimental method is devoid of methodological limitations. Most notably, applying psychological research to the legal world raises concerns over its *external validity*, that is, the degree to which the findings can be generalized beyond the experimental setting to the naturalistic environment.[55] Psychologists, who are habitually attuned to situational influences on human behavior,[56] are the first to acknowledge that experimental findings are sensitive to the specifics of the experimental design.[57] Critics of legal-psychological research observe that the controlled environment of the laboratory differs from the real world in important ways. The research has been criticized for overstating the import of experimental results, and more specifically, for the nonrepresentativeness of the participants, the disconnectedness from institutional contexts, and the inconsequentiality of the tasks.[58] This critique places a serious burden on researchers' shoulders. It does not, however, warrant a wholesale dismissal of the research.[59]

The concerns over the external validity of this body of research are largely allayed by its *convergent validity*.[60] The convergent validity of this research refers to the combined empirical support derived from replications of the results from studies that test different stimuli, on different populations, in different laboratories, and focusing on different facets of the issues. The convergent validity is enhanced also by triangulating a variety of methodologies, namely, basic- and legal-psychological experimentation, survey data, field studies, and archival research.[61] To be sure, not every finding mentioned in this book has been subjected to the complete panoply of external-validity verification, though the available data invariably indicate consistency and convergence in the findings.

One valid criticism of the experimental method is that it cannot fully capture the richness of human performance, which is invariably multi-determined. By design, psychological experiments focus on only one or two aspects of the task, while keeping all the other dimensions under tight control. The research, then, is not capable of explaining how any of its observations would fare if the focal aspect were allowed to interact with each of the numerous other aspects that were controlled in the particular study. This limitation must be acknowledged, but it does not lead to the conclusion that this body of experimentation necessarily exaggerates the problems with the criminal justice process. In fact, it seems more likely to underrepresent them because many of the hidden interactions actually detract from the accuracy of the process.[62] The experimental environment tends to block out biasing factors such as the actors' motivations, incentives, subcultures, and personalities, as well as adverse social dynamics, emotional arousal, prejudice, and the like.[63] Moreover, many of the human processes involved in operating the criminal justice process are basic-psychological phenomena. People's performance on these tasks is barely amenable to improvement, but is very susceptible to contamination from poor procedures.

Still, there are reasons to guard against overstating the conclusions that can be drawn from the research results. First, the prevalent criterion for the validity of experimental findings is the statistical probability that they are attributable to the experimental treatment, as opposed to mere chance. This criterion does not speak to the strength of the treatment or to its absolute values.[64] Second, difficult cases contain an unspecifiable fraction of the array of factors that have the potential to skew the process. These factors vary in strength, and they do not all sway the process in the same direction. With the exception of extreme cases, the net effect of the biasing factors is unknowable. Thus, the experimental findings are best understood as heightened propensities, or tendencies. It would be imprudent to attempt to determine unequivocally the exact effect of any factor or whether a particular outcome was accurate or mistaken. The research can, however, enrich our understanding about which factors present a risk of error and how best to avoid them.

Toward Reform: Accurate and Transparent Evidence

The primary objectives of this book are to energize the debate about the accuracy of the criminal process and to suggest reforms that would enable it to better meet its exacting goals. Given the depth of the foregoing critique, one might well be tempted to advocate a thoroughgoing restructuring of the criminal justice system. A fundamental institutional redesign, however, is not a proximate objective of this book. Deep institutional reforms would relinquish much of the reformative potential of the psychological research. Unlike most other disciplines that are employed in the analysis of the legal system, experimental psychology operates at a granular level that enables offering direct and immediate solutions to specific problems. It would be a mistake to forego the benefits that these solutions can yield. Over the years, a number of scholars have proposed profound institutional changes to the criminal justice process. Most of these proposals have entailed adopting elements from the inquisitorial system practiced in continental European countries.[65] These proposals warrant serious consideration, but they run against the grain of the current Anglo-American legal culture,[66] and would likely require deep legislative changes and perhaps also constitutional amendments.[67] Hence, these proposals seem unlikely to be implemented in the foreseeable future. In the vein of pragmatism, the recommendations offered in this book will be limited to reforms that are practical, feasible, and readily implementable in the short or medium term. Most of these reforms are targeted directly at law enforcement officials, lawyers, and judges, and they could be adopted at the departmental level and even by the individuals themselves.[68]

The reasons for reducing the incidence of false acquittals hardly need mentioning: escaping a deserved criminal sanction negates the very purpose of the criminal justice system, and thus can undermine the foundation of an ordered society. There are also strong reasons for reducing the incidence of false convictions to the lowest feasible level. Most obviously, inflicting punishment on innocent people constitutes a grave moral transgression, and it can also devastate that person's family and dependents. Preventing false convictions also serves a public safety interest, in that every conviction of an innocent person effectively averts the pursuit and incapacitation of the true perpetrator. By the same token, uncovering false convictions can lead to the apprehension of the actual perpetrators. In almost one-half of the DNA exonerations, the evidence that cleared the innocent suspect also inculpated the true perpetrator.[69] In the long run, minimizing false verdicts is bound to enhance the legitimacy of the criminal justice system.

Reforming the criminal justice system is a delicate and complex endeavor, particularly given the pointed adversarialism that tends to pervade all things related to criminal justice. Reforms must be designed not to reduce the overall rate of convictions or acquittals, but should be targeted as narrowly as possible at *false* convictions and acquittals.[70] Accurate evidence and correct verdicts, rather than partisan advantage, should be the goal. The two central recommendations made throughout the book are designed to address the most serious problem that affects the accuracy of criminal verdicts, namely, the problematic quality of the evidence presented in many criminal trials.

First, criminal investigations ought to be conducted meticulously according to best-practice procedures. Best-practice investigative procedures will ensure that criminal verdicts and plea bargains will be based on the most accurate account of the criminal event that can be obtained. Specific recommendations for some best-practice procedures will be offered at the end of each chapter.

In determining which procedures ought to be considered "best practice," one ought to think through the implications of the proposed reform for both false convictions and false acquittals. Contrary to widely held beliefs, criminal justice reform is not always a zero-sum game in which reducing one type of error necessarily increases the opposite one. Indeed, some of the key recommendations proposed in this book are designed to improve the quality of the evidence across the board and thus reduce both types of error at once. These win-win reforms include the use of computerized systems in eyewitness identification procedures, resorting to sophisticated interviewing protocols such as the cognitive interview, and, as discussed below, the creation of a complete record of the investigative process. A proposed reform should be noncontroversial also when it reduces one type of error substantially while causing a marginal increase, or none at all, in the opposite error. Reforms should be deemed justified also when they entail a moderate increase in the opposite error, when the marginal cases are based on evidence that is nominally correct, but unreliable.[71] It is, however, inescapable that some policy decisions entail tradeoffs between the two types of error, where the respective evidence is of similar reliability. The calculation of such tradeoffs is a complex undertaking because of the unknown distribution of truly guilty and innocent defendants in the mix of the cases and the perplexing weighting of the social costs of the respective errors. A full discussion of all possible costs and benefits of each of the recommended reforms lies beyond the scope of this book. While even the more controversial of these recommendations seem to strike a correct balance, they could benefit from further analysis and debate.[72]

Second, all encounters with witnesses should be recorded in their entirety and the recordings should be made openly available to all parties. In other words, the goal is to make the evidence as transparent as possible. It is important to appreciate that courtroom testimony is usually proffered months, sometimes years, following the criminal event.[73] During this time, witnesses typically have numerous encounters with the legal process. They interact with investigators, cowitnesses, lawyers, and other people who have a stake in the outcome of the case, and they are subjected to procedures that have the potential to induce error. Over the natural course of the process, testimony often changes, as previously unreported details come to be included in witnesses' statements, narratives are crystallized, gaps get filled, ambiguity fades away, and tentativeness is replaced by certitude. In other words, the *synthesized* testimony that is presented at trial often differs from—and is invariably stronger than—the witnesses' *raw* statements they initially gave the police. Although raw testimony is usually the best approximation of the truth, verdicts are invariably based on the inferior synthesized version.[74]

Enhancing the transparency of the evidence should have a very favorable impact on the process. Creating a reliable record of the criminal investigation stands to improve the investigation itself. The record will provide law enforcement agencies with a tool for training, oversight, and quality assurance. This should promote adherence to best practices and deter misconduct. The record could also serve as an informational tool by capturing forensic details that would otherwise be missed. Importantly, the record will provide access to the witnesses' raw statements and thereby offer a way around the effects of memory decay, contamination, and any biases or distortions arising from the investigative and pretrial processes. The availability of a record should also have a direct effect on the witnesses themselves because their testimony could be checked against their statements to the police. Effectively, courtroom testimony will be given under the shadow of the witnesses' own raw statements. The availability of the record should also reduce any pressures applied on the witnesses to alter their testimony, and when necessary it could be used to supplement or replace the testimony given in court. Transparent procedures will enable fact finders to focus on drawing correct inferences from the evidence, rather than conjecturing about its reliability. Greater transparency should also help jurors determine whether the testimony might have been induced or otherwise biased by the investigation itself.

The combined effect of heightened accuracy and transparency has tremendous potential to improve the performance and enhance the integrity of the process. More accurate and transparent evidence is bound to improve the ability of all decision makers—investigators, prosecutors, defense attorneys, judges, defendants, and jurors—to make more informed and well-reasoned decisions. Most notably, criminal verdicts are bound to be more accurate, and plea bargains are expected to be fairer and better calibrated with the defendant's actual guilt. Greater accuracy and transparency are bound to increase the legal actors' trust in the evidence and limit their ability to distort and hide it, which should lead to a reduction in the distrust between the adversarial parties and a softening of the contentiousness of the process. The range of plausible claims will be curbed, narrowing the opportunities for both unjust prosecutions and frivolous defenses. Greater accuracy and transparency should reduce the need to sort out murky facts through the costly, cumbersome, and imprecise process of litigation. One can also expect that the heightened level of factual clarity will result in fewer appeals, *habeas* proceedings, civil suits, and damage payouts.

However promising, the proposed recommendations should be constantly subjected to reassessment. Future research may yield somewhat different findings and contribute new insights to the policy debate. While the available psychological literature is neither perfect nor fixed in stone, it offers a wealth of sorely needed insight into the workings of the criminal justice system and it can show the way toward important reforms.

2

"WE'RE CLOSING IN ON HIM"

Investigation Dynamics

The criminal process is as good as the evidence on which it feeds. In all but the simplest of cases, the fact finder at trial is bound to be presented with a mixed fare, containing unknown shares of accurate and inaccurate testimonies. A central claim of the next four chapters is that the single most important determinant of evidence accuracy is the police investigation. This chapter examines the dynamic process by which evidence is sought and evaluated. It highlights the risk that investigations will arrive at faulty conclusions, even absent any malicious intent. The following three chapters examine the accuracy of the types of evidence that are commonly used in criminal prosecutions. These examinations emphasize both the risk of spontaneous error by the witness and the proneness of the investigation to induce and shape their testimony. Understanding the workings of police investigations is thus key to an appreciation of the verdicts they propagate.

The case of Ronald Cotton provides a rare opportunity to peer into the investigative process and to appreciate how closely the psychological research maps onto real-life investigations. Early in the morning of July 29, 1984, Jennifer Thompson, a white twenty-two-year-old student in Burlington, North Carolina, awoke to find a stranger hovering beside her bed. The man put a knife to her throat, forced himself on her, and sexually assaulted her. Throughout the ordeal, Thompson made an effort to memorize any feature that could help her identify her assailant. At some point, Thompson managed to convince him to allow her to go to the kitchen to fix them drinks. She seized the opportunity to escape through the back door, and ran for shelter in a nearby house.

A tip communicated to the police implicated Ronald Cotton, who was out on parole for a conviction for breaking and entering. Cotton, who was African-American, had been convicted as a juvenile for attempting to rape a fourteen-year-old white girl. Cotton was tried twice and convicted. At his second trial he was convicted for sexual crimes against both Thompson and a second woman who was assaulted in a nearby apartment that same night. He was sentenced to life plus fifty-four years in prison, and his conviction and sentence were ultimately held up on appeal.[1]

The evidence produced at trial amounted to a compelling incrimination of Cotton. Thompson provided forceful testimony, which included a confident identification of Cotton as her assailant. Police investigators and the prosecutor stated that she was the best witness they had ever put on the stand. At the second trial, Cotton was also identified by the second victim. Both victims provided similar descriptions of the man, and both reported that he was wearing a distinctive navy blue sports shirt with white stripes circling the arms. A bystander witness testified that around the time of the crime she saw Cotton riding a bicycle near Thompson's apartment and wearing the blue shirt described by the victims. The restaurant owner for whom Cotton had worked testified that Cotton had worn a similar blue shirt to work, and that he had also been seen wearing white gloves similar to the distinctive gloves described by Thompson. The employer testified also that Cotton had a habit of fondling white female waitresses and talking to them about sex. The prosecution's case was bolstered by physical evidence collected from Cotton's residence: a flashlight that was said to be similar to a flashlight removed by the assailant from the second victim's apartment, and sneakers that appeared to have been the source of a piece of foam found in Thompson's apartment. Cotton's defense was based on testimony by his family members stating that he was at home that night, watching TV and sleeping on the living-room couch. That alibi was undermined by the fact that Cotton had previously given the police an alibi that turned out to be untrue.

Some ten years after his arrest, a DNA test proved that Cotton was not the man who assaulted Jennifer Thompson. He was exonerated and released from prison after serving more than ten years of his life sentence. The biological evidence was traced to a convicted rapist, Bobby Poole, whose name as a suspect arose after Cotton was already in custody. It turns out, then, that the bulk of the evidence implicating Cotton—if not every material bit of it—was flawed. Thompson's identification of Cotton was wrong, as was the identification by the second victim. It is most likely that Cotton's employer never saw him wearing that distinctive shirt or uncommon gloves. The flashlight picked up from Cotton's residence was not the one taken from the second victim's house, and his sneakers were not the source of the foam found in Thompson's apartment.

How did all of this inaccurate evidence come into play? A static snapshot of the prosecution's case cannot provide an answer to this question, as evidence does not normally provide an account of its own production. What is needed is a dynamic account of how the case evolved from the initial report to the police through the adjudicative process. This case is exceptionally informative thanks to the uncommonly frank and detailed reports provided by Thompson and police detective Mike Gauldin. There is every reason to believe that Thompson's testimony was sincere and that Gauldin's investigation was performed conscientiously.[2]

The key to this prosecution lies in the fact that from the inception of the investigation, Thompson had apparently only a faint memory of the face of her assailant, Bobby Poole. As discussed in Chapter 3, the frailty of her memory was likely due to the dim lighting, the stressful assault, and the fact that her assailant was a member of a different race. That memory was soon cluttered and possibly also morphed by the arduous task of constructing the facial composite sketch. The investigation gained considerable momentum once Cotton's photograph was placed in the photo array, and it escalated considerably once Thompson picked it out. The identification bore the markings of a weak recognition: it was tentative, doubtful, and protracted. Any qualms that she might have harbored were probably allayed by Gauldin's assurance that she chose the man whom they had suspected. By the same token, Thompson's identification emboldened Gauldin, placing Cotton in the crosshairs of the investigation. Gauldin's search of Cotton's residence yielded the physical evidence that further implicated him in the act. After arresting and questioning Cotton, he also discovered that Cotton's alibi was untrue. Thompson, in return, was emboldened by Gauldin's findings.

The case against Cotton was boosted further when he was picked out by Thompson at a live lineup (he was the only person included in both procedures). Again, Thompson's identification was hesitant, slow, and insecure. Once again she was reassured and relieved by Gauldin's confirmation that she had chosen the same man. With the investigation closing in on Cotton, information that indicated the possible involvement of a convicted rapist, Bobby Poole, was disregarded. The case became stronger after the bystander stated that she saw Cotton near the crime scene wearing the particular blue shirt, and Cotton's employer linked him to the shirt and to the gloves described by Thompson. At some point, the second victim claimed that she recognized Cotton as her assailant despite having picked someone else at the lineup.

This dynamic account indicates that the mass of evidence against Cotton was triggered by the tip that connected Cotton to the composite sketch and was solidified and energized by Thompson's initial recognition of Cotton in the photographic array. That flimsy and erroneous identification propelled a process that ultimately produced a confident identification by Thompson herself, a reversal of a key witness's testimony (the second victim), another misidentification (the bystander witness), statements about Cotton's clothing that were probably false (from Cotton's employer), and two items of misleading physical evidence. Importantly, the investigation had a parallel effect on Thompson herself, transforming her initial hesitance into a formidably confident and persuasive testimony. By the end of the process, that initial error had escalated into a powerful prosecution that easily convinced two juries and passed the muster of an appellate court.

The case of Ronald Cotton epitomizes the phenomenon of the *escalation of error*. At bottom, even the most compelling prosecutions can be the product of a flimsy or erroneous piece of information that became amplified and reinforced as a result of the dynamics of the investigation. Similar escalations are observed in the investigations that resulted in a large number of DNA exonerations.[3] To understand better how investigations can go awry, we turn to criminological and psychological research that illuminates the investigative process.

The Investigative Task

Any discussion of criminal investigations in the United States must be qualified by the fact that investigations vary widely among the some 20,000 law enforcement agencies at the federal, state, and local levels. Most criminal investigations are performed by the 13,500 local police departments, many of which comprise just a handful of officers, with few if any trained and specializing in investigative work.[4] The following discussion will refer generally to investigators, a category that encompasses mostly police detectives, but also forensic examiners and even patrol officers, who perform a great deal of evidence gathering. Much of the discussion pertains also to prosecutors, who are often involved in one way or another in major investigations, and who are subjected to similar incentives and pressures in the performance of their role. In many respects, the investigative and prosecutorial processes share similar dynamic properties.

It must be appreciated that investigating crimes is a genuinely difficult task. Crimes that receive investigative attention lie mostly in the gray zone between easy cases and unsolvable ones. In many instances, investigators have too little information to generate leads, while in others they are inundated with information that is contradictory or dubious.[5] Investigators are entrusted with a great deal of discretion,[6] much of which is not readily teachable.[7] For example, investigators have discretion in deciding whether a crime occurred, which leads to pursue, what physical evidence to collect, which witnesses to question, which testimonies to trust, when to make an arrest, when to declare the case solved, and when to give up on it. Investigations follow an array of formal and informal policies, practices, and idiosyncratic habits.[8] The investigator's work is encumbered and complicated by departmental directives,[9] public expectations,[10] media exposure,[11] and the passage of time,[12] as well as by limited resources and departmental politics. The prevailing legal rules are onerous,[13] and often confusing, at least until interpreted by courts many months, even years, down the road. Most importantly, as described below, police investigators are encumbered by strong conflicts that pervade their roles. Overall, investigations are conducted in an environment that is hardly suited for the delicate and solemn task. The blue-ribbon committee commissioned by the National Research Council was rather pessimistic about the prospects of reforming the investigatory environment or improving the capabilities of the police to solve crimes.[14]

The accuracy of criminal investigations is bound to be determined by the interrelated cognitive and motivational dimensions of the task. The former pertains to the inferential reasoning involved in any investigative endeavor, while the latter pertains to the particular context of police investigative work. Each of these aspects can contribute to investigative breakdowns.

Cognitive Factors

Abductive Reasoning

In any investigative task, the process of winnowing the field of possible hypotheses to the single substantiated conclusion entails a conceptual problem. To determine the validity of a hypothesis, one needs to obtain evidence that supports or refutes it. Conversely, because it is impossible to seek and test the infinite amount of evidence that might have any bearing on the case, one needs a hypothesis in order to decide which evidence to test. Hence the circular nature of investigative reasoning: evidence is necessary to test hypotheses, while hypotheses are necessary to decide which evidence to pursue. This dialectical tension makes the investigator's task a most delicate cognitive endeavor.

A form of bootstrapping, known as *abductive* reasoning, is probably the only feasible method suited for conducting criminal investigations.[15] Abductive reasoning is a recursive process of generating and testing hypotheses, geared toward eliminating invalid hypotheses and substantiating the correct one. The testing of hypotheses has two components: a *search* for information, followed by its *evaluation,* that is, the drawing of correct inferences from that information. While the evaluation of the information entails logical inference, the generation of hypotheses and decisions about which information to pursue require intuitive and conjectural thinking. Hence, police investigative work is described not only as a science, but also as a craft, even an art.[16] Following in the mold of Sherlock Holmes, investigators are valued, even valorized, for the creativity of their intuitions.[17]

Performing this bootstrapping task correctly requires fine balancing. A lack of imagination will generate too few hypotheses and thus stands to miss useful information. Excessive creativity, on the other hand, is bound to drain resources on improbable hypotheses and, more importantly, it can lead the process astray. The primary concern is that the evaluative task may be swayed by both cognitive limitations and the motivational aspects of the investigative task.

The Confirmation Bias

A serious concern with the integrity of the investigative process stems from the potential stickiness of the focal hypotheses. While to some degree all reasoning processes rely on underlying knowledge and beliefs,[18] unwarranted conformity of incoming information to extant beliefs is a cause for concern. Investigative hypotheses are, by definition, merely hypothetical scenarios, generated for the sake of exploring particular lines of inquiry. The focal hypotheses must be readily abandoned when they are not adequately supported by the evidence, correctly construed. The threat of bias borne by inertia in investigative reasoning is highlighted by the experimental research on the relationship between extant beliefs and the evaluation of new evidence.

The research indicates that even flimsy thoughts can easily gain traction in people's minds. A number of studies show that merely providing hypothetical explanations or reasons for an imagined scenario strengthens one's belief in the likelihood of its occurrence. For example, asking people to explain why a particular sports team will win a future game increases their belief in the likelihood of that team's victory.[19] Similarly, asking people to imagine a certain outcome of a political election increases their belief in the occurrence of that outcome;[20] and asking people to explain why a particular mental patient might end up joining the Peace Corps (or, conversely, committing suicide) increases their belief in the corresponding future scenario.[21] The research demonstrates also that people tend to anchor their judgments on salient values even when those values are patently arbitrary[22] and adhere to newly formed beliefs even after the evidence that purported to support them has been debunked.[23]

Research on the *confirmation bias* verifies what Francis Bacon described as the "pernicious predetermination" that ensures that one's "former conclusion may remain inviolate,"[24] and what Arthur Conan Doyle's fictional character depicted as the "twist[ing] of facts to suit theories."[25] The key observation of this body of research is that incoming evidence is evaluated in a manner that conforms to the person's extant beliefs.[26] The bias is defined as the "inclination to retain, or a disinclination to abandon, a currently favored hypothesis,"[27] and has also been dubbed the *belief bias*,[28] and the *prior belief effect*.[29] Researchers have also identified the reciprocal *disconfirmation bias,* by which evidence that is incompatible with one's prior beliefs is judged to be weak and thus unlikely to disrupt them.[30]

Confirmatory reasoning has been demonstrated in a number of classic studies. Scientists refereeing an article for publication were more accepting of it when the results comported with their own beliefs than when they contradicted them.[31] The academic performance of a child was judged more favorably when participants were led to believe that she was a high-performing student than when they expected low performance.[32] The bias is strongest in the absence of alternative plausible theories,[33] thus confirming the adage that "nothing is more dangerous than an idea when it is the only one you have."[34] The research on the confirmation bias spans a breadth of domains, including judgments of people,[35] public policy,[36] scientific research,[37] consumer products,[38] and real estate.[39] The bias is observed among novices and experts alike. Doctors and medical students have been found to generate hypotheses at very early stages of the examination, and to adhere to them even in the face of counterevidence.[40] Indeed, premature diagnoses are a leading cause of faulty medical decisions.[41] Psychotherapists have been found to detect psychopathology when observing normal people whom they mistakenly believed to be psychiatric patients,[42] and to interpret ambiguous psychiatric test results as consistent with disorders that were tentatively suggested to them.[43]

The confirmation bias has also been observed in studies conducted with police personnel, some of whom were experienced investigators. A series of studies with Swedish police officers found that incoming evidence was judged to be stronger when it confirmed the officers' preliminary hypotheses than when it disconfirmed them. For example, eyewitness identifications were deemed more accurate and photographic evidence was deemed more reliable when they supported the investigators' notions than when they contradicted them.[44] A study conducted with Dutch police crime analysts found that even when special analysts are assigned to challenge the investigative team's prevailing theories, they tend to endorse those theories, at the expense of more plausible alternatives.[45] A small study found that a majority of international fingerprint experts judged print matches in a manner that conformed to (misleading) information about the case. In doing so, most of the experts negated their own previous judgments of the same prints.[46]

In the context of criminal investigations, confirmation biases have been labeled *tunnel vision*.[47] The incidence of tunnel vision in criminal investigations is boosted by the fact that the majority of arrests are made in the early stages of the investigation, often by the responding patrol officer.[48] That means that the bulk of the investigatory work is performed well after the suspect has been named and placed under arrest. In other words, investigations are often conducted under strong prior hypotheses regarding the identity of the perpetrator. The guilt-proneness of the bias is probably strengthened also by law enforcement personnel's prevailing attitudes toward questions of law and order. The research suggests that the bias is strongest when the prior beliefs are positively related to the person's stable attitudes toward the topic at hand.[49] Law enforcement personnel tend to subscribe to tough-on-crime worldviews, and are thus more inclined to prioritize the value of crime control over the countervailing values attached to the protection of innocence.[50] It follows that they are also more likely to infer guilt.

In sum, the confirmation bias can wreak havoc in the delicate dialectical task of abductive reasoning. When the evidence conforms to the hypothesis rather than serving to check it, the reasoning process can lose its internal backbone and become even more susceptible to other biasing factors, in particular to the motivational forces discussed below. As with the majority of psychological phenomena discussed in this book, the confirmation bias need not be driven by conscious or explicit errors. Rather, it occurs almost automatically, under the level of conscious awareness,[51] and is likely to be sincerely denied.[52] Like most other biases, the confirmation bias is most likely to occur when the evidence itself is ambiguous.[53] When the evidence is clear-cut, people are less susceptible to be swayed by biases.

Motivational Factors

Conflicting Roles

Even greater threats to the integrity of investigations stem from motivational factors pertaining to police investigative work. The criminal investigation is a delicate endeavor also in that investigators are entrusted with two distinct tasks. For one, investigators must solve the crime. In whodunit cases, that typically amounts to identifying and locating the perpetrator. In this vein, investigators are expected to search for the best explanation for the event. In addition, investigators are entrusted with constructing the case in preparation for the state's prosecution of the suspect. This task of case construction typically starts at the point at which the suspect is named or taken into custody, and intensifies as the investigation progresses toward its conclusion. The investigative task, then, contains an inherent tension between an objective inquiry and an adversarial-like endeavor of building a case against the suspect.[54] This duality can cause a palpable role conflict. Similar role conflicts are apparent in the work of forensic examiners, whose primary task is to apply scientific methods to discover the truth, but do so almost exclusively on behalf of law enforcement agencies, by whom they are typically employed.[55] Prosecutors, too, are burdened with a dual role, bearing both the responsibility to act as an adversarial advocate and as a "minister of justice."[56] Operating under these discordant goals might prove to be a tall order. The concern is that under some circumstances, the truth-seeking goal will be eclipsed by the adversarial one.

Research on *motivated reasoning* shows that people's reasoning processes are readily biased when they are motivated by goals other than accuracy. These *directional goals* pertain to any "wish, desire, or preference that concerns the outcome of a given reasoning task."[57] Distortions borne by motivated reasoning have been observed in the way people interpret information suggesting a threat to their health,[58] handle challenges to their competence,[59] perceive the performance of their preferred political candidate,[60] judge the sportsmanship of their sports team,[61] predict their future performance,[62] and assess the odds of winning a bet on a horse race.[63] Motivated reasoning has been observed also outside the laboratory.[64]

It does not take much motivation to skew a reasoning process. A recent study simulating an investigation suggests that the mere assignment to an adversarial role can trump the objectivity of the process. The study found that participants assigned to investigate a case either for the prosecution or for the defense were motivated to see their respective side win the case, and endorsed a biased view of the evidence that was consistent with their role. Those assigned to the prosecution side judged the suspect to be more guilty, whereas the opposite assignment led to more judgments of innocence. A third group of participants, assigned to investigate jointly for both parties, judged the case around midway between the two polarized versions, a result that suggests that they were more neutral in the evaluation of the facts and their judgment of the suspect's guilt.[65] This adversarial mindset was accompanied by a distrust of the (fictional) investigator assigned to work on behalf of the opposite side.[66] These adversarial tendencies were observed in a relaxed experimental setting, in the absence of incentives or tangible goals, and despite an instruction to be fair and objective.

The motivations in real life are considerably stronger. Not unlike any other professional group, criminal investigators take pride in their vocation and derive satisfaction from the execution of their professional duty, namely, solving crimes. For example, fingerprint analysts in the United Kingdom reported feelings of satisfaction, pride, and "a buzz" when finding a match.[67] Yet the motivation to clear the case runs deeper. Most law enforcement personnel identify themselves as fighters in the War on Crime.[68] Bringing criminals to trial is the noble cause to which they devote their careers and for which some risk their lives.[69]

Perhaps the strongest goal motivating investigators stems from the pressure to clear cases—that is, to arrest and charge the suspect.[70] In a public announcement of the arrest in the case of Darryl Hunt, the chief of police of Winston-Salem, North Carolina, stated: "We spent hundreds of man hours on this case but of course, our objective, from the very beginning was to make a charge, and we have accomplished that."[71] Clearing cases is the most common measure of departmental effectiveness.[72] At the level of the individual investigator, clearing cases is a measure of personal success. It reflects on her professional reputation, standing among her peers, and prospects for promotion.[73] By the same token, the failure to close cases can be costly at the departmental and personal levels. Low clearance rates are used as a key tool in disciplining management within police departments.[74] Low rates can also result in demotion of investigators to positions of lesser status.[75] Indeed, the pressures to clear cases has led to occasional distortions and misrepresentation of crime data by police departments in the United States and the United Kingdom.[76] The costs of failure are particularly steep in cases considered to be high-profile. Such cases are not limited to sensational or heinous crimes. Most violent crimes—especially rape-murders, sex offenses against children, and serious felonies committed in small towns or neighborhoods— have the potential to destabilize the community and generate heightened pressure for its resolution.

The pressure to clear cases is exacerbated by the generally low rate of solving cases through detective work. As mentioned in Chapter 1, only half of the serious crimes committed are reported to the police, and only one in five of these are cleared by arrest. A landmark study by the RAND Corporation found that a majority of the serious crimes that get cleared are solved during the first encounter with the responding patrolman. Even serious crimes are often resolved with the provision of the name of the suspect by victims or witnesses, thus obviating the need for detective work.[77] Many crimes that cannot be solved promptly will never be cleared.[78] Thus, detectives walk away from a great many crime scenes knowing that they are unable to do anything to solve them.[79] This reality flies in the face of the pragmatic, action-oriented, and getting-the-job-done culture that pervades investigative units.[80] The frustration of the investigators' goals is likely to increase their motivation to clear the relatively few crimes that are actually investigated.

Effects of Emotion

It is not hard to see how investigators can get emotionally involved in their cases. For one, investigators can develop personal relationships with the victims or their families, thus strengthening their resolve to apprehend the perpetrator.[81] Investigators are often exposed to the human tragedy inflicted by crime and confronted with gruesome crime scenes. This exposure has the potential to arouse intense negative emotions, particularly anger and also disgust.[82]

The research indicates that high levels of anger arousal tend to result in shallow processing of evidence and hostile judgments of other people. Specifically, anger has been found to result in stronger attributions of personal blame for negative outcomes, higher propensities to perceive other people's conduct as intentional, lower thresholds of evidence, and a stronger tendency to discount alternative explanations and mitigating circumstances.[83] Anger has also been found to increase reliance on stereotypes,[84] desire for retaliation,[85] and motivation to take action to remedy the transgression.[86] In a study simulating fingerprint analysis, participants displayed a heightened tendency to find positive matches after being shown gruesome photographs of the putative murder victims.[87] A study of experienced Swedish police officers showed that the arousal of anger resulted in superficial processing of information and a lack of sensitivity toward exculpating evidence.[88] In all of these studies, the person being judged was unrelated to the source of the anger. In other words, when in a state of anger, people are more harsh in their judgment of *any* other person. It is not hard to see how people would react angrily toward a person who is believed to have committed a heinous crime.

Group Membership

Another notable feature of criminal investigations is that they are performed within the social setting of group membership. Investigators generally view themselves as belonging to the group of people working for law enforcement agencies, and who share the common goal of fighting crime. This in-group includes detectives, patrol officers, forensic examiners, prosecutors, and sometimes also victims and witnesses for the prosecution. Importantly, the in-group contrasts itself starkly with the outgroup, consisting primarily of criminal offenders—who are generally deemed to be bad people, often referred to as "scumbags"—and sometimes also their defense attorneys. Suspects can readily be lumped into this out-group, whether because of their status as the presumed perpetrator or because of their criminal history.

The research indicates that group membership constitutes an important component of people's identity and is integral to their self-concept.[89] People tend to consider their groups to be trustworthy, competent, moral, and peaceful, while out-groups are generally regarded as untrustworthy, competitive, and aggressive. This *in-group favoritism* and *out-group derogation* have been observed in numerous laboratory studies as well as in anthropological work.[90] This polarization is fueled by the adversarial nature of the legal process.

The group setting has the potential to sway criminal investigations toward conclusions of guilt. Group members tend to share similar world-views, beliefs, and stereotypes about out-group members.[91] Groups tend to exert cohesive forces on their members when working toward the group's shared goal,[92] which in the case of criminal investigations is fighting crime. The joint endeavor makes the members more prone to reach a consensus and to conform to group norms.[93] Reflecting on the successful prosecution of a man who was subsequently exonerated by DNA evidence, the prosecutor stated: "Maybe I was too willing to believe what the law-enforcement officers told me. Maybe I got caught up in the sense that the prosecutor and the investigators are all on the same team."[94]

Groups, particularly homogeneous groups, have been found to search for information in a selective manner,[95] display the confirmation bias,[96] and respond to threats with arousal of anger followed by superficial processing of information.[97] Excessive cohesion can reach the pathological state of groupthink.[98] Importantly, the group setting has disinhibiting effects on its members, enabling them to overcome inhibitions that would normally prevent them from acting in their individual capacities.[99] For example, people are more likely to engage in binge drinking when that conduct is an acceptable norm of their group.[100] Groups have been found to be more aggressive than individuals in electrocuting another person,[101] and in forcing adversaries to eat hot sauce.[102] This heightened aggression is accompanied by a reduced sense of moral responsibility.[103] Group members are particularly prone to shed moral responsibility when they can attribute primary responsibility for aggressive behavior to other members of the group.[104] Group membership also makes it easier for individuals to discount, overlook, or turn a blind eye to the misdeeds of other members of the group.[105]

Commitment

Another potential problem stemming from the dynamics of police investigations is that as the process unfolds, investigators become increasingly invested in the focal hypothesis. They devote significant time and resources to pursuing their theory of the crime, and sometimes they invest personal capital in proving it to be correct. This sense of personal investment is likely to be heightened when a suspect has been placed under arrest, something that happens routinely once he has been named.

The admission of an error poses a threat to the ubiquitous need to maintain a positive self-conception,[106] particularly in regard to one's competence,[107] morality,[108] and consistency.[109] This motivation is understood to serve both private and social needs, that is, to maintain a positive conception in one's own eyes as well as in the eyes of others.[110]

A substantial body of experimental research demonstrates that people tend to adhere to their prior courses of action, even in the face of indications that they were wrong in the first place.[111] One explanation for this *escalation of commitment* stems from a favorable distortion of one's original course of action, which serves to negate any prior fault.[112] Studies show also that committed people tend to search selectively for information to justify their prior decisions rather than prepare themselves for future ones.[113] Committed people tend also to interpret incoming information in a distorted manner that serves to justify those decisions.[114] The escalation of commitment has been observed also in naturalistic settings. A study of NBA teams reveals that costly players receive preferential treatment that is not warranted by their performance on the court,[115] bank managers tend to be committed to bad loans that they had personally approved,[116] holders of theater season passes are more likely to attend the shows if they paid full price for them,[117] and managers provide inflated ratings of employees whom they hired.[118] Commitment effects were observed in a study that simulated a criminal investigation. The mere naming of the suspect at an initial phase of the study led participants to a stronger belief in that suspect's guilt, which resulted in a failure to explore alternative theories adequately. These participants sought additional information to confirm those initial hypotheses and evaluated it in a way that corresponded to those beliefs.[119]

The research has identified a number of task features that exacerbate the escalation of commitment, many of which are likely to be present in criminal investigations that go astray. Commitment has been found to increase along with increases in the actor's responsibility for the original error,[120] the room for concealing the failure,[121] the adversity of the outcome of the original decision,[122] the perceived threat entailed by the exposure of the error,[123] and the publicity of the original error.[124] Paradoxically, the more egregious the error and the longer it has persisted, the less likely it is that it will be corrected.[125]

Commitment to a faulty course of action is bolstered also by the group setting. Groups are prone to escalate their commitment to failing courses of action,[126] at times more so than individuals.[127] More importantly, groups exert strong disciplining powers on their individual members. Group deviance draws criticism, hostility, and ostracism, as evidenced by the typically harsh reaction to whistle-blowers.[128] Groups also retaliate more forcefully than individuals.[129] The more cohesive the group, the more strongly it condemns its deviants.[130] Thus, any doubt expressed by a law enforcement agent might be regarded as a challenge to the group's consensus and thus also as a breach of loyalty, a value that is valorized in police culture.[131]

Admitting error is complicated further by investigators' sense of commitment to the soundness of their investigative methods. A botched investigation punctuates that eyewitnesses cannot always be trusted, memories can be mistaken, confessions can be elicited from innocent people, and forensic tests can be off the mark. These prospects could be disconcerting, especially given that investigators live by these methods, defend them in court, and are bound to use them in investigations to come.

In sum, the commitment effect can deflect incoming information that challenges the focal hypothesis, that is, evidence that either indicates the innocence of the suspect or implicates a different person in the crime. Commitment can thus make it difficult to upend an advanced investigation or indictment, not to mention a conviction.[132] While it does not take much to become the target of a criminal procedure, it can be very difficult to reverse that status.[133] Strong commitment is observed also in the behavior of prosecutors, most notably when they proceed to prosecute defendants even after the latter have been exculpated by compelling evidence such as DNA testing.[134] For example, prosecutors in Orange County, California, went forward with the prosecution of an innocent man on charges of carjacking and armed robbery even though he had been excluded by both DNA and fingerprint tests. In defending the decision to prosecute, Assistant District Attorney Marc Rozenberg explained: "If nobody had identified him, we wouldn't have prosecuted this case."[135] Prosecutors persisted with the prosecution of some fifteen other defendants in the face of exculpatory DNA tests, all of whom were subsequently exonerated.[136]

Motivations Combined: The Adversarial Pull

The discussion thus far has indicated that in contested cases, investigators experience a cumulative set of motivations that drive them toward conclusions of guilt. In actuality, the picture is more nuanced. Investigators are undoubtedly motivated also by the goal of finding the true perpetrator and avoiding the incrimination of innocent people. Balancing these opposing pulls places investigators in the thick of a difficult and potentially stressful[137] role conflict.[138] Just how investigators resolve the conflict will depend on a host of circumstantial and personality factors.

The concern is that in the demanding circumstances of contested investigations, the truth-seeking goal will hold less sway. First, from the investigator's perspective, the need to avoid false charges is an abstract principle, not a concrete incentive. It is a constraint that is often experienced as a hindrance to the goal of clearing crimes, hardly a desideratum in its own right. Investigators get rewarded and recognized predominantly for making arrests, not for refraining from charging innocent people (imagine a chief of police convening a press conference to announce that although a dangerous perpetrator remains on the loose, the department succeeded in not arresting any innocent persons). Second, the opposing goals have very different feedback mechanisms. As mentioned, a failure to clear the case can bring immediate and tangible negative repercussions upon both the officer and the department, especially under the spotlight of the media. In contrast, a mistaken suspicion of an innocent person might well go undetected. Ironically, mistaken suspicions can be buried under compelling (yet mistaken) evidence that was induced by them. The prospect that mistakes may come to light months, years, or decades down the line tends not to weigh heavily in the rough-and-tumble exigencies of the moment.[139] Third, not unlike most other people, investigators are likely to hold unrealistically positive views of their own performance,[140] and thus tend to believe that they have not erred. Indeed, law enforcement agents and judges tend to believe that virtually no innocent people are convicted, at least not in their jurisdiction.[141] Finally, investigations often gravitate toward the usual suspects, that is, people with criminal records. These suspects are often engaged in some form or another of criminal activity, and may be deemed to have escaped punishment in the past. The investigator might feel less troubled by a false charge made against such suspects, and perhaps even welcome the opportunity to rectify their impunity for past misdeeds.

In sum, it is not hard to imagine that under certain circumstances, the truth-seeking objective will be overridden by goals and motivations that lead investigators toward a more adversarial, conviction-prone stance.[142] This *adversarial pull* was captured by Justice Robert Jackson's characterization of "the often competitive enterprise of ferreting out crime."[143]

To be sure, there are differences in the degree of adversarial pressures generated across jurisdictions, departmental procedures, and local professional cultures. There is variance also among the people who conduct investigations. Investigators differ in their professional temperament, which is probably affected by their introspection, integrity, conformity, and susceptibility to incentives. There is reason to believe that most law enforcement personnel in most police departments withstand the adversarial pressures, and conduct thorough and fair investigations. The adversarial pull, however, is likely to wreak havoc in investigations conducted under intense pressures and performed by those who lack a disciplined professional temperament. The adversarial pull is evident in the inculpatory bent of the scientific methods developed by forensic scientists. Many of these methods lack adequate scientific grounding, and some are plainly junk science.[144] The truth-seeking objective is most likely to be overridden in high-profile cases, where the pressures to solve the crimes are the strongest.[145] In some instances, the adversarial pull results in deliberate police malfeasance,[146] and even entails lying outright in court, a practice known as *testilying*.[147] Recall, however, that we are interested primarily in conduct that does not involve deliberate dishonesty.

Over time, the adversarial pressures that develop in the course of criminal investigations and prosecutions are bound to become internalized in the prevailing culture and practices of law enforcement agencies.[148] This internalization helps explain the gradual strengthening of tough-on-crime attitudes among police officers.[149] These attitudes, in turn, contribute to the inclination to infer guilt.

The Coherence Effect

One of the distinctive features of difficult cases is that they entail drawing inferences from multiple evidence items, all of which need to be integrated into a singular factual assessment and expressed in the form of a binary conclusion. This task is no light matter given the uncertainty, incommensurability, and conflict within the information that is often encountered in the course of investigations. For example, an analysis of the evidence presented in the trial of Sacco and Vanzetti identified more than 300 facts and propositions.[150] A cognitive process is needed also to integrate the available information with other aspects of the task, including the person's motivational and emotional responses to it. The cognitive process that performs this integrative task poses another threat to the accuracy of the investigative task.

The integration of evidence in complex decision tasks lies at the core of the body of research on the *coherence effect*. This psychological phenomenon can be encapsulated by the Gestaltian notion that *what goes together, must fit together*. Complex tasks can be solved effectively and comfortably when they are derived from coherent mental models of the case at hand,[151] that is, when the conclusion is strongly supported by the bulk of the evidence. This coherence effect is driven by a bidirectional process of reasoning: just as the facts guide the choice of the preferred conclusion, the emergence of that conclusion radiates backward and reshapes the facts to become more coherent with it.[152] This process occurs primarily beneath the level of conscious awareness.[153] The coherence effect has been observed in decision-making tasks as well as in tasks that involve general cognitive processing such as memorization of information or recounting it to another person.[154] In itself, the coherence effect is probably adaptive, in that it enables people to reach conclusions and make decisions even when the task is most complicated and difficult. Still, this phenomenon has serious implications for both the investigative and adjudicative processes.

First, coherence is achieved by spreading the evidence apart into two (or more) clusters, each corresponding to a different conclusion. The evidence supporting the emerging conclusion becomes stronger, while the evidence supporting the rejected conclusion wanes. Thus, the cognitive process transforms the evidence from an initial state of conflict into a lopsided evidence set that clearly supports the decision. In other words, the evidence comes to cohere with the emerging decision. This *spreading apart* results in the dominance of one conclusion over the other, thus enabling confident action. For example, one study presented participants with a theft case that contained a range of unrelated evidence items, including an eyewitness identification, a possible motive, an unexplained possession of money, and an alibi claim. The study found that people tended strongly to evaluate the evidence in a coherent block, all pointing toward either inculpation or exculpation.[155] The spreading apart enables people to reach concrete conclusions even when they originally perceived the evidence as ambiguous and conflicting. It must be appreciated that to some degree, the apparent strength of the evidence that enables confident action is an artifact of the cognitive process rather than an objective assessment of the case at hand. Thus, investigators will tend to perceive the evidence that supports their conclusion as stronger and more corroborative than it really is.

In itself, the coherence effect is nondirectional, in that it can inflate judgments of guilt and innocence alike. However, in combination with other biasing factors—notably, motivations and confirmatory biases—it can sway the judgments of the entire case in the direction of those factors.[156] The coherence effect can be seen operating in the abovementioned study of the confirmation bias in judgments of Swedish police investigators. When the witness's account was consistent with the investigators' theory of the crime, the investigators also judged her to be more reliable, the witnessing conditions to be better, and the memory loss over the seven-day interval to be less harmful.[157] Similarly, the abovementioned study that simulated an investigation found that the ambiguous fact pattern was evaluated in a manner that cohered with the participants' assigned roles.[158]

A second feature of the coherence effect is that information items are not evaluated independently, but rather according to how they fit into the mental model of the task. As a result of the interconnectivity of the Gestaltian process, any evidence item can impact all other items, and ultimately the entire case. One important facet of this *nonindependence* feature is that including an evidence item that is strongly inculpating can make the entire evidence set appear inculpating, just as including an exculpating item can result in a conclusion of innocence. This nonindependence naturally adds a directional dimension to coherence shifts, driving the entire set of evidence toward the corresponding conclusion. This phenomenon of *circuitous influences* was observed, for example, in the abovementioned study of a theft case. Adding information that placed the suspect near the scene of the crime resulted in a higher rate of convictions, as one would expect. Interestingly, it also resulted in more inculpating evaluations of all the other evidence items, such as greater trust in the eyewitness's identification, and a weaker belief in the defendant's explanation for his possession of money days after the theft.[159] Similarly, describing the defendant in a libel suit as motivated by good intentions led to the strengthening of various legal and factual reasons supporting his defense, whereas portraying him as motivated by greed resulted in opposite inferences.[160] In the absence of any direct relationship between these extraneous manipulations and the rest of the case, one must infer that these influences occurred through the circuitous connections of the cognitive system.

Circuitous influences were observed incidentally in a number of studies that showed how extraneous evidence can contaminate witnesses' statements. Eyewitnesses were more likely to pick the suspect at a lineup when they were told that he had confessed to the crime, and were less likely to identify him when told that another suspect had made a confession.[161] In a series of studies discussed in Chapter 3, eyewitnesses who identified the wrong person at the lineup were provided with (fictitious) affirmation of their identifications ("Good, you identified the suspect"). In addition to inflating the witnesses' confidence in their identifications, this feedback also distorted a range of judgments surrounding the witnessing of the criminal event, including the witnesses' assessment of how good a view they got of the gunman, how well they were able to make out the specific features of the gunman's face, how much attention they were paying to the gunman's face, how easy it was to identify him, and how quickly they picked him out at the lineup.[162] These judgments can be of considerable significance to the outcome of the case, in that they are typically viewed by third parties—investigators, prosecutors, and jurors—as indicators of testimony reliability. Given that all these identifications were wrong (actual targets were not placed in the lineups), the apparent corroboration is misleading.[163]

Circuitous influences were observed incidentally also in studies conducted with experienced criminal investigators. Polygraph examiners were more likely to interpret ambiguous physiological data as indicative of deception when told (fictitiously) that the suspect had confessed to the crime.[164] Fingerprint examiners from a number of countries were likewise influenced by (fictitious) knowledge that the suspect had confessed to the crime or that he was under arrest at the time.[165] The contaminating potential of circuitous influences poses a serious concern in police investigations, as it does for jury decision making as discussed in Chapter 6. Investigators are often exposed to a variety of information of varying reliability from informants, fellow detectives, witnesses, media reports, and physical evidence. Exposure to any such erroneous information can sway the evaluation of the incoming evidence and thus influence the direction of the investigation.

Five Mechanisms of Biased Reasoning

It would be helpful to briefly describe five common mechanisms by which biasing processing operates. Recognizing these mechanisms could assist in identifying biased reasoning processes. The mechanisms can work independently or in combination.

Selective framing strategy. One way of enhancing the compatibility of evidence with a preferred conclusion is to frame the inquiry in a manner that affirms the salient hypothesis. This mechanism, observed early on by Jerome Bruner and colleagues,[166] has been replicated in numerous studies and been labeled the *positive test strategy*[167] and the *verification bias.*[168] The strategy has been described as looking for "features that are expected to be present if the hypothesis is true."[169] For example, when people are instructed to determine whether a conversation partner is an introverted person, they tend to ask questions that confirm introversion (for example, "In what situations do you wish you could be more outgoing?"), and to phrase the questions in the opposite form when being asked to determine whether the person is an extrovert (for example, "What would you do if you wanted to liven things up at a party?").[170] It is not hard to see that different ways of framing the investigative task will result in different courses of action. As discussed in Chapter 4, subtle differences in the phrasing of questions can readily affect the responses given by witnesses. A positive test strategy will naturally yield leading questions that drive the witness toward affirming the interviewer's implicit assumptions. As discussed in Chapter 5, a study simulating an interrogation found that interrogators who were led to believe in a higher likelihood of guilt asked more guilt-presumptive questions, which in turn elicited responses that made the suspect look more culpable.[171]

Selective exposure. Another way to reach particular conclusions is to choose which evidence to examine for the purpose of testing the chosen hypotheses. The research indicates that people tend to selectively expose themselves to information that confirms their focal hypothesis and shield themselves from discordant information.[172] This pattern is readily apparent in people's choices of news media (compare the political attitudes of the viewers of Fox News and MSNBC).[173] Likewise, recent car purchasers tend to read advertisements of the car they bought more often than of other cars they considered but did not buy.[174] Experimental evidence includes findings that people are more likely to seek favorable rather than unfavorable information about themselves.[175] The selectivity of exposure becomes more acute when the information is scarce,[176] which is often the case in criminal investigations. Selectivity can also take the form of actively seeking evidence that is expected to inhibit a countervailing hypothesis.[177]

Selective scrutiny. Desired conclusions can also be derived by altering the standard for validating the incoming information. The research demonstrates that people tend to scrutinize information that is incompatible with their conclusion, but apply lax standards when assessing the validity of compatible information.[178] When people contest adverse positions, they spend more effort, generate more refutational thoughts, and muster more redundant counterarguments.[179] People who receive unfavorable results from a putative intelligence test tend to challenge its validity, but accept it at face value when they receive a favorable score.[180] Likewise, people react skeptically to a medical diagnostic test when it indicates that they are susceptible to a disease, but tend to accept it readily when it finds no such indication.[181] A study of peer reviewers of a scientific publication found that the referees were more likely to notice a typo in the submitted article when the result of the research contradicted their beliefs.[182]

Biased evaluation. The objectivity of the evaluation is key to the integrity of any investigation. Yet the most ubiquitous form of biased reasoning occurs through a distorted evaluation of evidence. Biased evaluation[183] features in the bulk of the abovementioned research, including evaluating a shove as either jovial or aggressive depending on the race of the actor,[184] maintaining that your preferred political candidate did better at a debate than his rival,[185] believing that a physical encounter in a football game was a foul if it was committed by the rival team but a legitimate hit if it was committed by a player on your favorite team,[186] and inflating the odds that your chosen horse will win a race.[187] Biased evaluation figures also in the studies that find distorted judgments in the testing of forensic evidence.[188]

Selective stopping. Finally, a limited body of research suggests that people tend to shut down inquiries after having found a sufficient amount of evidence to support their leading hypothesis.[189] This means that police investigations might be aborted prematurely. In particular, the inquiry might be stopped before information that tends to refute the police's hypotheses has been adequately considered.[190] As a veteran Dallas detective explained after learning that his investigation had incriminated an innocent man, "You think you have a slam-dunk case, and so you don't go in there and dot your I's and cross your T's." The detective added that it is only after the conviction has proved to have been mistaken that it "comes back to bite you."[191]

The Opacity of Investigations

There is reason for hope that investigative errors would be corrected by the mechanisms of oversight that are embedded in the criminal justice process. After all, the investigator's work product is subjected to the judgments of superiors, prosecutors, judges, defense attorneys, and jurors, all of whom are designated to assess the evidence with a critical eye. This institutional oversight parallels the psychological construct of *accountability*, wherein people anticipate being called on to justify their performance to others. The construct implies that one expects to gain praise or suffer negative consequences depending on how she is deemed in the eyes of an intended audience. As developed in the research of Philip Tetlock and his colleagues, accountability can improve otherwise inferior performance through a process of preemptive self-criticism, by which people anticipate and preempt the expected objections of their would-be critics. Accountability has been found to lead to closer attention to evidence, higher calibration between confidence and accuracy, increased sophistication of thought processes, and lower effects of emotions on unrelated judgments.[192]

Still, despite the multilayered oversight built into the criminal justice process, accountability might not yield its intended effects. Naturally, the ameliorative effects of accountability are limited to situations in which the relevant audience is well informed about the issue at hand.[193] Accountability is not a viable construct for people whose conduct remains out of sight. In other words, accountability depends on transparency, but criminal investigations are invariably opaque. Recording practices vary among investigative agencies, but are rarely complete or objective. By their own admission, 33 percent of lineup administrators fail to keep any written reports of the lineups, and 27 percent do not keep a photographic record of the procedure.[194] In many jurisdictions, only 7 percent of administrators videotape the lineup procedures.[195] This opacity deprives outside reviewers of information such as witnesses' choices, confidence, other statements about the suspect, the speed of the choice, and any statements made by the administrator. As discussed in Chapter 6, this information could be vital to the assessment of the identification. In about one-half of the eyewitness identification cases that have been decided by the U.S. Supreme Court, the Court noted the incompleteness of the record of the procedure (yet proceeded to discuss the reliability of the identifications—invariably, favorably—with no apparent concern over the missing information).[196]

In the bulk of interviews with cooperative witnesses, the record consists mostly of retrospective paraphrases jotted down by the investigator. These practices result in a loss of a considerable amount of information provided by the witness in almost all of the questions asked. For example, an experiment with forensic and child service interviewers found that between 20 percent and 40 percent of details provided by children and more than 80 percent of the interviewers' questions were omitted from the interview reports.[197] Similarly, a field study that tested real-life interviews of child abuse cases found that even when taking contemporaneous verbatim notes, interviewers missed about one-quarter of the details reported by witnesses and omitted more than one-half of the substantive questions that they had asked.[198] A study with experienced police investigators in Florida found that their reports missed some two-thirds of the information stated by the witnesses and did not include any of the questions that they had asked.[199] There is little reason to expect that witnesses will remember much more. This opacity is problematic, since errors can be induced in barely noticeable ways, such as by subtle phrasing of questions or mere hints of suggested information. The absence of a reliable record is particularly acute in the context of interrogations of suspects, where disputes often arise over both the content of the statements attributed to the suspect and the investigative means used to elicit them. As investigators are aware, in the bulk of these *swearing contests,* their word is trusted over the suspect's. In sum, the opacity of investigations obscures much evidence from the legal actors and gives investigators little reason to be worried about accountability.[200]

The Investigation of Brandon Mayfield

The investigation of Brandon Mayfield, an Oregon lawyer suspected of involvement in an Al Qaeda terrorist attack, provides a good illustration of the potential of police investigations to go astray. This case is instructive in that it has been the subject of especially thorough inquiries, one conducted by the FBI and one by the Office of the Inspector General of the Department of Justice (DOJ).[201] The Mayfield affair jolted the fingerprint identification community, which has long insisted on an error rate of zero, a claim that has been endorsed repeatedly by the courts.[202] The affair also demonstrates that even highly regarded professionals in a flagship law enforcement laboratory can get swept up in the dynamics of an investigation gone awry and ultimately insist on improbable conclusions.

In March of 2004, the FBI was called on to assist the Spanish National Police with the investigation of a massive terrorist attack by Al Qaeda on commuter trains in Madrid. A computerized fingerprint identification suggested Mayfield as a possible match with the latent prints of a person implicated in the attack. It is not hard to see why Mayfield seemed like a fitting suspect. Mayfield, an army veteran, had converted to Islam and was married to an Egyptian woman. He had previously represented a Muslim man convicted of terrorist conspiracy in a child custody dispute.[203]

A high-ranking FBI fingerprint specialist examined the prints and concluded a positive match. The match was subsequently confirmed by a retired FBI examiner with over thirty years of experience. The process was overseen by a specialist who headed the FBI's Latent Print Unit. Two weeks later, federal prosecutors applied to federal court for a warrant to search and detain Mayfield as a "material witness." The application was based primarily on FBI affidavits stating that the match provided a "100% identification of Mayfield."[204] Mayfield was arrested, and reportedly was told that he was being investigated in connection with crimes punishable by death.[205] The FBI's conclusion was subsequently confirmed by another fingerprint analyst who was appointed by the court. Soon thereafter, however, the Spanish Police found that the latent prints actually matched an Algerian national by the name of Daoud Ouhnane. After reviewing the indisputable match with Ouhnane's prints, the FBI withdrew its identification of Mayfield and released him.

From the moment that Mayfield's prints were declared a match with the Madrid train bomber, the investigation rolled ahead like an unstoppable freight train. As the author of the FBI report stated, "Once the mind-set occurred with the initial examiner, the subsequent examinations were tainted."[206] The FBI's motivation to name Mayfield as the suspect is also apparent. It is not a fancy speculation to state that the FBI was keenly interested in cracking the identity of the Madrid train bombings. Identifying the terrorists would have been beneficial in securing the cooperation of the Spanish government, then a reluctant ally of the United States in the Iraq war. The prospect of solving an Al Qaeda attack perpetrated on the soil of a friendly European country would also have been a boon for the United States in its Global War on Terror. Finally, linking an American Muslim to an Al Qaeda ring would have provided a justification for the government's domestic antiterrorism efforts and garnered support for its controversial legislative agenda, notably the Patriot Act. Indeed, the high profile of the Mayfield case was cited in the FBI report as a central reason for the faulty fingerprint match.[207]

The Mayfield investigation manifests the FBI examiners' selective exposure to the available evidence. As the DOJ report points out, some of the print similarities considered important by the FBI were visible in only one of the several sets of Mayfield's prints that were available.[208] In other words, the examiners focused on the source of information that provided evidence that confirmed the hypothesis, while ignoring equally reliable information that contradicted it. The examiners also treated the evidence with selective scrutiny. The comparison of the prints relied on a number of similarities within extremely tiny details of the prints ("Level 3" details), whose validity is considered controversial.[209] Unhindered by these concerns, the Mayfield examiners cited similarities in numerous tiny details to justify their match.[210] At the same time, they completely dismissed the fact that the entire upper left portion of the latent print did not correspond with Mayfield's print.[211]

Biased evaluation permeated this investigation. The FBI claimed to have found fifteen points of similarity between the sets of prints. According to the DOJ report, the examiners interpreted some murky and ambiguous details in the latent print as similar to Mayfield's.[212] It also turned out that the latent print originated from Daoud's right middle finger, whereas the FBI matched it to Mayfield's left index finger.[213] The examiners also engaged in "backward" reasoning that led them to "find" additional similarities that did not exist.[214] The case also manifests the effects of group membership. As noted in the FBI report, the analyses of the second and third FBI examiners were likely constrained by the pressures of cohesion: "To disagree was not an expected response."[215] The effect of group membership was evident also in the FBI examiners' apparent overconfidence and sense of superiority to their Spanish counterparts.[216]

Perhaps most notable in this case was the FBI team's commitment to the initial identification of Mayfield. Days after learning of the FBI's conclusion, the Spanish police notified the FBI that the match was "negativo." This red flag failed to spur a reexamination of the FBI's findings. Rather, the agency elected to arrange a meeting with its Spanish counterparts in Madrid to persuade them of the validity of the match. The meeting, held eight days later, did not go well. As reported by a Spanish official, the FBI insisted that the prints shared fifteen similar "points," whereas the Spaniards found only seven similarities.[217] The Spanish representatives kept pointing out discrepancies between their analysis and that of the FBI, but these "did not seem to sink in with the Americans." "They had a justification for everything," explained the head of the Spanish fingerprint unit, "But I just couldn't see it."[218] At the conclusion of the meeting, the FBI extracted a promise from the Spaniards to reexamine the prints. The pressure from the FBI persisted. As the Spanish official explained, for three weeks following the meeting, the FBI "called us constantly," "they kept pressing us."[219] The Mayfield case also punctuates the problems that stem from the opacity of the investigation. Even though this investigation was conducted in the comfort of an FBI facility, the examiners did not record the reasons that led them to their conclusions.[220] The precise reasons for this investigative debacle thus remain unknown.

This case also demonstrates that a commitment to an erroneous investigation can cause a secondary contamination of the adjudicative procedure. In attempting to justify the faulty investigation to the court, FBI personnel and their lawyers made unfounded and distortive statements in support of Mayfield's arrest warrant. The government misrepresented the uncomfortable discrepancy with the Spanish police analysis, stating that the Spaniards had "felt satisfied" with the FBI's conclusions and promised to reexamine their findings.[221] The FBI was also hard pressed to show that Mayfield had actually traveled to Spain: there was no record of his travel, and he did not own a passport. With no evidence to support the claim, the federal government's affidavit stated: "It is believed that Mayfield may have traveled under a false or fictitious name."[222] In an apparent attempt to link Mayfield with the Madrid bombings, federal agents claimed to have confiscated "miscellaneous Spanish documents" from Mayfield's office and home. According to a source close to Mayfield, these documents were his young children's Spanish homework.[223]

It is worth noting that the evidence produced by the FBI would probably have sufficed to have Mayfield convicted and sentenced to death. He was confronted with unwavering inculpating evidence from the most prestigious crime laboratory in the land, grounded in scientific testimony and backed up by a court-appointed expert. Under normal circumstances, it would have been close to impossible to uncover the FBI's error. Absent the verifiable and indisputable match to the true suspect, Mayfield's fate could have been quite different.

Recommendations for Reform

This chapter has examined the manner in which police investigations are conducted and has emphasized their dynamic properties. The discussion indicates that properly conducted investigations require delicate cognitive processing that might not be afforded in the harsh realities of contested criminal investigations. In themselves, the cognitive biases are mostly nondirectional, in that they merely bolster investigative conclusions regardless of whichever conclusion they support. However, the process can be swayed strongly by a variety of motivational forces, which tend to pull investigations toward adversarial, guilt-confirming conclusions. In reality, the cognitive and motivational phenomena often operate contemporaneously, producing a potent recipe for biased processing.

The foregoing analysis has focused on the investigators themselves, particularly how they seek, test, and evaluate information. It must be acknowledged that this discussion speaks to only one dimension of the dynamic process. It omits the crucial dimension pertaining to the impact of the investigation on the evidence that it produces, primarily, on human testimony. The next three chapters examine how investigative beliefs can seep into witnesses' testimony and induce it to conform to them. Hence the escalating dynamic of investigations: investigators' hypotheses tend to generate confirmatory testimony that bolsters those hypotheses and turns them into firm conclusions. As discussed in Chapter 6, this *pseudo-corroboration* can have a strong impact on criminal outcomes. Investigations that begin with an initial mistaken conception of the case are prone to perpetuate that error. This is mostly likely to occur in investigations in which the adversarial pull is particularly strong.

While adversarialism is one of the hallmarks of the Anglo-American adjudicative process, it seems hardly controversial that it is fundamentally unsuitable in the investigative phase of the process. To have any chance to succeed as a fact-finding device, adversarialism requires a contest between opposing accounts of the facts. In reality, investigations are virtually monopolized by the police and other state investigative agencies. The state has virtually exclusive access to the crime scene, the physical evidence, the databases, the victim, and most witnesses. The state also has exclusive power to search, seize evidence, place people under arrest, and wield its prosecutorial power as a threatening device. In contrast, the defendant is afforded a very limited scope for conducting investigations, especially when she is incarcerated. Yet even if suspects enjoyed equal investigative powers, the vast majority of non-white-collar suspects could not afford to avail themselves of them. Effectively, investigations are driven by a one-sided quasi-adversarial process, on which the accounts of the state go largely unchecked and unopposed. Like one hand clapping, this one-sidedness guts any virtue that the adversarial procedure might have harbored, yielding an unfitting method of truth discovery. The following discussion examines possible avenues to enhance the accuracy of police investigations.

Debiasing: Considering Alternatives

A natural approach to tackle the confirmation bias is to debias it. One possible way to do so is by promoting a healthy skepticism and lateral thinking, that is, by introducing mechanisms for the generation of alternative hypotheses.[224] Suggestions along these lines have been introduced in police training in the United Kingdom,[225] and have been mandated by Canadian courts.[226] One concrete experimental intervention that has been used with some success is instructing people to "consider the opposite" hypothesis.[227] Instituting this practice in criminal investigations could be done via forcing investigators to consider alternative hypotheses and elaborate on the reasons for rejecting them.

To be sure, this intervention should be welcomed, but it should be acknowledged that its effectiveness will likely be limited. Debiasing instructions have been found to be successful in correcting relatively weak cognitive failures, such as where lines of thought were neglected because of lack of sufficient attention.[228] They have proved less successful in correcting reasoning processes where cognitive biases were compounded by motivational factors.[229] There is reason to suspect that debiasing instructions will fall short of overcoming the strong motivational biases that are often present in contested criminal investigations. Moreover, this intervention can backfire, resulting in the bolstering of the focal hypothesis.[230]

Functional Separation

Another possible way of promoting the integrity of investigations is to introduce procedures designed to provide a critical appraisal of the focal hypothesis. The objective would be to scrutinize investigations and correct them when they go askew. Dialectical reasoning is an intervention that designates some of the team members to offer a countertheory to the prevailing focal hypothesis in order to instigate a structured debate about the merits and weaknesses of the vying hypotheses.[231] This technique has been found to reduce commitment to prior choices.[232]

Although functional separation is an elegant solution, in practice it is a complicated proposition and there is reason to doubt whether it will reap the intended benefits. The interventions can be effective when the designated intervener is driven by authentic dissent to the emerging hypothesis, but are ineffective when the dissent is contrived through techniques such as role-playing.[233] Genuine separation is difficult to generate, especially when the personnel designated to propound opposing views actually share the same viewpoints. In the context of criminal investigations, the designated dissenters will typically come from the ranks of the same agency as their counterparts, and they are likely to have undergone similar training and to hold similar attitudes toward issues of law and order. A failure of separation appears to have been the case in the study with the Dutch police crime analysts, whose function is to serve the role of devil's advocates. Recall that the critical contribution of those analysts was undermined by their tendency to confirm the investigative team's prevailing theory, while ignoring plausible alternative hypotheses.[234] Similar problems seem to be limiting the effectiveness of magistrates in the French legal system.[235]

Even if successful, functional separation might not endure. Dissenters are generally disliked,[236] and that could render them less influential in the long run. Moreover, genuine psychological separation is bound to be accompanied by the pathological features of intergroup conflict, which could encumber the investigative process and obstruct meritorious investigations. Furthermore, failed interventions might even backfire. Acknowledging countertheories and summarily refuting them might provide decision makers with a hollow sense of having addressed all objections, and thus result in heightened confidence in the correctness of their conclusions.[237] That appears to have happened in the Brandon Mayfield investigation. Recall that the expert appointed by the court arrived at the same erroneous conclusion as did his FBI colleagues, thus bolstering the FBI's blunder.

Still, with careful design and in the correct cultural climate, functional separation can operate successfully. The office of the District Attorney of Dallas County, under the stewardship of Craig Watkins, is a promising example. Watkins has brought the question of accuracy to the fore, and in 2007 he established an internal Conviction Integrity Unit. This unit is designed to review and re-investigate legitimate claims of innocence by convicted inmates.[238] Within four years of its operation, fourteen convicted inmates have been exonerated.[239] Other jurisdictions have established innocence commissions, which are quasi-judicial entities designed to reexamine convictions of inmates who can show a plausible case of innocence.[240] Functional separation would be most effective and beneficial if it prevented innocent people from being charged and convicted in the first place.

Restructuring the Investigative Authorities

The most ambitious way to defuse the quasi-adversarial nature of investigations is to revamp the institutional incentives and motivations under which investigators operate. Most importantly, eliminating the goal of clearing crimes should go a long way to reduce the institutional pressures on them to reach conclusions of guilt. This reform would replace the current incentive structure with one driven by the goal of truth-seeking. To achieve this, one could imagine transferring the investigative responsibilities from the police to an authority that is not directly responsible for fighting crime. A good candidate would be a judicial branch body established for this purpose.[241] Investigations would be overseen by specially trained judges and conducted by professional investigators. Criminal investigations would be conducted much like investigations of aviation accidents conducted under the authority of the Federal Aviation Authority. Investigative reports would contain a full exposition of both inculpating and exculpating evidence, and would be shared with the prosecution and the defense.

This proposed reform would require a sweeping overhaul of large bureaucratic entities. As discussed in Chapter 1, deep reforms of this nature ought to be considered seriously. The recommendations offered in this book, however, focus on changes that are feasibly implementable in the short and medium term, and that can be adopted even at the departmental or personal level.

Transparency: Electronic Recording of Investigations

The most promising and feasible avenue for enhancing the objectivity of criminal investigations is to make them transparent. This is one of the two single most important recommendations proposed in this book. All interactions with would-be witnesses—including all lineups, interviews, and interrogations—should be recorded and preserved in their entirety. Meticulous records should be made also of other investigative procedures, especially forensic testing. The recording should be made in the best available medium, which would normally be audiovisual. The recordings should also include unfruitful investigative efforts, even if they are not used in court, such as interviews with witnesses whose statements do not support the prosecution. Importantly, the record should be made available to all parties involved in the case.

As discussed in the following chapters, the creation of a complete and reliable record of investigations is bound to soften their quasi-adversarial bite and enhance the twin objectives of accuracy and transparency. In addition to improving the quality of evidence consumed by the entire criminal justice process, transparent investigations are expected also to improve the investigative process itself. The availability of a record would increase investigators' sense of accountability for their work. The awareness that their performance will be exposed to the critical eye of other actors should make investigators think harder when deciding which hypotheses to generate, which information to test, how to collect that information, and how to evaluate it. Transparency would help ensure that investigators adhere to best practices by providing law enforcement agencies with a tool for training, oversight, and quality assurance. Transparency should also help deter police misconduct.[242] Furthermore, recording investigations is bound to serve as an information-gathering tool. A complete and accurate record is bound to capture forensic details that would otherwise go unnoticed or be forgotten.[243]

The following recommendations seek to further promote more accurate and transparent evidence, and to diminish the adversarial pull.

1. Investigative departments should professionalize and systematize their investigative procedures. The procedures should be based on best-practice protocols.
2. Investigative departments should create full recordings of their investigative processes.
3. Investigative departments should encourage and reward open-minded thinking, and appoint personnel who demonstrate a temperament that is suited for the complexities of the task.

4. Investigative departments should promote greater sensitivity toward the possibility of error.
5. Investigative mistakes should be debriefed candidly.

Chapters 3–5 will offer specific recommendations for conducting best practices with respect to the most common types of evidence used in criminal trials.

3

"OFFICER, THAT'S HIM!"

Eyewitness Identification of Perpetrators

One morning in Tallahassee, Florida, a young man walked into a bank. After filling out a deposit slip, he approached the teller and asked her to cash a $10 money order made out by the United States Postal Service. The teller noticed immediately that the sum stated on the money order had been crudely altered in blue ink to $110. When she refused to cash the money order, the customer insisted that the post office had made a mistake, and showed her that the alteration was initialed. When the teller continued to rebuff the customer's request, he became irate and hurried out of the bank. The entire exchange took about one and a half minutes. Four to five hours later, a woman entered the bank, introduced herself as a police officer, and asked to interview the teller about the event. After recounting the event, the teller was asked to identify the suspect from a six-photograph array.

What the teller did not know was that she was one of forty-seven who had just participated in a field experiment run by eyewitness researchers from Florida State University. Overall, 55 percent of the tellers made correct identifications; in other words, close to half of them identified a wrong person or failed to pick the suspect. Notably, even when the arrays did not contain the suspect's photograph, 37 percent of the tellers picked someone. Naturally, those identifications were all wrong.[1]

This chapter deals with eyewitness identifications of people as the perpetrators of crimes. By definition, singling out the defendant is the key issue in identity cases (*whodunit* cases). Although suspects can be identified by means other than eyewitnesses, such as DNA or other biological matches, surveillance cameras, and electronic records, identification by eyewitnesses is the most common form of identification, and thus is an indispensable device in the investigative and prosecutorial toolboxes. By one estimation, some 77,000 suspects are identified by eyewitnesses in the United States every year.[2] The identification of the suspect typically constitutes a pivotal moment in an investigation in that it tends to concentrate the investigation on the identified suspect, and oftentimes seals the outcome of the case.

Picking out the perpetrator at a lineup is typically only a subset of the information provided by eyewitness. Eyewitnesses also provide a great deal of information to support their identification, such as the lighting conditions, the distance to the perpetrator, the duration of the exposure, and their confidence in the choice they made at the lineup. Eyewitnesses also provide a wide range of information about the criminal event, such as descriptions of the acts perpetrated and, importantly, a variety of specific details that can tie the suspect to the crime. Memory for the criminal event will be discussed in Chapter 4. This chapter deals only with the identification of the perpetrator, specifically identifications that are based on facial features, which are the most common cues people use.[3]

A voluminous body of experimental research seeks to better understand the vexing issue of eyewitness identification. How good are people at identifying strangers? What causes people to make mistaken identifications? To what extent are identifications influenced by investigative procedures? And ultimately, what can law enforcement agencies do to enhance the reliability of identifications? As it turns out, this seemingly simple task is profoundly complex. Despite the extensive research effort that has been invested in this field—more than 450 lineup studies and well over 2,000 face-recognition studies, all published in scientific journals[4]—we are still far from grasping the full extent of the issues involved. Given the sheer vastness of the factors implicated in identifications, it is unlikely that researchers will be able to fully explore all the factors involved, not to mention all the interactions among them.

The repertoire of identification procedures includes mugshot books, showups, photographic arrays, and live lineups. Mugshot searches are used primarily when the police do not have a suspect in mind, as a means of generating leads to the perpetrator. The witness is asked to recognize the suspect from a large number of photographs of people who are a priori suspects, but are not known to have any connection to the crime under investigation. Showups are identification procedures that contain only the suspect, with no foils. The witness is asked to state whether she does or does not recognize that particular person as the perpetrator. Showups are typically unstructured procedures conducted out in the field, in police cars, at crime scenes, and in hospitals. Photographic arrays (also called photographic lineups or photospreads) and live lineups are the most structured and trusted identification procedure. Lineups, whether photographic or live, are conducted when the police have a suspect in mind and seek to confirm his identity. In these procedures, the suspect is embedded amid five or more people who serve as foils, or fillers. The witness is asked to identify the perpetrator from this group of targets. The experimental research focuses primarily on photographic arrays and live lineups, as will this chapter. Unless specified otherwise, the term *lineups* is used here to refer to both procedures.

The basic design of identification studies consists first of the witnessing of the target person. Simulated witnesses are exposed to a video depicting the target committing a crime, or they witness an enactment of a crime in a real-life situation (such as bursting into a classroom and stealing the professor's bag). At the second stage, the witnesses are asked to pick that target out from a lineup. In some of the experimental procedures, the true target is included in the lineup (target-present lineups), which is designed to simulate situations in which the police have found the true perpetrator and have placed him in the lineup. In other experimental settings, the target person is deliberately left out of the lineup (target-absent lineups). These latter procedures emulate cases in which the police mistakenly suspect an innocent person, and have placed him in the lineup instead of the true perpetrator. The fate of the investigation then rests on the ability of the witness to state that that the perpetrator is not present.

A witness's response can be one of the following five types. When the witness correctly picks out the target, the identification is considered a true-positive, or a hit, which is a desirable outcome. In real life, true positives contribute to accurate convictions. When the person chosen is an innocent foil rather than the target, the identification is considered a false-positive, or a false alarm. In real life, it has the potential to lead to a false conviction. Every choice of any person in target-absent lineups is by definition a false alarm, because the target was not placed in the lineup. Witnesses can elect also to decline to choose anyone. One type of non-choice is to state that the target is not present, and thus to reject the lineup. When the perpetrator is truly not in the lineup, the rejection is considered a true-negative, and it correctly sends the police back to the drawing board. When the perpetrator actually is present, a rejection by the witness is considered a false-negative, with the possible effect of letting a guilty person go free. Finally, the witness can state that she does not recognize anyone in the lineup, but cannot rule out the possibility that he is there.

Overview of Identification Accuracy

The single most important observation from the research on eyewitness identification is that it is substantially less accurate than generally believed. Many thousands of observations of witnesses in real-life cases and experimental studies reveal a relatively stable pattern of performance. Overall, data from real-life cases show that just under 45 percent of witnesses pick the suspect, about 35 percent decline to make a choice, and about 20 percent pick innocent fillers.[5] Most of these data come from police records in the United Kingdom, where identification procedures are generally superior to those used in the United States, and where police records are more accessible to researchers. The limited available data from the United States show a similar pattern. Identification procedures conducted in Sacramento County over a twelve-year period show that 50 percent of the witnesses chose the suspect, 26 percent declined to pick anyone, and 24 percent chose innocent fillers.[6] These naturalistic data are remarkably similar to the results obtained in the laboratory. A meta-analysis of ninety-four experiments shows that 46 percent of the witnesses choose the perpetrator correctly, 33 percent decline to choose, and 21 percent choose innocent foils.[7]

The abovementioned experimental data pertain to lineups in which the suspect is present. These lineups correspond to cases in which the police have managed to find the perpetrator and have placed him in the lineup. In real life, however, the person suspected by the police is not always the true perpetrator. Thus, to obtain a more reliable measure of witnesses' testimony, one must also examine their performance when the target is not included in the lineup. In these target-absent lineups, the only correct answer is that the target is not there. Yet a large body of research shows consistently that almost one-half of witnesses (48 percent) pick someone, who is, by definition, an innocent filler.[8]

It is not hard to see how witnesses' difficulties to identify strangers can hurt the prospects of convicting truly guilty people. Even when the target is present in the lineup, one-third of witnesses fail to pick anyone out (recall that 35 percent decline to choose anyone). Of the witnesses who do pick someone, about one-third pick innocent fillers instead of the target (the 20 percent false picks out of the 65 percent who choose someone).

Thus, in total, about one-half of truly guilty perpetrators who are placed in lineups will go unidentified, and probably unpunished (the 35 percent non-choosers plus the 20 percent false picks). The research also provides insight into the risk that innocent suspects will be misidentified as the targets, which opens the door to the possibility of a false conviction. First off, identifications are not always correct. The data from the target-present lineups suggest that the only two-thirds of the witnesses who choose someone identify the correct target (the 45 percent correct identifications out of the 65 percent who choose someone). Thus, even when the true target is in full view, one of every three people chosen is actually innocent.[9] The rate of picking innocent fillers is particularly high in target-absent lineups, where 50 percent of the witnesses choose someone, inevitably a wrong person. As discussed later on, the high rates at which witnesses pick people whom they have never seen indicates that the identification of strangers is plagued by an *over-inclination to choose*. The risk of innocent people being falsely convicted is highest in the pervasive showup procedures, where every mistake tends to inculpate the suspect.

There is another reason to be concerned about the reliability of identifications. A second way to assess the reliability of an identification is to determine how the witness would have responded had the suspect been absent from the lineup. This assessment can be done by comparing the performance of witnesses picking from target-present lineups and witnesses picking from otherwise identical target-absent lineups. To be considered reliable, a witness who correctly picks the target when he is present in the lineup should decline to choose anyone when the target is absent. As it turns out, barely half of the correct identifications meet this double criterion of reliability. The other half manage to pick out the target correctly when he is present, but pick an innocent filler when he is absent.[10] Correct identifications that fail to meet the double criterion of reliability are fickle, and as suggested by Steven Penrod, they are little more than educated guesses.[11] Convicting defendants on the basis of such identifications raises serious policy issues because, however fickle, these identifications are habitually presented at trial with great confidence.

In sum, the data from both the laboratory and the field paint a rather bleak picture of the accuracy of identifications. One-third of picks are plainly wrong, and half of the correct ones are fickle. It follows that, in total, just one-third of the picks are reliably correct. Convicting defendants on the basis of identifications should thus cause us to treat this type of evidence with much caution. As discussed later, doubts about the reliability of identifications strengthen the case for reforming lineup procedures, even when these reforms entail a small decrease in the number of correct identifications.

Despite its problematic reliability, eyewitness identification testimony typically has a strong impact on the outcomes of cases. The identification of a suspect is bound to intensify the investigation efforts to prove his guilt, and, as discussed in Chapter 2, it can potentially lead to the collection of more evidence that corroborates that conclusion. The identification is bound also to persuade prosecutors to press charges and offer tough plea bargains, to weaken the tenacity of defense attorneys, and to strengthen the resolve of trial court judges. As discussed in Chapter 6, third-party fact finders tend to place a great deal of trust in the accuracy of identifications. Fact finders are generally insensitive to the numerous factors that hurt the reliability of identifications, and are thus not adept in distinguishing between accurate and inaccurate witnesses. It is hardly surprising that eyewitness misidentification has long been recognized as the most common cause of false convictions.[12] This observation is echoed in the known exoneration cases, of which almost three-quarters can be attributed to mistaken identifications.[13] In a large number of these cases, a mistaken identification was the only evidence presented against the defendants.

The Underlying Memory Process

The remainder of this chapter deals with the processes that explain the accuracy of eyewitness identifications and the factors that influence it. At bottom, the identification of a stranger is an exercise of memory. Witnesses are called to determine whether the suspect they see at the lineup matches their memory of the person they saw at the crime scene. Generally speaking, memory processes consist of three subprocesses: encoding, retention, and retrieval.[14] The research concludes that the accuracy of identifications is complicated by factors that can disrupt the process in each of these three phases.

Encoding. Memories begin with an encoding, which amounts to acquiring information about the object, person, or event. The memory of a person's image is contingent foremost on the encoding of his appearance. The simple truth is that people are not naturally adept at encoding the faces of strangers. There is reason to believe that the evolution of our memory system has disinclined us to expend resources on remembering the images of the tens, hundreds, and even thousands of strangers we encounter on any given day.[15] Encoding is hindered by the often sub-optimal viewing conditions at the criminal event.

Retention.   Following the encoding phase, memories are stored pending retrieval. During this retention period, memories typically weaken as a result of decay. Retained memories are also susceptible to contamination from a variety of sources, such as exposure to the image of the suspect in the media, on a wanted poster, or in court. Contamination can be caused also by exposure to information about the perpetrator obtained through communication with cowitnesses or the investigative interview.

Retrieval.   The culmination of a memory process is marked by its re-trieval, that is, the recovery of the memorized image into conscious aware-ness. Retrieval occurs at various points during the process, such as when the criminal event is spontaneously recalled, or when one recounts it to friends or to a police detective. In the context of identifications, retrieval is performed at the identification procedure, where the witness is asked to determine whether she recognizes any of the people presented in the lineup as the man who perpetrated the crime. Ideally, identification proce-dures would merely elicit the witness's memory and facilitate a straight-forward match with the target. In reality, the procedures amount to a most complex and multifaceted task that introduces a host of difficulties and potential biases. The procedures pose a threat to the accuracy of iden-tifications because people are naturally inclined to choose someone even in the absence of a reliable memory of that person. This *over-inclination to choose* is especially strong when the witness assumes that the perpetra-tor is present in the lineup and when the suspect is somehow singled out from the fillers. Thus this tendency can be readily exacerbated and manipulated by the identification procedure.

The over-inclination to choose is manifested in studies that give wit-nesses a second chance to identify the suspect after being informed that they picked out the wrong person on their first attempt. Rather than ad-mitting that their memory is faulty and shying away from the task, some 60 percent of witnesses actually proceed to pick someone else out.[16] The over-inclination to choose is a robust phenomenon that can easily be dem-onstrated even in informal settings.[17] The phenomenon was illustrated by a study that asked participants to perform an identification from a target-absent lineup just minutes after viewing the powerful *Frontline* documen-tary of the Ronald Cotton case. No fewer than 71 percent of participants picked someone, all of whom were necessarily innocent foils. This rate was no different from that of participants who did not view the film (74 percent).[18] Indeed, Jennifer Thompson herself was apparently overly inclined to identify her assailant (see Chapter 2). Both of Thompson's identifications were based on a weak (and wrong) recognition. At the photographic array, she eliminated four of the six photographs and was left pondering: "I think it was those—I know it was that one, but that one too." She then stated to Detective Gauldin: "I think it's these two."[19] Thompson was hesitant also in choosing Cotton at the live lineup eight days later. After spending some time examining an innocent college student standing in place #4, she turned to Gauldin and said that it was "between #4 and #5." It was only following a second effort that Thompson picked out #5, who was Ronald Cotton.[20]

A large body of research seeks to explain the causes of misidentifications. Contrary to popular belief, human memory is very different from video tape recorders. Like most facets of human cognition, eyewitness identifications are influenced by a nonspecifiable combination of a variety of factors. These factors can have a strong impact on the accuracy of the memory. For illustration, one study found that altering the witnessing conditions of the same target at the same event resulted in swings in accuracy levels from 14 percent to 86 percent.[21] The factors that influence the process will be labeled *accuracy factors* (although when present they typically reduce accuracy).

One type of accuracy factors, labeled *incident factors,* is concerned mostly with the encoding of the memory. These factors pertain to the witness' viewing of the criminal incident itself, including, for example, the illumination at the crime scene, the distance separating the witness and the perpetrator, and the duration of the exposure. For the most part, misidentifications caused by incident factors are spontaneous errors, that is, errors that occur without any direct involvement of the investigation procedures. The second type, *system factors,* pertain to retention and retrieval phases of memory. These factors encompass the procedures conducted by the police to obtain an official identification of the perpetrator. As demonstrated by the research discussed below, system factors have the potential to induce witnesses to make a pick at the lineup where they otherwise would not have done so, and even to induce the identification of the specific person suspected by the police. By their nature, system factors are within the control of the criminal justice system and are thus susceptible to reform. Since the publication of an influential article by Gary Wells in 1978, system factors have been receiving the bulk of scholarly attention. The field is thus placing a greater emphasis on future-looking, systemic reform rather than judging cases ex post facto.[22]

Incident and system factors also interact with one another. The weaker the memory trace, the stronger its susceptibility to biasing factors during the retention and retrieval phases. While badly conducted lineups are unlikely to affect a witness who has a solid memory of the perpetrator, they might well sway the witness who barely remembers him. Indeed, contamination is found to be strongest when the memory for the target is weak.[23] It follows that the passage of time does double damage, in that it both weakens the memory and makes it increasingly susceptible to contamination.

Like many other types of human error, mistaken identifications consist of concomitant failures of *cognition* and *metacognition*. Generally speaking, metacognition pertains to what people know about their knowledge states, such as their beliefs, judgments, and memories. A large body of research shows that errors that can hinder the operation of the criminal justice process tend to be accompanied by metacognitive errors. For example, people are generally incapable of recognizing mistakes in their memory, and are likely to experience incorrect memories as being true.[24] Thus, even the most confident and damning misidentification of an innocent person can arise from an honest mistake.

Observing the Suspect: Incident Factors

A memory can be no better than the information that is initially encoded. Before examining the factors that hinder the encoding, it is worth noting that the encoding of stranger's faces is not strong even under optimal conditions. A series of studies found that people encounter difficulties in recognizing faces they saw just five seconds previously, and even in matching faces seen contemporaneously.[25]

Poor encoding is observed in a series of studies that substitute a person with another person in the middle of a conversation with a third party. In one such study conducted on a college campus, a confederate stopped pedestrians to ask for directions. In the middle of the conversation, two other confederates carrying a door passed abruptly between the two conversants. While obscured by the door, one of the men carrying the door exchanged places with the original confederate, and continued the conversation with the pedestrian. The studies found that almost half of the participants failed to notice that the person with whom they were conversing was not the same person they had been facing just seconds earlier.[26] This finding has been replicated in a variety of situations, such as when a person serving the witness bends down momentarily behind a counter and is replaced by someone else.[27] In another study, some 60 percent of participants failed to notice a change of the target person in a video depicting a theft from a supermarket.[28]

Poor encoding of faces was demonstrated also in a Swedish study in which participants were shown headshots of two people and were asked to choose which one looked more attractive. Immediately after participants announced their choices, the experimenter surreptitiously exchanged the photos and, while showing the rejected photograph, asked participants to explain why that person was more attractive. Here, too, only a minority noticed the substitution, a result again suggesting that the participants had only a weak memory of photographs they had seen a brief moment earlier. Furthermore, the participants' explanations of their choices seemed reasonable, even convincing, though they were—unwittingly—providing reasons that were contradictory to their true choices.[29] This latter finding warrants attention because it manifests a broader phenomenon: people are inclined to provide seemingly good reasons for their putative beliefs, judgments, or behaviors, even if they are erroneous or imaginary. In other words, when explanations are needed but unavailable, people will concoct them, a phenomenon that has been dubbed *telling more than we can know.*[30]

In these studies, the viewing conditions were good: the witnesses had an unobstructed view of the targets, from a close distance, under good illumination, and for a substantial period. In most cases in real life, viewing conditions fall short of this ideal. Each of the incident factors listed below is bound to contribute to weakening the reliability of the identification. While the factors mentioned here play a prominent role in many cases, the list does not exhaust all possible factors.

Distance and illumination. Naturally, encoding an image requires that the visual system first perceive it. Two obvious factors that influence the perception of any object are the distance between the witness and the target, and the amount of illumination at the crime scene. The effect of these factors is familiar: the smaller the object and the dimmer the lighting, the weaker the perceived image. A group of Dutch researchers led by Willem

Wagenaar has sought to provide some guidance as to the magnitude of the two factors. The general findings are that reliable diagnosticity—that is, the ratio of correct to incorrect identifications—loosely follows the "rule of 15," reaching acceptable levels at illumination levels of above 15 lux (slightly above the level of lighting in an urban area illuminated by bright streetlights) and at distances of below 15 meters. Notably, accuracy drops as the distance grows to 20 meters, and worsens at 40 meters.[31] The decrease in identification accuracy with the increase in distances was observed also in a field study conducted in Canada.[32]

The Dutch study revealed also that accuracy declines precipitously once the lighting drops to 3 lux (equivalent to an urban area with bad street lights), and is no better than chance level under full moonlight. The rate of false alarms was high even when one of the two features was good, that is, when the distance was short and the illumination weak, or vice versa. This appears to have been the case in the identification of Ronald Cotton, as Jennifer Thompson observed her assailant from a close distance, but under poor lighting.[33] The likely explanation is that the one strong factor made participants feel that their identification was better than it actually was. This explanation is consistent with the idea that the decision to pick someone is influenced not by the objective strength of the memory, but by the person's beliefs about his own memory—that is, the person's metamemory—which in itself is subject to error.

One ought to be cautious about applying these data too literally in assessing specific cases. For one, they provide rough categories, rather than precise criteria. They also capture the upper boundaries of the viewing conditions, which are often reduced as a result of less-than-optimal values of other factors. More importantly, applying this research to actual cases is complicated by the fact that in most instances there is no objective measure of distance and illumination. For lack of a better alternative, investigators and fact finders must rely on witnesses' self-reports. This reliance can prove to be a problematic source of information. Research on distance estimations reveals disappointing performance, especially when the estimation is done from memory. The consistent finding is that people tend to underestimate distances, and this underestimation increases as the distances grow larger.[34] The participants in the Canadian field study underestimated the distances by about one-third, and when they used ranges to describe their estimations, the true distances fell outside the estimated ranges in more than half of the cases.[35] Underestimating the distance to the target makes the viewing conditions appear better than they really were, which leads to an overestimation of the accuracy of the viewing.

It is similarly risky to rely on witnesses' self-reports of the degree of illumination. The human eye adjusts automatically to the ambient level of light. Within the range of nonextreme lighting, people are generally unaware of the level of illumination in their environment. The fact that the lighting is low in a cozy coffee shop is typically not apparent until one walks out into the daylight. One of the weaknesses of the U.S. Supreme Court's jurisprudence on the question of eyewitness identification is that it relies heavily on witnesses' self-reports of their viewing conditions.[36]

Duration of exposure. A similar line of research has demonstrated the effect of the duration of exposure to the target. As one would expect, the findings show that the briefer the exposure, the lower the accuracy of identification. One study found that shortening the exposure time from forty-five seconds to twelve seconds decreased the level of accuracy by a factor of three.[37] Again, in real-life cases, reliable measures of duration are difficult to obtain given that people tend to overestimate the length of exposure to targets, thus making their identifications seem stronger than they really are. In the bank teller experiment described above, the mean time estimation reported by the tellers was 4.2 minutes, even though the event took on average only ninety seconds. In a different study, a thirty-second exposure to a robber was estimated by witnesses as lasting on average eighty-two seconds.[38] Duration overestimation tends to be particularly pronounced in stressful events.[39] More fundamentally, the bank teller study also demonstrated that time estimation is highly contingent on the method by which it is estimated. When mentally simulating the duration of the encounter with a stopwatch, the tellers reported times that were on average almost four times shorter than their spontaneous estimates.[40]

Witness stress. Another factor that has been found to affect the accuracy of identifications is the witness's level of stress at the time of observing the event. A meta-analysis of laboratory studies has shown that up to a point, increased anxiety improves identification accuracy, but higher levels impair it. High levels of stress have a negative effect on both identification accuracy and memory for the criminal event.[41] Given that the stress of experiencing a crime in real life is far greater than what can be generated in the laboratory, identification accuracy in real criminal settings is likely to be lower than that observed in experimental settings. The negative effects of stress were replicated in the naturalistic field setting of the U.S. Army survival school training program, which contained two types of interrogations, one of which was more stressful and violent than the other. Trainees subjected to low stress interrogations were more than twice as often correct in identifying their interrogators and were considerably less likely to choose innocent fillers.[42] Similar effects were observed in a field study conducted in a frightening exhibit in the tour of the London Dungeon.[43] Likewise, people receiving inoculation injections were more prone to misidentify the nurse who administered the injection than a person with whom they subsequently interacted in a nonstressful situation. Identification accuracy was lowest for those whose pulse rates increased the most.[44] Although Jennifer Thompson appeared never to have lost her composure at the time of her assault, she reported experiencing considerable stress. In her words, she was preoccupied with "whether I was going to live or die."[45]

Weapon presence.   A particular source of stress is the presence of a weapon. The research has shown that the accuracy of identifications is reduced somewhat when the target person is brandishing a weapon, especially when it is aimed at the witness.[46] The likely explanation for this phenomenon is that the weapon attracts the witness's attention, thus deflecting it from the person's facial features.[47] A study that tracked witnesses' eye movements found that the reduction in identification accuracy was directly related to the eye fixation on the weapon.[48] There is reason to believe that in real-life situations, a live weapon pointed at the witness will have an even stronger effect on the witness's level of stress.

Source confusion (transference errors).   Misidentifications can occur when witnesses confuse a familiar but innocent person with the perpetrator. In other words, witnesses correctly recognize the target, but err in associating the memory with the correct situation, time, or place where that person was seen. Confusion between an innocent encounter and a crime scene can turn an innocuous familiarity into inculpating testimony. Errors of this kind are explained as failures in monitoring the source of the memories (discussed in greater detail in Chapter 4).

On occasion, witnesses confuse the perpetrator with an innocent person whom they saw in a different context. This may be a person who happens to work or live near the witness, or a bystander seen in the proximity of the crime. This phenomenon, known in the literature as *transference errors* or *unconscious transference,* was the likely cause of the futile search for John Doe 2, thought to have participated in the bombing of the Alfred P. Murrah Federal Building in Oklahoma City in 1995.[49] The transference effect has been demonstrated also in the laboratory. In one study, participants received a massage from a licensed masseuse and also spoke to a researcher who was in the room. Four weeks later, almost half of the participants confused which of the two people was the masseuse and which was the researcher.[50] In another study, witnesses viewed a video depicting three women in a supermarket, one of whom was viewed shoplifting a bottle of wine. When asked to identify the shoplifter from a lineup that did not include the thief, more than half of the participants picked one of the bystanders, and one in five confused the bystanders with one another.[51]

Own-race effect. A considerable amount of research has been devoted to the phenomenon of the *own-race effect,* or *cross-race bias.* People are less accurate in identifying members of races or ethnicities other than their own.[52] A meta-analysis of ninety-one studies, representing data from almost 5,000 participants, revealed that the cross-race bias is relatively strong and robust. Across these studies, it was found that people are 1.4 times more likely to correctly identify a face from their own race than one from another race. By the same token, the rate of erroneously choosing an unfamiliar face from another race is 1.5 times higher than choosing from one's own race. The cross-race bias is symmetrical; that is, it applies similarly to members of different races.[53] Although the reasons for this phenomenon have not yet been fully explored, they probably involve a combination of cognitive and social factors.[54] There are indications that this effect is moderated by the degree of interracial contact; that is, the more contact people have with members of another race, the weaker the bias.[55] By the same token, witnesses are less accurate in identifying targets from different age groups.[56] This *own age bias* would suggest that cross-age group identifications in real life are less accurate than the average findings from laboratory studies, most of which are conducted with people of similar ages.

Idiosyncratic distinctive features. The outcome of an identification can depend also on the idiosyncratic features of the suspect. The research shows that people share certain stereotypes for faces and voices, which typically converge around positive categories or negative ones, such as criminals.[57] Under certain conditions, people whose physical appearance happens to match a criminal stereotype are more likely to be chosen at a lineup.[58] Other idiosyncratic features may involve distinctive physical attributes such as a noticeably hooked nose or very large ears, or even being considered "good looking." In principle, highly distinctive perpetrators are more likely to be identified correctly simply because they are better remembered by the witness. At the same time, distinctive-looking suspects might receive less fair lineups because it is more difficult to find a sufficient number of fillers with a similar appearance.[59] It is also possible that a perpetrator with a highly distinctive feature will be confused with an innocent person who happens to share that feature.

Identifying the Suspect: System Factors

Other research examines factors that are introduced by the police investigation and sometimes also by pretrial proceedings. By definition, these are system factors in that they are directly controlled by law enforcement agencies. The following discussion demonstrates the sensitivity of identifications to the manner in which the procedures are conducted. The discussion will first focus on factors that occur during the retention period that precedes the official identification procedure, and will then examine the complex array of factors that influence retrieval of the memory at the identification procedure itself.

Pre-lineup Factors: The Retention Phase

Face composite construction.   In investigations in which the police have no initial leads, witnesses may be asked to construct a composite image of the perpetrator. Composites are intended primarily to provide a recognition cue for other people who might be able to identify the perpetrator. Composites can be created by means of graphic kits or computerized programs, or they can be drawn by sketch artists. Two aspects of this seemingly sensible practice warrant attention. The first concerns the limited resemblance of composites to the image of the recalled face. One study found that only one in every four people shown a composite of a target was successful in identifying that target from a lineup, which was barely higher than chance level (one-sixth).[60] The likely explanation for the low resemblance has to do with a discrepancy between the methods employed to construct composites and the cognitive mechanisms by which faces are stored in memory. Composites are constructed via a feature-based process, performed by incrementally adding discrete facial features to the emerging image. In contrast, memory for faces tends to be a holistic, Gestalt-like process.[61]

The second issue has to do with the fact that the construction of the composite can weaken and contaminate the witness's original memory of the perpetrator. This concern was demonstrated by an experiment that showed that constructing a composite resulted in lower levels of accuracy in identifying the target, along with higher rates of filler identifications and nonidentifications.[62] Recall that Jennifer Thompson's mistaken identification followed a construction of a composite. The task took about one and a half hours, and she reported finding it "confusing."[63] Thompson's composite seems to bear resemblance both to Ronald Cotton and to the true perpetrator, Bobby Poole.[64]

Descriptions of suspects. The course of an investigation will often be determined by the description of the perpetrator given by the witness. Reliance on witness descriptions, however, is not always helpful and can be a source of error. As a general matter, people's verbal descriptions of strangers tend to be poorly diagnostic.[65] The holistic impression of facial memory cannot readily be captured by verbal descriptions. A large archival analysis conducted in the Netherlands found that descriptions tend to be nondescript, providing information mostly about general and non-individuating characteristics, such as gender, race, height, and age, and temporary features such as clothing and jewelry. Only 5 percent of the descriptions provided referred to specific facial features, of which more than one-third were found to be incorrect. Almost all the descriptions of facial hair (beards and mustaches) did not match the photographs contained in the police database. The study found no cues to distinguish correct from incorrect descriptions. Specifically, the completeness or degree of elaboration was found to be a poor indicator; detailed descriptions were no more accurate than less detailed ones.[66] Likewise, the bank teller field study discussed above found no relationship between the witnesses' descriptions of the suspect and their ability to identify him correctly.[67] A number of other studies have found that the relationship between description accuracy and subsequent identification accuracy is generally weak and inconsistent.[68]

Memory decay. One obvious factor that affects outcomes of identification procedures is the amount of time that has passed since witnessing the perpetrator. A most basic phenomenon of human memory is that memories decay over time, which means that shorter retention times are bound to lead to more accurate identifications.[69] A recent meta-analysis shows that the memory weakens relatively sharply soon after encoding, but the rate of forgetting decreases gradually until it flattens out. The studies reveal a strong decrease at about one week from the time of encoding.[70] The discontinuity around one week is consistent with naturalistic data from 640 identifications conducted by the London Metropolitan Police, which showed a decrease of about one-half in suspect identifications between viewings one week and one month after the event.[71] A more moderate forgetting effect was observed in the archival data from Sacramento County, California, where the rate of suspect identifications dropped from 55 percent in the first week to 45 percent thereafter.[72] The passage of time is related also to the changes in people's appearances. As one would expect, the more the targets change, the less likely they will be recognized.[73]

Successive viewings. The criminal investigation process often entails multiple identification procedures, comprising any combination of mugshot searches, showups, photographic arrays, live lineups, and in-court identifications. The problem is that mere repetition can alter witnesses' memory and make unseen people look familiar. Effectively, memories can be tested reliably only once. Experimental studies have shown that participants who were exposed to mugshot books that contained an innocent filler are more prone to choose that filler in a subsequent lineup and are less likely to choose the true perpetrator.[74] These findings were confirmed by a meta-analysis aggregating thirty-two studies testing more than 1,600 participants.[75] This phenomenon has been referred to as the *mugshot effect,* but since it applies equally following photo lineups[76] and showups,[77] it is better conceived of as the *successive viewing effect.* Evidence from memory research would suggest that errors arising from the successive viewing effect are generally not conscious; that is, the witness does not consciously recall seeing that person in order to feel that he seems familiar.

The detrimental effects of successive viewings are supported by archival data. In the study of police procedures conducted in Sacramento County, the rate of suspect identifications in the second procedure was significantly higher than the rate for comparable first-time identifications. Almost half of the witnesses who failed to identify the suspect on the earlier occasion made an identification at the later procedure.[78] This is a troubling phenomenon, since for the most part the passage of time weakens rather than strengthens memory.[79] A plausible explanation for the increase in identifications over time is that the witnesses' memories were contaminated by the successive viewings.[80]

One of the underlying causes of the successive viewing effect stems from cognitive aspects of memory. Memories can be altered by mere exposure to a target. Thus, exposure to an image of a suspect at the police station can interfere with the memory of the perpetrator from the crime scene, and make the former image seem familiar to the witness. This *familiarity effect* makes it hard for the witness to remember whether the subsequent recognition stems from viewing the target at the crime scene or at the previous police procedure.[81] Another cause of the successive viewing effect stems from the social aspects of having positively chosen a person in the first procedure. This *commitment effect* is understood to be driven by the pervasive motivation to appear consistent, reliable, and competent. Commitments made publicly have been found to exert a greater effect than private commitments.[82] Moreover, the repeated presence of just one target in successive viewings might well be interpreted by the witness as a cue from the detectives that this is their suspect. Witnesses might also experience repeated lineup procedures as pressure to be more cooperative and helpful in bringing the investigation to a close.

The distortive effect of successive viewings is a serious matter. If each of the successive viewings were an independent test of the witness's memory, one could interpret the consistent identification of the same suspect as a testament to the witness's accuracy. But given the biasing effect that each test has on all subsequent ones, the repetition is hardly diagnostic. It could just as easily signify a rehashing of the same error. In numerous DNA exonerations, the suspects were misidentified following repeated procedures. Invariably these suspects were the only person who was included in all of the identification procedures. The practice of successive viewings has long been a source of frustration among defense attorneys, who have labeled it "photobiased lineups."[83] Successive viewings become especially perilous when witnesses demonstrate poor memory of the perpetrator in their first attempts. Hesitant, tentative, and slow identifications are generally indicative of weak recognition. Recall that Jennifer Thompson's identification of Ronald Cotton was the product of successive viewings following a weak recognition. There is reason to suspect that her identification was bolstered by the commitment effect. Reflecting on her second identification, Thompson explained: "For me that was a huge amount of relief, not that I had picked the photo, but that I was sure when I looked at the photo that was him and when I looked at the physical line-up I was sure it was him. And again, as a credible witness, you had to have the two go together."[84] Whether Thompson's lineup identification was distorted by the prior identification or not, she was clearly unaware of that possibility. As she testified in court, "I didn't choose him because of a photo lineup and I didn't choose him because of just a physical lineup. I chose him because he was the one in my apartment."[85] Over the course of the investigative process, Thompson's weak memory trace of the assailant transformed and strengthened into a formidably confident and persuasive testimony. Her true memory of Bobby Poole had been supplanted entirely by Cotton's image. Even after coming to terms with her mistake, she stated: "I still see Ronald Cotton. . . . I would do anything to erase that face out of my mind, but I can't. It is just in my head."[86]

The least reliable witnesses are those who first choose an innocent filler and subsequently change their identification to choose the police's suspect. It is fair to say that these witnesses have a poor memory of the perpetrator, are overly inclined to choose, and are susceptible to influence from the police. In short, these witnesses are utterly unreliable and they should take no part in the identifying the suspect.

Extraneous information.   A witness's visual memory of the perpetrator can be contaminated by sources other than successive viewings. Researchers have shown that exposing witnesses to visual images that resemble the target person can interfere with the original memory. For example, showing witnesses composite images that resemble the target person but contain erroneous features increases the rate of choice of innocent fillers who share those features.[87] A recent study with military personnel enrolled in survival school training found that exposing trainees to photographic images that were associated (falsely) with their interrogators resulted in a substantial decrease in their ability to identify their interrogators.[88] Identifications can be contaminated also by exposure to verbal information. Verbal contagion was demonstrated in a study that found that merely mentioning that the target person had a mustache (when he did not) increased choices of innocent foils who had mustaches.[89] This contamination went on to affect choices at a later lineup that contained the true target.[90] Verbal contagion also affected the verbal descriptions given by witnesses and the composite images they drew.[91] Contamination has likewise been found to be caused by exposure to misleading questions.[92] The danger of contamination must be taken seriously given that in real life, witnesses are often exposed to information from a range of sources, including cowitnesses, police investigators, and depictions of the suspect in published composites or in the media.

Pre-lineup confidence. The decision whether to conduct an identification procedure is often influenced by cues from witnesses, especially their stated belief in their ability to identify the perpetrator. High levels of pre-lineup confidence can encourage a detective to conduct a lineup when she might otherwise not have done so. Pre-lineup confidence may also affect the detective's belief in the suspect's guilt, potentially raising her hopes and expectations from the impending identification procedure. The available research, however, shows that pre-lineup confidence is not diagnostic of the witnesses' ability to make correct identifications. In other words, witnesses who predict that they will successfully identify the target are not significantly more accurate than those who expect less from themselves. In the Ronald Cotton case, Detective Gauldin was strongly impressed by Jennifer Thompson's confidence in her ability to recognize her perpetrator.

Identification Procedures: The Retrieval Phase

There is wide variability among and within the almost 20,000 law enforcement departments nationwide as to which identification procedures they use and how they conduct them.[93] The available data indicate that showups constitute about one-half of the identification procedures used in criminal prosecutions,[94] and about three-quarters of the remaining lineups are photographic.[95] Thus, live lineups—which are considered to be more accurate than other procedures—account for only a small fraction of the identifications.[96] More importantly, showup procedures are the wild card of identification procedures: they are the most widely used, the least studied, and probably the most error prone.

The key question is the extent to which witnesses' responses are influenced by the procedures used to elicit them. It is important to keep in mind that most misidentifications do not result in false convictions, because the innocence of the fillers is known to police. The concern is that the witness will pick out the person suspected by the police even though she does not recognize him from the crime scene. This will occur randomly in one-fifth (or more, as discussed below) of filler choices, and it will occur also when the police's suspect is somehow singled out or the witness is otherwise steered toward him. These errors provide fertile ground for false convictions.

Lineup Design

Showups.   The most expedient identification procedure is the *showup:* presenting the suspect alone to the witness and asking her for a simple yes/no statement of recognition. Showups are an advantageous procedure in that they can be arranged quickly, before the witness's memory decays and the appearance of the perpetrator changes. They also benefit from the fact that they entail categorical judgments of recognition, known as *absolute judgments:* is this person the suspect or is he not? As discussed below, absolute judgments are generally perceived to be superior to *relative judgments.* Nonetheless, the procedure has some serious drawbacks. The absence of fillers undermines the possibility of distributing errors among many targets, and deprives the administrator of a means of gauging the reliability of the identification. Most importantly, the absence of fillers can result in strong suggestive effects, as witnesses are effectively told by the police that the target is their suspect.

Laboratory findings indicate that showups and lineups produce similar rates of correct identifications, but the former are more prone to yield false identifications,[97] especially when an innocent suspect resembles the target person.[98] There is good reason to suspect that in real life, showups are less accurate than the laboratory data. Showups are often conducted on the fly, under conditions of urgency and hot pursuit, when the prevailing objective is to apprehend the suspect immediately and the witness's emotions are running high. The procedure is usually conducted by patrol officers who are rarely trained in identification protocols. Moreover, showups are often conducted under heightened suggestibility, such as when the handcuffed suspect is sitting in the back seat of a patrol car or standing in the beam of police searchlights. The potential for bias appears to be borne out by the archival data set from Sacramento County, which shows that the rate of identifications of suspects in showups is considerably higher than in other types of lineups (76 percent vs.

48 percent, respectively), and is highest in photographic showups (83 percent).[99] Given the extensive use of showups in real-life cases, there is good reason to believe that they are a major source of misidentification.

Simultaneous and sequential design.   Once an investigator has decided to conduct a lineup, he must decide whether to present the targets simultaneously or sequentially. In *simultaneous lineups,* all targets are presented at the same time, typically standing alongside one another. The witness views them at whichever order she chooses and at her own pace, until she is ready to make a choice. This is the classic lineup format that is often depicted in popular culture. *Sequential lineups* resemble a series of showups. In these procedures, the witness is shown one target at a time, and is asked for a discrete positive or negative identification before the next target is shown. The choice in simultaneous lineups is understood to be based on *relative judgments,* by which witnesses are assumed to choose the person who resembles the perpetrator more than the other people in the lineup with little regard to the strength of the similarity. The concern is that when the perpetrator is not in the simultaneous lineup, witnesses will be overly inclined to pick the innocent filler who happens to resemble the perpetrator most.[100] In contrast, sequential lineups entail *absolute judgments,* which are deemed superior in that they force the witness to determine the resemblance of each target with their memory of the perpetrator independently of all other targets.

The research indicates that sequential lineups are more accurate overall than simultaneous ones, though their exact effect is not entirely clear. The laboratory data show that sequential procedures lead to mixed outcomes because they reduce the propensity of the witness to choose across the board, resulting in fewer choices of innocent fillers in target-absent lineups (32 percent vs. 54 percent), and to a lesser degree, also in fewer correct identifications in target-present lineups (44 vs. 52 percent).[101] A preliminary report of recently conducted field studies shows even greater advantages to sequential over simultaneous procedures, in that they result in a drop in false identifications without decreasing the rate of identifications of the suspects.[102]

Lineup Composition.   The reliability of an identification is very sensitive to the composition of the lineup, specifically, to the similarity between the suspect and the foils. Lineups are maximally diagnostic when the probability of the witness's choice is spread roughly evenly over the entire array of targets. Choosing a suspect from a well-composed lineup offers useful investigative information. Lineups that single out the suspect fail to provide a meaningful test of the witness's memory and are of limited probative value. More importantly, they stand the risk of focusing the investigation on an innocent person.[103] It does not take much to single someone out. For example, in a target-absent lineup study that contained only one individual who resembled the target, 79 percent of witnesses picked the designated innocent individual.[104] At the same time, lineups containing fillers that look overly similar to the suspect are nonprobative in that they make the recognition too difficult. In real life, such lineups are rare.

Most lineups conducted in the United States contain five fillers.[105] Fillers must be chosen so that they match the verbal description of the perpetrator and do not stick out markedly from the appearance of the other fillers.[106] When only a subset of the fillers matches the description, the risk of error is concentrated around that subset, which increases the probability that one of them will be picked out. Composing the lineup with foils who are noticeably dissimilar from the target increases the chances that the target will be picked out.[107] Thus, the diagnosticity of a lineup should be measured not by its nominal size, but by the number of fillers who match the suspect's description and who could realistically be chosen.[108] Typically, limiting the number of these fillers stacks the deck against the suspect.

One experimental method that highlights the limited diagnosticity of ill-designed lineups is the *mock witness* paradigm. In these studies, participants who never saw the suspect are asked to identify him from a lineup, solely on the basis of the verbal description provided by the witness. Given that these participants have no visual memory trace of the suspect, they should not pick the suspect at a rate higher than the inverse number of targets, usually one-sixth of the time. More frequent choices of a particular target suggest that the lineup was biased against him. Laboratory tests of ten real-life lineups found that the suspects were chosen by mock witnesses at a rate of 40 percent, which is equivalent to a random error in a lineup of 2.5 targets. The diagnostic value of these lineups was no better than if the suspects had been placed in lineups with an average of just one and a half fillers.[109]

Lineup bias is even more blatant when the suspect is chosen at high rates by participants who did not view him and were not given any description of him. With no memory nor any knowledge of the suspect, these identifications are apparently based on nothing but suggestive cues stemming from the distinctiveness of the individual or of the photo (such as suggestive markings on the photos or an odd pose).[110] These procedures lack any diagnostic value whatsoever[111] and are deeply troubling. Suspects can be singled out also when they are wearing clothes that resemble the perpetrator's clothing.[112] This effect is particularly strong for showup procedures in which the suspect's clothes are distinctive.[113]

It is important that lineups include only one suspect and that all fillers be beyond suspicion. Placing more than one suspect in the lineup provides no real test of the reliability of the identification, increasing the likelihood that any suspect selected will become the presumed perpetrator.

Lineup Administration

The identification procedure itself might appear to be an innocuous and straightforward task. In actuality, identification procedures are replete with opportunities to induce witnesses to pick someone and inflate their confidence, regardless of their memory or lack thereof.

Wording of instructions. One of the manifestations of the precariousness of identifications is their susceptibility to nuances in the wording of the instructions given to witnesses by the lineup administrator. The research shows that merely mentioning that the perpetrator "may or may not" be in the lineup alters witnesses' choices, with an overall increase in the rate of accuracy. While there is some inconsistency in the data, it appears that the inclusion of this notification reduces false identifications while also causing a moderate reduction in correct identifications.[114] The likely reason for the effect is that, by default, witnesses tend to assume that the perpetrator is present, an assumption that tends to lower their threshold for making a pick. This assumption is likely also to encourage the use of relative judgment strategies, which further increases the inclination to choose. The inclusion of this instruction has become a basic expectation in eyewitness research; instructions that do not contain it are labeled "biased."

Suggestive communication. At times, the police have a strong suspicion about the identity of a perpetrator, but they lack the formal proof that can be used in court. Conducting a lineup in these circumstances poses a risk to the investigation, as the witness might not pick out the suspect, or worse yet, she might pick out an innocent filler. Recall that in real life, one-third of witnesses do not pick out anyone and one in every three picks is wrong. The risk of jeopardizing the investigation might tempt investigators to somehow prompt the witness to pick out the suspect.

Explicitly communicating the identity of the suspect to the witness is bound to be the most effective way to steer her to choose that suspect. It is also blatantly inappropriate. Yet the identity of the suspect can also be conveyed subtly, in both verbal and nonverbal ways. The findings from a modest body of research show that when the lineup administrator is aware of the identity of the suspect, witnesses are more likely to choose that person, regardless of whether the target person was in the lineup.[115] These findings are most pronounced when the inclination to choose is strongest, that is, in simultaneous lineups using biased instructions.[116] Administrators who knew the identity of the suspect were more likely than blind administrators to engage in communicative gestures such as encouraging the witnesses to take another look at the lineup following a no-choice and removing the suspect's photo slowly if the witnesses did not choose him, and were perceived also to apply more pressure on the witnesses.[117] The strength of the suggestiveness was found to be influenced by the degree of the administrators' involvement in conducting the lineup and their physical proximity to the witnesses.[118] Another experiment demonstrated that identifications by one witness can affect identifications by a second witness in a separate procedure conducted by the same administrator. The lineup administrators were the likely conduit of this information, despite being blind to the identity of the suspect.[119] All of these effects seem to have been obtained without any conscious awareness, let alone malicious intent. Both administrators and witnesses reported that they neither conveyed nor received any suggestive information.

Suggestion can also be communicated outside the lineup procedure, by providing the witness with extraneous information that could sway his identification. This is most likely to occur in showups in which the police provide the witness with incriminating evidence, such as that the suspect was apprehended at the crime scene or caught in possession of the stolen wallet. Such suggestions can also influence witnesses' performance at lineups. For example, witnesses' lineup choices were influenced by learning that the person they originally identified had a solid alibi,[120] or that someone else had confessed to the crime.[121]

Confidence inflation. As discussed in Chapter 6, witness confidence plays a strong role in the adjudicatory process in that it strongly influences the way third parties—most importantly, jurors—assess the reliability of identifications. Confidence is used also by police investigators and prosecutors to ascertain the strength and viability of their cases. To a certain degree, witness confidence is indeed diagnostic of the accuracy of the identification. That diagnosticity, however, relies on a true and unbiased measure of confidence, which is not always available. Confidence is a malleable construct, and can readily be distorted by the investigative process. For example, confidence can be inflated or deflated depending on whether a cowitness identified the same person or failed to do so.[122]

A substantial body of research has shown that witness' confidence is easily manipulated by feedback from the lineup administrator. This research focuses not on suggesting the actual identity of the suspect, but on the seemingly innocuous feedback given to witnesses in response to their choice at the lineup. Telling witnesses (fictitiously) that their identification confirms the police's suspicion ("good, you identified the suspect") causes a substantial increase in confidence.[123] The robustness of this feedback effect has been established in a meta-analysis covering twenty studies, with more than 2,400 participants.[124] It is noteworthy that the artificial boost in confidence is accompanied by a concomitant increase in other aspects of the memory, such as the witness's account of the conditions of viewing the perpetrator, the attention he paid to the perpetrator, and the clarity of his memory.[125] These reports have the effect of further bolstering the apparent strength of the eyewitness's testimony. Moreover, according to the Court's jurisprudence, these reports are deemed to be reliable indicators of the witness's accuracy and are taken to support the admissibility of identifications obtained from flawed and suggestive identification procedures.[126] The distorting effect of feedback occurs beneath the level of conscious awareness, as the effects are equally strong for participants who deny being influenced by the feedback and for those who acknowledge its influence.[127] These concomitant changes are another example of the coherence effect, discussed in Chapters 2 and 6.

The effect of feedback on confidence was tested also in the real-life identification procedures conducted by the police in the United Kingdom. After making the choice and reporting their confidence, witnesses were given truthful feedback from a police officer as to whether they had picked the suspect or an innocent filler. The results showed a clear pattern of the feedback effect, depressing the confidence of those who had picked fillers while boosting the confidence of those who had picked the suspect.[128] Jennifer Thompson's identifications provide a clear example of the effects of administrator feedback. She recalls that immediately after choosing Cotton's photograph, "they looked to me and they said, 'We thought this might be the one.'" Similarly, following the live lineup, "I walked out of the room, then he looked at me and he said, 'That's the same guy. I mean, that's the one you picked out in the photo.'"[129] This feedback probably played a role in the inflation of Thompson's confidence over the course of the process.

Lineups in the Wild

Absent national standards of best practices, the nation's almost 20,000 law enforcement departments are largely free to conduct lineups as they see fit. Many departments appear to have no standing policies or procedures,[130] and the training of the officers who conduct the procedures is haphazard and nonuniform, at best.[131] A recent survey of more than 500 police officers reveals an inadequate and inconsistent knowledge of the factors that influence the accuracy of identifications, with correct responses ranging from 12 percent to 91 percent. Notably, only 30 percent of officers were aware of the steep drop in memory with the passage of time, half of them were unaware that exposure to mugshots could influence identifications in subsequent procedures, and almost half believed that it is possible to conduct fair lineup following an initial suggestive or biased lineup. At the same time, more than 80 percent were familiar with the weapon effect, and three-quarters of them were aware that heightened stress can impair identification accuracy. Similar knowledge levels were observed in the manner in which these officers conducted identification procedures. For example, 30 percent of the officers would show a lineup based only on a hunch that the suspect is the perpetrator, fewer than one-quarter of them videotape the procedures, some 95 percent provide witnesses with post-identification feedback. On the positive side, more than 80 percent of officers inform the witness that the suspect may or may not be in the lineup.[132]

A quick review of some known false convictions illustrates the many ways in which identifications can go awry in real life. In all of the following cases, the suspects were convicted at trial largely, if not entirely, based on eyewitness misidentification. Subsequently they were all exonerated on the basis of DNA evidence.

In some instances, the misidentification was spawned by incident factors, that is, by spontaneous errors, typically by source confusion (transference errors). In these cases, the contribution of the investigative process to the error was limited mostly to the failure of detecting the witnesses' mistakes. For example, a number of people were spontaneously recognized by witnesses while shopping in stores,[133] walking down the street,[134] or in an elevator.[135] An Illinois man was identified as the assailant for a crime that occurred three days after he came to the victim's house to see a motorcycle that the victim's son was selling.[136] A Virginia man who worked in a hospital was misidentified by a victim who was a nursing student at that hospital.[137] Witnesses have erroneously identified people who lived down the street from them,[138] worked for the same company,[139] resided in the same apartment complex,[140] or previously visited the victim's apartment or building.[141] In some instances, witness errors were induced by exposure to media reports. That was the likely cause in the cases of Kirk Bloodsworth and Darryl Hunt, in which key witnesses identified these suspects after seeing them on television.[142]

In the majority of known false identifications, however, witnesses' errors were more closely intertwined with the investigative process. The following examples demonstrate the breadth and depth of the contribution of police practices in inducing, exacerbating, or bolstering erroneous identifications. Because of the overall poor recording of investigative procedures, we have only partial knowledge of what exactly transpired behind the scenes. Still, the limited available evidence is sufficient to cast a serious doubt on the procedures that led to these convictions.

A number of falsely identified people were chosen at lineups in which they were the only target who fitted the description of the witness, such as being the only Hispanic[143] the only blue-eyed white male,[144] or the only man with blond hair.[145] Other suspects were identified in procedures where they stuck out relative to the other fillers. A Missouri man was identified from a lineup in which he was the only person dressed in an orange jail jumpsuit.[146] In a Wisconsin case, the suspect was placed in a lineup in which he was the shortest, youngest, and fairest person. A number of fillers were dressed in professional attire and wore neckties and eyeglasses, whereas he was dressed as a working-class man and did not wear glasses.[147] A Texas man was chosen from a lineup in which, according to the witness, he was the only person who was "anywhere near" resembling her attacker.[148] Other suspects were picked out from suggestive showups. For example, a California man was identified in a showup in which he was standing on his front lawn, shirtless, handcuffed, and surrounded by a SWAT team.[149]

In other procedures, lineup administrators engaged in conduct that was grossly suggestive of the identity of the suspect. A Pennsylvania man was convicted for rape after being chosen from a photographic array in which his picture was marked with the letter "R," a marking used by the police to denote people who had been arrested for rape.[150] An Ohio man was identified from a photographic array that listed his height, weight, and age, which matched the description given by the victim.[151] A Mexican national was convicted in an Illinois court on the basis of an identification from a lineup in which the detective singled him out and asked the victim whether he was "the one."[152] A California man was chosen by the witness only after she was shown a wanted poster bearing his photograph.[153] A Texas woman who was raped by a shirtless man identified her perpetrator from a photo lineup that was mailed to her a year after the crime. The suspect was one of the only two shirtless men in the lineup.[154] A New York rape victim declined to identify her assailant in a showup. After being prodded by the police and shown a four-year-old photo of the man, the victim returned to the showup and identified him as the perpetrator.[155]

Despite the habitual absence of lineup records, a number of cases reveal the use of biasing instructions. In a California case, the detective overcame a witness's reservations by assuring her that the perpetrator was present at the lineup and encouraging her to make a selection.[156] At a Texas trial, the witness reported that the lineup administrator "said I couldn't think it was him. He said I had to make a positive ID. I had to say yes or no." The hesitant witness then proceeded to identify the suspect.[157] Lineup instructions have also been used to soothe witnesses' doubts about their memory. In a press interview following the exoneration of Peter Rose (discussed in Chapter 1), the victim explained that she went along with the police because she thought that they "had other evidence against Rose."[158] Similarly, Jennifer Thompson felt reassured by the existence of the physical evidence that tied Cotton to the crime.

Misidentifications induced by the police investigation are apparent in the many cases in which the information provided by witnesses changed over time. In some instances, witnesses chose suspects who were noticeably different from the descriptions they initially gave the police. In a Missouri case, the victim described her assailant as being clean-shaven, 6'2" tall, and having a "David Letterman–like" gap between his front teeth. Seven days later she was shown a lineup of four people and identified an innocent suspect who had a full mustache, was 5'10" tall, and had a broken tooth.[159] An African-American man was convicted in a Texas court and sentenced to life on the basis of the identification by a rape victim, even though she initially told the police that her assailant was a white man.[160] An Illinois man was identified by a witness who first told the police that her attacker wore a diamond earring, had a tattoo, and spoke English. The man she identified had neither a pierced ear nor a tattoo, and he spoke only Spanish.[161] A Massachusetts man was identified by a witness who described her attacker as a clean-shaven man with crossed eyes, even though he had a mustache and goatee and no crossed eyes.[162] The notorious "Bird Road Rapist" who operated in Florida was described by multiple victims as an English-speaking Latino, weighing approximately 200 pounds, and at least six feet tall. Luis Diaz, who was convicted for the crimes, weighed 134 pounds and stood 5'3" tall. He spoke no English at the time.[163] In some cases, witnesses chose the suspect even after telling the police that they did not get a good look at their assailants. Examples include the cases of Peter Rose and Walter Snyder, discussed in Chapter 1.[164] In numerous cases, the witnesses' testimony in court made their identifications at the lineup sound much stronger than they really had been.[165]

In many cases, witnesses chose innocent suspects only after successive viewings, having failed to identify them in previous procedures. Invariably the innocent suspect was the only target to appear in all the procedures. A Texas witness failed to identify the suspect in several photo arrays. She then identified him from a sketch, and later identified him in a live lineup.[166] A New York witness failed to identify the defendant one day after the crime, but picked him out forty-five days later.[167] A witness in an Indiana case failed to identify the suspect in two live lineups, but eventually picked him out in a photographic array.[168] A Georgia man was convicted on the basis of testimony by one witness who identified the suspect in a photo array but later failed to identify him in a lineup, and by another witness who identified him in the lineup but not in the photo array.[169] In a West Virginia case, a rape victim was interviewed by the police repeatedly over the course of eight months. At the third interview, the witness ruled out the defendant from a photographic array, stating that she knew him, "and it wasn't him." Four months later, following a number of police interviews, she identified the man at a live lineup. In court, she stated that there was no doubt in her mind that he was the person who had assaulted her.[170] A Virginia man was convicted for burglary and the rape of a thirty-five-year-old woman. Initially the victim told the police that the room had been too dark to see the face of the assailant. At a photographic lineup conducted one day after the crime, she failed to pick out the defendant's photograph. After discussing the case with the detective and learning information about the defendant, the victim reexamined his photo and stated that his eyebrows seemed familiar. In court she identified him with complete confidence.[171]

More troubling, some suspects were picked out by witnesses who had chosen a different person at a previous procedure. Men from Georgia[172] and Oklahoma[173] were sent to prison on the basis of such identifications. In a Tennessee case, the victim failed to choose the defendant from a photographic array, and her boyfriend selected a filler. At the live lineup, she identified the suspect, but the boyfriend again selected a filler. Nevertheless, at trial both identified the suspect.[174]

The potential of poor procedures to contaminate identifications is most obvious in cases in which an innocent defendant is identified by multiple witnesses. The Florida man convicted for serial rapes attributed to the Bird Road Rapist was identified by at least eight victims.[175] Kirk Bloodsworth was identified by five people.[176] Ronald Cotton was identified not only by Jennifer Thompson but also by the second victim and another bystander. Multiple misidentifications have occurred in numerous other cases.[177]

The danger of misidentification is punctuated by the precariousness of the circumstances that lead to the inclusion of innocent people in police lineups. It did not take more than being spotted wearing a particular item of clothing,[178] having a photo on record from a minor traffic violation,[179] bearing a resemblance to a composite sketch,[180] acting strangely at a coffee shop about a mile from a crime scene,[181] skating at an ice rink where the perpetrator was believed to be present,[182] living near the victim,[183] bearing the same name as a wanted person,[184] or being named by a jailhouse informant.[185]

Recommendations for Reform

The research covered in this chapter points to a problematic mismatch between the frailty of human memory for strangers' faces and the societal need for identifying perpetrators, particularly when the identification is the key to a successful prosecution of serious crimes. As the research demonstrates, the identification of strangers is plagued by a complex and often-unnoticed slew of cognitive and social factors that contribute to this process. In reality, memories for faces vary widely from faint to strong, and witnesses' identifications range from plainly spurious to highly accurate. Identifications are often based on weak encoding, and are thus likely to result in nonidentifications and misidentifications. Memories are also malleable and ephemeral mental states—constructed, stored, and retrieved by mechanisms that lie beneath the level of awareness and well beyond human control. Gary Wells and colleagues have argued that memories ought to be preserved, not unlike other kinds of trace evidence such as blood samples or pieces of fiber that can be damaged or destroyed by mishandling.[186] In fact, this argument should be taken one step further. Unlike a blood sample secured in a sealed vial or a fiber locked in a hermetic plastic package, memories are fragile and porous, and are susceptible to decay and contamination. As such, memories warrant even greater care. A more accurate analogy would be a mischievous recording device that gradually fades and blurs images, confuses images from different scenes, blends images from different sources, and alters its images under pressure. The memories produced through this apparatus can be even more treacherous in that they are subjectively experienced by the person as accurate and unadulterated. It is easy to appreciate how, with the weight of the conviction on her shoulders, the witness will end up choosing a person who seems to be the suspect, even absent a reliable memory trace.

A major challenge facing eyewitness researchers is how to employ the research in the service of the criminal justice process. One potential use of the research is to assist in ex-post assessments of the reliability of identification testimony.[187] These assessments could assist police investigators in gauging the strength of their case and devising future lines of investigation. The assessments could likewise be sought by prosecutors to help in decisions regarding indictments, settlement negotiations, and trial strategies. Assessments of identification accuracy could also be used by fact finders to assist in determining the defendant's guilt. Both incident and system factors have the potential to inform these ex-post evaluations of specific identifications. It should be clear that incorporating all these factors to produce a discrete judgment of the accuracy of a given identification is an exceedingly difficult task. In all but extreme instances, no eyewitness researcher would venture to offer an unequivocal judgment of the accuracy of any particular identification. Still, cognizance of the effect of these factors is bound to help reach a somewhat more nuanced and realistic assessment than unquestioning trust in the identification.

Another way in which the research can assist law enforcement agencies is by suggesting valid indicia of accuracy. A number of studies have found that witnesses' response time and raw confidence are promising indicators of the accuracy of an identification. Witnesses who pick a person quickly are generally more accurate than those who take more time to decide. Studies have found that accurate identifications are more likely to be made under 30 seconds.[188] Recent research indicates that assessments of accuracy can be further improved by combining the witness's response time with her confidence in the choice. One study found that choices made within 10 seconds and accompanied by high confidence are considerably more accurate than slow and low confidence choices.[189] A large field study conducted in Germany found large differences between witnesses who decided within six seconds and expressed confidence levels above 90 percent, and witnesses who were slower and less confident.[190] Pending further replication, detectives and prosecutors might be in a position to place a greater deal of trust in quick and confident decisions (assuming of course that the procedures were conducted properly and that the witness's memory was not contaminated in any way). By the same token, decisions that take more than a minute or so and are not accompanied by high levels of confidence ought to be treated with circumspection.[191]

The most important payoff of the research is to generate policy recommendations, specifically, the prophylactic use of system factors to prevent police from inducing erroneous identifications in the first place. Some eyewitness researchers have been working in collaboration with law enforcement agencies in pursuit of policy reform. The first major step in this direction was the 1998 publication of the Scientific Review Paper of the American Psychology-Law Association, also known as the White Paper.[192] This led to the development of the *Guide for Law Enforcement,* issued by the Department of Justice's National Institute of Justice.[193] Reforms of this kind are gradually percolating into the practices of law enforcement, as a growing number of states and counties have implemented some version of reformed procedures.[194] There is good reason to believe that these reforms will gradually spread.

The following recommendations seek to provide best-practice protocols. The recommendations are directed at the twofold goal of maximizing the accuracy of identifications and the transparency of the procedures used to elicit them.

1. To the extent possible, construction of composites should be avoided.
2. Lineups should be preferred over showups; live and video lineups should be preferred over photographic arrays.
3. Suspects should not be placed in identification procedures absent an appreciable threshold of guilt.[195]
4. Prior to the lineup, witnesses should not be exposed to any identifying information about the suspect from any source.
5. Lineups should be conducted as soon as possible after the witnessed event.
6. Lineups should include only one suspect and five or more fillers whose innocence is beyond doubt.
7. Fillers should match the witness's description of the perpetrator and not be noticeably dissimilar from the suspect.
8. The suspect should be allowed to determine his place in the lineup and to change places between lineups.
9. The witness should be instructed that the perpetrator "may or may not be" in the lineup, and that it is appropriate to respond "perpetrator is not present," and "don't know."
10. Targets should be presented sequentially (rather than simultaneously).
11. All identification procedures should be "double blind": the administrator must be kept unaware of the identity of the suspect; the witness should be informed that the administrator does not know the suspect's identity.
12. The administrator should refrain from any communication or behavior that could be interpreted as suggestive or revealing of the identity of the suspect.
13. The witness should announce his recognition or nonrecognition, followed immediately by a confidence statement. The witness should not be given any feedback before completing the statement.
14. The time it took the witness to announce recognition should be measured and recorded.
15. To the extent possible, witnesses should participate in only one identification procedure; in cases that require successive viewings,

every effort should be made to include the same foils in all procedures.

16. Witnesses who at any time pick someone other than the suspect should not be allowed to provide any identification testimony about the suspect.

17. Witness who fail to identify the suspect, make a hesitant decision, or express low confidence at the initial identification should be deemed to have a weak memory of the suspect.

18. The procedure should be recorded in its entirety, preferably on videotape. Recording should include the images used and the instructions given. The witness should be videotaped throughout the procedure.[196]

A number of these recommendations are relatively uncontroversial, in that they increase accuracy across the board. There is little reason to suspect any loss of accuracy through practices such as placing only one suspect in the lineup, allowing the suspect to determine his place in the lineup, refraining from providing feedback before the witness has stated her confidence, and measuring the time the witness takes to announce the choice.

Other recommendations are likely to entail a tradeoff between the intended objective of reducing false identifications and the unintended effect of losing correct identifications. Some of these tradeoffs are nonetheless noncontroversial, for example, ensuring that the foils match the description of the suspect and that the administrators be blind to the identity of the suspect.[197] These recommendations do not raise serious dilemmas because the purpose of identification procedures is to test the witness's memory, not to confirm police hunches. Making the suspect stick out in the lineup and enabling administrators to leak his identity to the witness gut the process of any diagnostic value and turn the procedure into a travesty. One should also be wary of the dynamic effects of such practices. A belief that witnesses can be induced to choose the suspect is likely to lead investigators to use less rigorous criteria in deciding when and how to conduct lineups, and perhaps also to leak the suspect's identity even when the evidence against him is weak. In the long run, such practices are bound to further erode the accuracy of identifications.

The tradeoff between reducing false identifications and reducing correct identifications is sometimes more problematic. Such is the case, for example, with the recommendation to substitute simultaneous lineups with sequential procedures, a reform that is bound to lead to a reduction in both false and correct identifications.[198] Normally, one would be reluctant to implement reforms that are expected to yield such mixed outcomes, even when their desired effects are larger than their unintended counterparts. One argument in favor of these recommendations is that the benefit of reducing false identifications is normatively weightier than the harm of reducing correct identifications. A familiar tenet of criminal justice policy is that we should be concerned more about convicting an innocent person than letting a guilty man go free. Yet there is a stronger argument in favor of these recommendations. Recall that identifications are most trustworthy when they meet the double criterion of reliability, that is, the witness is capable of picking out the target when he is present *and* of rejecting the lineup when he is not. Recall also that only about one-half of the witnesses who correctly identify the suspect actually meet this standard of reliability. The other half of the identifications are fickle, and thus provide a shaky basis for condemning people to prison.[199] It follows that a moderate reduction in the marginal (and likely the most shaky) correct identifications ought not to be considered a valid reason to thwart otherwise desirable reforms.

The recommendation to create a complete record of the lineup procedures is most important. This should include the images used, the instructions given, the witness's choice and other statements, the response time, and the environment surrounding the witness during the lineup. The availability of a reliable and complete record of a well-conducted identification procedure will minimize the effects of memory decay, contamination, and any other biases induced by the investigation and pretrial procedures. The recording of the lineup should minimize if not eliminate any suggestions by investigators or lineup administrators, at least during the lineup itself. The availability of a record should also bind witnesses to their original responses, and thus shield them from any pressures to alter their testimony. In other words, the record will help to maintain the testimony in its *raw* state. This should provide fact finders and other decision makers with the best possible information for assessing the reliability of the identifications.

It would be most advantageous to incorporate all of the proposed recommendations into an authoritative and binding operating protocol, much like the *Guide* published by the Department of Justice. A prescribed protocol would provide police investigators with a benchmark for appropriate investigative methods. The protocol might also assist fact finders in assessing the procedures used in a given case. One study showed that lay participants were largely insensitive to substandard lineup procedures, but they came to recognize the low reliability of the identifications when the flaws in the lineup procedure were shown to constitute deviations from the formal guidelines of the Department of Justice.[200]

A Quantum Leap: Computerized Lineups

The headway that is currently being made in reforming identification procedures in a variety of jurisdictions is most welcome and important. However, this piecemeal approach has its limits. The reforms implemented thus far have been the product of strained compromises between researchers and law enforcement agencies. As a result, only a limited range of improvements have made their way into police stations in all too few jurisdictions. Notably, the Department of Justice *Guide* falls short of recommending the important policies of double-blind administration and videotaping of the procedure. It is incumbent on us to consider whether different approaches could better realize the potential of the research.

The time is ripe for a paradigmatic shift away from the core cause of system failures, namely, human involvement in constructing and administering lineups. Lineups should be conducted instead on computers. The possibility of conducting identification procedures on computers has been mentioned in passing by some researchers,[201] and a number of computer programs have been developed for that purpose.[202] Computerized lineups are being conducted in a series of field studies currently underway in collaboration with four police departments.[203]

Following is a blueprint for a computerized system that is designed to attain superior accuracy and transparency of identifications. This system incorporates, improves, and obviates some of the conventional recommendations discussed above. The proposed system should take care of virtually all the system factors through an automated, self-operated, and easily configurable computerized system. Naturally, the system would be incapable of correcting for errors arising from incident factors, but it could potentially reduce the adverse effects of memory decay and partially prevent contamination from extraneous information. Witnesses would conduct the procedure independently, on a dedicated desktop or laptop. The images of the targets, ideally video clips, would be displayed on the screen. As in current practice in the United Kingdom, lineups would be constructed from video images drawn from a very large database (statewide, perhaps nationwide), all retrievable on the basis of the description of the suspect, and analyzed for visual similarity. The composition of the lineups could be performed by a computerized program, under the supervision of an identification specialist, who is not connected to the investigation.[204]

The procedure would be conducted without direct involvement of law enforcement personnel. All instructions would be provided in text and audio from the computer, and offered in multiple languages. As a result of the large databases of fillers, the lineups would contain a substantial number of fillers (eight or more). Where relevant, voice samples could also be included. Witnesses would input their choice into the computer, and the time it took them to make a choice will be recorded.

While many details remain to be worked out, and stumbling blocks will inevitably abound, the proposed system has tremendous potential for correcting many of the faults inherent in current procedures. First and foremost, the system would serve the core objective of increasing identification accuracy. Lineups would be conducted according to standardized protocols that correspond to best practices, encompassing the recommendations listed above, and probably others based on future research. Lineups could be prepared and administered very quickly, thus minimizing memory decay, and reducing the need for the controversial showup procedure. Accuracy would be increased also by the use of video images, which provide more and better visual information than the frequently used photograph arrays.[205] The capability of including audio information provides an additional advantage in cases in which the identification could be aided by voice recognition, fluency, intonation, dialect, and speech impairments. Importantly, by providing a quick and reliable test, the system would all but obviate the need for successive procedures. By removing police personnel from the process, the system would effectively provide fully blind procedures, thus shielding witnesses from suggestive cues or communications from the lineup administrator.

Such a system would also provide all the benefits of heightened transparency. Throughout the procedure, a video camera and microphone mounted on the screen would record the witness and her environment. The computer and the videotaping of the witness would generate a full account of the entire procedure, including the images used, the instructions given, information communicated to the witness, and a precise account of the witnesses' responses: their pick, confidence, response latency, and any verbal statements that could convey their choice strategy, hesitations, qualifications, or changes of mind.

The proposed system would make identification procedures more convenient, easier to administer, and less expensive than they are today. The abundant supply of fillers would obviate the demanding searches for appropriate fillers to make the lineup diagnostic. When necessary, lineups could be conducted over the Internet, at remote locations such as in hospitals or at witnesses' homes, all under appropriate supervision. In this regard, the system would be more expedient and effective than the system in the United Kingdom, where the procedures are performed in only a small number of specialized identification sites.[206] Without having to convene the witnesses, suspects, detectives, and lawyers at the same time, lineups could be arranged quickly and scheduled flexibly. The filming of the suspect should not take longer than a few minutes,[207] and the computerized preparation and administration should be rather quick. The absence of the live suspect should relieve the fear and anxiety occasionally reported by witnesses, particularly rape victims and abused children. The system would be flexible enough to allow different jurisdictions to program the system to fit their preferred procedures, and even to tailor procedures to specific circumstances. Modifications of procedures would require little more than software updates, thus obviating costly and cumbersome retraining of personnel and revisions of written procedures, and minimizing the fallout from investigative failures.

The feasibility of implementing this system is enhanced by the fact that it is likely to be palatable to law enforcement officials. The switch to a computerized system will be portrayed genuinely as a desirable and inevitable technological advancement. This portrayal is devoid of any condemnation or disapproval of law enforcement personnel.

It must be kept in mind that all parties involved have much to gain and little to lose from increasing the accuracy and transparency of identification procedures. Law enforcement agencies will be better able to identify true perpetrators and to rule out innocent suspects. Prosecutors will be in a better position to convince juries that the identifications are accurate and the procedures are fair. Prosecutors should also appreciate the fact that the system virtually eliminates blunders by detectives and lineup administrators. By the same token, defense attorneys will have stronger grounds to prove the innocence of their innocent clients, and will be less inclined to pursue frivolous claims of lineup impropriety.

4

"OFFICER, THAT'S WHAT HAPPENED"

Eyewitness Memory for the Criminal Event

Chapter 3 dealt with witnesses' ability to recognize and identify the people they saw perpetrating a crime. This chapter deals with the broader range of testimony that witnesses provide about the criminal event. Event testimony typically describes *what happened* in terms of the time, place, statements uttered, sequence of actions, physical objects used, and numerous other factors that help determine what was perpetrated and by whom.[1]

Event memory pertains to both culpability cases and identity cases. A witness's account of the event can assist in determining the culpability of a known defendant. Correct testimony of the perpetrator's utterance can establish his intent, and an accurate report of a lethal bar fight can assist in ascertaining what transpired during the melee. By the same token, misremembering the words uttered by the perpetrator can make an accident appear to be an aggravated assault, and a confusion of the sequence of the bar fight can turn a justified act of self-defense into first-degree murder, and vice versa. Thus, erroneous event memory has the potential to result in false acquittals, or in convictions for noncriminal acts or convictions on charges that are more severe than warranted by the defendant's deeds.

Event memory can be crucial also in identity cases. Sometimes event memory is the primary or exclusive means of identification. For example, a Louisiana man (subsequently exonerated by DNA evidence) was linked to a capital homicide primarily on the basis of two witnesses' identification of his car.[2] More often, event memory serves to connect the suspect to the crime by corroborating other evidence that implicates the suspect, typically an identification of the suspect at a lineup. As discussed in Chapter 2, a mistaken memory played a role in corroborating the identification of Ronald Cotton. Recall that the second victim recognized the red flashlight retrieved from his apartment as similar to the one that was stolen from her by the perpetrator.[3] An Ohio man was convicted for the rape and murder of his mother-in-law. His niece, the primary prosecution witness, testified that the murder followed a dispute over family matters.[4] Other convictions have been based in part on witnesses' recognition of defendants' clothing,[5] boots,[6] tattoo,[7] gloves,[8] car,[9] and various objects such as a knife[10] or a toy gun.[11] In all of these cases the defendants were convicted at trial and exonerated years later on the basis of DNA testing.

It is theoretically possible that all these testimonies were based on accurate memories, and that it was a mere coincidence that these innocent people shared features with the actual perpetrators. The innocent suspect might well have owned a similar car, worn the same clothing, and sported the same tattoo as the perpetrator. It is also theoretically possible that all of these mistaken memories were caused by spontaneous error. In all likelihood, however, these testimonies were actually false memories that were induced through the witnesses' interaction with the criminal justice system. The effect of induced error is most conspicuous in cases in which it would be impossible for the witness to have generated the mistaken memories absent any involvement of the police. For example, a six-year-old rape victim identified the house of the defendant's grandparents where the rape allegedly occurred, and provided an accurate and detailed account of its interior. Given that a different man was matched to the crime by DNA, it became apparent that the victim had never seen or visited the house that she described.[12]

The effect of induced error is conspicuous also in cases in which the witness changes his statements over time to match the police's suspect. For example, Walter Snyder was convicted by a Virginia court for burglary and the rape of a thirty-five-year-old woman. At trial, the victim's identification of Snyder was corroborated by her testimony about her assailant's distinct odor: "a combination of oil and a basement—a musky smell." This testimony fitted Snyder perfectly. As revealed over the course of the investigation, he lived in the basement of his parents' house and came into contact with oil in his job as a boiler technician. It seems clear that the witness's memory had evolved to fit the facts known about Snyder. In her first statements to the police, she said that her assailant smelled of sweat, alcohol, and possibly cigarettes.[13] Two Tennessee witnesses stated to the police that the perpetrator limped only after learning that he had a walking disability and wore a leg brace.[14] Edward Honaker of Virginia was convicted for abducting and sexually assaulting a young woman, and was sentenced to three life sentences plus thirty-four years. In the initial police report, the victim stated that she "hadn't been able to see her attacker clearly throughout the entire ordeal." She told the police that the perpetrator wore a large crucifix, and that he drove a light-colored car that had a patch of rust on the passenger door. None of these facts matched either Honaker or his car. Still, at trial the victim claimed to identify Honaker; to recognize his crucifix, which was actually small; and to recognize his car, which was blue and had no rust stain.[15] Again, in all of these cases the suspects were convicted at trial and were subsequently exonerated by DNA evidence.

Memories of specific details about an event are often nonverifiable after the fact. Absent an electronic recording of the criminal event or unequivocal physical traces, it is all but impossible to verify crucial facts such as the exact words the defendant uttered before striking the victim at the bar fight, the precise sequence of the blows, and whether the victim carried a gun. Without reliable exogenous proof, event memory errors are often irrefutable.

This chapter deals with obtaining memory testimony from victims and cooperative witnesses, who are not under suspicion. Questioning of this type goes under the label *interviewing*. Chapter 5 will deal with the questioning of people who are suspected of having committed the crime, which is typically labeled *interrogation*.

Accuracy and Completeness

At the most general level, event memory has two important features: *completeness* and *accuracy*. Memories are deemed reliable when they contain all the details necessary to provide a comprehensive account of the event, and when those details are correct. To be sure, the accuracy of witnesses' memories is crucial to the integrity of the verdicts that rely on them. Accuracy is the primary focus of the research performed by both memory researchers and legal-psychologists. The research shows that not unlike eyewitness identification, event memory ranges widely from flatly inaccurate to highly accurate, depending on the myriad of incident and system factors that will be discussed below. Still, one can obtain a general sense from a large body of laboratory and field studies. The best—though admittedly crude—estimate of the rate of accuracy for event memory in forensically relevant tasks ranges between 65 and 95 percent, with most studies converging around the level of 80 percent accuracy. This rate has been found in a meta-analysis of fifty-five studies that included over 2,400 participants, using different interviewing protocols.[16] Similar levels of accuracy were found in studies conducted with English police trainees and Scottish police officers,[17] and with people who witnessed actual crimes in real life.[18]

Although this rate of accuracy is encouraging, two caveats must be kept in mind. First, these findings mean that about one in every five details reported by witnesses is false. For cases that hinge on a particular crucial detail, this rate of error can be troubling. More importantly, these rates represent the accuracy under relatively favorable conditions. As discussed below, induced memory errors are most likely to occur when the witness fails to provide the crucial details for solving the case and the police attempt to obtain the missing facts by means of vigorous interviewing techniques.

The pervasive focus on memory accuracy stands to miss a critical aspect of the forensic application of event memory, namely, the completeness of witnesses' memories.[19] Forensic investigations often hinge on specific, sometimes minute, details of the kind that we tend to ignore in our daily life: a particular word, the last two digits of a license plate number, a logo, or a piece of jewelry. Naturally, incomplete memories will often provide detectives with less information than is needed to solve the case. As a result, the crime might go unsolved and the perpetrator could walk free. Memory incompleteness also bears an indirect, but important, effect on the accuracy of memories in that the evidence shortfall often precipitates intensive investigations, and thus increases the prospects of inducing false memories.

While researchers tend not to study memory completeness per se, a number of studies have included measures of completeness that were incidental to the research objectives. Overall, these studies find that people typically remember about one-quarter of the specific details that could realistically make a difference to a criminal investigation.[20] In other words, witnesses' memories tend to omit a majority of the specific details that could be pivotal to the resolution of criminal cases.[21]

It should not be surprising that memories for forensically relevant events are rarely complete. People have limited attention capacity and cannot attend to every single detail of a situation. When viewing a bar fight, a witness might be looking at one of the brawlers and neglect to notice that a different person brandished a knife, and a witness concentrating on a brawler's jewelry might fail to notice his tattoo, and so on.

The research suggests that viewing a complex event entails a certain tradeoff: attending to one aspect reduces the attention to other dimensions of the event. Notably, a tradeoff has been found between memory of the perpetrator and memory of the event.[22]

Naturally, at the time of the event it is impossible for the witness to know which details will be needed to solve the crime. If the case turns on a claim of self-defense, it will be important to remember who started the fight; if the defendant claims an alibi defense, it might be important to remember the exact time of the event; and if the victim gets stabbed, it will be important to remember which of the brawlers drew the knife. The fate of the investigation, then, relies on the somewhat random probability that the witness accurately notices and remembers the specific fact that will eventually be crucial to the resolution of the case.

By frustrating the prospects of a quick resolution of the crime, incomplete memories tend to prompt detectives to engage in an intensive process intended to extract memories for the missing details that they believe can solve the case. Detectives will conduct multiple interviews in which they tend to repeat their questions, convey a sense of urgency, and lean on the witness to provide more information. A central feature of this intensified interviewing is that the witness is strained to engage in *memory work*, which is believed to enable the elicitation of the missing information. Under a narrow set of circumstances, intensified interviewing can actually yield accurate memories for the missing details. As discussed below, on occasion people actually recall facts that were previously deemed irretrievable.[23] More frequently, however, the witness's failure to retrieve the specific detail coveted by the detectives stems from his lack of memory for that detail. Under these circumstances, intensified interviewing can lead to one of three outcomes. First, when the interviews yield no results, the case is bound to go unsolved. Second, memory work can lead to confabulation, that is, to false memories produced by the witness to fill in the missing spaces. As these memories are generated in response to investigative pressures, they are likely to coincide with the detectives' theories of the case. Third, memory work can induce false memories by providing fertile conditions for contaminating the witness's memory with information provided by the detectives. The ensuing testimony thus dresses police hunches as bona fide eyewitness memory.

After a discussion of some general features of human memory, this chapter examines the incident and system factors that are known to strengthen and weaken memorial accounts. As in the domain of eyewitness identification, the research is most useful as a prophylactic device to advise law enforcement agents to maximize the completeness and accuracy of memories and to prevent eliciting false ones. Secondarily, one may utilize the factors to estimate the veracity of particular memories, although with the exception of extreme instances, drawing hard conclusions would be inadvisable.

Human Memory: General Features

Human memory capabilities are intriguing. The memory system plays a crucial role in human cognition. One can only marvel at the ability to recall innumerable life events, to harbor volumes of general knowledge, to command languages, and to spell thousands of words. At the same time, our memories fail us quite regularly. Think of situations like forgetting the name of your conversation partner at a dinner party only minutes after being introduced, or failing to recall where you placed your car keys. Many people cannot describe the face of their watches or the dashboards of their car. Memory failures are present also in important facets of our lives. Studies show that patients forget about half of the medical advice given by their physicians soon after the office visits.[24] This is true even for chronically ill patients.[25] People also tend to have poor recall of their own medical histories.[26]

As the research shows, memory for events cannot be characterized as generally good or bad, as it is highly contingent on a wide range of characteristics related to the circumstances surrounding the encoding, retention, and retrieval. As observed by Daniel Schacter, human memory can be both powerful and fragile.[27] The challenge that faces the criminal justice system is that many verdicts cannot be decided without relying on testimony that originates in this mystifying, often precarious, human capacity.

Popular conceptions of human memory are quite naïve. In a survey administered to over 1,000 jury-eligible citizens in Washington, D.C., some three-quarters of the respondents claimed to have an excellent memory. Almost half agreed that a memory for a traumatic event was like a video recording that can be recalled as if it has been "imprinted or burned onto one's brain."[28] This sanguine view is not limited to lay people. Similar responses were given by one-third of surveyed police officers.[29] A belief in the camera metaphor was expressed also in a survey of experienced Canadian police officers.[30] Some three-quarters of surveyed English police officers stated their belief that witnesses are rarely incorrect.[31]

The sanguine view of memory objectivity has long been repudiated by research that demonstrates that the brain does not merely copy and duplicate memorized events. Decades of research show that the memory system *constructs* memorial accounts from fragments of memories of the observed event. The memory system integrates information from multiple sources and generates information on its own to construct comprehensible and usable memories.[32] These processes, it should be noted, produce both accurate and false memories.

The constructive nature of memory was demonstrated in the seminal work of Cambridge psychologist Fredrick Bartlett. Bartlett asked his students to read a Native American folktale called "The War of the Ghosts," then tested their memory of the text. The reported memories included many details that were not contained in the original story and lacked other information that was contained in it. The most typical divergences from the original story were the addition of narrative elements that seemed familiar to these English students, and the removal of unfamiliar ones. Even specific words were altered, as participants replaced "canoe" with "boat," and "hunting seals" with "fishing." In other words, the memories of the story morphed into something that better fitted the students' own schemas, that is, their patterns of knowledge about the world and expectations from narratives of the kind.[33] While the reconstruction of the story apparently made the narrative more amenable to comprehension and memorization, it entailed a distortion of the original text.[34]

A central characteristic of the memory system is that memories are not monolithic entities. Rather, memorized events comprise an ad hoc grouping of memory traces. According to *fuzzy-trace theory,* event memory consists foremost of a *gist,* that is, the core occurrence that gives the event its criminal significance. In the example of the bar fight, the gist would refer to the fact that people brawled, someone pulled a knife, and a person got stabbed. A memory consists also of *verbatim* traces, which capture surface-level sensory aspects of experience that generally correspond to the specific details of the event, such as the exact words used, the license plate number, and the logo. One of the central observations of fuzzy-trace theory is that the gist and verbatim traces are not encoded or stored in the same manner, and are not retrieved with the same cues. Gist and verbatim traces are also forgotten at different rates, with the latter decaying much faster than the former.[35] Thus, even as witnesses retain memories of the general contours of crimes they observed, they often forget the many specific details that may be needed to solve the case.

Another important theoretical contribution to the understanding of memory is the *source monitoring framework,* developed by Marcia Johnson and her colleagues. The premise of this approach is that for a memory to have any practical meaning, it needs to be attributable to its source. For example, a memory of a knife being drawn is of little meaning if it is not connected to the time, the place, and the context in which it was observed. To serve as a useful memory, it would be necessary to recall whether the knife was seen at the bar fight that is being investigated, at some other bar fight, in a movie, in a dream, or in one's imagination. Thus, the ability to remember an event depends on the person's ability to relate the memory to the physical context of the witnessing experience, as well as to the thoughts, images, and feelings that accompanied it. In other words, to remember something correctly, one needs to be able to monitor and verify the source of the memory.[36] A common cause of false memories is that they become disjoined from their sources, opening the door to intrusions and interferences from other sources. Failures in monitoring memory sources can lead to *source confusion,* that is, mistakenly recalling elements from one event as belonging to another event.[37] Thus, the witness to the bar fight might confuse the jacket worn by the assailant with a jacket worn by someone else at the same bar the night before, or confuse a statement made by the assailant with something said by a different brawler.

Given the fragmented nature of memories, a key feature in their accuracy and endurance is the degree of *binding* all its fragments—the gist, the peripheral details, and the memory sources—into a comprehensive memory.[38] A failure in binding, or its unraveling over time, is a primary cause of both memory loss and memory error. The research helps identify the factors that contributes to both the incompleteness and the inaccuracy of memories.

Incomplete Memories

An obvious type of memory problem is the absence of one. As mentioned, memories for events typically contain only a fraction of the details that could be forensically relevant, which means that witnesses do not always have a genuine memory of all the details that may ultimately turn out to be crucial to solving the case. The reasons for memory incompleteness are numerous. First, as mentioned above, perception of events is constrained by people's limited attention capacity. Unnoticed details do not enter the perceptual system, and thus cannot be remembered. The selective nature of visual attention is demonstrated by a compelling study that shows that when participants are given a distracting cognitive task while watching a video clip, a large number of them fail to notice substantial facts, such as a person dressed in a gorilla suit thumping his chest in the middle of the frame. This phenomenon has been dubbed *inattentional blindness*.[39]

Still, attending to a fact and encoding it do not guarantee that memory will be retrievable at any given point in the future. People retain access to only a small fraction of the events and details they perceive, primarily because memories decay with the passage of time.[40] A large meta-analysis, covering research conducted over more than a century, shows that memory retention over time generally follows a logarithmic function, with retention dropping relatively precipitously soon after the event, and then decreasing at a gradually lower rate.[41] Memory decay is quickest for weakly encoded and poorly bound memories. As mentioned, even when a witness remembers the gist of events, she might have forgotten the often important verbatim details.

One notable exception to the normal forgetting curve is that some memories are better recalled on a subsequent test, a phenomenon known as *reminiscence*.[42] Memory improvements are most likely to occur when the subsequent test uses different retrieval cues.[43] Reminiscence might indeed advance a criminal investigation by providing evidence of the crucial missing details, but its benefits are infrequent and limited.[44] The contribution of reminiscence is likely to be diminished by the effect of memory decay that occurs between interviews.[45] A troubling offshoot of reminiscence is that it provides investigators with a reason to intensify the pressure on witnesses, which is oftentimes the trigger for the creation of false memories.

Autobiographical memories are another exception to the normal forgetting curve.[46] People tend to have better memories for significant and personally relevant episodes than for the impersonal items that are often used in laboratory research. Criminal events are likely to generate autobiographical memories for witnesses and victims for whom the criminal event is often of great personal significance. Memories of criminal events are likely to be mentally repeated many times, with the effect of strengthening and rebinding the memory traces. One strand of research has claimed to show that people have exceptionally accurate and durable memory for unique autobiographical events, particularly incidents that are unexpected, emotionally laden, and consequential. On the basis of studies of events like the Challenger disaster and the September 11 attacks, this line of research suggests that the memory system imprints unique events along with the peripheral details almost indelibly, much like a photograph taken under the bursting light of a flashbulb.[47] In the forensic context, *flashbulb memories* have been taken to show that witnesses have very strong memories even for the peripheral details of criminal events. This claim seems to be exaggerated. First, the research results have been mixed.[48] Second, the types of details tested in these studies typically consist only of autobiographical details that are of little forensic significance in solving difficult factual cases.[49] Finally, flashbulb memories can introduce error in that they have been found to lead to higher levels of confidence and perceived vividness of false details.[50]

False Memories

A major concern with event memory is that, under some conditions, people report memories of things that they never actually witnessed or that never occurred. False memories can occur spontaneously, or they can be induced externally, that is, due to an interaction with another person or exposure to contaminating information. The inclination to report false memories is highlighted by the fact that people tend to provide positive responses about events that they do not or cannot remember, even when they are given the option to state "don't know" or "can't remember."[51] This phenomenon resembles the over-inclination to choose in the context of eyewitness identification. People, it seems, are disposed toward providing information—accurate, false, or imagined—rather than none at all.

Spontaneous false memories. Naturally, memories rely on an underlying perception. People have been found to be generally inaccurate in estimating physical properties, systematically underestimating distances,[52] overestimating duration of time,[53] and misestimating speeds.[54] People also tend to perform poorly in estimating properties of other people, such as judgments of height, weight, and age.[55] Furthermore, human perception has been found to be contingent on the person's schemas and stereotypes,[56] as well as on his motivations and goals.[57]

Spontaneous memory errors are evidenced by research that suggests that people distort their memory to make events easier to comprehend, memorize, and make sense of the world. Recall that in Bartlett's study, the memories of English university students morphed from an unfamiliar Native American folktale into a narrative that was more familiar to them. A similar phenomenon was found in studies showing that people's pragmatic interpretations of events tend to intrude on their memories, thus substituting memory of the observed event with their own constructions of it. For example, people who are asked to memorize a sentence about a spy who "threw the secret document into the fireplace" tend to report remembering that the spy had actually burned the document;[58] and people asked to remember sentences such as "The flimsy shelf weakened under the weight of the books" tend to report remembering that the shelf had collapsed.[59] While these are not unreasonable inferences, they do not accurately account for the observed event and are thus false memories. Moreover, they can be wrong, such as when the spy merely hid the document in an unlit fireplace, and when the flimsy shelf remained intact. Another series of experiments shows that when asked to recall discrete sentences that share a narrative theme, people tend to blend them into a single memory.[60] It has also been found that memories of a narrative can be distorted by the story's outcome. Participants who were told a story about a couple's date that ended with the man raping the woman recalled the date as being more dangerous and promiscuous than did participants who were told that the same event ended with a marriage proposal.[61] Given that outcomes of criminal cases are invariably adverse, witnesses might tend to recall the suspect's conduct as more consistent with that outcome.

People's memories are also influenced by stereotypical beliefs. This was demonstrated in early studies by Gordon Allport that showed how stereotypes creep into the retelling of stories.[62] Another study found that describing a woman as a waitress or a librarian changed people's memories of various details concerning her lifestyle, taste in music, home decor, and more.[63] In a field study conducted in Tokyo, store clerks reported remembering that a particular customer's briefcase was black (the most typical color), though in reality it was green.[64] People also tend to have a better memory for facts that are consistent with their hypotheses[65] and the decisions they make.[66]

Strong evidence of spontaneous false memories comes from a line of studies labeled *crashing memories*. On October 4, 1993, a cargo plane crashed into an eleven-story apartment building in Amsterdam. Television crews arrived on the scene within an hour and thereafter provided extensive coverage of the crash site and the fire that ensued. Because the crash occurred unexpectedly, there was no television film depicting the plane in flight or at the moment it crashed into the building. Ten months later, Dutch researchers surveyed people about the event, asking respondents whether they saw the television film of "the moment the plane hit the apartment building." Fifty-five percent of the participants reported remembering seeing the nonexistent film,[67] thus providing memorial accounts for facts that were impossible to remember. This group of respondents was then asked about a specific detail about the crash, namely, when the fire broke out. Two-thirds of the respondents provided an (imagined) answer describing the outbreak of the fire. In a second study, about three-quarters of respondents reported remembering the airplane's angle of flight preceding the crash. Again, since there was no video recording of the plane before the crash, these participants could not have had genuine memories of the onset of the fire or of the plane's flight path.[68] Another group of Dutch researchers found impossible memories of a (nonexistent) televised depiction of the assassination of a politician days before the 2002 national elections.[69] Likewise, almost half of a group of English respondents claimed to have seen the (nonexistent) video depicting the car crash that took the life of Princess Diana.[70]

Spontaneous memory errors can occur also when people blend features from different memories, a phenomenon known as *memory conjunction.* For example, a conjunction error occurs when, after being presented with the words *blackmail* and *jailbird,* one reports remembering the word *blackbird* on a subsequent memory test.[71] Conjunction errors can also lead people to confuse similar venues, times, and events.[72] When tested for events recorded in their own diaries, people were found to mix facts between one event and another, and to confuse which people were present at which event.[73] People have also been found to confuse memories for actions they merely imagined doing with actions they in fact performed.[74]

Induced false memories. Memories can also be induced by external sources, such as when cowitnesses share their accounts of the crime, the witness learns about the event from the media, or when he is fed information from police investigators. In these instances the witness is likely to testify about facts that he does not really remember or may never have seen. When those sources happen to be accurate, the memories they induce can actually increase the accuracy of the testimony. Though it must be appreciated that the unwitting witness will serve as a mere mouthpiece for the investigator's theory, providing it with a phony mantle of credibility. The situation becomes more troubling when the inducing influences are wrong, thus leading to false induced memories. False memories of this kind not only stand the risk of leading to incorrect verdicts, but they can readily corrupt the investigation and serve as a conduit for disseminating error.

Induced memories can occur absent any ill will, such as when a witness receives information from a cowitness or happens to watch a crime report on television. Induced memories can stem also from an unintentional exposure by the police, typically as a result of substandard investigative techniques. More ominously, false memories can be induced deliberately by zealous police investigators, who plant vital information to reinforce and even fabricate their case.

The central line of research on induced false memories shows that exposing people to false information about an event that they witnessed can interfere with their original memories of the event. When witnesses have no memory of a particular fact, the exposure can lead them to believe falsely that they actually recall it. The exposure can also alter witnesses' memories of facts that they did see, causing a substantial proportion of participants to report memories that contain some of the erroneous misinformation provided to them. The studies that test this phenomenon, known as *postevent misinformation,* typically comprise three phases: participants first witness an event (usually a video clip, a staged event, or a slide show), then they are exposed to information that is inconsistent with the witnessed event, and then they are tested about the event.

The classic work in this line of research was conducted by Elizabeth Loftus and her colleagues. After viewing a slide show depicting a car accident, participants were presented with a questionnaire about the accident. For some of the participants, one of the questions presupposed an incorrect visual fact (for example, implying the existence of a stop sign at the intersection, even though the slide actually showed a yield sign). On a subsequent memory test, a substantial proportion of participants reported having seen a stop sign.[75] In another study, participants were shown a video clip of a car traveling along a country road and were asked to estimate the car's speed "when it passed the barn." In reality there was no barn in the clip. One week later, one of every six participants reported having seen a barn.[76] Memories can be altered also by means of slight variations in the semantic content of the postevent interview. After viewing a video depicting a car accident, participants who were asked to esti-mate the speed of the cars when they "smashed into each other" reported higher speeds than those asked to estimate the speed when the cars "hit each other."[77] Likewise, asking witnesses what kind of gloves the robbers were wearing was found to increase reports of seeing the (nonexistent) gloves, and asking about the appearance of the fourth robber increased reports of seeing a fourth robber (even though only three were actually seen).[78] This finding has been replicated in numerous other studies using different methods of exposure, including media reports, discussions with cowitnesses, and information provided by investigators.[79]

Postevent misinformation has been found to be particularly effective in changing people's memories for peripheral details. One study showed that misinforming participants about the object that was shoplifted in the stimulus scene had little effect on their memories; 93 percent of par-ticipants stated correctly that it was a bottle of wine, and not a pack of cigarettes, as suggested in the postevent narrative. However, providing misinformation about details in the background of the scene led about three-quarters of participants to report false memories.[80] In another study, misinforming participants about peripheral details resulted in ac-curacy rates that were about half of the rate when the misinformation pertained to central objects.[81]

Another body of research has shown that misinformation can go as far as to distort the gist of people's memories, and even falsely implant mem-ories of entire events. This line of research, labeled *implanted memories,* originated with a study by Loftus and Pickrell that showed that people could be led to report childhood memories of unique events that never happened to them. In these studies, participants are asked to recount vari-ous incidents that, as verified by their parents, never occurred, such as getting lost in a mall. At first the participants invariably deny having any recollection of these events. However, by the second or third interview, between one-quarter and one-half report remembering them.[82] Across a number of studies, participants were led to report false memories of riding in a hot-air balloon,[83] being saved by a lifeguard from drowning,[84] having a nurse remove a skin sample from their little finger,[85] being seriously at-tacked by an animal,[86] and running around at a wedding and knocking a punch bowl over the bride's parents.[87] In another study, about one-third of participants were led to recall meeting a live Bugs Bunny character at a visit to Disneyland—a highly implausible event, given that Bugs is a War-ner Brothers character.[88]

This line of research pertains most directly to the debate over the cases that involve claims of recovered memories, that is, criminal prosecutions that are based primarily on childhood memories that are said to have been repressed for many years. Memories of completely fictional events tend not to play a significant role in conventional criminal cases, as it is rather rare that people are charged with committing crimes that were only imagined. Still, this body of research is important in that it manifests the susceptibility of the memory system to suggestion and highlights the conditions that facilitate the generation of false memories.

Distinguishing between True and False Memories

The forensic implications of false memories depend to a large extent on witnesses' awareness of their inaccurate nature. There would be little reason for concern about false memories if witnesses were cognizant of the tenuous or erroneous nature of their memorial accounts. That awareness would presumably enable them to withhold or qualify their testimony accordingly. As with all other aspects of cognition, the memory system is closely linked to the person's metacognitive system, also known as *metamemory*. Metamemory judgments are related to people's ability to monitor the source of their memories, which could help to determine whether the memorized fact was genuinely perceived at the event, induced by postevent information, or generated internally. The research shows that metamemorial failures are not uncommon.[89]

There is some evidence to support the belief that people's experience of true memories is distinguishable from false ones. Some studies have revealed that true memories are more vivid and coherent, richer in detail, and held with higher confidence.[90] Such was the case, for example, in some of the false memories generated in the implanted memories paradigm.[91] These differences, however, are not robust and do not hold strong across the board.[92] Difficulty in distinguishing between the two kinds of memory is probably related to the fact that they are produced by the same mechanisms.[93] Distinguishing between false and true memories is particularly difficult when the memories are bonded weakly to their source or have been worn out by decay. Metamemorial differences tend to be blurred by repeated retrievals, which is commonplace following unique and personally relevant experiences.[94]

One of the puzzling aspects of both false and incomplete memories is that they tend to be replete with specific details. People who could not recall their daily activities from the previous week tended to offer (false) memories of their activities.[95] Participants who were asked about cars crashing into each other (as opposed to hitting each other) also tended to report seeing (nonexistent) broken glass at the scene of the accident.[96] As mentioned, a majority of the Dutch participants who reported seeing the (nonexistent) video of the Amsterdam plane crash also recalled that the fire started immediately, and that the plane was flying level before crashing into the building.[97] Participants who were led to falsely recall riding in a hot-air balloon also tended to report various details of the experience, including being fearful and feeling the wind blowing in their face.[98] Similarly, participants who falsely recalled having a skin sample removed from their little finger reported that the infirmary smelled horrible,[99] and participants who remembered knocking over the punch bowl at the wedding reported that it caused a big mess and they got into trouble for their mischief.[100] Some two-thirds of the participants who falsely reported meeting Bugs Bunny in Disneyland said that they shook his hand, and almost half reported hugging him. Others remembered touching his ear or tail or hearing him say "What's up, Doc?" One participant even reported remembering feeding him a carrot.[101] The invention of details to fill in false and incomplete memories is yet another example of the *telling more than we can know* phenomenon.

The details that accompany false and incomplete memories are not generated randomly, but tend rather to be based on information that is plausible and typical of the situation. In other words, people tend to fill in the missing details with what they normally expect to see in situations of the kind, on the basis of their knowledge schemas.[102] For example, people are prone to report that during the previous week they did what they do on typical days, and that they saw broken glass in the scene of a car crash.[103]

The filling in of false and incomplete memories with detailed and familiar accounts can affect the outcomes of criminal cases. As discussed in Chapter 6, memories containing rich details are more likely to be believed by third parties. Rich and detailed memories are prone also to strengthen the witness's metamemorial confidence in her own memory.[104] The schematic knowledge that is used to fill in false and incomplete memories is often wrong. For example, in the crashing memories study, a majority of respondents stated that they saw the airplane flying horizontally before crashing into the building, probably because people are most familiar with airplanes flying horizontally while approaching and taking off from urban airports. In this case, however, the false memory was incorrect, as the plane was in an almost vertical nosedive as it slammed into the building. Similarly incorrect were participants' memories of the wind blowing in their faces during the (nonexistent) hot-air balloon rides. In reality, the ambient air is still when one is riding in hot-air balloons.[105] The challenge, then, is to discern which of the witness's statements reflect facts that he actually perceived.

Event Memory Factors

It should be clear by now that the workings of human memory are too complicated and variable to enable general judgments about the reliability of any given memory. The vast body of memory research has revealed a large number of factors that are likely to affect the accuracy of memorial accounts in difficult investigations. Again, it will be useful to draw on the distinction between *incident factors* and *system factors,* while bearing in mind that some factors can belong to both categories. While both types of factors can shed some light on the reliability of a memory in a given case, system factors warrant particular attention in that they can guide law enforcement agents toward the prevention of false memories in the first place. Except in extreme cases, single factors rarely determine the veracity of a given memory by themselves. Rather, the robustness or fragility of a memory depends on a combination of factors, typically both incident- and system-related ones.

As a general matter, the effect of memory factors on a given memory depends to a large degree on the strength of the underlying memorial trace. Strong memories tend to be more stable and are retained longer. They are also more resilient to alteration, interference, and confusion, and are thus less likely to be contaminated or to be supplanted by false memories. By the same token, weak and decayed memories are most susceptible to the influence of memory factors. As discussed in Chapter 6, memory strength is not a monolithic property. While a witness may have a strong and accurate memory for some aspects of an event, she might have only poor memories or none at all for other facets of the same event.

Incident Factors

As discussed in the context of eyewitness identification, errors influenced by incident factors are typically spontaneous errors. Spontaneous errors occur, for example, when a witness fails to pay attention to the specific detail that is crucial to the investigation, forgets the detail, or, absent any external involvement, infuses the memory with a detail from a different event. The most important cluster of incident factors pertains to the viewing conditions at the time of encoding. As discussed in Chapter 3, the relevant viewing conditions include the illumination, distance to the event, duration of exposure, weather conditions, and the like.[106] The following discussion covers a range of additional incident factors.

Emotional arousal. The strength of encoding is heightened by the event's emotional intensity and its personal significance to the witness. Many crimes, especially violent crimes, are extreme and unique events in people's lives and lead to high levels of emotional arousal. Brain research using functional magnetic resonance imagining (fMRI) and hormonal tests shows that intense negative emotions leads to stronger memories for the event.[107] However, high arousal also narrows the focus of the attention, typically at the expense of the peripheral details. A field study conducted at a police training college in England found that arousing events resulted in memories that included more accurate, but fewer, details.[108] Similar findings were observed in a study of Scottish police personnel.[109] Another study found that arousal increases the memory for a violent segment of the event, but it weakens memory for what preceded and followed that segment.[110] In other words, arousal seems to enhance memory for the gist of events, but reduce memory for peripheral details, a phenomenon known as *tunnel memory.*[111] Emotionally arousing events have been described as "attention grabbing."[112] The assassination of Abraham Lincoln by John Wilkes Booth is a telling example. Although the murder was witnessed by a sizable crowd, there was little agreement on what exactly transpired during the stressful event.[113]

Memory consolidation. Once encoded, the resilience of the ensuing memory will depend largely on the successful binding of its fragments, that is, gluing the gist, peripheral details, and memory sources together. Memory binding is enabled by the process of consolidation that follows perception.

Memory consolidation is influenced to a large degree by the number of times the memory is retrieved. Laboratory studies show that repeated retrievals delays memory loss,[114] and strengthens the sense of familiarity with it, or *fluency,* which in turn increases the likelihood of its recollection.[115] Memory consolidation can also be enhanced by means of narrating one's memories to others, which has similar effects to those of reiterating the memory to oneself. Given the dramatic and sometimes traumatic nature of criminal events, witnesses and victims are generally prone to share their experience with others, including cowitnesses, family members, friends, therapists, the media, and even strangers.[116] In many instances, these narratives will later be shared also with police investigators and prosecutors.

The narration of memories can affect the content of witnesses' memories. People share their stories for a variety of reasons, often serving multiple goals concurrently. Survey data reveal that stories are told not only to convey information, but also to entertain, elicit sympathy, gain attention, and the like. Almost half of all stories are retold differently on different occasions, primarily because of changes in the audience. The respondents reported that their narrations often contain some sort of distortion, such as exaggeration, minimization, selectivity, or supplementation of information. These variations were driven by the goals of the narration.[117] These survey data are consistent with experimental findings. Telling a story in different ways has the effect of conforming subsequent memories of the story to that narrative,[118] a phenomenon labeled *saying-is-believing*.[119] One possible reason for this phenomenon is that narration entails selective rehearsal of the features of the event that cohere with that particular goal.[120] There is good reason to expect that the repeated narration of a witness's story will affect the testimony given in later stages of the criminal investigation and in court.

Memory content. The quality of people's memories is dependent also on the type of memorized event. Memory for conversations is forensically important in that many trials contain some evidence of verbal communication.[121] Utterances can be central to solving culpability cases, for example, as a means of determining the defendant's mental state. Testifying whether the defendant stated "I'm going to kill you, Jack" or "I'm going to tell on you, Jack," can have serious implications for determining the speaker's intent, especially if Jack eventually turns up dead. Memory for conversations is naturally dependent on the listener's comprehension, which can be diminished by the semantic ambiguity of the words used. The statement "We're expecting another load" will have different implications depending on whether it was said in the context of a drug transaction or doing laundry.[122] Comprehension of conversations can also be limited when the listener and the conversants do not share the same perspective, dialect, or discursive practices.[123]

The forensic value of verbal communication is typically embodied in the verbatim statements uttered. Consistent with fuzzy trace theory, the research demonstrates that the accuracy of memories of conversations differs greatly between the gist of the statement and the words actually uttered by the conversants. Interpersonal communication is driven by a search for meaning, which readily discards traces of the exact words used and leaves behind only traces of the gist. As a result, people tend to have poor memories of conversations. A study that tested for memory of a conversation about a criminal conspiracy found that participants averaged a recall of almost 15 gist items, but only 0.5 verbatim items.[124] Studies show that readers are capable of recognizing the exact wording used in the text for only short periods. Specifically, verbatim memory for written text tends to be forgotten within eighty syllables, without necessarily impairing the memory for the meaning or content of the text.[125] Memories for conversations are found to be poorly remembered even by the conversants themselves. Women participants were found to encounter difficulties in remembering conversations they held with their four-year-old children four days earlier. The mothers tended to forget both what their children had said and what they themselves had said, and were sometimes confused as to who exactly uttered certain statements.[126] Another study shows that people can report remembering saying things that they had intended to say, but never actually uttered.[127] Again, the events surrounding the murder of President Lincoln are instructive. Lincoln survived the night of his assassination in critical condition, lying in a small room in a nearby boardinghouse, surrounded by numerous aides and physicians. The next morning, after drawing his last breath, Lincoln's secretary of war, Edwin Stanton, uttered what has become a famous epitaph. The curious thing is that none of the people crammed into the small room could verify whether Stanton said "Now he belongs to the ages" or "Now he belongs to the angels."[128]

The timing and sequencing of events is another type of information that can be forensically important. Knowing when an event occurred might implicate a person who was at the crime scene, just as it might exculpate a person known to have been somewhere else. The research indicates that people encounter considerable difficulty in remembering exact dates and times, and are thus prone to commit *time-slice errors*.[129] When asked to remember what they did on a particular day a few weeks earlier, most people will need to resort to some extramemorial aid, such as consulting their calendar or family members.[130] The problem stems from the fact that the memory system contains no mechanism for tagging memorial events with a time stamp, which means that we have no reliable way to sequence the moments of our lives. This lack of a temporal account weakens access to the source of memories and contributes to conjunction errors between one event and the next.[131] Even when witnesses have strong memories for an event, they often have poor memories for the timing of that event.[132] Time-slice errors can readily lead to mistaken sequencing of events. For example, people's recollections for the events of September 11 were found to contain sequencing errors.[133] In the forensic context, time-slice errors can readily lead to inaccurate descriptions of events, and, as discussed in Chapter 6, they can also make it difficult for innocent suspects to reconstruct their own actions and to produce accurate alibis.[134]

Witness motivations. Witnesses' motivations can affect their willingness to provide information in the first place. At a deeper level, people's memories have been shown to be colored by personal goals, including the ubiquitous need to enhance one's prestige and sense of self-worth. For example, a comparison of college students' recollections of their high school grades with official transcripts revealed that 80 percent of the participants reported grades that were higher than the ones they had earned, while only 6 percent deflated them.[135] Similarly, memories for scores on standardized college entrance exams were far more frequently overstated than understated, particularly by lower-performing students.[136] Recall that people's memories are distorted toward decisions they make.[137] Memories are susceptible to motivational influences also because perception itself can be shaped by motivation.[138] In the forensic context, there is an added concern that witnesses will be inclined to provide information even if their memories are weak or nonexistent because of their desire to assist the investigation, see the defendant get punished, or bask in the spotlight. This inclination can result in the development of spontaneous false memories, and it can also increase witnesses' susceptibility to induced false memories.

Cowitness influences. A witness's memory can be influenced by information exchanged with other people who witnessed the event.[139] Survey data from Australia show that a large majority of people who witnessed dramatic events engage in spontaneous exchanges with cowitnesses, typically before being interviewed by the police.[140] Sharing memories can artificially inflate or deflate one's confidence in the memory.[141] More importantly, conversations with cowitnesses can cause blending of the content of the memories, a phenomenon known as *memory conformity*. Studies have shown that discussing the evidence with a cowitness prior to a memory test has caused people to report seeing a crime being committed that they never actually witnessed,[142] an accomplice that did not exist,[143] and a gun that was never shown.[144] Memorial reports have been found to be distorted also when cowitnesses are questioned together.[145] These influences are particularly strong for witnesses who have only weak memories of the event.[146] Memory conformity was in play in the case of the Oklahoma Federal Building bombing.[147] Clearly, cowitness influences can introduce both true and false memories.

System Factors

As stated above, the accuracy of event memory is influenced by incident factors, system factors, or a combination of both. Recall that system factors consist of the investigative procedures and actions taken to elicit the witness's memory. When exercised correctly, system factors might provide detectives with important information, just as incorrect interviewing exacerbates the risk of lost and false memories. Think of an investigation of a serious crime that is stalling because of a shortage of evidence to ascertain the identity of the perpetrator. The detectives have formed a theory and have a suspect in mind, but the eyewitness has not been able to provide the particular piece of evidence needed to arrest and prosecute him. In such cases, the incompleteness of the eyewitness's memory is the only thing preventing the clearing of the case. Lacking adequate training and appropriate procedures, most detectives in the United States and elsewhere commonly resort to questioning techniques that they intuitively believe can jog the witness's memory and elicit facts that the witness could not provide. This typically entails increasing the investigative intensity and prodding the witness to engage in *memory work*. This practice is problematic because, typically, the witness has no genuine accessible memory for the coveted detail. Invariably, details borne by memory work are the product of induced memories, and they reflect the witness's confabulation or guesswork, or the information suggested by the investigator. This generation of false memory can readily be driven by any of the commonly used interviewing techniques, absent any conscious intent by the detective. Either way, such memories stand to subvert the investigatory process, cloaking detectives' suspicions as the genuine memories of a seemingly trustworthy witness.

Interviewing techniques. A sizable body of research has shown that people's ability to recall memories is dependent on the manner in which the retrieval is attempted. Naturally, good interviewing techniques cannot produce facts that the witness does not remember, but bad interviewing protocols can easily degrade the completeness and accuracy of the reported memories. Notably, research has shown that the memorial account is hurt by asking close-ended, mutlipart, and short answer questions as well as by rapid questioning and interruptions.[148] As it turns out, police personnel habitually resort to such inadequate interviewing techniques. These patterns have been observed in the work of detectives and investigators in the United States,[149] the United Kingdom,[150] Canada,[151] Germany,[152] and Norway.[153]

Another troubling prospect is that the police interview itself will contaminate the witness's memory by leading the witness to report facts that were actually suggested by the interviewer. The body of research on postevent misinformation described above has shown that people's memorial accounts are easily contaminated by suggestive information. Recall, for example, that asking witnesses how fast the car was traveling when it drove by the barn leads people to report seeing a barn that did not actually exist in the film, and asking people about the color of the robber's gloves leads them to remember seeing gloves even though the robber was not wearing gloves.[154] Recall that such *postevent misinformation* can be caused also by exposure to media reports, discussions with cowitnesses, and any other source of information about the case. Witnesses can be misled also about the memories that they allegedly reported at previous interviews. Misrepresenting witnesses' past memory reports was found to distort their subsequent reports in a way that conformed with that manipulation.[155]

The available data from real-life interviewing practices gives much reason for concern over the possibility of suggested memories. In a study of real-life interviews conducted by English police officers, some 15 percent of the questions asked were found to be leading.[156] A survey of experienced Canadian police officers revealed a general acceptance of leading questions, with some justifying them as being necessary to remind witnesses of relevant facts.[157] Twenty percent of questions asked in real-life child-abuse interviews in the state of Washington were found to be suggestive of abuse.[158] A study of a simulated interview conducted by experienced forensic and child protective interviewers revealed that one of every six questions asked was leading, half of which were incorrect, and therefore misleading.[159]

Over the course of an investigation, opportunities for exposing witnesses to postevent misinformation are widespread. Misinformation can be conveyed by means of physical objects, visual images, or narrative accounts.[160] Witnesses and detectives have ample opportunity to communicate, and these conversations go unrecorded and they are typically not shared with the defense. In some cases, prosecution witnesses, particularly victims, remain in close and continued contact with law enforcement personnel. Jennifer Thompson, for example, testified that she communicated with Detective Gauldin about twenty times before the trial.[161] Recall that suggestive influences can be communicated without conscious awareness. Even a fleeting statement or accidental exposure to an image can alter a witness's memory and thus induce error.

Repetition and effort. One key ingredient of memory work is repeating the questions asked of the witness. Repeated questioning is particularly dangerous when it conveys leading or suggestive misinformation. The reiteration of suggested details has been shown to make them seem more familiar and thus more easily confusable with true memories.[162] Repeated retrieval attempts was a key feature in the implanted memory studies. In the hot-air-balloon study, for example, none of the participants reported any memory of the ride at first. By the third interview, conducted one week later, half of the participants reported information about the fictitious ride.[163] Likewise, in the punch bowl experiment, none of the subjects recalled knocking over the bowl when first asked about it. By the end of the first interview, one in every six participants reported the memory, and by the end of the third interview, the number increased to more than one-third of the sample.[164] Repeated questioning also strengthens witnesses' confidence in their memory, regardless of its accuracy.[165] The adverse effect of repeated questioning is heightened when it is conducted over a number of interview sessions. The passage of time between interviews further weakens witnesses' capacity to monitor the source of the memory, and thus increases the likelihood of incorporating false information.[166] Moreover, the repetition of questions can be interpreted by the witness as a signal that a different response is called for, and thus lead her to compliantly provide the desired response. In such cases, the repetition changes the witness's statements without actually altering her memory.[167]

Another commonly used technique for jogging memory is urging witnesses to try harder in their retrieval efforts. Invariably, the extra effort is counterproductive. The research shows that exhortations to increase effort in retrieval contributes to the generation of false memories.[168] The research shows also that retrieval performance is not improved by incentives. For example, offering witnesses monetary incentives to report more details does not improve retrieval, but it does boost witnesses' estimates of accuracy and confidence.[169]

Imagination and confabulation. Another strategy used to assist memory retrieval is to encourage witnesses to reconstruct the event in their imagination. This technique, however, frequently results in the creation of false memories. For example, false memories are created when witnesses are asked to elaborate on the physical appearance of unseen facts,[170] and when they are asked to elaborate on how they would react emotionally to imagined events.[171] Forcing people to guess or to confabulate facts that they cannot recall leads to false memories on subsequent memory tests. This result held both for questions about things they saw but did not remember, and for impossible memories, namely, things they had never seen.[172] Instructions to imagine the false events were central to the implanted memory studies. In the punch bowl study, for example, instructions to imagine the false event yielded considerably higher rates of false memories than did comparable instructions to merely think about it.[173]

Overall, the likelihood of false memories is enhanced by the compounded effect of multiple incident and system factors. For example, the effects of imagination are exacerbated by (misleading) positive feedback,[174] and the effects of confabulation are boosted by repetition.[175] Repetition has also been found to increase people's reports of remembering that they performed an action that they imagined doing, but did not actually do.[176]

The likelihood of false memories is related also to witnesses' specific states at the time of memory retrieval. Sleep-deprived participants were found to be more susceptible to suggestion but no less confident than well-rested participants.[177] People have also been found to be more suggestible when they believe that they are drunk.[178] The likelihood of false memories is related also to witnesses' personality traits. A series of experiments has revealed a heightened vulnerability to suggestion by witnesses who score high on measures of acquiescence[179] and fantasy proneness.[180]

Confidence and Confidence Inflation

A general phenomenon associated with memory is that people tend to be overconfident about their memories. For example, one study found that memories that were 60 percent accurate were reported with 90 percent confidence.[181] Another study found that 25 percent of inaccurate memories were reported with maximal confidence.[182] People are overconfident also with respect to the completeness of their memories. One study found that although witnesses recalled only 15 percent of the details of a crime scene, they believed that they recalled 71 percent.[183]

An important forensic implication of police interviewing is that the interviews can inflate witnesses' confidence in their memories, regardless of accuracy. A number of studies have found that confidence, but not accuracy, is boosted by repeated questioning. This effect was strongest for incorrect responses[184] and for impossible memories, that is, putative recollections of facts that were not seen.[185] Instructions encouraging participants to imagine events have been found to result in higher levels of confidence for false memories,[186] a phenomenon called *imagination inflation*.[187] Positive confirming feedback given to (wrong) guesses resulted in increases in witnesses' confidence.[188] As noted, confidence for false memories has been found to be inflated also by communications with cowitnesses,[189] and exertion of greater effort at retrieval.[190]

As discussed in Chapter 6, heightened levels of confidence that accompany false memories are particularly detrimental in that prosecutors are more likely to pursue cases with confident witnesses, and fact finders are more likely to believe them. Moreover, inflated confidence can spur other errors. For example, complimenting witnesses on their memories resulted in an inflation of their confidence about their performance on a subsequent identification lineup.[191]

Retrieval: The Police Interview

Memory retrieval is a relatively simple cognitive task as long as the person has a good memory for the fact to be retrieved. When the underlying memory is weak, not to mention nonexistent, the attempted retrieval involves a process that is far more complex and susceptible to error and contamination. Whether a person will report remembering a fact will often depend on the plausibility of the memory report and its consistency with the person's personal knowledge schemas. For example, people are more likely to mistakenly report remembering that medically related statements were uttered by a doctor rather than by a lawyer,[192] and that conservative political statements were uttered by a Republican rather than by a Democrat.[193] People also resort to logical inferences or heuristics such as: "Sam was the only person there who would have said this sort of thing, so he must have said it."[194] Retrieval is likely to depend also on the correspondence of the memory to other available information, which can be manipulated by the interviewer. For example, it has been found that showing participants a doctored photograph of the Tiananmen Square protest changed their memory reports for the events,[195] and showing photographs of a village devastated by a hurricane made them more likely to mistakenly recall reading about human casualties.[196] Memory retrieval is influenced also by the threshold criterion used by the person to distinguish between correct and incorrect memories, that is, the witness's sensitivity to the relative costs of over- or underreporting.[197]

Memory retrieval is sensitive also to the social dynamics surrounding retrieval. Research shows that people tend to adjust their memory reports to the expectations of the recipients of the reports, a phenomenon known as *audience tuning*.[198] Retrieval is sensitive also to interviewer feedback. Falsely labeling witnesses as having a poor memory increases their suggestibility to misinformation[199] and the rate of false memories they report,[200] and it can even increase false memories at subsequent interviews.[201] False memories have been exacerbated also by misleading the witness to believe that he should be able to remember an (actually impossible) event.[202] Suggestion is most effective when offered by someone who is deemed to be knowledgeable.[203] All these effects are bound to be more pronounced under the stressful social dynamics that are frequently present in intensive police investigations of unsolved serious crimes. The interviews are typically dominated by the detectives, who represent the authority of the state and are usually more knowledgeable about the case. The well-intended, cooperative, but not entirely helpful witness might well feel an urge to do his utmost to assist the investigation.

Recommendations for Reform

Event memory furnished by eyewitnesses is present in almost every criminal investigation, in both culpability and identity cases. A witness's memories of certain details often hold the key to the outcome of the case. The memory system that makes event testimony possible is a powerful feature of human cognition. At the same time, it is a delicate system that can easily go awry, and thus result in both types of erroneous verdicts. A witness's failure to provide memories of essential incriminating facts will normally not lead to a conviction or even reach a jury, and is thus likely to contribute to the dismissal of charges or the acquittal of true perpetrators. However, witnesses' statements that include false memories can readily lead to the incrimination of innocent people. The detrimental impact of false memories is made possible by the fact that most people, including many of those who operate the criminal justice system, do not fully appreciate the frailties of human memory and its susceptibility to the retrieval techniques. In the quest for crucial details, too much trust is placed in the problematic interviewing procedures that are habitually employed in police investigations.

At bottom, errors arising from memory failures stem from the fact that solving crimes often requires information that cannot be recalled by the witness, whether because it was not perceived or encoded, forgotten, or contaminated. Difficult investigations often hinge on minute details of the kind that people tend not to notice, quickly forget, or easily confuse. Memory shortfalls often prompt detectives to apply pressure on the witness to engage in memory work, in the hope of somehow squeezing out the desired information. The research shows that the ensuing interviewing yields only marginal increases in the remembered facts, but can readily lead to substantial increases in false memories.

The research offers guidance for reducing both these types of error. Police interviewers need to be sensitized and made aware of the fragile nature of human memory and the havoc they can wreak by mishandling it. As mentioned in Chapter 3, memories ought to be treated like an especially delicate type of trace evidence, which naturally decays and is constantly exposed to the risk of contamination. Interviewers ought to expect that witnesses' memories will often fall short of investigative needs, especially with respect to peripheral details, verbatim conversations, times, and dates. Special attention should be paid to the fact that bad interviewing techniques stand to contaminate the witness's memory.

The most important recommendation is that police interviewers adhere to the *Cognitive Interview* protocol, developed by Ron Fisher and Edward Geiselman.[204] This nuanced and research-based technique has been shown to generate somewhat more detailed memorial accounts without compromising accuracy.[205] The cognitive interview should serve also to enhance the professionalism of police interviews and to restrain investigators from engaging in divergent methods of questioning. The Cognitive Interview has been adopted by police in the United Kingdom as the recommended protocol for interviewing cooperative witnesses.[206] Other best-practice recommendations include the following:

1. Interviews should be conducted as soon as possible after the event.
2. Witnesses should be interviewed separately, warned not to talk to one another, and, if possible, sequestered from one another.
3. Witnesses should be encouraged to try to distinguish between what they perceived themselves and what they learned from other sources.
4. Interviewers should adjust their questioning to the state of witnesses (e.g., fatigue, alcohol dependence) and their personality types (e.g., heightened compliance, fantasy proneness).
5. Interviewers should refrain from conveying any information about the investigation to the witness.
6. Interviewers should not ask leading questions or suggest the desired response in any way.
7. Interviewers should refrain from urging or exhorting witnesses to try harder or to engage in memory work, including imagination, speculation, and guesswork.
8. Interviewers should not give the witness feedback or encouragement, and should not express disappointment over memory lapses.
9. Successive interviews should be conducted only when necessary. Interviewers should not ask about the same facts in more than one interview, unless they employ a valid mnemonic that was not previously used.
10. All interviews should be recorded electronically in their entirety.

The importance of the recommendation to record all interviews in their entirety cannot be overstated. For one, this practice is bound to provide more complete accounts of witnesses' memories. Much of the gist of witnesses' responses and virtually all the verbatim details are lost to the interviewer well before the conclusion of the session. Recall from Chapter 2 that studies with professional interviewers found that post-hoc summaries of conversations omitted more than half of the relevant facts provided by the witness. Electronic recordings are bound to capture some of these details. Electronic recordings should also improve the quality of the interview. Rather than devote attention to taking notes or trying to memorize witnesses' statements, detectives could concentrate more on assimilating information and planning future lines of inquiry. The availability of the record should also provide a useful tool in the training and monitoring of investigators' performance. This oversight is warranted because of the prevalence of inferior forms of questioning by police investigators in the United States and abroad.

Recording interviews should provide fact finders with a particularly useful aid in evaluating the accuracy of witnesses' memorial accounts. The record will provide firsthand exposure of the interview in its *raw* form, conveying the witness's narrative flow, confidence, and fluency, as well as the coherence and consistency of the account. The record will also provide insight into the investigative methods used to elicit the statements, including pressure from the investigator, repetition of questions, exhortations, and requests for imagination or confabulation. Importantly, the record will help determine whether the stated memories were truly recalled by the witness or were suggested by the investigator.

5

"JUST ADMIT IT, YOU'RE GUILTY"

Interrogating Suspects

A type of testimony that is widely used in criminal prosecutions consists of self-incriminating statements furnished by the defendants themselves. Typically these statements are made during interrogations conducted in police custody. Confessions are often the evidence of last resort, affording the only means of prosecuting cases in the absence of conventional types of evidence. It is thus not surprising that throughout history the extraction of confessions has often entailed serious abuses of a suspect's rights and bodily integrity. U.S. Supreme Court Justice Hugo Black lamented that "The rack, the thumbscrew, the wheel, solitary confinement, protracted questioning and cross questioning . . . had left their wake of mutilated bodies and shattered minds along the way to the cross, the guillotine, the stake and the hangman's noose."[1]

On its face, confessing to a crime invariably entails subjecting oneself to serious criminal punishment. It follows that making a confession is an exceedingly self-defeating proposition, regardless of one's actual guilt. Such behavior is especially perplexing given that the law currently insists that admissions of guilt be made voluntarily,[2] and that the suspect has the right to refuse to talk to investigators and to stop the investigation at any point.[3] Still, suspects confess with some regularity. The best estimates suggest that incriminating statements or confessions are obtained in about 50 percent of all interrogations.[4] This makes the interrogation an intriguing investigative tool. The fact that interrogations occasionally yield confessions from innocent people makes it a disquieting tool too. This chapter focuses on the accuracy of the interrogation process.

Self-incriminating statements range from admissions to specific incriminating facts to full-blown confessions for having committed the crime. The following discussion will focus on interrogations that lead to confessions, but it applies similarly to interrogations that yield limited self-incriminating statements and interrogations that deflect the blame from the suspect to his cosuspects. The term *interrogation* refers to police questioning of people suspected of perpetrating the crime, and who are typically uncooperative, in contrast to the subject matter of Chapter 4, which examined interviews with cooperative witnesses who typically are not the suspects. Interrogations can also be designed to bring the suspect to incriminate somebody else.

Interrogations that fail to obtain a confession tend to weaken the case against the suspect and may even result in the dropping of charges against him. When the suspect is actually guilty, that will constitute to a false acquittal, though when the suspect is innocent that will amount to a correct outcome. As with all other types of testimony, confessions can be either accurate or false. True confessions have the virtue of leading to the conviction of actually guilty suspects, whereas confessions obtained from innocent suspects can readily result in false convictions.

The potential of interrogations to generate false confessions is now indisputable. For example, five teens confessed to the rape and brutal assault in the infamous case of the Central Park Jogger.[5] Jeffrey Deskovic of New York confessed to the rape-murder of a high school classmate.[6] Bruce Godschalk (mentioned in Chapter 1) confessed to two incidents of burglary and rape. Six people were convicted in Beatrice, Nebraska, for a rape-murder based on multiple confessions.[7] Since these convicted persons were subsequently exonerated on the basis of DNA testing, it is inescapable that their confessions were false. False confessions have been observed in 15–25 percent of the known exonerations.[8] An archival study published in 2004 examined 125 reported cases of indisputable false confessions,[9] and the number of cases has grown considerably since. In a narrow category of instances, false confessions are made voluntarily, typically by suspects with mental impairments, or by suspects who cover up for someone else's guilt. In other instances, innocent suspects somehow come to believe in their guilt over the course of the investigation. Most frequently, however, innocent suspects confess despite their full knowledge of their innocence.[10] Invariably these confessions are induced by the interrogation process.

The technique for questioning suspects that is used most widely by American law enforcement agencies is the one marketed by John E. Reid & Associates, a Chicago-based commercial entity. Over the years, the Reid Technique of Interviewing and Interrogation has been taught to well over 100,000 law enforcement agents. One large survey of law enforcement personnel found that more than half of the responding officers had received training in the Reid method.[11] The Reid method is put forth in the company's textbook *Criminal Interrogation and Confessions,* now in its fourth edition.[12] According to the company's website, the book "is considered by the courts and practitioners to be the 'Bible' for interviewing and interrogation techniques," and it has been translated into Chinese, Japanese, and Turkish.[13] The corporation's website boasts an almost perfect record in courts' decisions to admit into evidence confessions obtained by its trainees.[14] The company also insists on the diagnosticity of the protocol. Joseph Buckley, the president of Reid & Associates, stated in a public forum: "We don't interrogate innocent people."[15] Notably, the corporation claims that investigators trained by this method can accurately identify liars 85 percent of the time.[16] Because of the prevalence of this method, it will be the focus of the following discussion.

Like other interrogation techniques, the Reid method seeks to attain the double objectives of distinguishing between innocent and guilty suspects, and obtaining confessions from the latter. The textbook prescribes a two-phase approach: a nonconfrontational preinterrogation interview that is dedicated mostly to the diagnostic task, followed by a confrontational interrogation that is designed primarily to obtain admissions of guilt.

According to the Reid method, the interview is intended to collect information from the suspect, build a rapport with him, and, most important, enable a decision whether to commence the interrogation process. The decision to interrogate is an important juncture because it triggers the deployment of the accusatory interrogation, which has the potential to yield confessions and thus all but seal the fate of the defendant. Investigators are advised to commence interrogations even in the absence of objective evidence of deceit, provided that they believe that the suspect is lying. Thus, the decision to escalate the process often rides on the investigator's ability to correctly determine that the suspect is being deceitful. In the absence of objective evidence undermining the suspect's story, deceit must be detected from the suspect's behavior.

Detection of Deceit

A considerable body of research has been devoted to people's capabilities in detecting deceit. Naturally, detection of deceit from behavior requires first that liars behave differently from truth tellers. Indeed, there are a number of theoretical reasons why telling a lie would result in phenomenological experiences that differ from telling the truth. Lying usually places people in unusual and potentially threatening situations, which can entail fear of getting caught or compunctions about being dishonest. This arousal is typically accompanied by physiological states, which may be observable by others. Unlike truth tellers, liars need to control their behavior to feign normal demeanor. Liars also expend extra cognitive effort to ensure that their story is plausible and consistent, and to monitor their apparent believability.[17]

Cues of deceit.   The question is whether these phenomenological experiences manifest themselves in unique and decipherable patterns of behavior. A comparison to the legendary hero of *The Adventures of Pinocchio* is helpful to appreciate the difficulties involved in this task. Pinocchio's lies are easy to detect because they are manifested by an ideal cue. The observer knows the cue ahead of time and thus does not have to scan for cues or spend time trying to identify the speaker's idiosyncratic indicia of deceitful behavior. Pinocchio's cue is exclusive, in that it is the only behavioral change that accompanies his lying. Thanks to the book's illustrations, the cue is also patently clear, so that we know how small the nose is when he tells the truth and how big it becomes when he lies. The cue also corresponds perfectly with the veracity of Pinocchio's statements, in that the nose grows when he lies, but does not when he tells the truth. Virtually none of these features apply in the real world.

To detect deceit in real life, one must first know which cues are actually associated with deceit. The list of potential cues that people use to detect deceit covers almost every imaginable facet of behavior, reaching a total of 158.[18] Most commonly, people resort to physical cues that are visually apparent, such as facial expressions, posture, head movements, and a variety of bodily movements. One cue in particular—gaze aversion, and its reciprocal, maintaining eye contact—is singularly prominent. The belief in the diagnosticity of gaze aversion appears to be pancultural: a survey of more than 11,000 respondents in fifty-eight countries yielded 103 spontaneously proposed cues believed to be associated with deceit. Of them, gaze aversion was cited by two-thirds of the respondents, more than twice the rate of any other cue.[19] Gaze aversion is used by children as young as six years old.[20] As discussed below, gaze aversion figures prominently in the teaching materials used in police training. Other cues pertain to the verbal expression of the target person, such as the richness of detail of the statement, the consistency of statements, and response length. Another type of cue consists of attributes that accompany speech. These paraverbal cues include voice pitch, response latency, pauses, and "ah" and "um" utterances.

The key question is whether the cues that people use are actually diagnostic of deceit. This question was the subject of a large meta-analysis covering data from 120 samples, totaling some 6,000 participants. The data showed that to the extent that liars behave differently from truth tellers, they do so in diverse and imperceptible ways. Of the 158 cues analyzed, the vast majority were found to be nondiagnostic of lying; that is, they were not shown by liars any more or less than by truth tellers. Invariably, physical cues—including gaze aversion—were found to be unrelated to deceit.[21] The findings also revealed that while people tend to believe that various physical behavioral cues are usually activated by deceit, in actuality they are often inhibited by it.[22] The few cues that were found to be valid were mostly verbal (notably, low richness of detail, discrepancies, ambivalence, uncooperativeness) and paraverbal (voice pitch and vocal tension).

Yet, even assuming that a reliable and universal set of diagnostic cues existed and that they were known to the observers, determining whether a particular statement is honest or deceitful would amount to a tall order. Investigators would need first to know which of the abundant cues are indicative of lying for the specific suspect. Next, they would need to know how the specific cue, say, body posture or hand movements, appear when that individual tells the truth and when she lies.[23] The observer would need to observe all the potential cues at once (Did I just observe a finger movement? Did she nod her head?), interpret them correctly (Does finger movement indicate truth, or deceit, or neither?), and combine all of the information into a discrete judgment, taking into account both the observed cues and those that were not observed (I noticed two finger movements and one suspicious head movement, but the suspect maintained eye contact much of the time, did not slouch, and crossed her arms only once). All of this must be done while the investigator is also busy phrasing questions, processing the information provided by the suspect, checking the responses against other evidence, and planning future lines of questioning. It seems clear that people are not equipped with the explicit knowledge needed to solve these intractable algorithms. Still, it is possible that this task can be performed implicitly.

Distinguishing between truth tellers and liars. A substantial body of research has been devoted to testing people's ability to distinguish between truths and lies. A large meta-analysis has examined data from 206 experiments, reporting results from more than 24,000 judgments of deceit. The analysis leads to a rather simple conclusion: people perform poorly in distinguishing truthful from deceitful statements. Overall, the mean percentage of accurate classifications is 54 percent. The highest reported rate in any sample was 73 percent, and the lowest was 31 percent.[24] These results are statistically better than flipping a coin, but barely so. The poor performance appears to be universal and equally distributed, with only minute differences in detection accuracy among people.[25] For example, of 125 participants asked to judge the truthfulness of a single witness, just over half (54 percent) judged him to be telling the truth, and the remainder (46 percent) reached the opposite conclusion.[26] As Aldert Vrij has pointed out, people are considerably better at telling lies than at detecting them.[27] The adverse effect of people's limited performance in detecting deceit is compounded by their overconfidence. A meta-analysis of eighteen studies found that people believed that they were accurate 73 percent of the time, while in reality their accuracy rate was 57 percent. Overall, the relationship between accuracy and confidence was close to zero.[28] As mentioned in Chapter 7, confidence in judgments of deceit is further inflated by deliberation, with no appreciable improvement in accuracy.

One could argue against the application of the abovementioned research to actual criminal investigations. It is quite possible that lies communicated to save one's freedom (or to cause someone else to lose his) will have stronger behavioral manifestations than lies told in experimental settings, and thus be more decipherable by the observer. Thus, one way to increase the external validity of this research is to look only at the subset of studies in which the targets were offered incentives for getting away with their lies.[29] Overall, these studies show that incentivizing liars makes only minor differences. Of the four cues that were significantly diagnostic, just one, voice pitch, had a more than minimal effect.[30] Gaze aversion was found to be significantly related to deceit, although the relationship was unstable and weak.[31] In fact the research suggests that greater motivation to be believed tends to increase suspicious behaviors and thus reduces one's credibility, regardless of the truthfulness of the testimony.[32] A second way to increase external validity is to look only at the subset of studies in which the participants were covering up for a transgression. These studies found four cues that were indicative of deceit, only one of which—nervousness—had an effect that was greater than minimal.[33] In this subset, gaze aversion was found to have no relationship to deceit.[34]

A key question concerns the performance of police investigators. There is reason not to expect superior performance from police investigators, given that they tend to report relying on the same deceit cues as lay people.[35] Gaze aversion is the most often-mentioned cue by professional lie catchers, including police patrol officers, detectives, customs officials, and prison guards,[36] although prison inmates are wary of relying on it.[37] Studies testing police officers and other expert lie detectors yield mixed results,[38] with some studies finding somewhat heightened accuracy levels of about 65 percent. The research gives reason to doubt that greater motivation to catch liars increases the accuracy of detection,[39] but it suggests that having knowledge about the context surrounding the event should lead to better performance than in laboratory settings.[40]

Investigator bias. The detection of deceit in real-life cases can be swayed by the dynamics of the investigation, in that the decision to interview the suspect is typically premised on a preliminary suspicion of the suspect.[41] That initial suspicion is likely to result in an *investigator bias,* that is, a propensity to view suspects as guilty of the charge.[42] As discussed in Chapter 2, such preconceptions can trigger confirmatory biases that tend to reinforce the initial suspicion. The circular nature of the investigator bias is manifest in a study that finds that people who are led (fictitiously) to suspect deceit overestimated the amount of gaze aversion that the target had actually displayed.[43] These preconceptions are apparently reinforced by the Reid method. In a training session attended by Richard Leo, trainees were informed by Reid instructors that "the rule of thumb" should be that the suspect is untruthful.[44] The textbook goes so far as to equate the investigator's suspicion with the actual truth. For example, suspects who deny responsibility are cautioned about the "futility of resistance to telling the truth."[45] An endemic feature of the investigator bias is that investigators tend to be overconfident in their determinations of deceit,[46] and thus more resolved in acting on their belief in the suspect's guilt.

New directions. Recently, researchers have begun developing more nuanced methods for deceit detection. One such way is by means of gathering more information from the suspect and using those statements against her.[47] For example, the Strategic Use of Evidence (SUE) technique suggests that rather than confront suspects with all the evidence at the outset, investigators should hold off on exposing their information until the deceitful suspect has made statements that can be refuted by the evidence. This method has been shown to increase the accuracy of judgments by both lay people[48] and police trainees.[49] Another line of experimental research suggests that deceit detection can be improved by increasing the suspect's cognitive load.[50]

The Behavioral Analysis Interview

Police protocols rely heavily on investigators' ability to detect deceit. The Reid method prescribes a protocol called the *Behavioral Analysis Interview* (BAI). For the most part, the interview is devoted to determining whether the suspect is lying, which is generally indicative of guilt.[51] The protocol begins with a list of deception cues, that is, behaviors that are said to distinguish between liars and truth tellers. The list comprises sixteen cues pertaining to attitudes, verbal responses, and paralinguistic behavior, and a number of specific nonverbal cues. The protocol then provides a structured interview consisting of fifteen questions about the criminal event. The questions are said to evoke different reactions from guilty and innocent suspects. These cues and reactions are to be used throughout the ensuing interrogation procedure.

The construct that underlies the Behavioral Analysis method is that telling a lie, or hiding the truth, generates anxiety and triggers a pattern of efforts to reduce it. The textbook states:

> During an interview lies result in anxiety, and many of the behavior symptoms revealed by a deceptive suspect represent his conscious, or preconscious, efforts to reduce this internal anxiety. This fundamental concept forms the basis for evaluating a subject's verbal, paralinguistic, and nonverbal behaviors. In essence, the mind, and subsequently the body, work together to relieve the anxiety associated with a lie.[52]

The proposed cues and predicted reactions to the questions all follow from this anxiety-based proposition. Notably, the protocol relies heavily on nonverbal cues, with a particular emphasis on the cue of gaze aversion: deceptive suspects "look down at the floor, over to the side, or up at the ceiling, as if to beseech some divine guidance when answering questions."[53] Guilty suspects are also expected to "display physical signs of guilt—shifting posture, crossing legs, brushing clothing as if to remove dust, slouching in the chair, or moving back in the chair in order to get as far away as possible from the investigator."[54] In contrast, the honest suspect will look the investigator straight in the eyes. His posture "will be upright in the chair and he will align his body with the interviewer so as to assure direct communication. During important statements, the truthful subject may lean towards the interviewer to emphasize the statement."[55]

One obvious problem with the protocol is that it relies heavily on nonverbal behavioral cues of deception, which, as mentioned above, are unlikely to help investigators to distinguish between liars and truth tellers. There are other grounds for doubting the diagnosticity of the protocol. The textbook offers investigators a vast array of suspect's statements—indeed, far too many to remember—that purport to distinguish deceit from honesty. Many of the statements rely on vague and conjectural assumptions. For example, the phrases "I swear," "Honestly," and "As far as I recall" are said to be indicative of deceit,[56] while "I didn't have anything to do with the crime" and "No way. I had absolutely nothing to do with [the crime]" are said to be indicative of honesty.[57] After asking the suspect whether she knows who might have committed the crime, investigators are advised to infer deceit from the response "I wish I did, but I have no idea whatsoever," and to infer honesty from the response "No I do not."[58] Investigators are said to be able to reach opposite judgments of veracity from the following pairs of statements: "I don't mind it at all" and "I'm nervous and scared" (in response to the question how they feel about being interviewed); "I could never live with myself if I did something like that!" and "It's wrong" (when asked for a reason why they would not commit the crime); "I'm sure you want to find out what I know about the arson at the warehouse" and "I suppose you want to talk to me about what happened at the warehouse" (in response to whether she knows the purpose of the interview). According to the protocol, the first response in these three pairs of statements is indicative of honesty and the second indicates deceit.[59]

Given the wide range of proposed indicators and their obscure relationship to veracity, it is not surprising to find contradictions among them. For example, innocent suspects are said to be more cooperative with the investigator and to hold more positive attitudes toward the interview because they perceive it as an opportunity to clear the suspicion of their involvement.[60] Yet innocent suspects are said also to express resentment toward the investigator's questioning,[61] to respond to the investigator's accusation in an angry and blunt manner,[62] and to state their case vehemently.[63] An oft-repeated prediction is that truthful suspects will offer confident, definitive, and emphatic responses,[64] but strong and bolstered denials are said to be indicators of deceit.[65] Innocent suspects are predicted to have given considerable thought to solving the crime prior to the interview ("The Sherlock Holmes effect"),[66] yet rehearsed responses are said to be indicative of deceit.[67] Likewise, delayed responses are deemed an indication of deceit,[68] yet a Reid executive insists that "it is much easier to lie to questions that are asked in a rapid-fire manner."[69]

Some of the precepts are too nebulous to be of any use. For example, the textbook states that even though truthful suspects "may be apprehensive, they show no concern about the credibility of their answers. Although attentive, their casual manner is unrestrained."[70] Deceptive suspects are said also to be more likely to interrupt the investigator and to precede the interruption with a gesture of "placing a forefinger of one hand on the finger of the other hand, in anticipation of expressing specific points of dissention."[71] The textbook evades advising how to reach the final conclusion regarding the suspect's truthfulness. It calls only for a "global assessment of the suspect's behavior,"[72] without offering guidance about how to score each response, how to weight them, how to handle ambiguous and contradictory responses, and what should be the criterion for determining deceit.[73]

Another serious drawback of the protocol is that it presents a cartoonlike image of deceitful suspects. Throughout, the guilty suspect is depicted as someone whose sense of guilt is exuding through her skin. For example, the guilty person will respond to the investigator's accusation "with a rather pleading look and answer in the form of a soft denial."[74] The guilty suspect also falls for transparent ploys such as endorsing a light punishment for the perpetrator and recommending giving him a second chance.[75] The textbook thus ignores the commonplace reality that liars routinely try to conceal their lies. Whether they do so successfully or not, liars frequently modify their behavior with the distinct purpose of appearing honest.[76] Developmental psychologists show that masking deceit begins as early as the age of three, and it continues to improve as the child develops.[77] The field of polygraph testing contains an established literature that deals with liars' attempts to mask their lies (countermeasures),[78] and with means of reading through those masks *(countering countermeasures)*.[79] As a corporation that markets polygraph training, Reid and Associates must be well aware of the problem with masking behaviors.[80] Yet the protocol does not share this issue with investigators and offers no way to distinguish between a suspect who looks the investigator straight in the eye because he is telling the truth or because he is trying to mimic a truth teller.

The BAI protocol is deficient also because it relies so heavily on the detection of anxiety. Recall that the protocol is based on the presumption that guilty suspects are anxious whereas innocent suspects are not. Yet this premise ignores the patent fact that innocent people, too, are likely to feel anxious when being investigated for a crime they did not commit. Remarkably, the protocol's authors acknowledge this possibility openly. They note that innocent people may be nervous because of the possibility of facing false charges, because of concern about the treatment they may receive, or out of fear that the investigation might unearth other indiscretions or embarrassing acts.[81] The authors briskly dispose of this concern by stating that the nervousness of innocent and guilty suspects is easily distinguishable by the duration of the nervous symptoms. This crucial claim is made in just two sentences: "As the interview progresses, and the innocent subject understands that the questioning is nonaccusatory, he becomes more relaxed and composed. Conversely, the deceptive subject's nervousness is maintained or sometimes actually increases during the course of the interview."[82] As with most of the claims made in support of the Reid method, the authors offer no evidence to support this assertion. Clearly, if this conjectural proposition is incorrect, one would have to conclude that the anxiety of honest suspects guts the protocol of any diagnostic value because innocent suspects who continue to feel anxious will be deemed guilty. Yet, even if this statement were accurate, it casts a doubt over the conclusions that could be drawn from the interview. The textbook fails to offer any guidance as to when the suspect's nervousness starts to become diagnostic and how that magical moment can be identified by the investigator. It would also follow that all inferences drawn up to that unspecified point in time are nondiagnostic and meaningless.

It is important to keep in mind that the cues and predicted behaviors offered by the Reid method were derived not via experimentation, but through informal observations by the company's personnel, dating back to the work of John E. Reid as a polygraph examiner for the Chicago Police Department in the 1940s.[83] Indeed, survey data show that the protocol's cues and predicted behaviors are very similar to lay people's intuitions.[84] Yet the corporation insists that its method is grounded also in scientific research. Specifically, it claims that its method can accurately identify liars 85 percent of the time. That claim is based primarily on a single, and deeply flawed, field study, published in 1994.[85] First, the study contained no control group and thus cannot say much about the effectiveness of the method. Second, the study contained no reliable measure of the *ground truth* of the suspects' veracity. The authors concede that the ground truth could be determined by "incontrovertible evidence" in only two of the sixty cases, both of which turned out to be innocent suspects.[86] In other words, the researchers could not classify reliably which suspects were lying and which suspects were telling the truth, a limitation that casts serious doubt on the study's internal validity. Third, the findings are not readily generalizable, as the data were generated by only a handful of participants, who were employees of the corporation or otherwise affiliated with it. Finally, the study has not been replicated adequately. Of the two known replications, one was published in a nonscientific journal and the other has not been published at all.[87]

The BAI protocol has been subjected to a more exacting laboratory study, which afforded the researchers full knowledge of the ground truth of the suspects' guilt, and tested the performance of participants drawn from a neutral subject pool and randomly assigned to a treatment condition and a control group. This study found that the BAI failed to distinguish between truth tellers and liars, and it was even contradicted by some of the observed behaviors. Truthful participants appeared less helpful, were more evasive, and showed more signs of discomfort, and they were more likely to cross their legs and to shift postures.[88] Another study found that training participants to use the BAI actually caused a decrease in the accuracy of their deceit determinations, but it inflated their confidence.[89]

In sum, the BAI protocol amounts to a cacophony of commonly held but poorly diagnostic intuitions. Its validity is hardly reinforced by its conjectural propositions[90] and folksy aphorisms.[91] Yet the protocol continues to be the leading interrogation tool used by law enforcement agencies across North America. It appears that for these agencies, the lure of the protocol lies with offering law enforcement personnel a pseudoprofessional framework for justifying their preconceptions and thus enabling them to proceed with the interrogation of the suspect at hand.[92] The protocol also validates police investigators' beliefs in erroneous cues of deceit.[93] Indeed, a number of false confessions were triggered by misguided and speculative determinations of deceit. For example,

Jeffrey Deskovic was deemed a suspect because he displayed too much emotion over the death of his high school classmate,[94] whereas Gary Gauger and Michael Crowe drew the suspicion of detectives because they displayed too little emotion in response to the death of their loved ones.[95]

Interrogations

If by the end of the interview the investigator believes that the suspect is deceitful, she will usually proceed to the interrogation phase. Given the self-defeating nature of admitting to a crime, suspects would be expected to strongly resist making a confession, regardless of their guilt. It follows that obtaining confessions would rarely succeed without subjecting suspects to a substantial amount of pressure. Since the outlawing of physical coercion as the primary method of obtaining confessions by so-called *third-degree methods* in the 1930s, interrogation methods have shifted to rely primarily on psychological pressures.[96]

There is no single method or style of interrogation. Interrogations vary from one interrogator to the next and from one police department to the other. They vary also from case to case and from suspect to suspect. Still, interrogations by American law enforcement agencies tend to follow a set of precepts that are shared by most investigators. These similarities stem either from commonly held intuitions or from training in similar methods. The typical interrogation conducted in the United States is an intensely confrontational affair. Interrogations are the most overtly adversarial part of the criminal investigation, and thus also the most inimical to the portrayal of the police's work as an impartial and objective search for truth. The intensity of interrogations is explainable in part by the fact that they tend to be conducted in high-stakes crimes—typically murder and other high-profile cases[97]—when the police have little other evidence to close the case. By this advanced stage of the investigation, investigators have typically invested considerable time and effort on the case, and have concluded that the suspect is probably guilty. The commitment to proving the suspect's guilt is likely reinforced further by the fact that interrogations entail a strong personal involvement from the interrogators. Thus, the process is bound to be driven also by the interrogators' concern over the ego-related and reputational implications of its success or failure.

As discussed in Chapter 6, confessions are a powerful type of inculpatory evidence. Yet, despite their potency—and, as discussed below, their susceptibility to error—the practice is regulated by a legal doctrine that is permissive and detached from the reality of the interrogation room. The doctrine also suffers from poor enforcement because of the habitual opacity of the investigative process and the quick deterioration of accusations of foul play into swearing contests.

Again, the interrogation method most widely used by American law enforcement agencies is Reid & Associates' protocol, the Reid Nine Steps of Interrogation.[98] The interrogation typically commences after the suspect has been read his *Miranda* rights and has agreed to waive them. The first step of the process is to confront the suspect with a blunt accusation of his involvement in the crime, an accusation that will be repeated persistently throughout the process. Interrogators are advised to block the suspect's attempts to deny the accusation and to prevent him from providing alternative narratives. Interrogators are advised also how to manage the suspect's mood. Finally, the protocol instructs interrogators how to induce the suspect to provide an admission of his wrongdoing, and how to turn that admission into a fully developed self-inculpating narrative. The crucial question is: How accurate are confessions obtained from interrogations that follow this protocol?[99] This inquiry is particularly important given the fact that, as discussed in Chapter 6, jurors tend to place a great deal of trust in confession evidence and do not appear to be adept at distinguishing between false and true confessions.

One way in which the interrogation process could lead to accurate results is by helping investigators assess the truthfulness of the suspect, and thus correct misclassifications of deceit made during the interview. There is little reason to place hope in this prospect, as the interrogation protocol does not add any tools for diagnosing deceit. Investigators are left to perform this task with the same (poorly diagnostic) tools they used in the preinterrogation interview. As investigators advance further with the process, their increasing commitment makes them less likely to seek and acknowledge signs of honesty. Indeed, the research shows that police investigators perform poorly in distinguishing between true and false confessions.[100]

Alternatively, the interrogation process could lead to accurate results if it had disparate effects on guilty and innocent suspects, that is, if it induced confessions from guilty suspects but not from innocent ones. To explore this possibility, it is necessary to closely examine the procedure and its likely effects on those subjected to it. This review will focus first on the literature that emanates from observational and archival research of real criminal cases, drawing mostly on the research of Richard Leo and his collaborators.[101] The discussion will subsequently turn to the experimental research, conducted mostly by the research groups of Saul Kassin and Christian Meissner.

Observational and Archival Research

The potential of the interrogation process to induce confessions appears to be driven by the combination of two features. First, the suspect must become willing to comply with the investigator's demands. Interrogations are conducted in specially designed rooms that are small, windowless, and secluded. This environment isolates the suspect and shuts down all means of communication, contact, and support from the outside world. The backbone of the interrogation is the insistence on the suspect's guilt. This accusation is to be hurled persistently and unwaveringly, and be accompanied by a flat and assertive rejection of the suspect's denials of guilt. Proclamations of innocence are to be attacked or cut off before they can be voiced and explained. The barrage of accusations and blunt repudiation of the suspect's denials are bound to make him feel trapped and overpowered by the interrogator. From the perspective of the hungry, tired, anxious, and despondent suspect, complying with the interrogator's demands might seem like the only way to terminate the ordeal and to gain the interrogator's favor. Indeed, numerous confessors have explained that they signed the confession just to stop the barrage of indignation, to get out of the room, or to go home (which, of course they were not permitted to do once they confessed to having committed a serious felony). For example, a New Jersey man confessed to killing his two children following thirty hours of questioning in a forty-hour period. "I just wanted the cops to leave me alone," he explained, believing that his innocence would come to light once more evidence was found.[102] Not surprisingly, many suspects recant their confessions immediately after the barrage of the interrogative process recedes.

Second, and more importantly, the interrogator must make the suspect perceive that confessing is the most beneficial course of action available to him. To bring the suspect to make the invariably illogical decision to confess, the interrogator must distort his perception of the situation, namely by making confessing appear to be more advantageous than refusing to confess. The distortion of the suspect's decision-making process was apparently on the Supreme Court's mind when it barred the use of physical violence, threats of harm and punishment, or promises of leniency, whether direct or implied.[103] As a consequence, interrogation protocols resort to alternative means in order to reach the same result. Notably, the Reid Method advocates the use of interrogative techniques that have been labeled *minimization* and *maximization*,[104] which have been deemed permissible by the Court.

The effect of minimization is usually achieved by means of presenting the suspect with a *theme* that reduces the import of the crime. Themes usually convey the interrogator's opinion that the crime was not so serious, that the victim deserved his fate, or that anyone else would have acted in the same way. For suspects who did in fact commit the crime, these themes might palliate their sense of guilt. More importantly, for both guilty and innocent suspects, the minimizing themes are prone to lessen the gravity of the charges they face. While in the eyes of the law the presentation of themes does not amount to an implicit promise of leniency, suspects might well perceive that to be the case, especially given the desperation of their situation. As discussed below, experiments show that minimizing themes are understood by lay people as implicit promises of leniency.

The dominant tone of the interrogation is one of maximization, that is, depicting the case against the suspect as being beyond any doubt. The implicit message is that the suspect is bound to be convicted even absent a confession, and that he faces harsh consequences, especially given the seriousness of the criminal charge (typically murder) and the severity of the corresponding punishment (life in prison or the death penalty). Cooperating with the interrogators is portrayed as the only possible way to mitigate the direness of his situation. Maximizing the likelihood of conviction is performed by means of presenting the suspect with powerful incriminating evidence, which typically lies beyond the suspect's ability to question or contest. The evidence may well be genuine, but in its absence, interrogators often fabricate it and deceive the suspect into believing that it exists. At times the evidence will be manufactured by means of a ploy, disguised as a way to help the suspect prove his case. For example, the interrogator might convince the suspect to undergo a truth verification test, such as a polygraph or some other (typically specious) contraption. Regardless of the actual results, the interrogator will invariably portray the evidence as proving that the suspect is lying. Like most other aspects of the interrogative process, lying to suspects and fabricating evidence have been condoned by the Court.[105]

When multiple suspects are suspected to have been involved in the crime, the interrogator will often use the confession of one suspect—whether an actual confession or a fabricated one—to induce a confession from another suspect. This form of maximization places the latter suspect in a literal prisoner's dilemma. It appears that the suboptimal option is chosen rather frequently: in some 30 percent of studied false confession cases, the police obtained confessions from more than one innocent suspect.[106] There is little doubt that the discussions that lead to the incrimination of codefendants contain promises and threats. In practice, some interrogators squarely violate the prohibition against issuing threats. A rare glimpse into the reality of interrogation rooms was provided during a recent debate over the abolition of the death penalty in the Illinois General Assembly. Representative Jim Sacia, a former FBI agent, argued unabashedly that the death penalty should be preserved because threatening suspects with death sentences can help the police solve crimes.[107] Against the prospect of a death sentence, succumbing to the interrogator's lures, however severe, can indeed be the most rational course of action.

After obtaining a statement from a suspect admitting to having committed the crime, the interrogator is advised to develop a full narrative, which serves to further commit the suspect to his admission and to create a "legally acceptable and substantiated confession that discloses the circumstances and details of the act."[108] As discussed in Chapter 6, confessions are more likely to be believed by judges, jurors, and lawyers when they reveal detailed knowledge of the criminal incident. In other words, the richness of the suspect's narrative is taken as an indication of the confession's reliability. This seems like a sensible cue, unless of course the narrative does not reflect the suspect's actual knowledge. Just as innocent people can be induced to confess to crimes they did not commit, they can be induced also to embellish their fictitious account with corroborating details. Indeed, almost all of the DNA exonerees who falsely confessed provided detailed accounts of their purported criminal act. Most of these confessions contained details that were not publicly known, and thus could have been known only by the true perpetrator and the police. It is inescapable that those details were somehow communicated to the ignorant innocent confessors, invariably by police investigators, whether deliberately or unwittingly.

Experimental Research

The methods of interrogation used by the police have been subjected also to experimental testing in the laboratory. It must be acknowledged that the experimental approach to interrogations raises particular concerns of external validity, due mostly to the difficulties in mimicking the intense, unfamiliar, and high-stakes experience of real-life interrogations. Still, the experimental findings can provide important insight into some specific aspects of the interrogative process. It is noteworthy that the experimental findings are consistent with the observational and archival research, as well as with personal accounts from real-life case studies.

The research has found that not unlike the other facets of the investigation discussed in Chapter 2, interrogations can be skewed by confirmatory biases. Specifically, studies show that an interrogator's initial belief in the suspect's guilt biases the interrogation and its likely outcome. In one study, simulated interrogators who were led to believe (fictitiously) that the suspect was guilty were more inclined to ask guilt-presumptive questions, to exert stronger pressure on the suspect, and to use a wider variety of techniques to induce a confession, including the presentation of false evidence and promises of leniency. That preconceived belief was not cured by the interrogation process. By the end of the process, investigators who were led to believe that the suspect was guilty were 23 percent more likely to confirm that belief than those who were initially told that the suspect was innocent. Moreover, the interrogators' initial belief had an apparent effect on the suspect's behavior, resulting in higher defensiveness in responding to the interrogator's questions.[109]

Other studies have examined the effect of the use of minimization and maximization. One study showed that minimizing themes are generally understood as an implicit promise of leniency, whereas exaggerating the strength of the evidence is taken to be an implicit threat of a more severe punishment.[110] A study in which participants were interrogated for actually having cheated found that resorting to the minimization technique almost doubles the rate of confessions from guilty suspects, but has a threefold increase on the rate of confessions from innocent suspects. Notably, this study demonstrated the powerful effect of cumulative interrogation techniques. Combining the minimization technique with a "deal" (implying a positive outcome for a confession and a negative outcome for continued denial) resulted in a large increase in false confessions.[111]

Other studies have examined additional aspects of the interrogation process. One experimental simulation found that innocent participants were twice as likely as guilty ones to waive their rights and agree to be interrogated in the first place. Almost three-quarters of the innocent suspects who waived their rights explained their waiver as based on their innocence; that is, they felt that they had done nothing wrong and had nothing to hide.[112] Another study tested the effect of presenting suspects with false incriminating evidence. The study found that presenting statements by a witness that (falsely) corroborated the accusation resulted in a heightened rate of confessions.[113] This finding was replicated in a Dutch study that imposed a monetary loss on subjects who succumbed to the pressure and admitted responsibility.[114] Another study found that the rate of false confessions was increased by bluffing, that is, pretending to possess some significant items of evidence, even without stating explicitly that it is inculpatory evidence.[115]

The Miranda Doctrine

One of the hallmarks of American criminal justice is the doctrine established in the Court's 1966 opinion in *Miranda v. Arizona*. The *Miranda* warnings inform suspects of their right to remain silent, that anything they say can be used against them in a court of law, that they have the right to an attorney, and that an attorney will be appointed free of charge if they cannot afford one.[116] The *Miranda* doctrine has traditionally been perceived as an encumbrance on criminal interrogations, and was received with much consternation by law enforcement agencies.[117] In practice, it seems clear that American interrogators have adapted rather well to life under the *Miranda* regime.[118] The simple truth is that very few confessions are ever excluded as a result of violations of the *Miranda* rule. Recall that Reid & Associates boasts that confessions performed by their trainees are admitted in more than 99 percent of the cases.[119] There is little evidence that the doctrine has caused a drop in the rate of interrogations that result in confessions.[120] The key statistic is that some 80 percent of suspects waive their *Miranda* rights or are legally deemed to have waived them.[121]

Oftentimes, suspects choose to talk to their interrogators, whether out of a desire to tell their side of the story or just to please the police. When the suspects elect not to talk, interrogators might try to induce them to waive the *Miranda* protections by trivializing the significance of the rights, by ingratiating themselves with the suspects, or by persuading them that the waiver is in their best interest because it offers them an opportunity to present their side of the story. At times, investigators interrogate suspects "outside of *Miranda*," that is, off the record. The putatively unofficial nature of such interrogations could lead suspects to believe that their statements cannot be used against them.[122] In actuality, the police can use the statements to obtain other incriminating evidence or to impeach the defendants' testimony in court. In the absence of a reliable record, it is also possible that interrogators will fraudulently claim to have read the *Miranda* warnings, thus leading to a *swearing contest,* which they invariably win.

As it turns out, the *Miranda* protections actually facilitate the interrogative process more than they inhibit it. Contrary to its original purpose of protecting suspects from coercion, the doctrine now serves mostly as a weapon to negate claims of coercion. Over the years, the Court moved away from hinging the admissibility of confessions on their reliability and now focuses instead on their voluntariness.[123] In doing so, the Court has condoned the antiseptic qualities of the *Miranda* warnings, by which suspects who waive their *Miranda* rights are deemed to have waived claims of coercion at any time during the investigation.[124] The Court has stated that granting suspects their *Miranda* rights amounts to "a virtual ticket of admissibility," and that the question of the voluntariness of a confession "tends to end with the finding of a valid waiver."[125] For all practical purposes, the voluntariness of the waiver seems to legitimize the questionable interrogative methods that follow in its wake and to absolve the interrogator of any responsibility for inducing the suspect to falsely incriminate himself.

The Prospect of False Confessions

The promoters of the Reid method stand by its accuracy. The textbook insists that "none of the steps is apt to make an innocent person confess," and it assures its users that "all the steps are legally as well as morally justifiable."[126] Joseph Buckley also makes the virtually irrefutable argument that "In the experience of most professional interrogators the frequency of false confessions is rare."[127] Yet the interrogative procedure is designed foremost to extract confessions from the suspect at hand, who is believed to be guilty. There is no indication that it is prone to induce confessions only from guilty suspects. Suspects are most likely to confess when they succumb to the coercive forces of the interrogation, that is, when the interrogator succeeds in beating them into submission and altering their perception of their situation. This eventuality is only loosely related to the suspect's actual guilt. Indeed, the research shows that the prospects of obtaining a confession are determined primarily by the scope and intensity of the coercive techniques employed, and by the duration of the interrogation.[128] The archival study of false confessions found that the median length of these interrogations was about twelve hours, which is many times longer than average interrogations.[129] The coercive nature of the interrogation is manifested also by the high proportion of vulnerable populations who succumb to it, namely, the mentally ill, the mentally retarded, and adolescents.[130] The typical suspect is very much unlike Hannibal Lecter, the cunning and composed character from the film *The Silence of the Lambs*.

Saul Kassin has argued convincingly that innocence itself might actually be a risk factor for false confessions.[131] Consistent with the phenomenon of the *illusion of transparency,* people tend to overestimate the extent to which their inner states are observable to the outside world.[132] Thus innocent suspects might naïvely believe that their innocence will set them free. They are likely to feel that they have nothing to hide and fear that noncooperation will make them appear guilty. Observational studies of interrogations indicate that suspects who have no criminal record are more likely to waive their *Miranda* rights and thus subject themselves to interrogations.[133] Recall that an experimental simulation found that innocent participants tended to feel that they had nothing to hide and were twice as likely as guilty ones to waive their rights and agree to be subjected to an interrogation.[134] In sum, there is good reason to believe that the interview and interrogation methods that prevail in the American criminal justice system have the potential to lead innocent people to confess to crimes they did not commit.[135]

The PEACE Method

The interrogation method currently used in the United Kingdom originates in reforms that were put in place following highly publicized convictions in the 1970s, which were subsequently found to have been based on faulty interrogations. In 1984 the English Parliament enacted the Police and Criminal Evidence Act (PACE), which introduced a sweeping reform of procedures for conducting criminal investigations.[136] In 1993 the Home Office took another major step forward by promulgating a framework for investigative interviewing that has come to be known by the mnemonic PEACE.[137] This approach is driven by the following principles (as revised in 2007):

- The aim of investigative interviewing is to obtain accurate and reliable accounts about matters under police investigation.
- Investigators must act fairly.
- Vulnerable people must be treated with particular consideration at all times.
- Investigative interviewing should be approached with an investigative mindset.[138]

The PEACE framework comprises two complementary methods of questioning: the Cognitive Interview (discussed in Chapter 4), which is intended for cooperative interviewees, and Conversation Management, which is intended for noncooperative interviewees.[139]

The Conversation Management method is based primarily on the use of information, much of which is collected from the suspect himself. Much of the interview is devoted to the suspect's account of the event. The investigator is instructed to play a largely passive and facilitative role, to ensure that the suspect's account is complete and fully understood. During this phase the investigator must not challenge anything the suspect says. She may, however, follow up with probing questions and take note of particular issues and contradictions in his account. If the suspect's account refutes the suspicions against him, the investigation into his involvement should be terminated. If the suspect's account fails to satisfy the investigator, she can proceed to the crucial phase of challenging its inconsistencies and contradictions. In sharp contrast to accusatory protocols that instruct interrogators to silence and shut down the suspect from stating anything but an admission, the Conversation Management method encourages the suspect to provide an abundance of information. This approach both offers the suspect a fair opportunity to make his case and provides the interrogator material for challenging that account. Importantly, the Conversation Management approach discourages aggressive treatment of the suspect, and it forbids resorting to minimization, maximization, intimidation, or any other technique that might be coercive.

Both the PEACE framework for interrogation and the Strategic Use of Evidence for deceit detection rely on a sophisticated use of information. This approach is reminiscent of the TV character Detective Columbo, played by Richard Falk. Rather than confront, accuse, or coerce his suspects, the chatty and affable detective would trap his suspects by exposing their lies and contradictions through various factual ploys, which he constructed mostly from the information that he culled from them.[140] Preliminary research indicates that noncoercive interrogations are more diagnostic of the suspect's guilt than accusatory interrogations that bear the hallmarks of the Reid method.[141]

The transformation of interrogative procedures in the United Kingdom from accusatory methods to information-centered methods did not occur overnight. The PEACE method was introduced following a critical evaluation sponsored by the Home Office in 1991, which revealed serious shortcomings in the conduct of interrogations. Despite the precepts of PACE, interrogations were found to be driven by an assumption of guilt and to contain an abundance of psychological pressure.[142] These findings triggered an extensive program for training police personnel, which was designed and monitored in a collaborative effort by police personnel and legal psychologists.[143] Recent surveys show that the method has gained broad support among English police investigators. Moreover, a study of transcripts of real-life interrogations shows that the police actually follow the core principles of the method. Notably, they shy away from using the prohibited techniques of minimization, maximization, and intimidation, and they refrain from highlighting the futility of the suspect's situation.[144] So far, researchers have not been able to ascertain the effect of the transition to the PEACE method on the actual rate of confessions, whether truthful or false.[145] Nonetheless, the widespread support of English investigators indicates that they do not feel obstructed by the method. The PEACE method has been adopted by the police forces of New Zealand[146] and Norway,[147] and it is enjoying increasing influence in Sweden and Denmark.[148]

Recommendations for Reform

Perhaps more than any other type of evidence, confessions go to the heart of the criminal justice process. Given the dark history of the practice and the risk to suspects' dignity in the interrogation room and beyond, one should be especially disconcerted by interrogative techniques that can lead innocent people to incriminate themselves. The research reviewed in this chapter calls for a more informed, self-conscious, and nuanced approach to both lie detection and interrogations.[149] The criminal justice system has much to gain from shifting from tough-cop interrogation methods to those of smart cops like Columbo. Specific recommendations for reform include the following:

1. Investigators ought to cease relying on physical cues in attempting to detect deceit. The Behavioral Analysis Interview and similar protocols should not be used until their validity has been demonstrated scientifically and their error rates have been measured and found to be acceptable.
2. In detecting deceit, investigators ought to rely more heavily on the information provided by the suspect, such as Strategic Use of Evidence technique.
3. Contingent on further research, investigators should make use of interviewing methods that increase the suspect's cognitive load.
4. In conducting interrogations, investigators should reduce their reliance on accusatorial and coercive methods and move toward less confrontational procedures that focus on information gathering.
5. The Supreme Court ought to rethink its permissive attitude toward the admissibility of contested confession evidence. In particular, it should forbid or severely restrict the use of interrogative measures that have the power to overcome the suspects' will.

Regardless of whichever techniques are used, it is vital that a complete and reliable record be created of the entire interview and interrogation processes. The call to record interrogations has been made by numerous commentators and professional organizations,[150] and it is already taking root in a number of states and hundreds of police departments.[151] Notably, some 80 percent of surveyed law enforcement personnel maintain that interrogations ought to be recorded from start to finish.[152] As discussed throughout this book, having access to what transpired in the interrogation room can go a long way to assist in the assessment of the fact-sensitive judgments of both the voluntariness and the reliability of confessions. Chapter 8 provides a discussion of the numerous advantages of this recommendation and a response to its detractors. It must, however, be acknowledged that the creation of the electronic record itself can introduce bias. Factors such as camera perspective, framing, lighting, and editing can shape the narrative impact of the film. The recording of interrogations should thus be done in a manner that minimizes the risk of any such biases.[153]

6

"WE FIND THE DEFENDANT GUILTY"

Fact-Finding at Trial

The preceding four chapters dealt with the investigative phase of the criminal justice process. This chapter and the next deal with the complementary part of the criminal process: the adjudicative phase—both the criminal trial and, more briefly, the role of post-trial judicial review.

Trials are the most symbolic embodiment of the rule of law. The U.S. Supreme Court has portrayed the criminal trial as a "decisive and portentous"[1] and "paramount" event.[2] Trials are considered "the central institution of law as we know it,"[3] the crown jewel of the legal system.[4] Amidst its multiple purposes, the essential objective of the criminal trial is to reach a factual determination whether the defendant did or did not commit the crime, that is, to distinguish between guilty and innocent defendants. In psychological terms, this is a *diagnostic* task. The guiding principles of the adjudicatory process follow the *rationalist tradition of adjudication,* which emphasizes the importance of drawing rational conclusions from the evidence adduced at trial.[5] The ultimate objective of the trial is the rectitude of the decision, or, put simply, getting it right.

The prevailing sentiment within the American polity and legal profession is that the trial is well suited to meet the expectations of the criminal justice system.[6] Although proponents will admit, as they must, that the system cannot be completely flawless,[7] this truism does not appear to make much impact on how the process is conducted. The Court routinely lauds the Constitution's unparalleled ability to arrive at correct verdicts,[8] the aptness of the adversarial process,[9] the truth-revealing power of cross-examination,[10] the auspicious effects of jury deliberation,[11] the oversight offered by appellate and *habeas corpus* courts,[12] and the overall suitability of juries—the queen bees of the system—for the task of fact-finding.[13]

Among their other strengths, jurors are deemed capable of comprehending and following judicial instructions,[14] handling untrustworthy evidence,[15] detecting lies,[16] ignoring biasing information,[17] overcoming prejudice,[18] and acknowledging any biases they might harbor.[19]

These two chapters examine whether the criminal trial can satisfy the high epistemic demands of the criminal justice system.[20] At its core, this inquiry focuses on the diagnostic capabilities of the process's fact finders, namely, jurors and judges. The question no longer centers upon the accuracy of the testimony itself—the subject of Chapters 2–5—but upon the ability of third-party fact finders to accurately assess that testimony. This discussion focuses mostly on the performance of jurors, who serve the fact-finding function in the large majority of criminal trials. Its purpose, however, is not to compare the suitability of juries for the task with that of judges. A mounting body of research finds that professional judges do not perform much differently from lay people in a number of important fact-finding tasks.[21] The limitations of human cognition observed in these chapters appear to exceed any possible differences between the two decision-making entities. The debate over the suitability of the jury as the preferred fact-finding body is thus left for another day.

The first part of this chapter discusses the main weakness of the criminal justice process: the evidence on which verdicts are based is of unknown, and often compromised, quality. The second part examines the research that pertains to people's ability to draw correct factual inferences from the types of testimony that are frequently presented in criminal trials. The third part examines other features that complicate that delicate task. Chapter 7 examines the efficacy of a number of legal safeguards which are built into the trial process, and which are designed to overcome some of the impediments to accurate fact-finding.

Problems with the Integrity of the Evidence

Substandard Investigations

The problems with the integrity of the evidence begin with the standard of police work during the criminal investigation. Recall from Chapters 2–5 that criminal investigations are performed by almost 20,000 different law enforcement agencies, each following its own procedures, practices, and training programs, which are often inadequate. As a result, the reliability of the evidence produced by an investigation is often idiosyncratic to the particular department, investigator, or case. Investigative procedures that do not meet the standard of best practices are prone to produce a high level of erroneous evidence and also have the potential to induce errors: misidentifications can be caused by poorly performed lineups, event memory errors can be triggered by suggestive questioning, and false confessions can be extracted by means of coercive investigative tactics. In short, the evidence generated by the conventional investigative procedures is bound to contain unknown quantities of error.

Synthesized Testimony

Recall also that the evidence presented at trial amounts to a *synthesized* version of the witnesses' testimony, which can differ substantially from the original statements that they gave the police. Over the course of the investigation and pretrial processes, evidence degrades, gets exposed to contamination, and loses many of its traces of accuracy. As the *raw* statements evolve into the synthesized testimony that is fit for the courtroom, the testimony tends to become more one-sided, comprehensive, and resolute. As discussed below, drawing correct inferences from testimonial accounts of contested criminal events is difficult under the best of conditions. Deciphering the truth from such synthesized renditions is a far less reliable endeavor.

Biased Testimony

In an ideal world, witnesses would be mere conduits of sensory information. In actuality, they are often intricately entangled in the social tragedy surrounding the criminal event, and at times they have strong desires with respect to the outcome of the case. Defendants who testify in their defense are habitually motivated to save themselves from criminal punishment, and are generally regarded with considerable suspicion for that reason. Victim-witnesses are generally viewed as reliable and are usually treated with sympathy. They, too, however, can be motivated toward a particular outcome, typically, to see the perceived perpetrators suffer punishment. Jennifer Thompson candidly articulated what most crime victims propbably feel: "I just wanted to nail [Cotton]. I wanted to make him go to jail for ever and ever and ever."[22] As discussed in Chapter 2, prosecution witnesses are often drawn into the intergroup conflict between the state and the defense and are typically included in the in-group of law enforcement personnel. Recall that group membership influences perceptions of facts, affective states, and motivations pertaining to the issue at hand.[23] Jennifer Thompson recounts being prodded by the prosecutor "to nail Cotton" and being praised for her compelling testimony.[24] Following Cotton's conviction, she was taken to the district attorney's office for a champagne celebration.[25] A witness's motivation can strengthen the persuasiveness of his testimony[26] and thus possibly affect the outcome of the case.

Even seemingly disinterested witnesses can get caught up in the adversarial process and find themselves aligned with one of the parties. One factor that can contribute to the swaying of testimony is the common, though troubling, practice of *witness preparation*. Lawyers routinely prepare witnesses before the trial. While this practice verges on subornation of perjury,[27] failing to do so can amount to a breach of the professional responsibility the lawyer owes her client. Lawyers are permitted to discuss the witness's probable testimony, to inform him of other testimony to be presented, and to ask him to reconsider his recollection in that light. A lawyer is also permitted to discuss the applicable law, prepare the witness for hostile cross-examination, ask him to rehearse the testimony, and also suggest alternative word choices.[28] In sum, lawyers have considerable latitude to mold the testimony to fit a particular conclusion, thus weakening its correspondence to the actual facts. One study found that after being interviewed by a simulated lawyer, the witness's testimony became skewed in favor of that lawyer's side. These effects were mediated by the manipulativeness of the individuals playing the role of the lawyers.[29] Another study found that forewarning a prosecution witnesses about an expected hostile cross-examination by the defense attorney resulted in a strengthening of the witness's inculpating testimony, which led in turn to higher conviction rates by a simulated jury. The effect was most pronounced for witnesses whose testimony was actually mistaken.[30] Testimony can be biased also by the fact that witnesses are summoned by one of the parties. One study found that the mere summoning of bystander witnesses to testify on behalf of one side swayed their testimony toward that side.[31] Over the course of the process, such an affiliation can evolve into camaraderie.

Pseudo-Corroboration

The assessment of evidence is further complicated by the unclear significance of corroboration. The convergence of separate evidence items in
support of the same conclusion is a familiar and ubiquitous cue for
drawing inferences. In principle, the larger the number of items and the
more strongly they corroborate one another, the more they are deemed
to support the conclusion. In practice, however, the appearance of corroboration can be misleading. As discussed in Chapters 2–5, the gathering and interpretation of evidence are strongly impacted by the dynamic
nature of the investigative process. In the normal course of an investigation, the accumulation of evidence follows and builds upon the evidence
already collected, until a sufficient accumulation of items converges on
the investigative conclusion. When the key piece of evidence that triggered the escalation is erroneous, it can set off an *escalation of error* that
sweeps through the entire investigation.

Thus, although a corroborating body of evidence can indeed reflect the
strong evidentiary support for a correct conclusion, it can also be a mere
artifact of the investigative process that conceals its erroneous nature.
This form of pseudo-corroboration was observed in a number of known
false convictions where the prosecution's case consisted of compelling and
corroborative sets of evidence items, all of which turned out to have been
false. The corroborative nature of the evidence in these cases might help
explain why only one of sixty-nine innocent convicts received relief by
contesting the sufficiency of the evidence (before the revelation of the exculpatory DNA evidence), and that singular case was subsequently reversed. Notably, fewer than half of DNA exonerees even bothered to raise
this claim.[32] The evidence in these cases was often deemed compelling also
by reviewing judges in appellate and post-conviction proceedings.[33]

Investigation Opacity

Another profound hindrance to the assessment of evidence stems from the
fact that police investigations are usually not recorded. The absence of a
reliable record of the investigation prevents access to witnesses' *raw* statements, which are typically the most accurate account of the criminal
event. The opacity of the investigation also prevents fact finders from being able to assess whether the testimony was induced by the investigation
process itself. Thus, fact finders have no way of knowing whether the ad-

ministrator of a lineup pointed out the suspect to the witness, whether a particular fact was first suggested by the witness or by the interviewer, and whether promises and threats were made in the interrogation room.[34] Recall from Chapter 2 that one-third of lineup administrators fail to keep any records of the lineups, only one out of four keep photographic records of the procedure, and only a small fraction record interrogations.[35] Investigators forget much of the relevant information provided by the witness before the end of the interview, and they have even weaker memory of the questions that they asked. This opacity of the investigation is particularly problematic given that the information provided by witnesses can be swayed by even subtle and unnoticeable features of the investigative procedures.

Still, detectives routinely testify about their investigations, often in great detail. That testimony is bound to be inaccurate at least in part because it is all but impossible to remember all the nuances of the process without a reliable record. Moreover, detectives' testimony is likely to be colored by the motivation to depict their investigative work as professional and trustworthy, if not by their motivation to see that the suspect is convicted. On the stand, detectives habitually deny influencing witnesses' responses. In some instances, these denials are genuine, whether because the detective did not engage in any behavior that could induce error, was not aware that her conduct influenced the witness's response, or has simply forgotten what exactly she said or did. In other cases, detectives lie outright about their conduct, a practice known as *testilying*.[36] Regardless of the source of the detective's denial, it often contradicts the defendant's account. Such discrepancies occur most frequently in the context of interrogations, one of the most veiled yet influential facets of the investigatory process. With no verifiable record in hand, these contradictory testimonies turn into swearing contests between police officers and defendants. For the most part, the former prevail.

In sum, the unavailability of the investigative record deprives jurors of a valuable means of ascertaining the accuracy of the testimony. With only incomplete and often biased information at their disposal, jurors are left with little choice but to trust one version of the truth blindly or, as discussed below, to resort to superficial and often misleading cues such as the witness's confidence and demeanor.

People's Performance in Evaluating Testimony

We next explore the research that examines people's ability to draw inferences from types of human testimony that are frequently presented in criminal trials. This research focuses primarily on situations in which the fact finder does not have verifiable information that is exogenous to the testimony, such as a DNA match or surveillance camera footage. The task, then, is to draw inferences from the witnesses' testimony itself. For the most part, this research pertains to testimony that was collected under favorable conditions, and thus is not afflicted by the factors discussed above. In other words, the research examines the performance of fact finders in deciphering testimony that is of higher quality than what actual juries face in real life.

Eyewitness Identification Testimony

As discussed in Chapter 3, three-quarters of the known false convictions were caused primarily or exclusively by a misidentification of an innocent suspect. Recall that thousands of naturalistic and experimental observations reveal that one-third of positive identifications are wrong. Some of the spontaneous errors do not reach the jury, such as when the chosen fillers are known to be uninvolved in the crime. At the same time, many of the induced misidentifications are likely to reach the jury because the inducing influences tend to lead the witness to pick the person suspected by the police. The key question is how adept courtroom fact finders are in assessing witnesses' identifications, that is, in distinguishing between accurate and mistaken identifications.

General beliefs about identification accuracy. A starting point for evaluating people's ability to assess identification testimony is to gauge their trust in human capabilities of identification at the general level. General beliefs are important in that they affect specific judgments: jurors who tend to trust identification generally are more likely to believe a specific identification. The consistent finding is that people overtrust human capabilities in this domain. For one, people overestimate their own capabilities. Recall that a large survey of jury-eligible citizens in Washington, D.C., revealed unrealistic beliefs, with two-thirds of the respondents agreeing with the statement "I never forget a face," and three-quarters maintaining "I have an excellent memory." Only one-half of the respondents disagreed with analogizing memories of traumatic events to video recordings.[37] People overestimate their capabilities also when asked to predict how they would perform on various experimental tasks. For example, 97 percent of respondents estimated that they would succeed in a task that involved an identification of a target person, which was performed successfully by only 50 percent of the actual participants.[38]

People tend also to overestimate the performance of others. In one study, participants overestimated the performance of people in identifying faces from blurry photographs.[39] In another study, one-sixth of the participants estimated that the witnesses would pick an innocent filler at a lineup, while the actual rate of erroneous picks was almost 80 percent.[40] Some 80 percent of jury-eligible Florida residents overestimated the performance of the store clerks who had participated in a field study. On the basis of these results, in about seven juries out of ten, at least ten jurors would be prone to overtrust the identification.[41]

Overtrusting identification performance has been found also in studies of simulated trials. For example, a study conducted in a provincial courthouse in Ontario, Canada, found that simulated jurors judged the identifications to be accurate and voted to convict in 69 percent of the cases, when the actual rate of correct identifications was only 50 percent.[42] In a similar study, 80 percent of simulated jurors believed the witnesses' identifications, although only 58 percent of them were actually correct.[43] Another study found a more moderate level of overbelief (68 percent), where the underlying rate of accuracy was 54 percent.[44]

Diagnosticity of identification accuracy. The key finding in this body of research is that people do not perform well at distinguishing between accurate and inaccurate identifications. One study found that simulated jurors were significantly more likely to believe accurate witnesses than inaccurate ones.[45] But in the study conducted in the Ontario courthouse, simulated jurors were no more likely to believe accurate witnesses than inaccurate ones,[46] and three studies have found that simulated jurors tended to believe witnesses who had misidentified the suspect more than they believed accurate witnesses.[47] Notably, a number of defendants in real-life cases were convicted based on eyewitness identification despite having already been excluded by DNA testing.[48] These men were exonerated years later, though typically not before the DNA was matched to some other credible suspect.

Sensitivity to accuracy factors. The likely explanation for this shortfall in diagnosticity is that people are largely insensitive to the factors that make identifications more or less accurate. Recall that identification accuracy is highly susceptible to the specific factors of the case, resulting in swings in accuracy rates from as low as 14 percent to as high as 86 percent for the same basic witnessing scenario.[49] It follows that to distinguish between accurate and inaccurate identifications, jurors need to be aware of these factors and the effect they have on the performance of witnesses.

Survey data show that people have limited knowledge of the accuracy factors. One survey found that students and jury-eligible citizens responded correctly to fewer than one-half of the questions about accuracy factors. This performance was significantly better than chance (25 percent) but overall rather poor.[50] Another series of studies compared responses from jury-eligible citizens and experts, and found agreement on only four of thirty items asked.[51] Poor appreciation for identification factors was revealed also in the abovementioned survey conducted with jury-eligible respondents in Washington, D.C. A majority of respondents overweighed the diagnosticity of witness confidence, almost three-quarters failed to realize the detrimental effect of biasing lineup instructions, and almost half failed to appreciate the advantage of conducting blind lineups.[52]

A large experimental study found that simulated jurors were flatly insensitive to nine factors that are known to impair identifications, such as the retention interval, the lineup instructions, and the number of foils. The participants were, however, influenced by the witness's stated confidence,[53] which, as discussed below, is of limited diagnostic value. Another study found overall insensitivity to the the influence of viewing conditions, such as the level of illumination, distance from the perpetrator, and duration of exposure.[54] Simulated jurors have also been found to be relatively insensitive to cross-race bias[55] and to biased instructions,[56] and only marginally sensitive to the similarity of the suspect to the fillers.[57]

Insensitivity to witnessing conditions is particularly manifested by a strong overbelief in identifications conducted under poor witnessing conditions. One study found that when the rate of correct identifications was merely 32 percent, the witnesses were believed by 62 percent of the simulated jurors.[58] Another study found no difference between judgments of accuracy of an identification made under superior conditions (71 percent) and identifications made under three different suboptimal conditions (65, 68, and 67 percent).[59] Moreover, as many as 42 percent of the respondents trusted identifications that were exceedingly unreliable.[60]

It should be added that even if jurors were appropriately sensitive to the factors that hinder identifications, in real life, their assessments would be impeded by a lack of reliable information regarding those factors. In many cases jurors must rely on the witnesses' own reports of properties such as distance, duration, and illumination at the time of the viewing, as the witnesses themselves are the only possible source of that information. As discussed in Chapter 3, the research casts doubt over these self-reports, as people tend to shrink assessments of distances, exaggerate estimates of duration, and fail to notice inferior illumination, all of which are bound to result in inflated assessments of accuracy. Moreover, these judgments are also susceptible to manipulation. Giving witnesses positive (fictitious) feedback ("good, you identified the suspect") leads them to report more favorable viewing conditions and having paid more attention to the culprit.[61]

Relying on witness confidence. A considerable amount of research indicates that jurors place much weight on witnesses' confidence in their identifications. One study found that eyewitness confidence was a stronger predictor of jurors' decisions than the actual accuracy of their identifications.[62] Simulated jurors have been found to trust identifications by confident witnesses twice as often as identifications by non-confident witnesses.[63] Witnesses who testified that they were "completely certain" were three times more likely to be judged accurate than those who reported being "somewhat uncertain."[64] In another study, conviction rates were almost 50 percent higher when the prosecution eyewitness stated that he was "100% confident" than when he "could not say that he was 100% confident."[65] In a different study, conviction rates were considerably higher (62 percent vs. 38 percent) when the eyewitness stated that he was "absolutely certain" in his identification of the perpetrator than when he stated that he was "not certain at all."[66] Witness confidence has also been found to wipe out jurors' sensitivity to witnessing factors.[67]

Reliance on witness confidence as a proxy for accuracy would be helpful if it were a good marker of accuracy. But the experimental findings cast some doubt over this proposition. The statistical relationship between identification accuracy and witness confidence is about 0.4.[68] Though positive, this correlation is not strongly diagnostic. For example, where the base rate of accuracy is 50 percent, a coefficient of 0.4

means that of the witnesses who claim to be absolutely confident, only 70 percent will in fact be correct.[69] More importantly, synthesized evidence is more likely to be reported with inflated levels of confidence, a result that further weakens the accuracy-confidence relationship. Recall also that confidence is a malleable construct that is sensitive to distortion from a variety of sources, such as identifications by cowitnesses, successive viewings, repetition, and knowledge about other inculpatory evidence against the suspect. Again, fictitious feedback from the administrator ("good, you identified the suspect") has been found to boost witness confidence, and also increase jurors' trust in those identifications.[70] Thus, at the point where the witness's confidence counts most, it is at best only weakly diagnostic of accuracy, with the effect of making identifications appear more reliable than they really are. Confident witnesses are likely to be overrepresented at trial because prosecutors are more likely to try cases when they have confident eyewitnesses.

In-court identifications.   Jurors' ability to evaluate the accuracy of identification testimony is hampered also by the ubiquitous practice of in-court identifications. Any doubt that jurors might harbor about the witness's identification at the lineup can be readily overwhelmed by the courtroom spectacle of the witness performing an identification in front of the fact finders' very own eyes. While some observers tend to dismiss in-court identifications as insignificant symbolic acts,[71] there is good reason to suspect that they exert a strong influence on fact finders. Observing an event firsthand is generally more persuasive than hearing a verbal account of the same event by a third party, a phenomenon called *seeing is believing.*[72] One study found that as many as 42 percent of respondents trusted an identification that was based solely on an in-court identification, even though the witness had previously failed to identify the defendant at a live lineup.[73] Moreover, in many instances identifications conducted in court are loaded with inculpatory rhetoric and accompanied by high levels of confidence. At an Illinois trial, for example, a witness identified the defendant and stated, "He raped me."[74] Another witness identified a defendant and claimed: "I will never forget the face, the color skin, and his voice."[75] A witness in a Georgia rape case identified the defendant in court, stating that she was 120 percent confident. At the sentencing hearing the judge stated, "I haven't seen many cases with any stronger eyeball identification," and sentenced the man to forty-five years in prison.[76] In a trial of another Illinois man, the rape victim stated in court:

"I still stand strong. No one was in that dark alley with me but Jesus and this person. There is a certainty, sir, and I am standing on that."[77] All of these defendants were convicted at trial and subsequently exonerated based on DNA testing. It is no surprise that prosecutors insist on conducting in-court identifications and defense attorneys dread them.

In-court identification has become a routine procedure in adjudicating identity cases. It is most likely that in every false conviction that contained an identification, the witness pointed to the innocent defendant and assured the jury that it was he who perpetrated the crime. Still, the practice receives only scant scholarly attention. This lack of attention should not be blamed on experimental psychologists, as the flawed nature of the practice is too obvious to warrant empirical investigation. The indifference of legal scholars and policymakers is, however, puzzling.[78] While the impact of in-court identifications on the verdict can be dramatic, its probativeness ranges from being poorly diagnostic to downright misleading.

Most notably, the procedure is patently suggestive. Given the layout of the courtroom, it is no secret who the defendant is. Put simply, the witness need only point to the person sitting at the defense table, next to the lawyer in the gray suit. This exercise can be performed successfully by anyone who never saw the perpetrator, even by a tourist who happened to stumble into the courtroom. The flagrant suggestiveness of this procedure is many times more powerful than factors that have been shown to bias identifications, such as imperfect instructions and nonverbal suggestive behavior by the lineup administrator.[79]

In-court identifications are naturally weakened by the lapse of time since the criminal event and are thus susceptible to both decay and contamination. In most cases, in-court identifications constitute a successive viewing. In fact, the procedure often constitutes the apex of a series of encounters with the suspect's image, which spans the investigation, pretrial hearings, and the trial itself. Permitting successive viewings rests on the assumption that witnesses can accurately trace the source of their memories and determine correctly that they recognize the suspect from the crime scene rather than from any one of the potentially contaminating identification procedures. Recall from Chapter 3 that this is a dubious proposition. Repeated exposure leads to a familiarity effect, by which witnesses are more likely to recognize previously viewed targets, even if they did not pick them out in the original procedure.

More importantly, the social environment surrounding in-court identifications produces an immensely strong commitment effect. A witness might well fear that failing to reidentify the defendant will make him appear incompetent, unreliable, or unhelpful to law enforcement. Nowhere is the commitment effect stronger than when a witness is standing in the spotlight of the courtroom, facing the authoritative judge and the assembled jury, knowing the importance of his testimony to the resolution of the case. Under these situational forces, it would be extremely unusual for a prosecution witness to break ranks and reverse what he had previously told the police and promised the prosecutor to repeat at trial.

The policy of permitting in-court identifications has been extended to permit a range of particularly troubling applications. In-court identifications are sometimes the first and only identification procedure by that witness. That is, witnesses are asked to identify the suspect in court absent any investigative procedure that tested their memory.[80] The practice is more troubling when the witness's statement in court conveys a recognition that is stronger or more confident than it was at the original lineup. Recall that Jennifer Thompson's identifications of Ronald Cotton at the lineups were very hesitant, but her identification in the courtroom was unwavering. It is very disturbing that in-court identifications are permitted when the witness had initially failed to pick out the suspect, even after he originally identified an innocent person as the perpetrator. These failures should serve as a categorical indication that the witness does not have a reliable memory of the suspect and should not be trusted with providing testimony on this point.

Most astoundingly, in-court identifications are used as a means of curing the ill effects of suggestive lineups. The Court has asserted that testimony borne by suggestive procedures should be admitted when it is said to have originated from a source that was "independent of" the flawed procedure.[81] In other words, flawed identification procedures can be cured by subsequent ones—typically, by identifications conducted in court. Effectively, the Court's position rests on the belief that witnesses can reliably state that they can trace their memory to the crime scene rather than to the flawed identification procedure. As discussed in Chapter 3, early identification procedures routinely contaminate subsequent ones, and witnesses perform poorly at determining the correct source of the sense of familiarity with the suspect. This practice ignores the serious risk that the in-court identification was actually contaminated by the flawed procedure that it is supposed to cure.

As if the procedure itself were not suggestive enough, in-court identifications have been permitted when supplemented with even more suggestive information. Courts have allowed identifications when the prosecutor showed the witnesses photographs of the defendant one day before the trial, some three years after the event;[82] the prosecutor gave the witness a pretrial tour of the courtroom during which he singled out the defense table;[83] and when the defendant was dressed in a jail outfit, bound by handcuffs and leg manacles, and surrounded by uniformed deputies.[84] Paradoxically, given the procedure's lack of diagnostic value under the best of conditions, it is unclear whether these excesses really make a difference.[85]

Given the habitual and ubiquitous admission of in-court identifications, defense attorneys have all but given up on challenging them on the grounds that they violate due process.[86] Still, a small number of defense attorneys have elected to contest the practice by means of subterfuge, specifically by seating someone other than the defendant in the defendant's seat. In the few reported cases of this kind, the witnesses botched the identifications by picking out the innocent substitutes. Invariably, judges have responded angrily, citing the counsel for contempt. In one Illinois case the trial judge scolded the lawyer for placing the substitute at the "customary location of a defendant," thus creating a misrepresentation that he was the defendant. In affirming the contempt conviction, the state supreme court added that the lawyer's conduct "derogates from the court's dignity and authority."[87] While the contempt citations are arguably justified in their own right, the courts' reactions are notable for ignoring the true import of these cases—that in-court identifications are a hollow and even detrimental form of proof.[88]

Event Memory Testimony

The bulk of the evidence presented at criminal trials consists of witnesses' accounts of the criminal event. The assessment of testimony for events can entail two distinct modes of judgment. When a juror has reason to suspect a witness's honesty, she is concerned mostly with trying to determine whether the witness is lying. When the juror does not suspect the witness's honesty, she is effectively concerned with evaluating the accuracy of the memorial account. The former task of deception detection has been discussed in Chapter 5 and will be discussed further below. For now, we focus on assessments of testimony from witnesses who might be mistaken but are not suspected of lying.

The assessment of a witness's memory for an event boils down to distinguishing between true and false memories. As discussed in Chapter 4, a large body of psychological research demonstrates that human memory is a powerful cognitive apparatus, but it can be fickle at times, and is vulnerable to error and contamination. For one, people's memories are invariably incomplete, in that they do not contain all the details that might be needed to solve a difficult case. Human memory is strongest in remembering the *gist* of events, that is, the deeper, more practical and meaningful aspects of the episode. Specific verbatim details are least likely to be noticed and encoded, quickest to decay, and most vulnerable to contamination. Moreover, people's memories are not always accurate. False memories can occur spontaneously, such as when people confuse facts from different events, fill memory gaps with mistaken information, and interpret events to match their schemas and expectations. False memories can also be induced by external sources, such as when the witness is subjected to faulty investigative procedures or exposed to postevent misinformation. The psychological research helps us to understand how, and how well, people assess other people's memory for events. A number of laboratory experiments reveal inconsistent and overall weak performance, with accuracy levels ranging from 50 percent to 75 percent (with 50 percent being chance level).[89]

One cue that people commonly use to assess other people's memories is the vividness of the memorial account, which often boils down to the *richness of detail* that it contains.[90] A series of studies showed that the believability of the testimony of a prosecution witness in a robbery-murder of a convenience-store clerk was influenced by the inclusion of trivial details. Testimony that explicitly detailed the items taken by the perpetrator before the shooting (Kleenex, Tylenol, and a six-pack of Diet Pepsi) made a greater impact than did an otherwise identical testimony that only mentioned "a few store items."[91]

A second accuracy cue that observers use is the consistency of the witness's memorial accounts.[92] A number of studies found that inconsistencies in witnesses' testimony influence the believability of the witness, estimations of probability of guilt, and the rate of guilty verdicts.[93] The third commonly used accuracy cue is the person's stated level of confidence.[94] As with judgments of identifications, fact finders are more likely to believe testimony that is accompanied by high levels of confidence. One study found that testimony from more confident prosecution witnesses ("I am absolutely sure" versus "I am reasonably sure") resulted in substantial increases in estimations of the probability of guilt and in conviction rates.[95] The effect of confidence has been replicated in a number of studies.[96]

The question, then, is whether these cues are actually indicative of memory accuracy.[97] Obviously, if the cues do not correspond to the accuracy of the assessment, or if they correspond only weakly, they stand to lead to mistaken conclusions. As it turns out, the research casts doubt over the diagnosticity of these cues. It seems appropriate to infer that a memory for a particular fact is more likely to be accurate if it is remembered in rich detail. But the richness of the memory for one detail should not be used to infer that the witness's memory is more reliable for any of the other details of that event. As discussed in Chapter 4, memories are not monolithic entities. Memories are constructed from multiple fragments that are bound with different memory sources, that have different significance to the person, that are stored in different parts of the brain, and that decay at different rates. It follows that an accurate memory for any one aspect of the event is not a valid indicator of other aspects of the witness's memory.[98] Thus, the fact that a witness is capable of recalling some trivial details, such as the specific items that the robber picked up before robbing the convenience-store clerk, says little about the witness's ability to identify the robber or to correctly remember the getaway car. Moreover, memories for different aspects of an event can even be inversely related. It has been found that the better the witness's memory of the peripheral details of a criminal event, the worse she performs in identifying the perpetrator of that crime.[99] Similar issues arise with respect to the usefulness of the consistency cue, as consistent recollection on one aspect of a memory is a weak indicator of the strength of the memory overall. Indeed, the statistical relationship between memory consistency and memory accuracy has been found to be a modest 0.3.[100]

Doubts also plague the diagnosticity of the widely used confidence cue. Memories tend to be reported with overconfidence. For example, people have been found to report 90 percent confidence when they are only 60 percent accurate[101] and to report as many as 25 percent of inaccurate memories with maximal confidence.[102] The accuracy-confidence correlation for event memory has been found to be unstable and often weak, ranging from zero to 0.6.[103] One set of studies revealed that even when the confidence-accuracy relationship was significant, observers tended to "overuse" the reported confidence, that is, to place more weight on it than warranted by its correspondence with accuracy.[104]

The three noted cues are even less diagnostic when assessing the *synthesized* testimony presented at trial. As described in Chapter 4, the decay of memory for verbatim and surface details leaves voids that people tend to fill. People replenish their incomplete memories with details that fit their schemas, expectations, and stereotypes, and that help them draw pragmatic inferences about the world. Memory lapses and gaps can also be filled with information suggested by other people or by a variety of external sources. Thus, rich memorial accounts stand not only to mislead the fact finder about the criminal event, but can easily inflate the perceived reliability of the witness' memory. Moreover, people's intuitive belief in the richness-of-detail cue can be manipulated at trial. Savvy attorneys can readily encourage witnesses to include trivial details, praise their witnesses' testimony for containing details, and attack opposing witnesses for failure to recount trivial details or for mentioning mistaken ones. The diagnosticity of the consistency cue is likewise questionable because synthesized memorial accounts are often reiterated and rehearsed repeatedly in preparation for trial.[105] This cue, too, is susceptible to manipulation as lawyers can praise witnesses for being consistent even if they are mistaken, and catch truthful witnesses in an inconsistency on some detail or another.[106]

Synthesized testimony also robs the confidence cue of much of its usefulness. The research indicates that numerous investigative procedures result in the inflation of witnesses' confidence for event memory, which typically coincides with the decrease in accuracy arising from decay and contamination. Recall that a number of studies have found that confidence, but not accuracy, is inflated by a variety of factors that are often present in real-life investigations, such as repeated questioning, communicating with cowitnesses, engaging in imagination and confabulation, and receiving confirmatory feedback from the interviewer. Providing witnesses with (fictitious) feedback has been found to reduce the confidence-accuracy correlation from 0.6 to zero,[107] and increasing the witness's motivation at retrieval has been found to reduce the correlation from 0.4 to 0.05.[108]

Confession Evidence

Another important type of evidence consists of statements obtained out of court, in which the defendant confessed to having committed the crime or provided other statements that implicate him in the criminal event. Confessions are generally believed to be powerful inculpatory evidence, "probably the most probative and damaging evidence,"[109] a "bombshell which shatters the defense."[110]

Confession evidence is widely perceived to be trustworthy, a notion that is reinforced in court by prosecutors.[111] Yet confessions are not always reliable, and thus pose a serious challenge to accurate fact-finding. As discussed in Chapter 5, confessions are usually extracted by means of interrogative methods that are not designed to distinguish between innocent and guilty suspects, and are deployed on the assumption that the suspect at hand is indeed the perpetrator. That assumption is typically based on a judgment that the suspect is lying to the investigator, which itself rests on shaky grounds. The prospect that a false confession will lead to a false conviction depends critically on the jury's ability to recognize it as such. The legal system places much faith in jurors' capabilities in this regard, and applies a liberal standard for admitting contested confessions into evidence.[112] Thus, it is important to determine how good jurors are in distinguishing true confessions from false ones. The limited available naturalistic data cast doubt upon jurors' performance in this regard. Two studies examined real-world cases containing confessions that were subsequently revealed to have been false. Of the cases that went to trial, three-quarters resulted in a conviction, which suggests that jurors believed three out of every four false confessions.[113] In a number of known false conviction cases, jurors trusted the confessions even in the face of compelling contradictory evidence. Jeffrey Deskovic was convicted despite the fact that he was excluded by a pretrial DNA test.[114] In the Central Park Jogger case, the teens were convicted despite the fact that they were excluded by DNA tests, and notwithstanding the inconsistencies within and among their statements.[115] In the case from Beatrice, Nebraska, the jury believed the confession evidence that stated that six men and women participated in the rape-murder, even though the investigation indicated that the crime was perpetrated by a single man acting alone.[116] One DNA exoneree was convicted by a judge despite the existence of an exculpating DNA test.[117]

The research indicates that lay people are rather sanguine about the prospect of false confessions. People tend to believe that the police do not interrogate innocent suspects or that even coercive interrogation techniques elicit true confessions but not false ones.[118] The insensitivity to the possibility of false confessions may stem from the fact that more than 90 percent of surveyed people maintain that they themselves would not confess to a crime they had not committed.[119] Extending this logic leads to the conclusion that people who confessed to committing a crime are likely to be guilty. Jurors might also be accepting of the coercive nature of interrogations because they believe that the use of unethical methods to elicit true confessions is justified.[120] Even when they are mindful of the effects of coercive interrogations, people do not always adjust their verdicts accordingly, including when they are admonished by the judge to disregard the impermissible confession.[121] As discussed in Chapter 7, jurors' decisions are often influenced by their personal values and beliefs, which are not always consistent with the law's dictates. Notably, judges, too, do not consistently follow the mandate of the law with respect to ignoring impermissibly coercive interrogations.[122]

Even if jurors were perfectly attuned to the risks of coercion, and even if they translated those concerns appropriately into verdict decisions, discerning the veracity of confessions in actual criminal cases would remain a tall order. The difficulty stems from the fact that interrogations in the real world tend to cover up their traces of reliability. A commonly used cue in assessing confession accuracy is, again, the richness of detail, especially regarding facts that were not made public.[123] Yet recall from Chapter 5 that false confessions invariably come fully packaged with detailed accounts of the confessor's purported criminal deeds. Indeed, one of the explicit objectives of police interrogations is to convert the defendant's admission into an elaborate narrative.[124] Thirty-eight of the forty confessions given by people who were later exonerated by DNA testing contained rich and detailed, yet false, accounts of those crimes. Invariably, the prosecutors highlighted the richness of the narratives at trial and emphasized that the facts were nonpublic and thus could have been known only to the true perpetrator.[125] One prosecutor stated that it was a "mathematical impossibility" that the defendant could have guessed so many details correctly,[126] and another dismissed the defendant's claim of coercion, emphasizing that he "supplied detail after detail after detail after detail."[127] Recall also that when confessions are ultimately determined to have been false, the most plausible conclusion is that the nonpublic information divulged by the defendants was somehow communicated to them by the police.[128] Still, in most DNA exonerations, the detectives denied in court having disclosed any facts to the suspects.[129] In some confession records, detectives include assurances from the defendant that the statement was made of their free will.[130] With this kind of evidence in hand, juries have no apparent reason to question the veracity of a confession, nor do they have the tools to do so.

Alibi Testimony

The assessment of alibi evidence poses yet another set of challenges for the fact finder. In principle, alibi evidence would seem to provide an effective tool for determining facts in some situations. As one cannot be in two places at once, the proof of an alibi should normally negate the suspicion of innocent defendants. In reality, however, alibi evidence is hard to produce and is readily misconstrued. The research on this issue is rather sparse, and relatively intuitive, but it helps highlight the difficulties with respect to both the construction of the alibi by the suspect and its subsequent believability by third parties.[131] Alibis play an obvious role in persuading jurors and police officers, and they can also affect the outcome of a case by convincing prosecutors, judges, and even defense attorneys. The assessment of alibis is closely related to judgments of deceit, as disbelieved alibis are typically deemed to be deceitful, and thus are readily taken to imply guilt. The current discussion focuses on assessments based on the content of the alibi claim, not on determinations of truthfulness.

In reality, constructing an alibi can be a difficult task for the innocent person. The simple fact is that human memory does not contain a reliable function for tracing time. As discussed in Chapter 4, people have poor memory for dates, times, and sequences of events, and sometimes confuse the details of one event with those of another or fail to recall which people were present at which event. Although the commission of a crime is invariably a memorable event for the perpetrator, it is typically of no significance to those who were not implicated in it. Innocent suspects rarely have a prepared account for their actions at the particular time, and they lack both the motive and the opportunity to prepare an alibi in advance of the interview. Innocent suspects might feel the need to furnish an alibi on the spot, without the benefit of having access to other people, calendars, or physical records. Innocent people might not be sufficiently cautious about offering an incorrect alibi, believing naïvely that the truth will eventually come to light. This lack of caution is particularly likely before the suspect has been informed of the severity of the charges, or when she is hoping to fend off the detective with a quick distraction. Constructing an alibi is particularly difficult for people who lead unstructured and undocumented lives, such as the self-employed, the unemployed, and the homeless. Almost one-third of the DNA exonerees did not raise an alibi defense at trial.[132] The failure to provide an alibi can be misconstrued by fact finders, as people seem to believe that when faced with the threat of severe punishment, innocent people will invariably be able to furnish a truthful and believable account of their whereabouts at the time the crime was committed. A lack of an alibi is thus seen as an indication of guilt.

Some innocent suspects will provide mistaken alibis. If refuted by the police, mistaken alibis create a strong appearance of guilt. In some instances, the suspect will seek to correct her mistaken alibi with information gathered on a subsequent occasion. Corrected alibis should improve the suspect's situation, but they are still likely to be viewed with heightened skepticism, since inconsistencies in testimony are generally perceived as a cue for unreliable memory, if not an indicator of deceit. It should also be noted that in some situations, innocent suspects will provide false alibis intentionally, as when covering up for someone else or trying to conceal some unrelated indiscretion. Thus, providing a false alibi to conceal a relatively minor transgression can readily make a suspect look guilty of a serious criminal charge.

Yet even when suspects manage to construct their whereabouts truthfully and accurately, they stand to be disbelieved unless they can offer satisfactory corroboration. Indeed, 68 percent of the DNA exonerees raised the alibi defense, but they were all disbelieved by the fact finders.[133] Failures to corroborate can be costly to defendants. One study indicates that the failure of a corroborating witness to support the defendant's alibi can actually backfire by increasing perceptions of the defendant's guilt.[134] Alibis can be corroborated by physical evidence, such as ticket stubs, passport stamps, and surveillance cameras. It is, however, rather rare to possess physical proof of one's whereabouts, since most people's lives are not documented and do not produce a constant stream of time-stamped physical traces. And even when corroborating evidence is available, it is often discounted, especially when it is perceived to be susceptible to fabrication.[135] An analysis of 125 American and Canadian alibi cases revealed that alibis were corroborated by physical evidence in fewer than one-tenth of the cases examined.[136]

Alibis can also be corroborated by human testimony, typically, statements that the suspect was with the corroborating witness somewhere else at the time the crime was committed.[137] Corroboration by witnesses is not always available, as people spend certain amounts of time by themselves, especially people who live alone. Moreover, corroboration is likely to fail when the corroborating witness himself cannot construct his whereabouts at the time of the crime, or when his own account cannot be corroborated reliably.

Most commonly, alibi testimony is discounted as a result of suspicion about the credibility of corroborating witnesses. A number of studies have shown that corroboration from strangers, neighbors, and store clerks reduces the rate of convictions, but corroboration by friends and family members does not.[138] These results are hardly surprising, as a majority of survey respondents believe that people would lie to the police rather than see a loved one go to prison, and they concede that they would do the same.[139] This incredulity makes corroborating alibis a difficult feat, given that people tend to spend the bulk of their non-solitary time in the company of the very people who are most disbelieved. In the abovementioned analysis of 125 alibi cases, only 2 of the alibis were supported by people other than friends and family.[140] The vast majority of the alibis offered by people who were ultimately exonerated by DNA evidence were corroborated (unsuccessfully) by family members, girlfriends, and friends.[141] At Ronald Cotton's trial, a number of his family members testified that he was at home on the night of the crime. One of the jurors reacted negatively to the fact that they all "said the same thing." She added: "You knew what the next one was going to say after about three or four of them had said that he was on the sofa. So that impressed me as . . . that they had been rehearsed, like they had been told what to say. Well, to me, that would make one think that somebody is guilty."[142] At the trial of Timothy Cole, who was exonerated posthumously by a DNA test, the prosecutor attacked the alibis given by Cole's brother and his friends, describing the witnesses as "brash, slick liars who would say anything to save their friend."[143] As prosecutors and defense attorneys know full well, although alibi testimony is intended as a shield, it frequently fails to protect innocent defendants and can even serve as a weapon against them. Whether present, absent, refuted, or altered, alibi testimony can easily hinder the fact finder's ability to determine the facts correctly.

Judging Deceit

Assessments of a suspect's statements are intimately intertwined with judgments about her truthfulness. Although honesty does not ensure accuracy, deceit is generally a strong indicator of falseness. Recall that the detection of deceit plays a key role in police investigations. It can also be critical in courtroom fact-finding. In many criminal cases, the witnesses testifying for the opposing sides provide widely disparate factual accounts, implying that at least some of them are probably lying. An effective way to win a trial is to paint the witnesses testifying for the other side as deceitful. Concluding that a witness lied on even a small detail can undermine the credibility of his testimony and can go so far as destroying that party's entire case. Judgments of deceit are often concentrated on the defendant herself, regardless of whether she testifies or not, as doubts about her honesty loom constantly in the background. Jurors are most likely to rely on determinations of deceit in difficult cases, where the ambiguous evidence leaves them in the uncomfortable state of indecision. Determining that a witness is lying provides a convenient way out of the decisional conflict. The absence of reliable extrinsic evidence in those cases usually means that the determination will be based on the witnesses' demeanor.

The legal system places a great deal of trust in jurors' ability to detect deceit. As the Court stated, "A fundamental premise of our criminal trial system is that the jury is the lie detector."[144] Jurors are explicitly instructed to rely on witness demeanor in assessing the credibility of the evidence.[145] As discussed in detail in Chapter 5, distinguishing between truth and lies on the basis of witness demeanor is a most difficult task. Performing this task successfully requires that liars and truth tellers emit different cues that reliably correspond to the veracity of their statements, and that the observers are capable of perceiving and interpreting those cues correctly. The scope of potential cues is extensive. For example, the definition of the term *demeanor* in *Black's Law Dictionary* enumerates twenty paraverbal and visual cues, including the witness's hesitation, smiling, zeal, expression, yawns, use of eyes, and "air of candor."[146] Recall that researchers have examined a slew of 158 cues that people use, and have found that the vast majority, including the universally trusted cue of gaze aversion, are plainly useless as indicators of deceit. To the extent that liars behave differently from truth tellers, they do so in ways that are diverse, idiosyncratic, and barely perceptible. Even if a universal set of diagnostic cues existed, it is doubtful that people could attend to them all at once, interpret them correctly, and integrate them into a discrete inference of veracity. Numerous studies have found consistently that people's judgments of deceit from demeanor are barely better than flipping a coin.

Deceit detection is particularly difficult in the courtroom, where nervousness is rampant, as most witnesses—innocent defendants perhaps more than others—are anxious to be believed by the jury. Other problems stem from the physical limitations of the courtroom. Subtle facial cues are unlikely to be detectable from the distance that separates witnesses from jurors, and movement of body extremities might not be observable from behind the witness box. Other cues, such as voice inflections, cannot be reliably determined without special instrumentation.[147]

The detection of deception is particularly difficult from the synthesized testimony that is habitually presented at trial. The numerous pretrial recitations of their testimony provide witnesses with the opportunity to practice and improve their story. There is good reason to believe that over the course of these renditions, the stories evolve toward a better fit with the extrinsic evidence and become embellished with details. Rehearsing the testimony might also assist liars in overcoming any ambivalence, non-cooperativeness, and hesitation, and in testifying with fewer pauses and shorter response latencies—all of which are deemed to be cues of deception.[148] Indeed, the research shows that observers are less accurate when judging prepared statements than unprepared ones.[149] One study found that over the course of successive interviews, deceitful witnesses' behavior came to appear more believable.[150]

The inherent difficulty in detecting deceit makes this judgment susceptible to biases and extra-evidential information. One study found that depicting the witness as being more reliable in a context that was unrelated to the particular testimony increased the testimony's believability, while an opposite depiction of him reduced it.[151] Another study found that witnesses who were judged to be friendly, likable, and attractive were also more likely to be believed, irrespective of the underlying truthfulness of their statements.[152] Recall also that determinations of deceit are accompanied by high levels of confidence that are not indicative of the underlying accuracy. Indeed, the observed confidence-accuracy relationship is very close to zero.[153] Moreover, the research shows that confidence in determinations of deceit is further inflated by group deliberation, with no appreciable improvement in accuracy.[154] In sum, the combination of poor accuracy and overconfidence, compounded by the severe consequences of erroneous judgments render the detection of deceit a problematic aspect of the adjudicative process. This conclusion calls into question the reliance of the adjudicative process on juries' judgments of deceit and the wisdom of encouraging them to engage in this endeavor.

The research also questions the reluctance of appellate and post-conviction courts to intervene in factual findings made at trial.[155] Studies find that judgments of deceit that are based on visual stimuli alone are least accurate, while judgments based on audiovisual presentations, audio recordings alone, and transcripts of the testimony share similar levels of accuracy.[156] In other words, the witness's physical demeanor makes no contribution over and above the verbal testimony that can be culled from the cold record.

Other Factors That Complicate the Fact-Finding Task

The fact finders' task is further complicated by various features of the environment in which they make their decisions. A courtroom is hardly an ideal setting for rational, astute, levelheaded decision making. The entire experience is replete with factors that have the potential to impair the process's capacity for the rational drawing of inferences from the evidence. There is good reason to believe that successful attorneys are familiar with the biasing potential embedded in these factors, even if only implicitly so. As these factors are generally unrelated to the defendant's actual guilt, the concern is that they will skew the fact-finding task. Cases that happen to contain potentially inculpating factors are more likely to command a harsh plea bargain and, if tried, are most likely to be won. By the same token, cases that lend themselves to exculpating biasing factors are more likely to be dismissed or to result in an acquittal.

The fact-finding task is affected also by selection of cases that occurs at the plea bargain stage. Recall that the vast majority of criminal prosecutions culminate in plea bargains. The cases that go to trial are the few that failed to settle. This selection has two implications for the pool of adjudicated cases. First, there is reason to believe that some innocent individuals prioritize proving their innocence over the cost-benefit calculations that generally dictate plea bargains. This phenomenon is supported by anecdotal evidence from real-life cases,[157] as well as by laboratory findings.[158] It follows that innocent defendants are more likely than guilty ones to go to trial in the face of compelling inculpatory evidence. Thus, among the cases that go to trial, the rate of innocent defendants is likely to be higher than their ratio in the entire pool of prosecutions. Second, the plea-bargaining calculus of both prosecutors and defense attorneys hinges to a large degree on their predictions of the jury's reaction to the evidence.[159] Thus, cases are more likely to go to trial when the jury's decision is not easily predictable, that is, where the evidence is least clear. In other words, a high proportion of the litigated cases present the jury with ambiguous evidence, and thus also with tough decisions. This also means that the litigated cases are more susceptible to biasing influences. Both experimental and archival data show that decisions are most resilient to extra-evidential influences when the evidence is clear and strong, one way or the other. The process becomes most vulnerable when the decision is close or when the evidence is of unknown reliability.[160] It is not hard to see how having to decide high-stake matters, based on ambiguous and conflicting evidence, and under the adverse and polarizing conditions of the trial, can impede on jurors' decision-making faculties.[161]

Courtroom Persuasion

One of the distinctive features of the Anglo-American criminal trial is its heavy reliance on live testimony and advocacy. At bottom, the trial consists of attempts by litigants to persuade fact finders to believe and endorse their side of the case. As such, litigation is an inescapably persuasive endeavor.

The most ubiquitous form of persuasion is storytelling. Narratives, more than isolated bits of information, transport the listeners mentally, temporarily altering their normal emotional and cognitive reactions to the information presented. By partly neutralizing the recipients' critical evaluation, the storyteller makes possible the acceptance of accounts that might otherwise be rejected.[162] A series of studies by Nancy Pennington and Reid Hastie shows that jurors naturally fit trial information into storylike formats. People make sense of complicated evidence sets by constructing narratives that are formed around intuitive and familiar schemas or scripts of human action.[163] Thus, evidence that lends itself to the story format is more likely to be taken to trial and is more likely to be convincing to a jury.[164]

To be sure, there is nothing inherently counternormative about the impact of narratives on courtroom persuasion, nor can one conceive how evidence could be presented without resorting to a narrative of one sort or another. There is also reason to believe that in reality, truthful evidence is more likely than untruthful evidence to produce a good narrative. Still, a good story is not necessarily an accurate one. There is a danger that factual inferences will be overpowered by the narrative force of a case, and by the narrative skills of the witnesses and attorneys who deliver it.

There are more serious concerns than mere storytelling. According to a body of social psychological research, people can be persuaded both through the *central* routes of persuasion and through *heuristic* (or *peripheral*) persuasion. The former emphasizes systematic presentation of facts and arguments intended to lead to rational inferences, and is thus consistent with law's avowed commitment to reasoned elaboration. The latter route consists of superficial persuasive devices, such as associations, similarities, metaphors, emotive appeals, and narrative ploys. The research shows that persuasion is often dominated by heuristic, superficial cues rather than by analytic inferences that can be sustained by the evidence.[165] Persuasion is affected by a host of heuristic routes that have little to do with accuracy, including emotional appeals,[166] metaphors,[167] irony,[168] rhetorical questions,[169] humor,[170] and the likeability of the speaker.[171] Persuasion is affected also by the listeners' characteristics, such as attitudes and group membership,[172] their affective states,[173] and confidence.[174] People have been found to place greater weight on anecdotal and personal experiences than on more reliable sources of information.[175] People are also affected by the medium through which visual information is communicated, such as video, color photography, or text.[176]

It is hardly surprising to find that attorneys resort to a variety of heuristic forms of persuasion in their adversarial endeavor. A brief glance at conventional trial advocacy manuals and professional education materials reveals how seriously the legal profession takes heuristic persuasion. For example, lawyers are advised to dress properly, maintain an appearance of absolute sincerity, entertain the jurors, tell them a story, be brief, keep a distance from the jury box, and, tellingly, not sound like a lawyer.[177] Another manual instructs lawyers to "be good," appear confident, maintain eye contact with the jury, dress to suit the jury's taste, and vary the tone, volume, and modulation of speech.[178] Titles of mainstream training manuals include "Theater Tips and Strategies for Jury Trials" and "What Can Lawyers Learn from Actors?"[179] Some lawyers undergo therapy in the hope of connecting better with jurors.[180] The potential for exploiting heuristic persuasion is one of the driving forces behind the emergence of the trial consulting industry. For example, the September 2011 newsletter of the American Society of Trial Consultants offers lawyers advice on topics such as artful dodging, capitalizing on jurors' cognitive biases, and using psychological techniques to better prepare witnesses for their testimony.[181] At the end of the day, factual determinations seem to be too susceptible to arbitrary features of the case, as well as to the rhetorical skill of the lawyers and the degree to which they are willing to employ nondiagnostic persuasive devices.

Extra-Evidential Information

A key feature of the Anglo-American trial is that the factual determination ought to be based on the evidence admitted at trial. Information about the case or the persons involved that was not admitted into evidence ought not to affect the decision.[182] Often extra-evidential information comes in the form of pretrial publicity, that is, media reporting about the case, most of which is propagated by the police or the lawyers. Extra-evidential information can also originate in questioning during the jury-selection procedure, utterances by witnesses, statements by lawyers, or courtroom gossip, and it can be the product of speculation by the jurors.[183]

The concern is that extra-evidential information will seep into the decision-making process and sway the verdict.[184] The effect of pretrial publicity has been observed in the laboratory as well as in the field. Field studies have found that prospective jurors' belief in defendants' guilt was positively related to their exposure to information about the cases.[185] A study of 179 Indiana trials revealed that greater exposure to pretrial publicity was associated with a higher rate of guilty verdicts.[186] The presence and impact of pretrial publicity is bound to be strongest in cases of high-profile crimes, especially in small communities. In one notable case, a poll conducted by an Oklahoma City TV station found that 68 percent of the respondents believed that the defendant was guilty before the trial even began. The defendant was indeed convicted and sentenced to death, only to be exonerated by DNA evidence ten years later.[187]

The effect of exposure to extra-evidential information has been observed also in the laboratory. Studies have shown that conviction rates rise after exposing jurors to inadmissible newspaper items that linked a defendant's gun to the murder,[188] reported the defendant's past suspicious conduct,[189] described the suspect as a friendless bully,[190] and provided information about an argument between the defendant and the victim on the day of her death.[191] A meta-analysis of forty-four empirical tests involving more than 5,000 participants found that exposure to extra-evidential information resulted in an overall increase of conviction rates by 16 percent.[192] Presenting pretrial allegations more graphically (on video) led to stronger biasing effects than did less graphic presentations (in print).[193] In some instances, judges seek to counter the effects of extra-evidential information by instructing jurors to ignore it. The limited effectiveness of these admonitions will be discussed in Chapter 7.

One explanation for the impact of extra-evidential information is that jurors consciously disregard the legal rules of admissibility in order to reach a result that seems just. Another explanation assumes that this effect occurs without conscious awareness, as indicated below in the discussion of the coherence effect. The impact of extra-evidential information is probably facilitated by a failure in *source monitoring,* as discussed in Chapter 4. That is, jurors cannot always recall whether a particular piece of information was presented as evidence at trial or was conveyed through some other source.[194]

Emotional Arousal

The tension between law's aspiration to rational fact-finding and the biasing effects of the evidence is perhaps most pronounced in cases that are emotionally charged. Given the ubiquity and inextricability of emotion in everyday judgments, it would be impractical and inadvisable to try to rid the decision making of all emotion. The situation gets more complicated when it comes to intense emotions. Jurors are occasionally exposed to cases that have involved heinous acts, which, as discussed in Chapter 2, tend to arouse high levels of anger, disgust, outrage, and indignation. Recall that states of intense anger tend to result in shallow processing of evidence and hostile judgments of other people. Specifically, anger leads to stronger attributions of personal blame for negative outcomes, higher propensities to perceive other people's conduct as intentional, lower thresholds of evidence, and a stronger tendency to discount alternative explanations and mitigating circumstances. Anger has also been found to increase reliance on stereotypes, desire for retaliation, and motivation to take action to remedy the transgression. To be sure, the legal system is well aware of the susceptibility of jury verdicts to emotional arousal, and jurors are routinely instructed not to be overtaken by it.[195] The problem is that these instructions are generally ineffective, and lawyers seem to be well aware of that fact.

Studies have observed that presenting gruesome evidence can bias jurors' decisions. One study found that exposing simulated jurors to gory photographs of a stabbed murder victim led to an arousal of negative emotions, including vengefulness, outrage, shock, and anxiety, and it resulted in a doubling of the conviction rate.[196] Similar findings were made in Australian studies that contained descriptions of severe brutality and mutilation.[197] Importantly, in these studies the issue in question was the identity of the perpetrator, which rendered the heinousness of the act entirely irrelevant to deciding the verdict.[198] These jurors, it seems, felt the need to punish somebody for horrible crimes, and the person standing trial was the natural candidate. In the terminology of evidence law, the heinous evidence bore a strong prejudicial effect while providing no probative value.[199]

Anger can be aroused also without graphic evidence, such as in the lawyers' opening statements and closing arguments. For example, the prosecutor in the trial of Darryl Hunt brought jurors to tears when describing how the victim of the rape-murder must have felt with the "thick yellow sickening fluid in her body? . . . Did she feel the life inside just trickle right out of her body right there on the grass?"[200] Confessions provide a particularly powerful mechanism for arousing anger because they often contain sordid details and purport to come straight from the mouth of the defendant. In the case of Chris Ochoa, as the detailed (though false) confession of a rape-murder was read aloud in court, the victim's mother exited the courtroom and vomited in the restroom.[201] In some trials, jurors' emotions are aroused by the normal unfolding of the process, such as when a victim of a sexual assault weeps on the stand while recounting her ordeal.[202]

Criminal verdicts are susceptible also to the arousal of valence judgments, that is, judgments of goodness or badness. It is not hard to imagine that jurors would experience positive or negative feelings toward the actors involved in the case—most prominently, the defendant and the victim—but also toward other witnesses, the police, and the lawyers. The research indicates that valenced judgments are capable of swaying people's decisions.[203] Indeed, much of the lawyers' efforts at trial are devoted to coloring the respective actors in either a positive or a negative light.[204] One innocent man was described by the prosecutor at trial as "as scary an individual as you'll ever see in your life."[205]

Racial Stereotypes

Another threat to the integrity of the fact-finding process stems from ethnic or racial stereotypes. Given that minority groups are subject to discrimination in various walks of life,[206] it is not surprising to find that they are also treated disparately by the criminal justice system. The experimental research shows that racial bias influences conviction rates when the crime charged is typical of the stereotype of the defendant's group. For example, white defendants are more likely to be found guilty than black defendants for embezzlement, but the reverse is true for auto theft and burglary. The research shows that the congruence between the crime and the stereotype leads to more superficial and confirmatory searches for information regarding the defendant's guilt, to attributions of the criminal behavior to the internal personality of the defendant, and to higher predictions of future criminal behavior.[207]

These results are consistent with data from the DNA exonerations, which come predominantly from convictions for rape, the crime that is probably most strongly associated with racial stereotypes. Although 73 percent of DNA exonerees convicted for rape are minorities, the overall proportion of minorities among people convicted for rape is about half of that.[208] This pattern is particularly pronounced in cases in which the victims are white. Although less than one in five rapes are committed by black men against white women,[209] almost half of the people exonerated of rape by DNA testing were convicted for cross-racial rape, mostly black men charged with assaulting white women.[210]

Racial effects are observed also in the meting of punishments, especially in the context of death sentencing. As discussed in Chapter 7, archival data show that black defendants who killed white victims are more likely to be sentenced to death than any other racial combination. It is also noteworthy that some black defendants appear to be treated more harshly than other black defendants. Specifically, studies show that black defendants with distinct Afrocentric facial features—notably, a broad nose, thick lips, and dark skin—are punished more harshly than black people who appear less stereotypically African.[211] This finding is manifested in archival data of prison sentencing,[212] as well as in death penalty sentencing.[213]

The Coherence Effect

The *coherence effect* (see Chapter 2) can play a substantial role in juror decision making. Recall that *coherence-based reasoning* offers an account of the cognitive process that integrates inferences from multiple evidence items and combines them to reach a discrete decision. This process is encapsulated by the Gestaltian notion that *what goes together, must fit together*. Complex decisions can be made effectively and comfortably when they are derived from coherent mental models of the case, that is, when the conclusion is strongly supported by the evidence. The cognitive system reduces complexity and decisional conflict by strengthening the evidence that supports the emerging conclusion and suppressing the contrary evidence. The process is performed by means of bidirectional reasoning, in which the facts guide the conclusion, while the emergence of that conclusion reshapes the facts to become more coherent with it.

Recall that one key feature of the coherence effect is that it entails the *spreading apart* of the evidence into two lopsided subsets, leading one verdict to be supported by strong and corroborative evidence, and the other to be weak and poorly supported. For example, when faced with a theft case containing a range of unrelated evidence items—including an eyewitness identification, a possible motive, an unexplained possession of money, and an alibi claim—people tended strongly to interpret all of the evidence items as a coherent block, pointing toward either inculpation or exculpation.[214]

There is good reason to maintain that this spreading apart is generally adaptive, in that it enables reaching a decision even in complex tasks. At the same time, however, it can have serious implications for the integrity of some types of decisions, including criminal verdicts. Notably, the spreading apart has the potential to sway the verdict toward convicting the defendant by making an inclination toward conviction appear considerably stronger and more corroborative than it would otherwise. First, when a juror leans toward voting for conviction, the weakening of inconsistent evidence will amount to a reduction in the strength of the exculpating evidence. Thus, evidence that might otherwise have given rise to a reasonable doubt can be reduced in the fact finder's mind to a mere negligible doubt. Second, the coherence effect results in high levels of confidence, even when the evidence itself was initially ambiguous and complex.[215] Confidence levels have been found to be correlated with the magnitude of the coherence shifts: the greater the spreading apart of the evidence, the higher the confidence.[216] In other words, confidence is an inevitable artifactual by-product of the cognitive process. It is not hard to see how both of these effects can undermine the protection offered by the heightened standard of proof:[217] the devaluation of exculpatory evidence and inflation of the confidence in the inculpatory evidence can boost a mere leaning toward conviction to surpass the requisite threshold for conviction.[218]

A second key feature of the coherence effect poses a challenge to one of the implicit normative principles of the rationalist tradition whereby each item of evidence ought to have an invariant informative value (so long as it is not logically dependent on other evidence items). Recall that because of the interconnectivity of the Gestaltian process, all evidence items are interconnected with all other items and ultimately with the entire decision. Hence the feature of *nonindependence,* by which evidence items can be influenced by the emerging verdict, and they can be influenced also by other items to which they have no logical relation. As a result of these circuitous influences, exposing fact finders to an evidence item that is strongly inculpating can make the entire evidence set appear inculpating, just as including an exculpating item can push the evidence toward a conclusion of innocence. The *circuitous influences* phenomenon adds a directional dimension to coherence shifts, driving the entire set of evidence toward the conclusion that corresponds with that particular item. Recall that in the abovementioned study of a theft case, adding information that placed the suspect near the scene of the crime resulted in more inculpating interpretations of the other (unrelated) evidence items.[219] Similarly, describing the defendant in a libel suit as motivated by good intentions led to the strengthening of all the legal and factual arguments supporting his case, whereas portraying him as motivated by greed resulted in opposite inferences.[220]

The nonindependence of evidence can be observed incidentally in a number of jury simulations that were designed to test other questions. Some studies have found that evidence items can be affected by (unrelated) items presented by the opposing side. For example, the inclusion of trivial details in one witness's testimony leads to decreases in the perceived believability of opposing witnesses,[221] disproving irrelevant details in a witness's testimony leads to increases in the credibility of opposing witnesses,[222] and increasing the confidence of a prosecution eyewitness results in a weakening of the credibility of the defendant's alibi evidence.[223] Similar influences were observed among evidence items supporting the same side: exposing simulated jurors to inculpating evidence made them more likely to conclude that an ambiguous composite drawing resembled the defendant.[224] It has also been observed that discrediting an evidence item results in the weakening of other evidence items supporting the same side.[225]

The nonindependence of evidence contributes to our understanding of the contaminating effect of extra-evidential information, such as pretrial publicity and innuendo.[226] Exposing jurors to inadmissible evidence or pretrial publicity can readily influence not just their verdicts, but also their interpretation of the rest of the evidence. For example, informing jurors that the defendant in a murder trial was a friendless bully resulted in more guilty verdicts and in more inculpatory interpretations of the testimony given by the patrol officer, the coroner, the victim's father, and the social worker.[227] Informing jurors of self-incriminating statements by the defendant led to more inculpatory interpretations of testimony from four other witnesses.[228] Similar effects were observed when jurors were exposed to the defendant's prior criminal record.[229] The coherence effect thus might help explain why judicial admonitions to disregard extra-evidential information are often futile, as will be discussed in Chapter 7. Even if people could obey instructions to disregard the impermissible information (in itself a difficult feat), the biasing effect of the exposure on the other legitimate evidence items is bound to be harder to overcome.

Recommendations for Reform

The research discussed in this chapter casts doubt upon the diagnostic capabilities of the criminal trial. The fact-finding task is hindered, foremost, by the unknown, and often inadequate, quality of the evidence on which verdicts are based. Yet, even with reliable evidence, the fact-finding task remains a tall order, as people often encounter difficulties in assessing the accuracy of the types of evidence that are typically presented at criminal trials. Drawing correct inferences becomes all the more difficult, given that the decision-making environment is replete with factors that have the potential to bias the verdicts it produces.

Since the core problem affecting the adjudicatory process is its heavy reliance on evidence that is of questionable integrity, reforms are best targeted at the process that is primarily responsible for producing that evidence, namely, the investigative phase. Providing juries with more accurate and transparent evidence will go a long way to make their task more manageable and their verdicts more accurate. The adjudicatory process, with its deeply ingrained traditions and adversarial trappings, is a less amenable forum for reform. Indeed, many of the problems discussed in this chapter do not readily lend themselves to effective and feasible reform. For example, there seem to be no workable solutions to counter the effects of good narratives, most forms of heuristic persuasion, and the normal arousal of emotion. It is also difficult to prevent racial stereotypes from creeping into the courtroom, and it is doubtful that the coherence effect can be eliminated or decreased substantially.[230]

Still, there is some potential for reform in the adjudicative process itself. The research offers ways to enhance the diagnosticity of the fact-finding task. As discussed in Chapter 8, jurors are better capable of assessing the accuracy of identifications when they are shown video recordings of the lineup and of the interview with the witness. Recall from Chapter 3 that identifications are considerably more reliable if they are made quickly and confidently. Thus, armed with the knowledge of the witness's speed and confidence, jurors would be in a better position to evaluate the accuracy of identifications. For this to happen, jurors would need to be educated about the effects of these accuracy factors. This educative task could be done by experts. Expert testimony stands to contribute to the fact finding task by dispelling nondiagnostic factors and calling attention to factors that actually are indicative of the truth. The limited research on the effect of expert testimony on fact-finding tends to show a moderate improvement.[231] In reality, however, expert testimony is beyond the reach of most defendants, and in many jurisdictions it is deemed inadmissible.[232] There is good reason to relax the restrictions on the admissibility of expert testimony. Other proposals for reform include the following:

1. Trial judges should adopt a stringent attitude toward admitting testimony obtained through flawed investigative procedures.
2. Eyewitness identifications arising from flawed lineup procedures should be ruled inadmissible.[233]
3. In-court identifications should not be allowed as a first identification, and they should not be allowed following any suggestive identification procedure, nor following a procedure in which the witness did not choose the suspect or chose a suspect other than the defendant.
4. Confessions should be admitted into evidence only if they are both voluntary and reliable.[234] Courts should not admit into evidence confessions that are deemed unreliable, regardless of their perceived voluntariness and the waiver of *Miranda* rights.
5. The admission of confessions should be based on a high threshold of proof (in lieu of the "preponderance of the evidence" standard currently used).
6. Trial judges should educate jurors about the perils of drawing mistaken inferences from alibi evidence.
7. The instruction advising jurors to use demeanor evidence to determine deceit should be abolished. Trial judges should educate

jurors about the perils of judging deceit from witnesses' demeanor and caution them against attempting to do so.

8. Judges sitting in appeals and post-conviction proceedings should not refrain from assessing the truthfulness of testimony from trial records.

9. Trial judges should be more vigilant in preventing the exposure of jurors to extra-evidential information.

10. Trial judges should prohibit the admissibility of heinous or other strongly emotional evidence, unless it is directly relevant and necessary for the disposition of the case.

7

"BOLTING OUT THE TRUTH"

The Trial's Fact-Finding Mechanisms

The preceding chapter examined a range of difficulties that hinder fact finders' ability to draw correct inferences from the evidence presented at trials of difficult cases. It must be conceded that much of that discussion was limited to human performance under somewhat decontextualized circumstances. Legal fact-finding might look different—and possibly better—when it is embedded in the institutional context of the legal process. The adjudicative process offers a number of mechanisms that are said to safeguard the accuracy of the verdicts. The ubiquitous reverence accorded the American criminal trial is premised on the assumption that these mechanisms perform their designated tasks successfully. The efficacy of these mechanisms is the subject of this chapter.

Cross-Examination

Cross-examination of a witness in open court is heralded as one of the hallmarks of the adversarial system. Cross-examination is one of the primary justifications for the right to confront one's witnesses and the right to assistance of counsel, both guaranteed by the Sixth Amendment.[1] In addition to its important symbolic and political dimensions, cross-examination is deemed a formidable diagnostic tool, which has long been believed to "beat and bolt out the Truth."[2] Quoting John Wigmore, the U.S. Supreme Court has repeatedly stated that cross-examination is the "greatest legal engine ever invented for the discovery of truth."[3] Cross-examination could conceivably improve the diagnosticity of the process by either deterring or exposing false testimony.

Deterring False Testimony

Cross-examination could have a prophylactic effect on would-be witnesses: the expectation of having to face tough questioning in open court could deter them from providing dishonest statements. It is clear that, to some extent, this deterrent effect does indeed contribute to the accuracy of the process. Still, the limitations of this effect ought not to be overlooked. For one, the deterrent effect might restrain would-be liars, but it is doubtful that it can have much impact on the more challenging cases that involve honest, yet mistaken, witnesses. As discussed in Chapter 4, memory research indicates that people tend to trust their memories, regardless of the underlying accuracy of those memorial accounts. Given that mistaken witnesses perceive themselves to be accurate, they are unlikely to be deterred from recounting false memories any more than accurate witnesses would be deterred from recounting their truly correct ones.

The deterrent effect is also likely to be diminished when the witness has little to fear from being exposed on the stand. Witnesses have little to fear when there is no reliable evidence that contradicts their statements. This occurs, for example, when the witness is the sole source of evidence, such as when she was the victim of a crime committed in private, or when she happened to be the only person to witness the criminal event. Also, there will be no reliable evidence to contradict a witness's statement when the witness's testimony is corroborated by the rest of the available evidence. However, as discussed in Chapter 6, the putative corroboration might be merely pseudo-corroboration, that is, a misleading artifact of the dynamic nature of an erroneous investigative process. Paradoxically, it is possible that the corroborating evidence itself was induced by an investigation that was thrown off course by the erroneous testimony now being corroborated. Police investigators who testify at trial will typically not be challenged by contradictory evidence. The opacity of investigations often means that any adverse facts will not be available to contradict their testimony.

Witnesses also have little to fear when they know that the jury is strongly disposed to believe them. This is often the case when the witness is a sympathetic victim or, in most jurisdictions, when she is a police officer or public official. Witnesses also have little reason to fear being exposed on the stand when they expect to be discredited no matter what.

This is the case for witnesses who perceive that the jury is predisposed to disbelieve them, and it is also generally true for expert witnesses who testify for hire. These experts tend to adopt the position of the party that hires them, and fully expect to be hammered by the opposing side.[4]

Exposing False Testimony

Another way in which cross-examination could improve the diagnosticity of the trial is by exposing mistakes or lies in real time, in the course of the cross-examination itself. It is beyond dispute that such exposures (call them Perry Mason moments) enhance the accuracy of the evidence presented to the jury. Yet these dramatic instances are few and far between. As discussed in Chapter 6, witnesses are habitually prepared by lawyers. The preparation process offers an opportunity to massage their testimony and make it appear as reliable as possible. This process is also likely to coach witnesses what to expect during cross-examination and how best to respond to it.

The infrequency of Perry Mason moments also stems from the strategic risks involved in seeking to expose witnesses on the stand. Attempting, but failing, to expose a witness as deceitful can be very costly. For one, repeated questioning gives the witness another opportunity to reiterate her statements. More importantly, weathering a cross-examination can make the testimony seem even stronger, and thus bolster the effectiveness of that witness. Hence the famous adage: "Do not ask questions for which you don't already know the answer."[5] The effectiveness of cross-examination is particularly limited for defense attorneys, who labor under an informational disadvantage. The vast majority of criminal defendants lack the resources, expertise, and legal authority to investigate crimes effectively. While the prosecution has a virtual monopoly on the evidence, its duties to share exculpating evidence are rather limited.[6] Thus, defendants are often denied effective use of what is touted as the prime tool of getting at the truth. Vigorous cross-examination can also be interpreted as a signal that one's case is weak. It can also be perceived as unduly hostile, and thus seem off-putting to the fact finder.[7] Again, this concern is particularly constraining for defense attorneys, as jurors tend to react negatively to the badgering of the common prosecution witnesses: victims, police officers, and bystanders.[8]

Moreover, cross-examination can hamper the diagnosticity of the process by undermining the testimony of even honest and accurate witnesses.[9] Indeed, some commentators argue that assailing the reliability of opposing witnesses is a professional duty that a lawyer owes her client in an adversarial system.[10] A recent study shows that subjecting (presumably honest) witnesses to a realistic cross-examination results in substantial changes in their testimony, with almost three-quarters of witnesses altering their responses on at least one of the four critical factual issues.[11] The changes in this study resulted in substantial decreases in the accuracy of the testimony, though, in principle, altering the testimony of a mistaken witness could actually enhance the accuracy of the evidence. One technique for undercutting a witness is to phrase the questions in convoluted language, pejoratively dubbed *lawyerese*. These questions come in the form of leading questions, questions phrased in the negative or double negative form, and multipart questions. Studies show that these questions increase the rate of erroneous and "don't know" responses.[12] Questions phrased in lawyerese have also been found to reduce the confidence of witnesses, regardless of their accuracy,[13] thus further weakening the diagnostic value of the witnesses' confidence.[14]

Occasionally, the quest to discredit witnesses injects a degree of acrimony and even viciousness into the proceedings. One manual for trial advocacy evokes images of hunting witnesses: "Close all the gaps he might try to slither through" and "pin him down—don't spring the trap too soon."[15] Needless to say, personal attacks on witnesses can further align them with the party for whom they are testifying and sway their testimony accordingly. Recall the study that showed that preparing a prosecution eyewitness for a hostile cross-examination bolstered the incriminating strength of that witness's testimony, resulting in an artificial inflation of guilty verdicts.[16]

Cross-examination can also compromise the process by influencing the selection of witnesses on grounds other than the accuracy of their testimony. Lawyers might well elect not to bring to the stand an honest and reliable witness because she might "not hold up well" to the vigor of cross-examination because of a personality trait, low intelligence, and the like. By the same token, a lawyer would be tempted to bring a witness who is expected to stand up to the task, even if she suspects his integrity or the reliability of his account. Thus, while cross-examination should help deter dishonest witnesses and expose the truth on the stand, its effectiveness and availability are limited, and it can even have an adverse impact on the accuracy of the process.[17]

Jury Instructions

A primary justification cited for entrusting jurors with the task of deciding criminal verdicts is that they infuse the decision-making process with common sense.[18] At the same time, a fundamental tenet in democratic regimes is that the imposition of guilt must be in accordance with the formal dictates of the law.[19] The primary means by which the legal process seeks to subordinate jury verdicts to the appropriate legal rules is to have the trial judge convey a formal set of instructions to the jury. In addition to the definition of the criminal charge, jury instructions contain numerous rules designed to delineate the framework for deciding the verdict, including the primacy of trial evidence, the presumption of innocence, and the standard of proof. To reach legally warranted verdicts, juries need to apply these rules in the prescribed manner. Sometimes juries deliberately disregard the instructions, thus engaging in jury nullification.[20] The following discussion, however, is concerned instead with unwitting failures in applying instructions.[21]

Driven by a fidelity to the law and by the fear of being overturned on appeal, trial judges typically provide jurors with instructions that adhere to legal rules, even when doing so entails issuing instructions that are beyond the grasp or capabilities of most people. Instructions are often complex, couched in alien terminology, and demanding of unfamiliar and even improbable mental exercises. Still, the legal system relies heavily on the assumption that juries conform to the instructions they receive, and the Court routinely proclaims its faith in their conformity: "A crucial assumption underlying that system is that juries will follow the instructions given them by the trial judge."[22] Underlying this faith is the belief that although jurors are endowed with a keen eye for discerning human behavior and a developed sense of morality, they are also remarkably malleable to the dictates of the law, even when it conflicts with their personal sense of justice. Just how well jurors comprehend and apply jury instructions is an empirical question. The following discussion tracks the two primary functions served by jury instructions: guiding jurors toward proper decision making, and protecting decisions from potential prejudice.

Guidance Instructions

One way to gauge the effectiveness of instructions in guiding jury decision making is to measure how well jurors comprehend them. A sizable body of research indicates that jurors' performance falls well short of law's implicit assumption of complete or near-complete comprehension. The studies find comprehension rates ranging from 13 percent to 73 percent, levels that are not always better than chance.[23] The data are mixed as to whether the instructions actually improve jurors' understanding of the law, with some studies finding modest improvement,[24] and others finding that instructed jurors are no more knowledgeable than their noninstructed cohorts.[25] The comprehension is particularly low for instructions about which jurors hold incorrect preexisting beliefs and that entail unfamiliar mental tasks.[26] A study conducted in England found that people tend not to acknowledge their limited levels of knowledge. While only 31 percent of respondents understood the judge's instructions, two-thirds of them maintained that they comprehended them correctly. Notably, the level of comprehension increased to almost one-half when the instructions were given in writing.[27]

Similar doubts arise when lay people are tested on their ability to apply jury instructions to legal situations. Studies with jurors in Washington state and Florida have found that instructed and uninstructed participants performed similarly in applying instructions.[28] Notably, studies have found that decisions are often unaffected by the instructions given. In deciding homicide cases, simulated jurors rendered the same verdicts under two discrepant definitions of the crime.[29] Similar ineffectiveness was found in experiments that compared discrepant instructions for the crime of rape[30] and for the insanity defense.[31]

Perhaps the strongest impediment to the instruction of juries is the jurors' own preconceptions of law and justice. People's decisions tend to conform more to their personal preconceptions than to the instructions they receive.[32] Even after receiving instructions on the definitions of crimes such as robbery, burglary, and kidnapping, lay people continued to apply their preexisting and often mistaken understandings of these offenses.[33] When explicitly instructed to use a standard-of-proof threshold of 90 percent, simulated jurors reported using an average standard of 85 percent, which appears to have been a compromise between the instructed threshold and the one they reported absent an instruction (78 percent).[34] Notably, judges, too, seem to subject their compliance with legal rules to their personal sense of justice.[35]

Curative Instructions

Another type of jury instructions is designed to "cure" the process of biases. Often curative instructions are administered to remedy the exposure of jurors to potent information that is not admissible as evidence. Such exposure can originate outside the courtroom, typically in the form of pretrial publicity, or it can derive from statements uttered by the lawyers in court, whether unwittingly or deliberately. At times, counsel will request the judge to call a mistrial, but such motions rarely succeed. More frequently the judge will either deny the motion outright or issue an instruction admonishing the jury to ignore the information.

A number of psychological reasons warrant suspicion about the curative potential of judicial admonitions. Research on ironic mental processes has shown that instructing people to suppress a thought is a difficult mental feat, which can even backfire by increasing the salience of the thought.[36] Likewise, research on reactance theory suggests that people respond negatively to restrictions on their freedom. One reactive response is to increase the value of the deprived freedom, which could amount to placing greater emphasis on the information that is supposed to be ignored.[37] Research on hindsight bias indicates that people have a difficult time imagining their state of knowledge in the absence of information they already have.[38] Research on the belief perseverance phenomenon indicates that people tend to adhere to beliefs that they have formed, even after learning that the information they used to form those beliefs has been discredited.[39] The lingering impact of prejudicial knowledge can also be explained by the coherence effect.[40]

The research findings on the effectiveness of curative instructions are somewhat muddled.[41] Some clarity can be attained, first, by appreciating the role of people's personal conceptions of justice, which pertain both to their individual policy preferences as well as to the perceived probativeness and reliability of the information. For example, instructions to ignore information were found to be effective when that information was deemed unreliable, such as when the wiretapped confession was barely audible[42] or when the source of the information was suspicious.[43] Conversely, admonitions failed to defuse the effect of information that was considered to be reliable and probative of the defendant's guilt.[44] Admonitions were ineffective also when the grounds for their exclusion could be considered "legal technicalities," such as when the incriminating conversation was obtained by means of illegal wiretap,[45] or when the murder weapon was obtained in an illegal search.[46] Curative instructions were also found to be ineffective when used to neutralize the effects of bad character evidence,[47] the joinder of multiple crimes into a single trial,[48] and extra-evidential insinuation.[49] In short, people appear to follow instructions to ignore evidence when doing so is consistent with their sense of justice, but do not ignore evidence when doing so would contradict it.[50] It is notable that judges behave in a similar manner. A study of sitting judges found that they cannot refrain from being swayed by probative information that they themselves ruled inadmissible.[51]

A second way to clarify the research on curative instructions is to distinguish between instructions to disregard evidence completely and instructions to admit evidence for limited purposes. *Limited-purpose* instructions arise from the need to reconcile conflicting policy considerations.[52] When it comes to admitting the defendant's prior criminal record, for example, the rules of evidence split the difference by positing that evidence of prior convictions cannot be admitted to support inferences about the defendant's propensity to commit the crime, but it can be admitted to prove other aspects of the charge or to impeach the credibility of the testifying defendant.[53] To address this palpable contradiction, the rules advise judges to "restrict the evidence to its proper scope and instruct the jury accordingly."[54] Limited-purpose instructions are premised on a belief in people's ability to exert formidable control over their cognitive processing. This assumption runs contrary to the research. Many social judgments occur automatically,[55] and thus resist conscious control.[56] Given that turning information on and off at will is an unnatural task that is unparalleled in everyday life, it is not surprising to find that this instruction is basically ineffective in preventing the drawing of impermissible conclusions. A number of jury simulation studies find that despite limiting instructions, exposing jurors to the defendant's prior criminal record results in higher conviction rates.[57] A meta-analysis shows that evidence of prior criminal behavior is generally resistant to curative instructions.[58] Paradoxically, the instruction limiting the use of prior criminal behavior bears only mixed and weak results with respect to its ostensibly justified objective, namely, impairing the credibility of the defendant's testimony.[59]

Courts have long been skeptical about the effectiveness of curative instructions. Justice Robert Jackson described them as an "unmitigated fiction,"[60] and Judge Learned Hand characterized them as a "mental gymnastic" that is beyond the jury's powers.[61] Judge Jerome Frank described them as "a kind of 'judicial lie' " that "damages the decent judicial administration of justice."[62] Ignoring inadmissible evidence has also been likened to "unringing the bell"[63] and to ignoring the smell of a skunk just thrown into the jury box.[64] This skepticism has rarely been acknowledged by the Court in recent years. The Court under the stewardship of Chief Justices Burger, Rehnquist, and Roberts has shown no hesitation in asserting that juries can and will disregard inadmissible evidence when instructed to do so.[65]

The practical implications of exposure to inadmissible evidence go beyond the limited effectiveness of curative instructions. The research shows that the judge's decision to admit the contested evidence can actually backfire by boosting its impact on the verdict.[66] The prospect of an adverse effect poses a serious dilemma for attorneys. Refraining from objecting to prejudicial evidence runs the risk of leaving the jury exposed to that information. Yet objecting to the evidence will, at best, result in a relatively ineffective curative instruction and, at worst, will actually boost the prejudicial effect. This perilous situation is often a double blow for the defendant in that the prejudicial fact—particularly a defendant's prior record—has possibly already contributed to the police's decision to investigate him in the first place and the prosecutor's decision to follow through with the charges.

Capital Sentencing

Nowhere do jury instructions play as critical a role in legal decision making as in the context of capital sentencing, and nowhere are the misconceptions of jurors' performance as consequential.[67] Since the 1970s, the primary focus of the debate over the death penalty has not been the constitutionality of execution per se, but the fairness of its administration. The current state of the law was forged by two landmark decisions of the Court. In *Furman v. Georgia* (1972), the majority of justices decried the extant unbridled jury discretion, determining it to constitute cruel and unusual punishment, and thus violative of the Eighth Amendment.[68] Four years later, in *Gregg v. Georgia* (1976), the Court reinstated the practice by endorsing Georgia's regime of *guided discretion,* a sentencing framework that sought to rein in the jury's discretion while maintaining enough latitude for individualized justice.[69] The Court heralded the proposed regime, characterizing it as a "carefully drafted statute that ensures that the sentencing authority is given adequate information and guidance."[70]

While the specific instantiations of the guided discretion regime vary somewhat over time and across jurisdictions, they share three key features. First, the jury must find at least one of the enumerated *aggravating factors* that increase the blame of the defendant (for example, murdering a police officer or killing multiple victims). Typically, the finding of aggravating factors must be made unanimously and be determined beyond a reasonable doubt. Yet even if aggravating factors are found, the death sentence is not automatic. The jurors must also consider factors that bode for sparing the defendant's life.[71] These *mitigating factors* can be established by the relatively low threshold of preponderance of the evidence (or no threshold at all) and do not require the unanimous agreement of the jurors. Mitigating factors need not be enumerated in the statute, but can encompass any fact that tends to lessen the defendant's blame. Finally, jurors are given a *decision rule* that prescribes how to weigh the aggravating factors against the mitigating factors in making the choice between a death sentence and the alternative punishment, which is typically life imprisonment without the possibility of parole.

The legality and legitimacy of the death penalty regime relies heavily on jurors' ability to abide by the procedure of guided discretion. Given that jurors find it difficult to comprehend and apply relatively straightforward instructions in noncapital procedures, it should come as no surprise to find that they fall short in mastering the intricate and unfamiliar mental procedure prescribed by the guided discretion regime. A series of studies by Craig Haney and Mona Lynch tested jury-eligible Californians for their comprehension of the state's death-sentencing instructions. Even after hearing the instructions three times, jury-eligible respondents were largely unsuccessful in defining the terms *aggravating* and *mitigating*. Fewer than half of the participants provided even partially correct definitions for the terms *aggravation* and *mitigation,* and only 8 percent provided definitions that were legally correct.[72] Of particular interest are the misunderstandings of mitigation, which typically offers defendants the only chance of coming out of the process alive. About one-quarter of the respondents mistook two of the mitigating factors to be aggravating factors, and more than one-third misinterpreted the most important mitigating factor—"any other circumstances that extenuate the gravity of the crime"—as grounds to buttress a death verdict.[73] Respondents also manifested low comprehension of the all-important decision rule. Only one-half stated (correctly) that a death verdict was impermissible when the mitigating factors outweighed the aggravating factors, and only 15 percent said the same (correctly) when the factors were balanced equally. Forty percent stated (incorrectly) that death was mandatory when the aggravating factors outweighed the mitigating ones.[74] A follow-up study by Haney has found that comprehension improves somewhat thanks to the psycholinguistically improved instructions that were put into effect in California in 2006, and it can be moderately improved even more by using instructions that provide jurors with thematic and case-specific examples, presented in a relevant and concrete manner. Still, even with these modified instructions, the level of comprehension remains rather low.[75]

Another series of studies was conducted by Richard Wiener and his colleagues, testing juror comprehension of the Missouri death penalty instructions. These studies found overall comprehension levels of 55–60 percent, which is just slightly better than guessing.[76] Particularly poor levels were observed with respect to some of the procedure's central features, including the need for unanimity in finding aggravating factors, the freedom to consider mitigating factors that are not enumerated in the statute, and the decision rule for weighing the countervailing factors.[77] Substandard comprehension was observed also in studies testing the instructions used in Illinois,[78] Florida,[79] Ohio,[80] and Tennessee.[81]

Given that the guided discretion regime works primarily to inhibit jurors' discretion to award death sentences, poor comprehension is prone to undermine the protections promised by this procedure. The misconceptions observed in the studies—notably, relaxing the limits on finding aggravating factors, narrowing the scope for establishing mitigating factors, and underappreciating the freedom to vote for imprisonment even in the face of aggravating factors—all result in higher rates of death sentences than intended by the law. Indeed, studies find a consistent relationship between comprehension and death sentencing: the less jurors understand the instructions, the more prone they are to vote for death.[82] Relatedly, comprehension is inversely correlated with jurors' support for the death penalty, in that those who strongly support the practice tend to display poorer comprehension.[83] Thus, the procedure of death qualification—which excuses jurors who express a strong aversion to voting for a death sentence—decreases the jury's overall level of comprehension, and thus further increases the likelihood of a death sentence.[84] Instruction comprehension also interacts with racial bias. Low comprehension has been found to be related to a greater tendency to sentence black defendants to death, particularly when their victims were white.[85]

The findings from the laboratory and field studies are notably consistent with data from the Capital Jury Project, which has conducted in-depth interviews with some 1,200 jurors who served on 350 capital sentencing cases in fourteen states. One of these studies found that almost half of the jurors fundamentally misunderstood the concept of mitigation, believing that under certain circumstances death was "the only acceptable punishment." Not surprisingly, jurors who failed to appreciate their duty to explore mitigating factors were five times more likely to decide prematurely on a death sentence than those who understood the instruction correctly. The influence of jurors' preconceived notions of justice was manifested by a greater endorsement of mandatory death (which is always incorrect) for more reprehensible murder charges.[86] A significant number of South Carolina jurors mistakenly stated that the law prescribed certain aggravating factors that were intuitively plausible, but which were not mentioned in the instructions.[87]

The most telling evidence of the shortcomings of the guided discretion regime comes from naturalistic sentencing data. A large body of econometric research shows that death sentencing in the post-*Gregg* regime continues to be performed in an unprincipled manner. The landmark study was conducted by David Baldus and his colleagues on death sentencing in the state of Georgia, where the cases of *Furman* and *Gregg* originated. This study, which examined the 2,484 homicide cases decided between 1973 and 1979, concentrated on racial discrimination, the most salient impermissible influencing factor. The study found that jury sentencing decisions were affected by the races of the defendants and their victims. White defendants were sentenced to death at a rate of 8 percent for killing white victims but only 3 percent for killing black victims. In contrast, 22 percent of black defendants were sentenced to death for killing white victims, but only 1 percent received death sentences for killing black victims.[88] The findings of this study were presented to the Court in *McCleskey v. Kemp* (1987), but they failed to shake the justices' trust in the restraining power of the guided discretion doctrine.[89] Racial discrimination in meting out the death penalty has been observed in a number of other jurisdictions, including northern states,[90] and has been confirmed by the General Accounting Office.[91] In sum, it appears that the touted regime of guided discretion provides little guidance, yet allows much discretion. Death penalty sentences continue to be meted in the prejudicial manner found to be unconstitutional in *Furman v. Georgia* (1972).

Jurors' Assurance of Impartiality

It is well established that people's decisions are affected by their attitudes, preferences, beliefs, moral convictions, and the like. The legal system is cognizant and accepting of these effects on juror decision making, and it would be quite impossible and indeed unwise to try to rid jurors of them. At the same time, there are good reasons to curb the excesses of idiosyncratic influences, since the integrity of the criminal justice process is compromised when the juror's decision in a given case is overpowered by her prior positions. Hence the Sixth Amendment's guarantee of the right to an impartial jury. Weeding out partial jurors is the primary ostensible objective of the jury-selection procedure.[92] A key factor in deciding whether to place a person on the jury is that person's assurance to the court that she can be unbiased. Assurances of impartiality are used similarly during the trial to allay any suspicion of contamination, such as following exposure to inadmissible information.

The shared wisdom within the legal system is that jurors are quite capable of assessing their objectivity. While the Court acknowledges the difficulty in knowing "the imponderables which cause one to think what he thinks," it insists that jurors can rise to the occasion: "surely one who is trying as an honest man to live up to the sanctity of his oath is well qualified to say whether he has an unbiased mind in a certain matter."[93] Whether jurors can reliably vouch for their own impartiality is an empirical question.

To meet this expectation, jurors would need, first, to be sufficiently introspective so as to be able to identify which factors actually influence their decisions. Psychological research has long distinguished between access to *declarative* and *procedural* types of knowledge. People have generally reliable access to the former, which enable fairly accurate reporting of the contents of one's thoughts, such as one's beliefs, decisions, and emotional states. At the same time, the cognitive mechanisms and processes used to arrive at those mental states are generally inaccessible to introspection.[94] Notably, people have only limited access to the situational factors that actually influence their decisions and behaviors.[95] Still, people habitually insist on their introspective abilities,[96] and when asked about the reasons of their decisions and behaviors, they readily provide spurious explanations, a phenomenon known as *telling-more-than-you-can-know.*[97]

The limitations on introspection are even more pronounced when it comes to the acknowledgment of bias. In a culture that places a premium on rationality, dependability, and predictability, the notion of bias carries a pejorative connotation. The ubiquitous motive of maintaining a positive self-conception and public image thus hinders any inclination to concede being biased. Notably, people tend to believe that they are fair and objective.[98] While people might be open to admitting in general terms that their judgment can be subject to occasional bias, they rarely concede bias in their current judgments, or in any specific judgment for that matter.[99] Limited introspection and the aversion to conceding bias combine to create an *illusion of objectivity.*[100]

The disinclination to admit to bias has been observed also in studies of jury behavior. Simulated jurors are consistently found to be swayed by extra-evidential factors even as they deny any such influence. Such findings were made in studies that exposed jurors to media publicity about the crime,[101] the defendant's prior record,[102] gruesome photographs,[103] and coerced confessions.[104] The motivation to appear unbiased is likely to be heightened by the courtroom environment and the avowed commitment to impartiality and fairness. In sum, while there is good reason to exclude from jury service people who say that they cannot be fair and objective,[105] the system should be less trusting of self-proclamations of objectivity.

The Prosecution's Heightened Burdens

One of the distinctive features of the criminal process is the imposition of heightened demands on the prosecution, namely, the *presumption of innocence* and the standard of proof *beyond a reasonable doubt.* The asymmetry underlying these two measures stems to a large extent from the legal system's avowed discrepant aversion to false convictions and false acquittals. As stated by the Court, "it is far worse to convict an innocent man than to let a guilty man go free."[106] This disparity was famously quantified by Blackstone's assertion that "the law holds, that it is better that ten guilty persons escape, than that one innocent suffer."[107] These measures are generally extolled in the legal discourse, yet their exact meaning and practical effects are far from clear.

The Presumption of Innocence

One possible conception of the presumption of innocence is that it is directed at law enforcement agencies and courts, as an overarching principle to govern their affairs throughout the criminal justice process. According to this formulation, all ambiguities and discretionary judgments should be resolved with an eye toward favoring the defendant. The Court, however, has rejected this interpretation. The Court insists that the presumption is directed only at the fact finder at the trial phase, as an aid in the process of deciding verdicts.[108]

One way in which the presumption of innocence could aid the decision-making task is to counter the possible suspicion that arises from the fact that the defendant is the subject of a criminal prosecution.[109] Even prior to the presentation of the prosecution's evidence, it would be rational for a fact finder to regard the accused as the likely perpetrator of the crime; why else would she be brought to trial? According to one survey, lay people estimate the initial probability of a defendant's guilt at close to 50 percent.[110] Although this estimate seems intuitively sensible, it is considerably higher than what a presumption of innocence would imply. Whether a judicial instruction is potent enough to counter this suspicion and anchor it at a level that befits the criminal system's precepts is an empirical question. The scarce available data leave this issue unsolved. For one, it is unclear whether jurors comprehend this instruction correctly. A Wyoming field study found that 40 percent of jurors who had received jury instructions indicated that the charges brought against the defendant were evidence of his guilt.[111] One laboratory simulation demonstrated that the presumption did have a constraining effect,[112] while another study revealed that simulated jurors did indeed assign low initial probabilities of guilt at first, but quickly abandoned them once the prosecution evidence started coming in.[113]

The presumption of innocence could also aid the decision-making task by instantiating the prosecution's *burden of production,* that is, the rule that places the onus of producing evidence on the prosecution and relieves the defendant of the need to prove her innocence. The research shows that jurors do not always comprehend the asymmetric allocation of the burden, a concept that has few parallels in everyday life. After being given Florida's pattern jury instructions, only half of the jurors surveyed in a Florida courthouse maintained that the defendant need not present any evidence to prove his innocence,[114] and only three in ten of another group of Florida jurors correctly understood the prosecution's burden.[115] A failure to understand the allocation of the burden was displayed also by two-thirds of a sample of Michigan jurors[116] and one-fifth of Wyoming jurors.[117] Finally, the presumption of innocence can be conceived as serving the role of tiebreaker, positing that if the evidence against the defendant does not meet the requisite standard of proof, she should be acquitted. Here, too, there is reason for concern. Almost one-quarter of instructed Florida jurors believed that when faced with two equally reasonable sets of evidence, the defendant should be convicted.[118]

The Standard of Proof: Beyond a Reasonable Doubt

The criminal process's signature standard of proof—beyond a reasonable doubt—has received a fair amount of scholarly attention over the years, yet it remains elusive and deeply disputed.[119] For one, there is considerable disagreement as to whether the standard should pertain to the fact finder's subjective state of mind or to a property of the evidence itself. Although most commentators agree with the former formulation,[120] there is disagreement as to whether the standard posits a numeric criterion for assessing the probability of guilt, or whether it prescribes a threshold for one's belief in the inculpatory power of the evidence.[121] The latter option, which figures more prominently in courtroom practice and legal literature,[122] is essentially a metacognitive judgment, not unlike a measure of confidence. There is also disagreement about the appropriate meaning of the reasonableness criterion, namely, whether it pertains to the strength of the doubt or to a substantive judgment of its underlying rationality.[123] Another controversy centers upon the appropriateness of providing jurors with definitions and explanations of the standard. Although some commentators and courts propose that the standard should be communicated to the jury without attempting to explain it,[124] others insist on the need to supplement the definition with explanatory language. Among the latter, some would focus on the doubt itself—for example, "not a possible doubt, a speculative, imaginary or forced doubt"[125]—whereas most instructions speak to the absence of such a doubt,[126] as in "firmly convinced,"[127] "an abiding conviction,"[128] "settled belief," and "near certitude."[129] In practice, many jurisdictions mix numerous definitions and explanations, thus making for unwieldy instructions. For example, a Louisiana death sentence was based on a jury instruction that defined the standard in no fewer than eight ways.[130]

The available research on the standard of proof leaves much unresolved. A number of surveys have sought to gauge its effect by asking people to express their conception of the standard in terms of a probabilistic threshold. The mean responses in most studies hover around 85 percent,[131] which is a little lower than the value of 90 percent plus that is commonly assumed in legal discourse.[132] Although the standard is conceived as invariant to the specifics of the case, varying the case characteristics in the same study has resulted in thresholds ranging from 79 percent to 94 percent.[133] Most notably, there is considerable variation in assessments of standard. One large sample of respondents reported an average of 64 percent,[134] whereas large numbers of respondents insist on complete certainty. Thresholds of 100 percent were reported by almost 70 percent of a sample of Michigan jurors[135] and by more than half of the 500 jury-eligible respondents in a Canadian study.[136] A large survey conducted in the United Kingdom obtained thresholds of 100 percent certainty from no fewer than half of the jurors and almost one-third of the legal professionals and magistrates surveyed.[137] Naturally, requiring absolute certainty should make convictions virtually impossible; this is clearly contradicted by experimental and naturalistic data. These high standards are also out of whack with lay people's intuitions regarding the appropriate ratio of false convictions to false acquittals.[138]

The limited experimental research testing the effect of the standard of proof on verdict decisions yields mixed results, but it appears that the standard does indeed exert its intended effect, even if only roughly and partly. Some studies have found that instructing jurors with the beyond a reasonable doubt standard reduced conviction rates relative to the *preponderance of the evidence* standard (as it should).[139] Another experiment found that the standard alone has no appreciable effect, but it reduces conviction rates when combined with the presumption-of-innocence instruction.[140] However, a field study of more than 300 actual trials conducted by the National Center for State Courts (NCSC) gives reason for pause. This study observed the relationship between the strength of the evidence and the verdicts in each case. As would be expected, the juries voted to convict at high rates when the strength of the evidence was described as strong. However, more than half of the juries convicted the defendant when they felt that the prosecution's evidence was of medium strength and, surprisingly, one in five juries voted to convict even when they felt that the evidence was weak. A similar pattern of judgments was obtained from the judges who presided over these cases.[141]

Yet, even if the standard of proof were found to perform the function of reducing conviction rates, it would not necessarily increase the accuracy of verdicts. The standard is merely a sorting mechanism, and is devoid of any diagnostic properties of its own. It relies on the fact finder's ability to correctly assess the accuracy of evidence in the particular case. If, as the research suggests, the fact finder's perception of the defendant's guilt does not correspond closely to the actual guilt, the standard can do little to differentiate guilty from innocent defendants. High standards are thus bound to result in the acquittal of both innocent and guilty defendants.

Jury Deliberation

The discussion thus far has focused primarily on the performance of individual jurors. Yet criminal verdicts are cast collectively by groups, following a process of deliberation. Vesting the decision-making power in the hands of juries embodies the ideals of a representative and deliberative democracy, and confers legitimacy on the process.[142] The important question for our purposes is whether juror deliberation contributes to the accuracy of the decisions made.

The field data pertaining to the effects of deliberation are very instructive. Post-trial interviews with real-life jurors reveal a very simple yet noteworthy finding: with very few exceptions, verdicts are determined straightforwardly by the distribution of votes on the first ballot. In total, in 94 percent of the cases the initial majorities won the day.[143] An early study by Kalven and Zeisel found that juries convicted defendants 94 percent of the time when more than six jurors first voted for conviction, and acquitted them 97 percent of the time when fewer than six jurors voted for conviction on the first ballot.[144] Similar findings were made in studies of 179 criminal trials conducted in Indiana,[145] and 43 in Kentucky.[146] Slightly more nuanced relationships between first-ballot votes and final verdicts were found in the NCSC field study.[147] The conclusion from these data is that juries behave democratically not in the nuanced deliberative sense of the term, but in the blunt majoritarian sense.[148] Heroic feats by lone jurors, as depicted in the classic film *Twelve Angry Men,* did not occur even once in the thirty-four cases that began with a split of eleven votes to one on the first ballot.[149]

Still, the overwhelming power of numeric majorities should not lead to the conclusion that deliberation has no desirable effect on the process. For one, deliberation serves the important function of identifying the median votes, thus eliminating much of the idiosyncratic bias of individual jury members. The question remains whether deliberation also improves the accuracy of the factual findings that underlie the verdicts. This is particularly important in cases in which the initial faction splits are close to equal. The contribution of deliberation is important also to our understanding of what transpires prior to the first ballot vote.

It is widely intuited that groups outperform their individual members. The underlying notion is the belief in collective wisdom, which posits that pooling knowledge and judgment produces the best that the group has to offer and discards the worst. The research, however, indicates that this belief does not always correspond with reality. The preponderance of the research suggests that judgment by groups cannot be said to be generally superior or inferior to the performance of their individual members.[150] On some tasks, groups do indeed outperform their members.[151] On other tasks, however, they perform comparably,[152] or fall short of their members.[153] The respective strengths and weaknesses depend on a host of contextual and group-specific factors.[154] Crucially, the effect of deliberation on the group's decision will depend on the accuracy of the faction that wins the day. Groups are bound to reach correct conclusions when the prevailing members hold the correct views, but when they are wrong, deliberation is bound to promote error.

Informational Persuasion

Generally speaking, consensus within groups can be achieved by means of two forms of persuasion: *informational influence* and *social influence*.[155] Informational persuasion is performed by means of conveying information and arguments that lead the listener to alter her position. The research points to three possible ways in which the exchange of information among jurors could contribute to the accuracy of verdicts.

Improving memory of trial evidence. One potential contribution of informational persuasion is to improve the jurors' memory of the evidence presented at trial. As it is impossible to remember everything presented over the many hours or days of testimony, jurors enter the deliberation room with memorial accounts that are incomplete and somewhat idiosyncratic.[156] Group deliberation could prove beneficial either by enhancing memory completeness through the pooling of the members' memories or by increasing memory accuracy through the correction of errors by members with better recall. With respect to the latter, the research indicates that deliberation hardly affects the accuracy of the recalled evidence, primarily because most facts recalled by jurors are accurate.[157] This is an encouraging finding. The issue of memory completeness, however, is more complicated. The research reveals that memories produced by collaborative recall are somewhat more complete than the recall of the average member, but less complete than the total nonredundant memories recalled by individual members.[158] Studies testing group recall in simulated jury trials indicate that deliberation offers only a modest improvement to the completeness of jurors' memories.[159]

Comprehending and complying with jury instructions. The exchange of information during the course of jury deliberation could conceivably improve individual jurors' comprehension of the jury instructions. A large jury simulation conducted by Phoebe Ellsworth found that deliberating jurors were no more knowledgeable than nondeliberating jurors, and their comprehension levels were no better than chance. Only half of the references to legal issues that were expressed during the deliberation were correct. When jurors were influenced to alter their understanding of the law, they were as likely to substitute accurate understandings with errors as they were to correct mistakes. Opinions expressed most forcefully tended to prevail, regardless of their accuracy.[160] A Canadian study found that in the few instances in which jurors discussed the judicial instructions, only 61 percent of the statements were legally correct.[161] The Missouri juror studies found that deliberation had a positive though weak effect on comprehension of death penalty instructions in one study, and no effect at all in another.[162] A study of California jurors found low comprehension of death penalty instructions following deliberation.[163] Another study found that deliberations improved comprehension of a death-sentencing instruction that was correctly understood by two-thirds of the respondents, but not of two other instructions that were correctly understood only by half or fewer.[164] Deliberation could promote accuracy also by improving jurors' ability to comply with curative instructions. Here, too, deliberation yields mixed effects at best. In some instances, deliberation mitigated the effects of extralegal evidence.[165] Yet in others it made no difference,[166] and even exacerbated the influence of the impermissible evidence.[167]

Drawing inferences. Finally, jury deliberation could promote verdict accuracy by improving jurors' ability to draw correct inferences from the evidence. The limited available research reveals only modest benefits in this regard. Social-psychological studies find that the effect of group deliberation on social judgments is ameliorative at times, but not always

so.[168] Studies on deceit detection found that groups were no more accurate than individuals, though group members were more confident
about their (actually poor) performance.[169] A recent study shows that
group deliberation does not reduce the coherence effect.[170]

Social Influence

Informational persuasion is most likely to succeed when there is a de-
monstrably correct and evident conclusion,[171] which is rare in difficult
criminal cases. In the absence of such favorable conditions, the requisite
unanimity will rely more heavily on social influence.[172] Indeed, a distinctive feature of jury deliberation is that unanimity is often achieved
through social pressure. The prevalence of social pressures is not altogether surprising given that jury deliberation is a nonstructured, non-
transparent, one-shot process among strangers, driven by a strong mandate to reach unanimity in cases that are often divisive.[173] The study by
the National Center for State Courts (NCSC) included interviews with
more than 3,000 jurors. These interviews indicate that the factors that
enabled juries to reach a verdict (as opposed to resulting in hung juries)
were predominantly social, not evidential. Reaching consensus was
found to be explainable by factors such as the perceived open-mindedness
and reasonableness of the other jurors, the domination of the deliberation by one or two jurors, and the degree of conflict on the jury.[174]
Moreover, this study revealed that the putative unanimity did not reflect
genuine consensus. In almost half of the juries that reached a verdict, at
least one juror voted with the majority against his or her personal judgment.[175] Acquiescence of minority jurors to the will of the majority has
been observed also in experimental studies.[176] Jurors who change their
mind tend to be the least confident, not the least accurate.[177] The strength
of social pressure tends to increase as the deliberation progresses,[178] and
is exacerbated considerably by judicial instructions designed to undo
locked juries, also known as dynamite charges.[179] It follows that jury
deliberation is potentially beneficial when the influential jurors have
reached valid conclusions, probably detrimental when they are wrong,
and of mixed results when they are evenly split.

Data from laboratory and field studies suggest also that social influence is affected by the race and gender of the jurors, especially of the
forepersons. The study of the 179 Indiana juries revealed that juries
convicted more frequently when the foreperson voted to convict, espe-

cially when the foreperson was white and male.[180] Likewise, studies conducted by the Capital Jury Project have observed the influence of white male jurors on the likelihood of death sentences.[181] This effect was observed also in a simulated deliberation in a death-sentencing study.[182]

Two additional aspects of jury deliberation are of note. First, there is preliminary evidence that the quality of the deliberation is affected by the jury's deliberation style, specifically, whether it commences with a discussion of the evidence (evidence-driven deliberation) or with a vote (verdict-driven deliberation). The latter style tends to be more argumentative, as jurors advocate for their espoused verdict. The resulting evaluation of the evidence tends to be more disjointed, the connections between the law and the facts are less developed, and the debate is less rigorous and congenial.[183] A large field study of real-life juries found that the juries that took a vote within the first ten minutes of the deliberation were more likely to hang than juries that deliberated for longer before their first vote.[184] Given the freedom jurors enjoy in structuring their deliberations in the real world, it is likely that different juries follow different procedures.[185]

Second, it is important to acknowledge that jury deliberation has a polarizing effect on the decision. A large body of research shows that discussing and deciding issues in group settings tends to strengthen people's positions in support of the chosen resolution.[186] Typically, this polarization also results in higher levels of confidence.[187] Studies of simulated juries find that deliberation increases jurors' confidence in their memory of the trial evidence (both accurate and inaccurate),[188] in their monitoring of the sources of their memory,[189] and in their judgments of the strength of the evidence.[190] As mentioned, group deliberation has also been found to inflate members' confidence in judgments of deceit.[191]

This polarization is bound to have two practical effects. First, polarizing a fractured jury is likely to deepen the rift between the subgroups, and thus weaken the prospect of informational persuasion. This effect, in turn, is bound to increase the use of social pressure in order to achieve putative unanimity. Second, jury polarization is likely to drive jurors to feel more strongly about their initial position. Not unlike the intraindividual polarization arising from the coherence effect discussed in Chapter 6, group polarization has the potential to alter the verdict of a juror who is moderately leaning toward conviction. The polarization of that inclination and the concomitant boost in confidence can drive her decision over the threshold of proof and result in a decision to convict.[192]

Appellate and Post-conviction Review

Another legal safeguard that is said to improve judicial outcomes is the subjection of jury verdicts to post-trial review proceedings. The two common forms of review are the direct appeal process that runs through higher state courts[193] and the collateral post-conviction proceedings, notably *habeas corpus*,[194] that are conducted in federal and state courts. Both processes are ultimately reviewable by the Court. In principle, post-trial review can contribute to the accuracy of the process by correcting for mistaken decisions at the trial level.

Appellate and post-conviction proceedings provide the opportunity to examine trial court verdicts from a more detached and authoritative vantage point and thus have the potential to increase the diagnosticity of the adjudicative process. Yet, as will be discussed in Chapter 8, the scope of review by appellate and *habeas* courts is limited by a range of stringent procedural barriers. Moreover, reviewing courts confine their inquiries almost exclusively to procedural issues and all but eschew questions of fact. When they do engage in factual examinations, courts view the evidence in the light most favorable to the prosecution, and subject their analysis to high thresholds of proof.

The meager scope for meaningful review of factual determinations is manifested by courts' treatment of the DNA exonerees prior to the discovery of the exculpating DNA evidence. Brandon Garrett has analyzed the appellate and post-conviction review that preceded the DNA exoneration in the first 250 DNA exoneration cases. Of the 165 cases with written decisions, 69 convicted inmates raised claims challenging the sufficiency of the prosecution's evidence, yet none of these inmates received relief that was upheld on appeal.[195] Neither was relief awarded to any of the inmates who presented claims based on newly discovered evidence of innocence.[196] Of the 70 misidentified people who challenged the integrity of the identification procedures, just five succeeded in undermining the reliability of the procedures[197] and only one of the 13 confessors who challenged the admissibility of their confessions was granted relief.[198] Of the 38 DNA exonerees who petitioned the Court, just one was granted review,[199] only to see his petition rejected by a majority of six justices. Tellingly, the petitioner's request pertained to the very piece of evidence that ultimately proved his innocence.[200] Overall, the reviewing courts tended not to reveal any qualms about the underlying convictions. In about half of the cases the courts made matter-of-fact references to the inculpating evidence, occasionally labeling it "overwhelming."[201] It is also notable that the DNA exonerees were no more likely to receive relief than a matching group of similarly situated inmates whose guilt was not refuted by DNA or by any other exonerating evidence (9 percent and 10 percent of noncapital cases, respectively).[202]

It is troubling to note that many of the innocent convicts did not even challenge the faulty evidence that led to their convictions. Of those falsely identified by eyewitnesses, only half contested the identification procedures, and fewer than two-thirds of those convicted on the basis of a confession challenged the legality of their interrogations.[203] In fact DNA exonerees did not challenge their convictions any more than did the inmates in the matching group (who were presumably guilty).[204] Whether the impassivity of these innocent people was due to a lack of resources, their mistrust of the system, or any other reason, the reality is that they did not benefit from the legal avenues that were ostensibly open to them.

Conclusion and Recommendations for Reform

The research discussed in this chapter indicates that, to a certain extent, the legal mechanisms put in place to promote the diagnosticity of the process do indeed enhance diagnosticity. However, under a wide range of circumstances they have mixed effects, are ineffective, and are even detrimental. Together, Chapters 6 and 7 lead to the conclusion that the adjudicatory process has only limited capabilities in distinguishing between accurate and inaccurate evidence. In light of society's high expectations of the adjudicatory process,[205] it is better characterized as *pseudodiagnostic*. To a large degree, criminal verdicts are determined at the investigative phase, with the trial serving primarily as a ritual that delivers more symbolic than diagnostic value.[206]

This conclusion is squarely inconsistent with the views of prominent commentators who laud the fact-finding capacity of the American criminal trial. First, proponents point to the research that indicates that judges and juries agree on verdicts in about three-quarters of cases.[207] This observation is indeed germane to the debate about the comparative suitability of juries and judges for the fact-finding task. Yet it hardly speaks to the actual diagnosticity of either one. In fact there is good reason to expect that when faced with the same trial evidence, judges and jurors will encounter similar difficulties in discerning the truth, and will produce similar verdict patterns.[208]

Second, proponents point to the research that shows that the strength of the evidence is the most important determinant of verdicts and is more influential than all other case characteristics.[209] The field data reveal correlations of about 0.5 between fact finders' assessments of the strength of the inculpating evidence and the rate of convictions.[210] The fact that the correlations are statistically significant is encouraging; yet their limited strength gives reason for pause. In contexts in which there is no reason to expect any relationship between two variables—say, between eating broccoli and academic performance—even a weak correlation would be considered a promising finding. The same cannot be said for contexts in which a powerful relationship is both prescribed and expected in the first place. Given the process's deep-seated dependence only on trial evidence for the drawing of factual determinations and its commitment to high rates of accuracy, it is troubling to find that more than half of the variance in verdicts cannot be explained by the evidence. It is inescapable that verdicts are driven to a large extent by extra-evidential and thus unwarranted factors. There is reason to maintain that the unexplainable variance is attributable at least in part to the limited diagnosticity of the adjudicatory process.

Recall from the discussion in Chapter 6 that the bulk of the reform effort should be directed at the investigative process, with the objective of presenting fact finders with more accurate and transparent evidence. Still, as mentioned there, reforming the trial mechanisms is bound to yield some benefit.

1. To make the adversarial trial more diagnostic, the informational asymmetry between the prosecution and the defense should be minimized.
2. Jury instructions should be drafted in plain language and be provided in writing. Jury instructions should include an explicit debunking of common misconceptions and, when possible, guidance on how to apply them to concrete examples.
3. When trial judges are asked to clarify the jury instructions, they should provide jurors with helpful explanations rather than merely repeat the (patently unclear) instructions.

4. Given the ineffectiveness of curative jury instructions, trial judges should be more assertive in limiting potentially biasing evidence and in preempting any other situations that might require resorting to such instructions. The use of limited purpose instructions should be discouraged.

5. The Supreme Court should acknowledge that the guided discretion doctrine fails to eliminate prejudicial administration of the death penalty and thus violates the Eighth Amendment's prohibition on cruel and unusual punishment.

6. Trial judges should be skeptical of jurors' assurances of impartiality and should apply greater scrutiny in empaneling jurors.

7. Jurors should be encouraged to deliberate thoroughly before taking the first vote.

8. Appellate and *habeas* courts should be more amenable to taking a fresh look at the evidence upon a substantial showing of innocence, and should apply less stringent criteria for assessing convictions.

8

TOWARD ACCURACY

The Accuracy Shortfall

The central observation that emerges from this book is that our understanding of the criminal justice process can be enriched by an appreciation for the psychological strengths and limitations of the people entrusted with its operation. Criminal verdicts can be no more accurate than the human input into the process that makes them possible. Chapters 2–5 focused on the investigative phase, which is the birthplace of the core problem that plagues the process: the questionable accuracy of the evidence on which criminal verdicts are based.

Chapter 2 examined the dynamic nature of investigations, by which facts are gradually accumulated and integrated into an investigatory conclusion. The reasoning process that lies at the core of criminal investigations is inherently susceptible to various cognitive biases that tend to confirm the tentatively posited conclusions. When triggered by an erroneous fact or an incorrect hypothesis, the process can readily escalate and produce a large set of strong and mutually corroborative—though mistaken—evidence. Criminal investigations are susceptible also to various motivational forces. Police investigators experience pressures imposed by the institutional goal of clearing crimes, emotional arousal, group membership, and the ever-increasing commitment to the initial course of action. Together, these motivations create a pull toward conclusions of guilt, giving the process a quasi-adversarial flavor. The pull of the investigation can be further reinforced by the coherence effect, the by-product of the cognitive mechanism that enables decisive action even on the basis of weak, ambiguous, or conflicting evidence.

The research on eyewitness identification examined in Chapter 3 demonstrates the weaknesses that pervade the task of identifying strangers. Witnesses are inclined to pick out a person at the lineup, even when they barely recognize him or merely imagine that they do. As a result, a substantial number of identifications are false, and many of the correct identifications are fickle. The accuracy of identifications is sensitive to a wide range of factors inherent in the witnessing conditions, and is highly susceptible to the manner in which the identification procedures are conducted. Nonetheless, police departments often resort to substandard and haphazard procedures while paying little attention to the psychological research. The widespread reliance on eyewitness identification, coupled with the strong effect it has on fact finders, makes this form of testimony fertile soil for false convictions.

Chapter 4 examined witnesses' memory for the criminal event. The research indicates that memories for events are invariably incomplete, and thus often fall short of providing detectives with all the specific details needed to solve difficult cases. Criminal investigations can be undermined also by false memories. False memories can occur spontaneously, as they do in everyday life, but they can also be induced by the investigative process. Specifically, the research shows that common interviewing practices that prod witnesses to report details they cannot recall can readily induce them to report false memories.

Chapter 5 examined police interrogations of suspects. The interrogation process is typically triggered by a determination that the suspect is lying, which is based in turn on poorly diagnostic and guilt-confirming police protocols. The research indicates that the accusatory interrogative methods used by most American police forces obtain confessions primarily through psychological coercion. These procedures are not sensitive to the suspect's actual guilt, and thus have the potential to elicit confessions from both the guilty and the innocent.

Chapters 6 and 7 examined the diagnostic capacity of the adjudicative phase of the process to distinguish between guilty and innocent defendants. These chapters dealt not with the accuracy of human testimony, but with fact finders' ability to assess that testimony and draw correct inferences from it. Chapter 6 pointed to the fact that the most fundamental problem with the accuracy of criminal verdicts stems from the unknown and inconsistent reliability of the evidence. En route to the courtroom, the witnesses' statements typically evolve from their raw state toward a synthesized version fitted for courtroom consumption. In the course of this process, the testimony tends to become more inculpatory and to lose its traces of reliability. Testimony can also be biased by the motivations of witnesses and the roles they are assigned to play in the process. The apparent corroboration of evidence is often just an artifact of the escalating nature of police investigations. As errors beget errors, even large sets of corroborative evidence can be entirely wrong.

Ascertaining the truth in difficult criminal cases can be challenging even with the benefit of reliable evidence. The research shows that people have a difficult time judging whether a witness identified the perpetrator correctly, whether memories of an event are accurate, and whether confessions obtained in police interrogations offer truthful accounts of the suspects' deeds. Alibi testimony can be hard to produce, and its absence is often misconstrued. Judgments of deceit are chronically mistaken. Chapter 6 showed also that drawing correct inferences is hindered by a variety of nonevidential factors that are present in the courtroom environment. These include excessive strategies of persuasion, pretrial publicity, emotional arousal, racial stereotypes, and the coherence effect, all of which are habitually intensified by the adversarial nature of the proceeding.

Chapter 7 concluded that the difficulties facing fact finders are not appreciably remedied by the mechanisms embedded in the legal process. Cross-examination falls short of its reputation as the greatest engine for the discovery of truth. Jury instructions are often misunderstood, misapplied, and overridden by the jurors' own beliefs about the law and by their intuitive sense of justice. Jurors are not well placed to vouch for their own impartiality, as they are often called to do. The effect of the prosecution's heightened burdens on the accuracy of the process is unclear and limited, and the effects of jury deliberation are generally weak and overall mixed. Appellate and collateral courts provide only scant review of the factual bases of trial court verdicts.

In sum, this analysis leads to the conclusion that the investigative process produces evidence that is bound to contain unknown quantities of truth and error, and the adjudicative process is ill equipped to distinguish between the two. The limited accuracy of criminal investigations, compounded with the limited diagnosticity of criminal adjudication, lead to the conclusion that the criminal justice process falls short of delivering the precision that befits its solemn epistemic demands and the certitude it proclaims. Chapter 7 integrates and advocates for the implementation of the proposed recommendations, in the vein of narrowing the process's accuracy shortfall. First, however, it is imperative to examine two important mindsets that help sustain the process despite its limited accuracy: the marginalization of factual accuracy and the denial of the process' shortcomings.

The Marginalization of Factual Accuracy

One of the most bewildering and underappreciated features of the criminal justice process is the low value it assigns to the accuracy of its factual determinations or, in legal parlance, to the discovery of truth. It would be naïve to suggest that determining facts—namely, who committed which crime—is the single desideratum of the criminal justice system. The process must fulfill a broader array of objectives, which include promoting the public's acceptance of verdicts, expressing society's values, asserting the authoritative power of the state, bringing closure to victims, and finalizing disputes.[1] The process must also comport with a number of constraints, such as expedience, cost-effectiveness, and timeliness, all the while abiding by constitutional and legislative dictates and protecting the privacy and autonomy of the people involved.[2] A key challenge facing any criminal justice system is how to balance the search for truth and these competing objectives and constraints.

The framework that has been adopted by the American criminal legal system is strongly committed to the tenets of the Anglo-American conception of adjudication, as enshrined primarily in the Sixth Amendment. Defendants are guaranteed a number of procedural rights, including the right to a trial by a jury, the right to confront and cross-examine opposing witnesses, and the right to the assistance of counsel. A key feature of this regime is the *principle of orality*, which mandates that testimony be delivered live, in open court.[3] While the U.S. Supreme Court concedes that the ultimate purpose of these provisions is to assist in the determination of truth,[4] it explicitly rejects the search for truth as the process's guiding principle. Defendants are promised procedural rights, not reliable evidence or accurate verdicts.[5] For illustration, the Court states: "The aim of the requirement of due process is not to exclude presumptively false evidence but to prevent fundamental unfairness in the use of evidence, whether true or false."[6] The Court explains that the ultimate goal of the right to confront one's accusers "is to ensure reliability of evidence, but it is a procedural rather than a substantive guarantee. It commands, not that evidence be reliable, but that reliability be assessed in a particular manner: by testing in the crucible of cross-examination."[7] To a large extent, the procedures themselves have become the ultimate value of the process.[8] The guiding principle of the Court's analysis is the fairness of the procedures. Yet this conception of fairness does not stand for the substantive principle that people ought to get what they deserve. Rather, it serves as a mechanical device for balancing out the litigants' tactical advantages in the adversarial contest. The process is deemed fair if the playing field is roughly level,[9] with little regard to what actually transpires on it.[10]

The marginalization of factual accuracy is manifested throughout the criminal justice process. As discussed in Chapters 2–5, investigative procedures are designed with little regard to scientific research or best-practice protocols. The procedures vary considerably among law enforcement departments and often fall short of acceptable standards. Commonly used forensic sciences lack a verifiable scientific basis, and are often misused and misrepresented in court.[11] Recall that the vast majority of criminal convictions are not determined through adjudication but are negotiated in private through the obscure process of plea bargaining. Although plea deals are followed by a public admission in open court, that symbolic gesture is hardly a guarantee of either the accuracy or the honesty of the plea. Recall that plea bargains are driven primarily by tactical considerations, which revolve around the expected outcomes of taking the case to a jury, regardless of the veracity of the charges. In many jurisdictions, jury selection is performed by litigants, whose primary goal is to empanel a jury they expect to decide in their favor, not a fair and unbiased one.[12] As mentioned in Chapter 6, lawyers commonly assist witnesses in preparing for their courtroom appearance, a practice that can easily sway the pending testimony.[13]

The adversarial form of litigation is touted for its ability to promote factual accuracy. This benefit is said to be served by the motivation of the litigants to collect and present the best evidence in support of their case.[14] That seems like an appealing presumption, but it is crucial to note that motivation also fosters bias.[15] Thus, the jurors' fact-finding task amounts to choosing between two biased and irreconcilable versions of the criminal event. Moreover, as lawyers are quick to explain, the trial is not concerned with what actually happened at the crime scene, but with what can be proven in court. Thus, in the practitioners' adversarial universe, the currency of testimony is measured not by its correspondence with the truth, but by the muscle it provides in the adversarial contest. A positive identification by a confident eyewitness, for example, is a powerful prosecutorial weapon, regardless of any doubts that cloud its accuracy or questions about its accompanying confidence. It should also be noted that the adversarial framework is a ripe environment for fostering mutual distrust between the adversaries. That distrust, in turn, can polarize their positions and thus distance them even further away from the truth.[16] The ability of the adversarial process to find the facts correctly is further limited by the parties' informational asymmetry. Recall that the prosecution has a virtual monopoly on the evidence, as most defendants lack the resources, expertise, and legal authority to investigate their cases. The prosecution also bears only a limited duty to share exculpating evidence with the defense.[17] Oddly, criminal defendants are entitled to considerably less information about the evidence poised to deprive them of their liberty than are litigants in simple contract or tort proceedings.[18]

The place of factual accuracy is especially obscure and perplexing at the pinnacle of the process—the jury's decision making. Jurors are required only to issue general verdicts,[19] are not expected to provide any reasons for their decisions, and are unaccountable for them.[20] Moreover, Federal Rule of Evidence 606(b) shrouds the deliberation process with a veil of secrecy by barring jurors from testifying about how the decision was reached and what transpired in the deliberation room.[21] Yet the system reserves the fact-finding task exclusively to the proverbial *province of the jury* and guards that dominion fiercely.[22] As the trial judge told an innocent man convicted for raping and murdering a high school classmate: "Maybe you're innocent . . . but the jury has spoken."[23]

Following the trial, convicted defendants face a number of routes for reviewing their convictions by both state and federal courts. While the criminal justice system is often faulted for affording convicted inmates too much access to appellate and post-conviction review, in reality the potential for the correcting erroneous factual findings at these proceedings is very slim. Indeed, a number of the DNA exonerees' cases were given extensive and repeated review by appellate and post-conviction courts prior to the discovery of the exculpating biological evidence.[24] Invariably, these costly and cumbersome proceedings failed to reveal the crucial point that these convicted inmates were innocent. Most likely, the factual guilt of these inmates was not on the judges' minds.

One reason for the limited effectiveness of appellate and post-conviction review is that the access to these courts is restricted by a host of intricate procedural conditions, such as filing deadlines, contemporaneous objection at trial, narrow categories of cognizable claims, and exhaustion of claims.[25] Meeting these conditions is a tall order, especially given that the majority of inmates conduct their post-conviction affairs without the benefit of legal counsel. Furthermore, the grounds for granting relief are stringent. Indeed, federal courts award relief in only 0.4 percent of the noncapital *habeas corpus* cases they review.[26] Of this slim yield, most interventions are based on legal errors, namely, procedural flaws committed during the investigation or trial; the rate of successful challenges on factual grounds is infinitesimal. A key obstacle to receiving relief on factual grounds stems from the strong aversion of appellate and post-conviction courts to intervene in factual determinations made at the trial level.[27] When they do extend themselves to examine factual findings, these courts rely on the record developed by the trial court and examine the evidence in the light most favorable to the prosecution,[28] which naturally tends to comport with the lower court's findings. These courts also apply high thresholds for intervention[29] and entertain only a "sharply limited" review of claims challenging the sufficiency of evidence.[30] For example, one state supreme court has ruled that the evidence required for post-conviction relief must be new, material, noncumulative, and conclusive; it must meet "an extraordinarily high standard"; and it must "undermine the prosecution's entire case."[31] The difficulties of overturning convictions are exacerbated by the hindrances on testing and considering new evidence. The Court has been reluctant to order states to provide convicted inmates access to the biological evidence that could substantiate their claim of innocence.[32] Finally, cases with lingering doubts are often punted onto the lap of the executive branch,[33] for whom the political costs of freeing convicted inmates—even ones who are most likely innocent—are particularly high.[34]

The marginalization of factual accuracy is manifested most bluntly by its subjugation to competing interests in the Court's rulings. The Court habitually prioritizes various interests—notably, bureaucratic considerations—over the protection against false verdicts. For example, the Court described the exclusion of questionable eyewitness identifications as a "Draconian sanction" to the prosecution, while making light of the risk that a misidentification posed to the defendant.[35] In denying the right to disclosure of exculpatory impeachment evidence during plea negotiations, the Court stated that such a constitutional obligation would "seriously interfere with the Government's interest in securing those guilty pleas . . . and the efficient administration of justice."[36] In denying an evidentiary hearing to investigate allegations that members of a jury consumed large amounts of alcohol and drugs during their jury service, the Court prioritized the interests of finality, frank deliberation (ignoring the risk of excessive frankness), and, oddly, the public's trust in the system.[37]

The Court's low regard for factual accuracy, coupled with its permissive doctrines for admitting evidence of questionable validity,[38] have provided fertile ground for the proliferation of inadequate investigative and adjudicative procedures. Most mystifying, the Court has yet to resolve its doubts whether the Constitution affords a freestanding claim of actual innocence to death row inmates who can provide a "truly persuasive" demonstration of innocence. The Court's hesitation stems from the concern that entertaining claims of actual innocence would have a "very disruptive effect . . . on the need for finality in capital cases."[39] The Court added that if this "assumed right" were recognized, the threshold for establishing it would necessarily be "extraordinarily high."[40] More recently, Justice Antonin Scalia reminded us that "This Court has *never* held that the Constitution forbids the execution of a convicted defendant who has had a full and fair trial but is later able to convince a *habeas* court that he is 'actually' innocent."[41] Moreover, even if the Court were to bestow innocent defendants the right not to be executed, it would probably not grant relief to innocent inmates convicted for a noncapital crime, many of whom spend decades or their entire lives in prison.

The primacy of proceduralism is manifested also in the scholarly debate and legal pedagogy. A quick glance at the contents of the leading American criminal procedure casebooks mirrors the predominance of constitutional and procedural rights, with only a small fraction of the curriculum devoted to the crucial question of accuracy. Notably, a substantial share of criminal procedure education and discourse is occupied by the search and seizure doctrine, which, by its nature, thwarts accuracy and works mostly to benefit factually guilty defendants.[42]

The Denial of Error

Despite the pervasive marginalization of factual accuracy, proponents of the criminal justice process swear by the correctness of its outcomes.[43] Proponents seem to believe in a convenient confluence, by which adherence to the procedural safeguards leads to factually correct outcomes.[44] As noted by an English jurist, the jury's "verdict does pass for truth."[45] Justice Sandra Day O'Connor posited that a person cannot be deemed legally or factually innocent if he was awarded the constitutional protections and found guilty by a jury of his peers.[46] This widespread faith was famously captured by Judge Learned Hand's assurance that while the criminal justice procedure had always been "haunted by the ghost of the innocent man convicted," that concern was merely "an unreal dream."[47] Justice Scalia has dismissed false convictions as an "insignificant minimum."[48] He also characterized them as a testament not to a failure of the process, "but its success,"[49] even though, in reality, a large number of exonerations were obtained despite bitter resistance by prosecutors and even judges.[50] Notably, the denial of error is prevalent also among law enforcement officials who operate the system on a daily basis. A majority of surveyed police chiefs, prosecutors, and trial judges insist that mistaken verdicts are nonexistent or that they occur at an infinitesimal rate, at least within their own jurisdictions.[51]

The proclaimed trust in the process intensifies in the face of challenges to the system's legitimacy. The defensiveness becomes particularly pointed when the adversarial system is compared unfavorably to the continental inquisitorial system, with its explicit commitment to the discovery of truth.[52] These critiques are typically met with counter-criticisms of the inquisitorial framework,[53] a form of *legal nationalism*.[54] In that same opinion, Justice Scalia lamented that the mere mentioning by the dissenting justices of the prospect of error would be "trumpeted abroad as vindication" of the criticism of America's death penalty regime by "sanctimonious" and "finger-wagger" nations, which he subsequently identified as members of the European Union.[55] Rather than fostering introspection, the critiques of the American system appear to embolden its resolve and entrench its aversion to acknowledging its deficiencies.[56]

The faith in the accuracy of the criminal justice process is necessarily founded on a profound trust in the ability of juries to determine facts correctly. The Court routinely lauds "the good sense and judgment of American juries."[57] One sitting judge has opined that "There is something almost mystical in [the juries'] collective ability to find the truth about a case."[58] Importantly, this unwavering trust in juries has led the Court to be nonchalant about presenting juries with flawed evidence. As the Court explains, "It is part of our adversary system that we accept at trial much evidence that has strong elements of untrustworthiness."[59] Untrustworthy evidence is said to be "customary grist for the jury mill."[60] The Court insists that decisions to exclude confession evidence are "not based in the slightest on the fear that juries might misjudge the accuracy of confessions and arrive at erroneous determinations of guilt or innocence."[61] In heralding the astuteness of juries, the Court goes so far as to undercut the importance of the evidence itself: "While identification testimony is significant evidence, such testimony is still only evidence, and . . . is not a factor that goes to the very heart—the 'integrity'—of the adversary process."[62]

There is little doubt that the self-assurance in the accuracy of the process caters to important psychological and societal needs. For one, people tend toward favorable assessments of the prevailing social order, deeming it to be just and legitimate.[63] More importantly, the mere notion that the state can wreck the lives of innocent people casts a disconcerting shadow over the integrity of the system and is bound to pose a threat to the psyche of the people involved in its operation.[64] Ironically, a natural response to threats of this kind is to deny their existence.[65] Thus, rather than addressing the weaknesses of this complex, vulnerable, yet potentially lethal process, the criminal justice system comforts itself with a palliative insistence on its exactitude. To paraphrase Justice Robert Jackson, the system is entrusted with dispensing the state's punitive powers not because it is infallible; it deems itself infallible because of the powers it possesses.[66]

Narrowing the Accuracy Shortfall

The prospects of reform are to a large extent contingent on the prospects of altering these two pervasive mindsets. The people who design, oversee, and operate the criminal justice process ought to place a higher priority on reaching accurate verdicts and acknowledge that, in its current form, the process cannot be expected to meet its objectives. Proponents of the criminal justice system argue that it operates well enough to be left alone.[67] Yet given the solemn nature of criminal punishment, it would be incumbent on the system to exercise its powers with heightened conscientiousness and diligence, even if its failures were few and far between. As Jerome Frank noted, convictions of innocent persons are legitimate "only if they are inevitable—that is, only if everything practical has been done to avoid such injustices. But, often, everything practical has not been done."[68]

The criminal justice system ought to grapple vigorously and forthrightly with the issue of factual accuracy, particularly with the risk of false convictions. Achieving the system's competing objectives—the public's acceptance of the verdict, the assertion of the state's authority, and the expression of society's values—cannot be done conscientiously without reducing the risk of mistaken verdicts to the lowest feasible level. Before being subjected to the state's punitive powers, people deserve more than procedural rights,[69] especially rights of limited efficacy. Criminal punishment should require proof of guilt beyond a reasonable doubt by a system that is seriously committed to the accuracy of its verdicts.

The research discussed in this book calls into question the blind faith in the prowess of the jury. In executing their difficult task, jurors should be enabled to focus on drawing inferences from the best available evidence, rather than on second-guessing the ill effects of arcane and inadequate procedures. There is no justification for the sanguine view that evidence "is still only evidence,"[70] whose questionable reliability can be readily ignored in favor of competing considerations. Evidence is the very matter on which the whole process subsists. As such, it both informs and contaminates the verdicts that we live by. The solution, then, must revolve around improving the integrity of the evidence.

One might be tempted to propose that the integrity of the evidence could be preserved by means of the extant evidentiary regime. Notably, Federal Rule of Evidence 403 permits the exclusion of evidence when its prejudicial effect is deemed to substantially outweigh it probative value.[71] In reality, the solution offered by the evidentiary regime is inadequate. For one, the rules of evidence are all but irrelevant in the vast majority of criminal convictions that are forged through the process of plea bargaining. Thus, evidence that is unreliable or prejudicial is unlikely to be filtered out of guilty pleas. Second, to ferret out unreliable evidence, trial court judges must possess a sound appreciation for the factors that influence the accuracy of the evidence. As it turns out, trial judges often lack that scientific knowledge. For example, one survey that tested judges on the factors that influence eyewitness identifications found considerable variance, with correct responses ranging from 19 to 94 percent, with an average of 55 percent.[72] These judges were no more knowledgeable than undergraduate students and were less knowledgeable than law students.[73] Another survey found that judges disagreed with experts on 60 percent of the questions.[74] Finally, and most importantly, collecting reliable evidence in the first place is far superior to discarding bad evidence at the trial stage, way down the road. It is possible that the presence of faulty evidence will induce other erroneous evidence and thus skew the entire investigative and pre-trial process. Moreover, the exclusion of evidence might entail dropping the charges, which amounts to a waste of precious resources. The mere prospect of having to drop the charges at this late stage might make judges less prone to exclude the evidence, and lead prosecutors to double their efforts in seeking to disprove or conceal its flaws.

Recall from Chapters 2–5 that the primary and antecedent causes of faulty evidence lie in the police investigation, and that the underlying errors are frequently induced by the substandard investigative procedures used. It follows that the criminal investigation both warrants improvement and is potentially amenable to it, and is thus a promising venue for reform.[75] As mentioned in Chapter 1, the reforms must transcend the contentious adversarial divide and be tailored as narrowly as possible to target *false* convictions and acquittals. Indeed, the recommendations proposed here are designed not merely to reduce false convictions, but also to increase the reliability and completeness of the evidence, reduce frivolous litigation, defuse excessive contentiousness, promote professionalism and candor throughout the process, and ultimately also increase convictions of true perpetrators. This enhancement of the integrity of the process should go a long way toward promoting the legitimacy of the criminal justice system.

One obvious way to enhance the accuracy of the evidence is to ensure that criminal investigations are conducted scrupulously according to best-practice procedures. Adherence to best-practice procedures should both focus the investigation on accurate evidence and minimize its propensity to induce erroneous evidence. Chapter 2 offered specific suggestions for managing the investigative process, and Chapters 3–5 proposed better ways to conduct lineup procedures, interviews with cooperative witnesses, and interrogations of suspects.

As discussed throughout the preceding chapters, another very promising and feasible way to enhance the integrity of the evidence is to make criminal investigations transparent. Transparency can be achieved by creating an electronic record of all investigative procedures and making it available to all parties. Recall from Chapter 2 that transparent investigations are expected to have an ameliorative effect on the investigative process itself. The availability of a record would increase investigators' sense of accountability for the way they conduct their investigations. The record would help ensure that investigators adhere to best practices by providing law enforcement agencies with a tool for training, oversight, and quality assurance, and it should also help deter police misconduct. The record is also bound to serve as an informational tool by capturing forensic details that would otherwise be missed.

The combined effect of best-practice procedures and transparent investigations will infuse the entire process with more reliable evidence and is thus bound to make a dramatic impact throughout the legal proceedings. More accurate and transparent testimony should enable prosecutors to offer plea deals that are more fair and justified, and allow defendants to better assess their situation before signing off on long terms of imprisonment. The heightened integrity of the evidence can be expected to reduce the need to sort out murky facts through the costly, cumbersome, and imprecise process of litigation. Ultimately, it should also result in fewer appeals, *habeas* proceedings, civil suits, and damage payouts.

When cases go to trial, the heightened quality of the evidence is bound to elevate the level of the proceedings. Greater evidential clarity should reduce the distrust between the adversarial parties and soften the contentiousness of the process. The range of plausible claims will be curbed, with the effect of narrowing the opportunities for unjust prosecutions and frivolous defenses. Prosecutors would be in a position to pursue strong cases more forcefully, just as defense attorneys would be better equipped to defend their clients against erroneous charges and to call out governmental misconduct. Indeed, law enforcement agencies that currently record interrogations report that the number of motions to suppress confessions has been reduced dramatically, and in some jurisdictions have been eliminated altogether.[76] Freeing police detectives from excessive court proceedings, hostile cross-examinations, and swearing contests should reduce the adversarial pressures they encounter and enable them to devote more effort to solving crimes.

Needless to mention, the heightened integrity of the testimony should have a direct effect on the accuracy of the verdicts produced at trial. Providing fact finders with evidence that corresponds more closely to the criminal event will place them in a better position to determine what actually transpired at the crime scene. The record will effectively capture witnesses' *raw* statements and thereby minimize the effects of memory decay, contamination, and any biases or distortions arising from the investigative and pretrial processes. The availability of a record should bind witnesses to their original statements and thus reduce any pressures that might be applied on them to alter their testimony. Fact finders should benefit also from gaining better access to the investigative procedures used to elicit the testimony. Indeed, a recent study found that simulated jurors can better ascertain the accuracy of eyewitness identifications when they are shown video recordings of the lineup and the initial interviews with the witnesses.[77] Moreover, access to the investigative record should also help fact finders determine whether the testimony might have been induced or otherwise biased by the investigation itself. For example, jurors will have much to gain from learning whether or not implicit suggestions were made at the lineup, leading questions were asked at the interview, or coercive techniques were deployed in the interrogation room. One would expect that fact finders would treat statements arising from biasing procedures with circumspection, and be more trusting of testimony obtained by sound investigative methods.[78]

The advantages conferred by recording investigations punctuate the realization that the methods that were available for the presentation of evidence in the eighteenth century in England are not necessarily the best ways of doing so today.[79] The deterioration and contamination of testimony en route to the trial, coupled with the technological capability to memorialize witnesses' statements, make the orthodox adherence to the principle of orality seem arcane and deeply misguided. Historically, the primacy of oral testimony was based on its perceived superiority over documentary testimony.[80] But that advantage is no longer germane, as the *synthesized* oral testimony given in court fares poorly in comparison with a digital recording of that witness's raw statements. The oral presentation of evidence will better serve the fact-finding goal if witnesses were to testify under the shadow of their own raw statements, and when need be, the courtroom testimony were supplemented by those recorded statements.

To be sure, the recommendation to create investigative records is bound to be met with some resistance from law enforcement agencies. The Federal Bureau of Investigation, for example, has steadfastly resisted taping custodial interrogations of crime suspects and sharing them with the defense.[81] The strongest objection to broad disclosure of prosecution evidence is that it will expose the witnesses to intimidation and bribery, and even put them in harm's way.[82] In 1975 the U.S. Senate rejected a legislative proposal for a limited disclosure of the prosecution's list of witnesses. The Senate relied mostly on the passionate objection of the Department of Justice, which described the measure as "dangerous, "frightening," and an invitation to "bribery and obstruction of justice."[83] Although a comprehensive debate about the merit of broader discovery is beyond the scope of this discussion,[84] it must be noted that this intuitively appealing argument is grossly overblown and, on balance, wrong. Witness harassment is hardly an issue outside a very narrow category of cases in which the defendant is a member of a regimented and violent criminal organization. The vast majority of serious crimes are committed by individual perpetrators, who are typically in custody throughout the duration of the legal process and simply do not have the logistic apparatus to pose a threat to witnesses. Indeed, a number of states, including Arizona, Colorado, New Jersey, and North Carolina, mandate broad discovery,[85] and others, notably Florida and Vermont, even give criminal defendants the right to depose the prosecution's witnesses ahead of the trial.[86] These states do not appear to have experienced any of the calamities predicted by the Department of Justice.[87]

For the rare occasions that pose a realistic reason to fear for a particular witness, the prosecutor could obtain a protective order to shield and protect that witness, as she would likely do absent a broader discovery regime.[88] Moreover, there is good reason to believe that the existence of a transparent record will actually deter harassment. Citing the recorded statements, witnesses will be in a better position to resist any pressures from defendants and their associates. Defendants will have less to gain by preventing the witness from testifying at trial. In the event that they manage to keep the witness out of court, the recorded testimony could be used to follow through with the prosecution.[89]

The logistics and costs entailed by recording investigations are hardly reasons to thwart this initiative. The recording of encounters with members of the public is becoming increasingly affordable and widespread, as patrol cars and even foot patrol officers are being equipped with electronic recording devices.[90] Resolving cases that are fully recorded will indeed consume more resources, especially the time it would take investigators, prosecutors, and defense attorneys to canvass the records. While this cost is undeniable, it should be offset by the resources saved by the reduction in frivolous litigation and in the occasional large payouts to falsely convicted individuals. More importantly, the costs are justified by the overall benefits to the integrity of the process that are bound to result from this reform, and by the lessening of the human suffering that follows from wrong verdicts. Moreover, many of the benefits of transparent evidence would be gained even if the record is not examined by the lawyers in every case. The mere knowledge that the investigation will be memorialized and made available to all is bound to make investigators feel more accountable, and thus likely to conduct better investigations.[91]

The strongest endorsement for recording investigations comes from those who already do so, namely, law enforcement agencies that currently videotape their interrogations. The uniform reaction of police personnel and prosecutors in these jurisdictions is nothing short of enthusiastic support. The recording of interrogations has turned out to be a beneficial tool in the hands of law enforcement, even as it continues to receive backing from defense attorneys.[92] As stated by a Minnesota official, the order by the state supreme court to tape interrogations was "the best thing we've ever had rammed down our throats."[93] Likewise, a North Carolina police chief explains that having "greater documentation and better evidence ... will be a greater thing when it comes to successful prosecution of the case."[94]

Ideally, the movement to reforming the criminal justice process would be spearheaded by the U.S. Supreme Court, which is the ultimate authority on individuals' liberties and the only body that has effective jurisdiction over the multitude of law enforcement agencies and state courts. The Court is also best positioned to set the tone regarding the prioritization of the goals of the criminal justice process and the place of factual truth. A good way for the Court to steer the system toward more accurate verdicts would be by breathing life into the largely dilapidated "freestanding" conception of the Due Process clauses of the Bill of Rights.[95] According to this approach, the Due Process provisions would be understood to provide criminal suspects and defendants the most basic and genuine form of protection, namely, ensuring that their life and liberty will be deprived only following a process that minimizes the risk of mistakes to an unavoidable minimum. This approach would deploy the Constitution to promote the integrity and accuracy of the evidence, even in the absence of police wrongdoing.

It must be acknowledged that the Court does not appear to be heading in this direction.[96] Thus, reform, if it comes, will need to be chaperoned by other entities. Fortunately, the Court's indifference toward the accuracy of criminal verdicts has not discouraged an ever-increasing number of state and local agencies throughout the country. Courts and legislatures in Illinois, New Jersey, North Carolina, Wisconsin, and other jurisdictions are leading the charge toward a more accurate criminal justice system.[97] Bold and entrepreneurial reforms have been instituted also by numerous local law enforcement agencies, such as the District Attorney office in Dallas County, Texas, under the stewardship of Craig Watkins;[98] the District Attorney office in Suffolk County, Massachusetts;[99] the police department in Northampton, Massachusetts;[100] and fifteen police departments in Santa Clara County, California.[101] The scope and potential for reform are vast. Most of the recommendations proposed in this book can be implemented straightforwardly by law enforcement officials and policy makers at almost any level, from individual police investigators, prosecutors, and judges to police chiefs, district attorneys, attorneys general, and state courts and legislatures.

The accuracy of criminal verdicts will forever be constrained by the imperfect human cognition that makes them possible. Still, the combination of best-practice investigative procedures and transparent investigations promises to enable the criminal justice process to achieve a higher degree of accuracy. Pending those much-needed reforms, we have no choice but to question the evidence we use and to live in doubt as to who we set free and who we punish.

NOTES

ACKNOWLEDGMENTS

INDEX

NOTES

1. Introduction

1. For a detailed account of the Rose case, see Rutenberg, S. (2006). Anatomy of a miscarriage of justice: The wrongful conviction of Peter J. Rose. *Golden Gate University Law Review, 37,* 7–37; Innocence Project, profile, Peter Rose. http://www.innocenceproject.org/Content/Peter_Rose.php.

2. On the Godschalk case, see Kreimer, S. F., & Rudovsky, D. (2002). Double helix, double bind: Factual innocence and postconviction DNA testing. *University of Pennsylvania Law Review, 151,* 547–617; Innocence Project, profile, Bruce Godschalk. http://www.innocenceproject.org/Content/Bruce_Godschalk.php.

3. *Commonwealth of Pennsylvania v. Bruce Godschalk,* 00934-87, Montgomery County, Jury Trial, May 27, 1987, pp. 138–139.

4. Junkin, T. (2004). *Bloodsworth: The true story of the first death row inmate exonerated by DNA.* Chapel Hill, NC: Algonquin Books; Dwyer, J., Neufeld, P., & Scheck, B. (2000). *Actual innocence: Five days to execution and other dispatches from the wrongfully convicted,* pp. 213–222. New York: Doubleday. See also Department of Justice (1996). Convicted by juries, exonerated by science: Case studies in the use of DNA evidence to establish innocence after trial. http://www.ncjrs.gov/pdffiles/dnaevid.pdf.

5. For early critiques of the process, see Borchard, E. M. (1932). *Convicting the innocent.* Garden City, NY: Garden City Publishing; Frank, J., & Frank, B. (1957). *Not guilty.* Garden City, NY: Doubleday.

6. As the large majority of the crimes discussed in this book are perpetrated by males, the text will normally adopt that gender.

7. It is estimated that only 48 percent of violent crimes and 38 percent of property crimes committed in the United States are reported to the police. Department of Justice, Bureau of Justice Statistics (data for 2006/2007). http://bjs.ojp.usdoj.gov/content/glance/tables/reportingtypetab.cfm.

8. The clearance rates are 45 percent for violent crime and 17 percent for property crime. The rates are 64 percent for murder, 55 percent for aggravated assault, 40 percent for rape, and 27 percent for robbery. Federal Bureau of Investigation (2008). *Uniform crime reporting handbook, 2008: Crime in the United* States, table 25. http://www2.fbi.gov/ucr/cius2008/data/table_25 .html.

The data are similar in the United Kingdom, where about one-half of serious crimes are reported, of which only one-fifth are prosecuted. Crown Prosecution Service (2002). *Narrowing the justice gap.* http://www.cps.gov.uk/publications /prosecution/justicegap.html.

9. Failures to punish guilty individuals can also be caused by legal rules that exclude reliable inculpating evidence or thwart the prosecution in the first place. See, e.g., Pizzi, W. T. (1999). *Trials without truth: Why our system of criminal trials has become an expensive failure and what we need to do to rebuild it.* New York: NYU Press.

10. For recent literature on the topic, see Gross, S. R. (2008). Convicting the innocent. *Annual Review of Law & Social Science, 4,* 173–192; Garrett, B. L. (2011). *Convicting the innocent: Where criminal prosecutions go wrong.* Cambridge, MA: Harvard University Press; Westervelt, S. D., & Humphrey, J. A. (2002). *Wrongfully convicted: Perspectives on failed justice.* Piscataway, NJ: Rutgers University Press; Gould, J. B. (2008). *The Innocence Commission: Preventing wrongful convictions and restoring the criminal justice system.* New York: NYU Press; Marshall, L. C. (2004). The innocence revolution and the death penalty. *Ohio State Journal of Criminal Law, 1,* 573–584 (p. 573).

11. See Gross (2008), *supra* note 10; Garrett (2011), *supra* note 10; Marshall (2004), *supra* note 10.

12. See Justice Scalia's concurring opinion in *Kansas v. Marsh,* 548 U.S. 163, 193, 200 (2006). Justice Scalia relies on an appealingly simple mathematical calculation proposed by Joshua Marquis: dividing the number of known exonerees by the number of people incarcerated across the country yields a quotient 0.027 of 1 percent (or 0.00027), which is indeed a small number. Marquis, J. (2005). Myth of innocence. *Journal of Criminal Law & Criminology, 95,* 501–522. See also Hoffman, M. B. (2007). The myth of factual innocence. *Chicago-Kent Law Review, 82,* 663–690.

This mathematical computation is flawed because the rate of false convictions (as opposed to exonerations) is obscure, and because the denominator should be limited to cases in which false convictions are realistically possible and the detection of error is feasible. While both the numerator and denominator resist accurate quantification, under any realistic assumptions they are bound to lead to an error rate that is dramatically larger than the values proposed by Marquis and Scalia. Sam Gross argues convincingly that the rate that Justice Scalia advocates is "flat wrong and badly misleading." Gross, S. R. (2006).

Souter passant, Scalia rampant: Combat in the marsh. *Michigan Law Review First Impressions, 105,* 67–72 (p. 69).

13. Innocence Project, http://www.innocenceproject.org/.

14. As there is no official record of exonerations, their exact number is unknown. Data compiled by Samuel Gross and his colleagues from the University of Michigan indicate that there were some 340 known cases of individual exonerations between 1989 and 2003. Since 2000, the rate of exonerations has been about 40 cases per year. Fewer than half of the cases were overturned through DNA testing. The remainder of the exonerations were spurred by factual findings made by means of conventional types of evidence. Gross, S. R., Jacoby, K., Matheson, D. J., Montgomery, N., & Patil, S. (2005). Exonerations in the United States 1989 through 2003. *Journal of Criminal Law & Criminology, 95,* 523–560.

15. Sam Gross and colleagues have found an estimated error rate of about 4 percent among death row inmates. This rate was estimated for inmates who were sentenced to death between 1973 and 2004 and who remained under threat of execution for up to twenty-one years. Gross, S. R., O'Brien, B., Hu, C., & Kennedy, E. H. (under review). The rate of false convictions among criminal defendants who are sentenced to death. Michael Risinger examined the rate of DNA exonerations in the category of capital rape-murders and found a minimal error rate of 3.3 percent, with a likely ceiling of 5 percent. Risinger, D. M. (2007). Innocents convicted: An empirically justified factual wrongful conviction rate. *Journal of Criminal Law & Criminology, 97,* 761–806. These errors are mostly taken from within the select one-third of capital verdicts and sentences that survived criminal appeals. Gelman, A., Liebman, J. S., West, V., & Kiss, A. (2004). A broken system: The persistent patterns of reversals of death sentences in the United States. *Journal of Empirical Legal Studies, 1,* 209–261. For a survey of these and other studies, see Zalman, M. (in progress). Qualitatively estimating the incidence of wrongful convictions—a postscript.

16. While the crimes of rape and murder account for fewer than 2 percent of the total felony convictions, they make up for 96 percent of the exonerations. See Gross et al. (2005), *supra* note 14. For all practical purposes, the probability of discovering mistaken convictions in other crimes is very slim.

17. It is clear that many innocent people plead guilty rather than go to trial. For example, 135 people most of whom were innocent pled guilty in the Rampart scandal in Los Angeles and in the infamous case of Tulia, Texas. See Burcham, D. W., & Fisk, C. L. (2001). Symposium: The Rampart scandal: Introduction. *Loyola of Los Angeles Law Review, 34,* 537–543; Open Society Policy Center (2005). Tulia: Tip of the drug war iceberg. http://www.soros.org/resources /articles_publications/publications/tulia_20050101/tulia.pdf.

Overturning a conviction is close to impossible for inmates who were convicted based on their pleas. These inmates are at a substantial disadvantage when it comes to tapping into the limited legal assistance resources, convincing prosecutors, judges, and even defense attorneys to entertain their claim of innocence. Most important, in many states these inmates are barred from testing the evidence that could exonerate them.

18. The average time it takes from conviction to exoneration is more than ten years. See Gross et al. (2005), *supra* note 14.

19. As discussed in "Identity Cases and Culpability Cases," exonerations are all but impossible in culpability cases. Almost all the false convictions that have come to light were in identity cases, that is, cases in which the wrong person was convicted.

20. It is estimated that with the exception of rape crimes, biological evidence is available in only a limited subset of cases, around 10–15 percent of serious felonies. Liptak, A. (2007). Study of wrongful convictions raises questions beyond DNA. *New York Times,* July 23. Quoting Peter Neufeld. http://select .nytimes.com/2007/07/23/us/23bar.html?_r=1.

21. For illustration, in Dallas County, Texas, the standard procedure has been to preserve evidence post-trial, whereas Harris County, Texas has historically destroyed the evidence. As of November 2011, Dallas County has exonerated twenty-two people on the basis of DNA tests, whereas only eight people have been exonerated in Harris County, which has almost double the population. In Virginia, eight innocent convicts have been exonerated on the basis of biological evidence preserved by the late Mary Jane Burton, who worked in the state's crime lab. Burton's habit of preserving evidence was contrary to the laboratory's policies. See Associated Press (2011). Man exonerated in 1979 Newport News rape. April 13. http://hamptonroads.com/2011/04/man-exonerated-1979-newport -news-rape.

22. Some exonerations were based on tests of physical evidence that was supposed to have been destroyed. Dwayne Dail of North Carolina was convicted for raping a twelve-year-old girl and was sentenced to more than two life sentences. Eighteen years into his sentence, Dail was told that the evidence from his trial had long ago been destroyed. Dail's lawyer, Christine Mumma, discovered that the since-deceased police detective had kept the victim's nightgown in a private storage unit. A DNA test of the gown excluded Dail and inculpated a convicted inmate. Mumma, C. (2009). Wrongfully convicted: One lawyer's perspective. *NIJ Journal* no. 262 (March). http://www.nij.gov/journals/262/one -lawyers-tale.htm.

In the abovementioned case of Pete Rose, the bulk of the evidence used to convict Rose was destroyed, but one sample of the semen had been left by mistake at a laboratory in Berkeley for nearly ten years. Rose was set free on the basis of a DNA test of that sample. Rutenberg (2006), *supra* note 1. In the case of Kevin Byrd, the exculpating evidence was preserved most likely as a result of a clerical error. Byrd served twelve years of his life sentence. Innocence Project, profile, Kevin Byrd. http://www.innocenceproject.org/Content/Kevin_Byrd.php.

In a Nebraska case, six innocent people were exonerated thanks to a police sergeant who preserved the biological evidence from another suspect (the real perpetrator) for twenty-three years. DNA tests clear 6 in 1985 slaying: Group's guilty pleas coerced, attorney general says (2008). KETV7.com, November 7. http://www.ketv.com/news/17936340/detail.html. Likewise, the biological evidence that exonerated Ronald Cotton (discussed in Chapters 2–4) was preserved only thanks to the personal initiative of Detective Mark Gauldin.

23. Alan Newton's exoneration for rape, assault, and robbery came twelve years after his first motion to conduct the testing. Dwyer, J. (2006). 22 years after wrongful conviction—and after 12 years fighting for access to evidence—DNA proves Alan Newton's innocence. *New York Times,* June 6. Likewise, in the case of Anthony Capozzi, Erie County Medical Center recovered the biological evidence fifteen years after his first request, following multiple subpoenas issued by the county's district attorney. Capozzi was exonerated after spending twenty-two years in a New York prison for two rapes. Staba, D. (2007). Located in hospital, DNA clears Buffalo man convicted in '80s rapes. *New York Times,* March 29. http://www.nytimes.com/2007/03/29/nyregion/29bike.html.

24. Good fortune was critical in the exoneration of Clarence Elkins, who was sentenced to life for murdering and raping his mother-in-law and raping his six-year-old niece. Elkins's requests for DNA testing were rebuffed by the Ohio courts. Coincidentally, Elkins was placed in the same prison block with the inmate who he suspected had perpetrated the crime. Surreptitiously, Elkins obtained a cigarette butt from the inmate and arranged for it to be tested. The DNA test inculpated that man and set Elkins free. He was released after serving seven and a half years of his sentence. Innocence Project, profile, Clarence Elkins. http://www.innocenceproject.org/Content/Clarence_Elkins.php.

James Curtis Giles became the suspect in a rape case based on a tip from an informant. He was subsequently identified by a rape victim in a photographic lineup, even though he was a decade older and much heavier than the man she had described to the police. Giles was given a DNA test only after the informant admitted that he had intended to inform on a different man by the name of James Giles, who turned out to be James Earl Giles. Giles was exonerated on the basis of a DNA test, while on parole, some twenty-five years after his conviction for a brutal rape. Bustillo, M. (2007). Texas men's innocence puts a county on trial. *Los Angeles Times,* April 9. http://www.latimes.com/news/nationworld/nation/la-na-exonerate9apr09,1,265991.story.

Roy Brown of New York was convicted for sexual assault and murder, and was sentenced to 25 years to life imprisonment. Due to a fire at the home of his step-father, Brown requested copies of the police reports and was accidentally given previously undisclosed reports that implicated the true perpetrator. Brown was ultimately exonerated based on a DNA test of the deceased suspect's daughter. Santos, F. (2006). With DNA from exhumed body, man finally wins freedom. *New York Times,* December 24. http://www.nytimes.com/2007/01/24 /nyregion/24brown.html; Innocence Project, profile, Roy Brown. http://www .innocenceproject.org/Content/Roy_Brown.php.

25. Some of the exonerations in cases that did not have DNA evidence were precipitated by very uncommon circumstances. For example, the innocence of an Illinois man convicted for murdering his parents came to light only because the actual perpetrators were caught bragging about murdering the couple while under surveillance in an unrelated investigation. On the case of Gary Gauger, see Warden, R. (2005). Illinois death penalty reform: How it happened, what it promises. *Journal of Criminal Law & Criminology, 95,* 381–426. After Anthony Porter's family began making funeral arrangements in anticipation of his execution, journalism students from Northwestern University managed to disprove his guilt and obtain a taped confession from the true culprit. See Warden (2005), p. 423. The innocence of two Illinois death row inmates was revealed only because a state attorney happened to recall that the actual perpetrator (who was also the prosecution star witness) had confessed committing the murder to him when they were co-workers at a summer job some years prior. On the case of Perry Cobb and Darby Tillis, see Warden (2005), pp. 412–413.

26. See discussion of such cases in the section "Lineups in the Wild" in Chapter 3.

27. Since much of human behavior is multidetermined, it is impossible to pinpoint a single, precise cause of any given error. Still, one can make rough distinctions between internal stochastic errors and ones that are triggered or exacerbated by a specific type of situation or an input from another person.

28. For example, one prosecutor reflected on his prosecution of an innocent man exonerated after serving twenty-four years in prison: "His name got up in a lineup, and she picked him out. It just turned out to be the wrong man." Another prosecutor commented on her prosecution of a man exonerated after serving sixteen of a forty year sentence: "the police thought they had the right man. And the victim thought she had the right man, and they were wrong." Interviews with Mike O'Connor and Lana Myers, former prosecutors in Dallas County, Texas, commenting on the false convictions of James Curtis Giles and Willy Fountain. Council, J. (2008). Witnesses to the prosecution. *Texas Lawyer,* June 9.

29. The victim agreed to identify Rose only after a protracted and testy exchange with the detectives, and the bystander witness followed suit. Rutenberg (2006), *supra* note 1; Innocence Project, profile, Peter Rose, *supra* note 1.

30. See Kreimer & Rudovsky (2002), *supra* note 2; Innocence Project, profile, Bruce Godschalk, *supra* note 2.

31. See Junkin (2004), *supra* note 4, chap. 12. Two of the witnesses were intoxicated when they saw the perpetrator, and identified Bloodsworth only after seeing him being paraded by the police on television.

32. Dwyer, Neufeld, & Scheck (2000), *supra* note 4, pp. 45–77; Innocence Project, profile, Walter Snyder. http://www.innocenceproject.org/Content/Walter_Snyder.php.

33. See Gould, J. B. (2008), *supra* note 10.

34. For an excellent work of investigative reporting, see Zerwick, P. (2007). Murder, race, justice: The state vs. Darryl Hunt. *Winston-Salem Journal,* November 16; Vertuno, J. (2009). Judge clears dead Texas man of rape conviction. *Austin American-Statesman,* February 7. The Hunt case was also the subject of a compelling documentary film; see Brown, K., Rexer, W., Stern R., & Sundberg, A. (Producers), & Stern, R., & Sundberg, A. (Directors). (2006). *The trials of Darryl Hunt* [Motion picture]. United States: Break Thru Films. See also Innocence Project, profile, Darryl Hunt. http://www.innocenceproject.org/Content/Darryl_Hunt.php.

35. See Castelle, G., & Loftus, E. F. (2002). Misinformation and wrongful convictions. In S. D. Westervelt & J. A. Humphrey, eds., *Wrongfully convicted: Perspectives on failed justice,* pp. 17–35. New Brunswick, NJ: Rutgers University Press; Innocence Project, profile, William O'Dell Harris. http://www.innocenceproject.org/Content/William_ODell_Harris.php.

36. For more examples, see cases listed in the section "Lineups in the Wild" in Chapter 3.

37. As mentioned above, Rose was identified confidently by two witnesses (Rutenberg 2006, *supra* note 1). Bruce Godschalk was convicted on the basis of an identification by a victim, testimony of a second victim, testimony of a jailhouse informant, forensic evidence of a blood test, plus his own confession (Innocence Project, *supra* note 2). The capital prosecution of Kirk Bloodsworth included identifications by five eyewitnesses, a shoe impression, and a putatively incriminating statement made by the defendant, all leading the prosecutor to describe the evidence as being "extremely strong" (Dwyer, Neufeld, & Scheck 2000, *supra* note 4, p. 222). Ronald Cotton, whose case is discussed in the following chapters, was convicted on the basis of identifications by two victims and a bystander, testimony of his employer, and physical evidence.

38. Saks, M. J., & Koehler, J. J. (2005). The coming paradigm shift in forensic identification science, *Science, 309,* 892–895. A similar analysis of the first 225 DNA exonerations done by the Innocence Project yielded a total of 376 percent; see http://www.innocenceproject.org/understands/. An analysis of the first 250 DNA exonerations indicates that invalid forensic testimony was present in about 60 percent of the cases that contained forensic evidence (80 out of 137 cases in which the trial transcripts are available), which amounts to about one-third of this sample of exonerations. Garrett, B. L., & Neufeld, P. J. (2009). Invalid forensic science testimony and wrongful convictions. *Virginia Law Review, 95,* 1–97.

39. As observed by Saks and Koehler (2005, *supra* note 38), false convictions are caused also by nonevidential factors: 44 percent of the cases involved police

misconduct, 28 percent involved prosecutorial misconduct, and 19 percent involved incompetent legal representation.

40. Julius Ruffin was convicted by a Virginia jury on rape and burglary charges. He was exonerated on the basis of a DNA test after serving twenty-one years in prison. Gould (2008), *supra* note 10.

41. See, e.g., Uviller, H. R. (1990). Acquitting the guilty: Two case studies of jury misgivings and the misunderstood standard of proof. *Criminal Law Forum, 2,* 1–43; Rosen, J. (1998). After "One Angry Woman." *University of Chicago Legal Forum,* 179–195.

42. In many instances, litigators and other courtroom observers will not risk predicting the jury's decision.

43. National Research Council (2004). *Fairness and effectiveness in policing: The evidence.* Ed. W. Skogan & K. Frydl, pp. 74, 227–228. Washington, DC: National Academies Press.

44. One type of systemic differences among types of people in relation to the criminal justice process is demonstrated in the research by Dan Kahan and his colleagues. See Kahan, D. M. (2010). Culture, cognition, and consent: Who perceives what, and why, in "Acquaintance Rape" cases. *University of Pennsylvania Law Review, 158,* 729–813; Kahan, D. M., & Braman, D. (2008). The self-defensive cognition of self-defense. *American Criminal Law Review, 45,* 1–65.

45. The rate of plea bargaining is high even for serious felonies such as rape (88 percent), robbery (89 percent), and aggravated assault (92 percent). Even for murder, almost two-thirds of convictions (61 percent) are obtained by plea bargain. Rosenmerkel, S., Durose, M., & Farole, D. (2009). Felony sentences in state courts, 2006—statistical tables. *U.S. Department of Justice, Bureau of Justice Statistics,* table 4.1. http://bjs.ojp.usdoj.gov/content/pub/pdf/fssc06st.pdf.

46. For critiques of the practice, see Alschuler, A. W. (1976). The trial judge's role in plea bargaining. *Columbia Law Review, 76,* 1059–1154; Stuntz, W. J. (2004). Plea bargaining and criminal law's disappearing shadow. *Harvard Law Review, 117,* 2548–2569. Cf. Church, T. W. (1979). In defense of bargain justice. *Law & Society Review, 13,* 509–525. On the heightened risk that plea bargaining poses for innocent defendants, see Alschuler, A. W. (2003). Straining at gnats and swallowing camels: The selective morality of professor Bibas, *Cornell Law Review, 88,* 1412–1424.

47. See Gross et al. (2005), *supra* note 14.

48. The Innocence Project identified police misconduct in thirty-seven of the first seventy-four cases. The misconduct included suppression of exculpatory evidence, undue suggestiveness, evidence fabrication, coercion of witnesses, and coercion of confessions; http://innocenceproject.org/understand/Government -Misconduct.php. As observed by Saks and Koehler (2005, *supra* note 38), police misconduct was present in 44 percent of the first eighty-six DNA exoneration cases.

49. Prosecutorial misconduct was identified in thirty-three of the first seventy-four DNA exoneration cases. The misconduct included suppression of exculpatory evidence, knowing use of false testimony, coercion of witnesses, improper closing arguments, false statements to jury, and fabrication of evidence; http://innocenceproject.org/understand/Government-Misconduct.php. Saks and Koehler (2005, *supra* note 38) identified prosecutorial misconduct in 28 percent of the first eighty-six DNA exoneration cases.

50. According to Saks & Koehler (2005, *supra* note 38), 27 percent of the first eighty-six DNA exoneration cases involved false or misleading scientific testimony. For disconcerting abuses of scientific testimony, see Garrett, B. L., & Neufeld, P. J. (2009). Invalid forensic science testimony and wrongful convictions. *Virginia Law Review, 95,* 1–97; Giannelli, P. C. (1997). The abuse of scientific evidence in criminal cases: The need for independent crime laboratories. *Virginia Journal of Social Policy & the Law, 4,* 439–478; Mills, S., McRoberts, F., & Possley, M. (2004). Forensics under the microscope—When labs falter, defendants pay. *Chicago Tribune,* October 20.

51. See Federal Rules of Evidence 403, 404(a), and 404(b); and Strong, J. W., ed. (1999). *McCormick on evidence* (5th ed.). St. Paul, MN: West Group.

52. Stuntz, W. (2011). *The collapse of American criminal justice.* Cambridge, MA: Harvard University Press.

53. The work of public defenders and appointed counsel is hindered by both excessive caseloads and limited compensation. For illustration, the estimated average hourly rate of court-appointed attorneys in noncapital felony cases ranges from $50 to $65, which is about one-fourth of the hourly rate of lawyers in private practice. Public funding for investigation is all but nonexistent. The Constitution Project (2009). Justice denied: America's continuing neglect of our constitutional right to counsel. http://www.constitutionproject.org/pdf/139.pdf.

54. For a good account on how law works in parts of the country, see Bach, A. (2009). *Ordinary injustice: How America holds court.* New York: Henry Holt.

55. For this body of research, there is less reason for concern over internal validity and construct validity, both of which speak to the extent to which the observations support the stated conclusions. See Aronson, E., Wilson, T. D., & Brewer, M. B. (1998). Experimentation in social psychology. In D. T. Gilbert, S. T. Fiske, & G. Lindzey, eds., *The handbook of social psychology,* vol. 1 (4th ed.), pp. 99–142. New York: McGraw-Hill.

56. See, e.g., Lewin, K. (1935). *A dynamic theory of personality.* New York: McGraw-Hill; Ross, L., & Nisbett, R. E. (1991). *The person and the situation: Perspectives of social psychology.* New York: McGraw-Hill.

57. See Simon, D. (2010). In praise of pedantic eclecticism: Pitfalls and opportunities in the psychology of judging. In D. E. Klein & G. Mitchell, eds., *The psychology of judicial decision making,* pp. 131–147. New York: Oxford University Press.

58. See, e.g., McCloskey, M., Egeth, H., & McKenna, J. (1986). The experimental psychologist in court: The ethics of expert testimony. *Law and Human Behavior, 10,* 1–13; Konecni, V. J., & Ebbesen, E. B. (1986). Courtroom testimony by psychologists on eyewitness identification issues: Critical notes and reflections. *Law and Human Behavior, 10,* 117–126; Yuille, J. C., & Cutshall, J. L. (1986). A case study of eyewitness memory of a crime. *Journal of Applied Psychology, 71,* 291–301.

For an uncharitable treatment of the research on the exclusion of jurors from death penalty panels ("death qualification"), see Chief Justice Rehnquist's opinion in *Lockhart v. McCree,* 476 U.S. 162 (1986). For a response, see Ellsworth, P. C. (1991). To tell what we know or wait for Godot? *Law and Human Behavior, 15(1),* 77–90.

59. See Diamond, S. S. (1997). Illuminations and shadows from jury simulations. *Law and Human Behavior, 21,* 561–571; Bornstein, B. H. (1999). The ecological validity of jury simulations: Is the jury still out? *Law and Human Behavior, 23,* 75–91; Simon (2010), *supra* note 57.

60. On the construct of convergent validity, see Aronson, Wilson, & Brewer (1998), *supra* note 55.

61. On the construct validity of legal psychological research, see Simon (2010), *supra* note 57.

62. Whether an experiment will overstate or understate the results will depend on the manner in which the controlled factors would have interacted with the focal factor in a natural setting. Controlling factors that would otherwise moderate the focal factor are bound to result in the overstatement of the finding, whereas controlling factors that would otherwise exacerbate it are likely to understate the finding. For illustration, a finding that individual jurors are susceptible to a certain bias might be said to exaggerate the problem for the criminal justice system because, in real life, that bias might be corrected by jury deliberation. On the other hand, the deliberation itself might exacerbate the bias, which would mean that the focal finding actually understates the problem.

63. As discussed in Chapter 7, the institutional context of legal adjudication is hardly a guarantee for the accuracy of the process.

64. According to the conventions of experimental psychology, a finding is deemed statistically significant based on the probability that the effect attributed to the experimental treatment was not caused by chance (typically, using a threshold criterion of 0.05). In itself, statistical significance does not distinguish between weak effects (for example, an increase in the rate of an error from 24 percent to 29 percent) and strong ones (an increase in the rate of the error from 24 percent to 60 percent). Nor does it speak to the absolute levels of the observed phenomena, namely, whether the treatment results in an error rate of 30 percent (up from 20 percent) or of 90 percent (up from 80 percent).

65. Lloyd Weinreb proposed the establishment of an "investigating magistracy." Weinreb, L. L. (1977). *Denial of justice*. New York: Free Press, p. 119. George Thomas proposed that criminal investigations and pretrial procedures be overseen by a "screening magistrate": Thomas, G. C., III (2008). *The Supreme Court on trial: How the American justice system sacrifices innocent defendants*. Ann Arbor: University of Michigan Press, pp. 193–227. Along similar lines, Keith Findley has suggested a system that blends the strengths of the adversarial and inquisitorial systems. Findley, K. A. (in press). Adversarial inquisitions: Rethinking the search for the truth. *New York Law Review*.

On the differences between Anglo-American and continental criminal justice systems, see Hatchard, J., Huber, B., & Vogler, R. (1996). *Comparative criminal procedure*. London: British Institute of International and Comparative Law; van Koppen, P. J., & Penrod, D. S. (2003). *Adversarial versus inquisitorial justice: Psychological perspectives on criminal justice systems*. New York: Kluwer Academic Publishing.

66. On the prevailing aversion toward inquisitorial systems, see Sklansky, D. A. (2009). Anti-inquisitorialism. *Harvard Law Review, 122,* 1634–1704.

67. It should be acknowledged that the inquisitorial system is no panacea, as its lofty goals of seeking the truth are not entirely immune to the harsh reality of criminal investigations. Jacqueline Hodgson has observed that the French system does not routinely meet the ideal of the inquisitorial model. Some 95 percent of crimes are investigated not by the magistrate *(juge d'instruction),* but by the regular police force under the supervision of a prosecutor *(procureur).* The latter process functions much like the one in the Anglo-American model, with perhaps weaker protection for suspects' rights. Hodgson, J. (2005). *French criminal justice: A comparative account of the investigation and prosecution of crime in France*. Oxford: Hart Publishing.

68. A small number of suggestions might require legislative intervention.

69. Forty-two percent of the first 250 exonerations resulted in positive identifications of the true perpetrators. Innocence Project (2010). 250 exonerated, too many wrongfully convicted. http://www.innocenceproject.org/news/250.php.

70. On the importance of protecting only innocent defendants, see Amar, A. R. (1997). *The constitutional and criminal procedures: First principles,* chap. 4. New Haven, CT: Yale University Press.

71. For an example of this type of tradeoff, see "Recommendations for Reform" in Chapter 3.

72. Designing reform should take into consideration the potential for unintended and unwanted consequences. As noted by Carol and Jordan Steiker, arguments based on actual innocence can be used as a double-edged sword, and they have been deployed successfully by the U.S. Supreme Court and by Congress to justify policies that deprive defendants of a fair review of their cases. Steiker, C. S., & Steiker, J. M. (2005). The seduction of innocence: The attraction and

limitations of the focus on innocence in capital punishment law and advocacy. *Journal of Criminal Law & Criminology, 95,* 587–624.

For a skeptical view of the need for reform, see, e.g., Allen, R. J., & Laudan, L. (2008). Deadly dilemmas. *Texas Tech Law Review, 41,* 65–92.

73. The median time from arrest to adjudication for various felonies including rape, robbery, and assault ranges from four to eight months, and for murder it is about one year. Cohen, T. H., & Kyckelhahn, T. (2010). Felony defendants in large urban counties, 2006. *Department of Justice, Bureau of Justice Statistics,* table 10. http://bjs.ojp.usdoj.gov/content/pub/pdf/fdluc06.pdf. In the cases that actually go to trial, the periods are oftentimes considerably longer.

74. There are exceptions to the superior accuracy of *raw* evidence. On occasion, a witness's original statement could have been mistaken, while the contamination from cowitnesses' statements can actually make his or her testimony more accurate. As a policy matter, planting accurate information in witnesses' testimony must be discouraged. The possible increase in accuracy cannot justify the host of legal, ethical, and practical concerns raised by this prospect.

2. "We're Closing In on Him"

1. The case is the subject of a moving book: Thompson-Cannino, J., Cotton, R., & Torneo, E. (2009). *Picking cotton.* New York: St. Martin's Press. The case was first exposed in a documentary film produced and directed by Ben Loeterman, *What Jennifer Saw, Frontline* series, PBS (1997). http://www.pbs.org/wgbh/pages/frontline/shows/dna/. The account of the case in the text is based also on the transcripts of the first trial (*State v. Cotton,* No. 257A85 Alamance Co. Super. Ct., January 7, 1985), and the appellate documents of the second trial (*State v. Cotton,* 318 N.C. 663 [1987], No. 257A85).

2. Although Gauldin's identification procedures do not meet the current best-practice standards, they are not much different from the way procedures are conducted today in many jurisdictions. Unlike many defendants lacking the means to afford effective counsel, Cotton was lucky to have been represented by a court-appointed attorney, Philip Moseley, who appears to have performed proficiently both at trial and on appeal.

3. For example, the interrogation that led to Bruce Godschalk's false confession came on the heels of his identification in a photographic array by one of the victims. Although this woman testified in court that she was absolutely certain in her identification, she had been very hesitant when she picked him out at a photographic array. She picked Godschalk only on the third viewing, each of which lasted twenty to thirty minutes. *Commonwealth of Pennsylvania v. Bruce Godschalk,* 00934-87, Montgomery County, Suppression hearing, May 26, 1987, p. 23.

4. National Research Council (2004). *Fairness and effectiveness in policing: The evidence.* Ed. Wesley Skogan & Kathleen Frydl, pp. 48–49. Washington, DC: National Academies Press. No fewer than 771 departments employ only one police officer. Bear in mind that police departments are also entrusted with noninvestigative tasks, such as enforcing the law (mostly through patrolling), maintaining order, and providing miscellaneous public services.

5. Innes, M. (2003). *Investigating murder: Detective work and the police response to criminal homicide,* p. 127. Oxford: Oxford University Press.

6. National Research Council (2004), *supra* note 4, p. 2; Skolnick, J. (1966). *Justice without trial: Law enforcement in democratic society,* pp. 66–68. New York: Wiley; Waegel, W. B. (1981). Case routinization in investigative police work. *Social Problems, 28,* 263–275.

7. See Brownlie, A. R. (1984). *Crime Investigation, art or science? Patterns in a labyrinth.* Edinburgh: Scottish Academic Press. Much of detectives' training is done informally on the job, effectively by means of apprenticeships with senior agents. Manning, P. K. (2006). Detective work/culture. In J. Greene, ed., *Encyclopedia of police sciences,* p. 394. New York: Routledge.

8. Innes (2003), *supra* note 5.

9. Skolnick (1966), *supra* note 6; Neyroud, P., & Disley, E. (2007). The management, supervision, and oversight of criminal investigations. In T. Newburn, T. Williamson, & A. Wright, eds., *Handbook of criminal investigation,* pp. 549–571. Portland, OR: Willan Publishing.

10. See U.S. Department of Justice, National Institute of Justice (2003). *Factors that influence public opinion of the police.* Washington, DC. http://www.ncjrs.gov/pdffiles1/nij/197925.pdf.

11. Handling the media in high-profile cases has become one of the more onerous tasks facing police investigators. Mawby, R. C. (2007). Criminal investigation and the media. In T. Newburn, T. Williamson, & A. Wright, eds., *Handbook of criminal investigation,* pp. 146–169. Portland, OR: Willan Publishing.

12. Innes (2003), *supra* note 5, p. 127. Investigations that fail to make progress in the "golden hour" stand the risk of contagion of crime scene evidence, deterioration and contamination of witness memory, and greater opportunities for the perpetrator to cover up his leads. Innes, M. (2007). Investigation order and major crime inquiries. In T. Newburn, T. Williamson, & A. Wright, eds., *Handbook of criminal investigation,* pp. 255–276. Portland, OR: Willan Publishing.

13. As observed by Skolnick, abiding by the rule of law can interfere with getting the job done. Skolnick (1966), *supra* note 6, chaps. 9–11. See also National Research Council (2004), *supra* note 4, p. 159.

14. National Research Council (2004), *supra* note 4, p. 3. Since the 1970s, the field of police investigation has been researched only sparsely in the United

States; ibid., p. 23. Much of the recent research has been performed in the United Kingdom.

15. A study of murder investigations conducted in the United Kingdom found that abductive reasoning was by far the most commonly used form of investigative logic. Innes (2003), *supra* note 5, p. 184. On abductive reasoning, see Anderson, T., Schum, D., & Twining, W. (2005). *Analysis of evidence.* 2nd ed. Cambridge: Cambridge University Press.

16. Carson, D. (2009). Detecting, developing and disseminating detectives' "creative" skills. *Policing & Society, 19,* 216–225.

17. Risinger, M. D. (2006). Boxes in boxes: Julian Barnes, Conan Doyle, Sherlock Holmes and the Edalji case. *International Commentary on Evidence, 4(2),* article 3.

18. Spalding, T. L., & Murphy, G. L. (1996). Effects of background knowledge on category construction. *Journal of Experimental Psychology: Learning, Memory, and Cognition, 22,* 525–538.

19. This effect has been labeled the *explanation bias*. Markman, K. D., & Hirt, E. R. (2002). Social prediction and the "allegiance bias." *Social Cognition, 20,* 58–86. This effect, however, can easily be swamped by motivation. For example, it does not hold up for participants who are fans of either one of the teams.

20. Carroll, J. S. (1978). The effect of imagining an event on expectations for the event: An interpretation in terms of the availability heuristic. *Journal of Experimental Social Psychology, 14,* 88–96.

21. Ross, L. D., Lepper, M. R., Strack, F., & Steinmetz, J. (1977). Social explanation and social expectation: Effects of real and hypothetical explanations on subjective likelihood. *Journal of Personality and Social Psychology, 35,* 817–829. For a review, see Koehler, D. J. (1991). Explanation, imagination, and confidence in judgment. *Psychological Bulletin, 110,* 499–519. See also Gilbert, D. T., Krull, D. S., & Malone, P. S. (1990). Unbelieving the unbelievable: Some problems in the rejection of false information. *Journal of Personality and Social Psychology, 59,* 601–613.

22. Tversky, A., & Kahneman, D. (1974). Judgment under uncertainty: Biases and heuristics. *Science, 185,* 1124–1130. For findings of inflated belief in conditional probabilities, see Koriat, A., Fiedler, K., & Bjork, R. A. (2006). Inflation of conditional predictions. *Journal of Experimental Psychology: General, 135,* 429–447.

23. This effect has been labeled *belief perseverance*. Anderson, C. A., Lepper, M. R., & Ross, L. (1980). Perseverance of social theories: The role of explanation in the persistence of discredited information. *Journal of Personality and Social Psychology, 39,* 1037–1049.

24. Bacon, F. (1620/1960). *The new organon and related writings,* p. 50. New York: Liberal Arts Press.

25. Doyle, A. C. (1891). The adventures of Sherlock Holmes: A scandal in Bohemia. *Strand Magazine,* July 1981, p. 2.

26. For reviews, see Klayman, J. (1995). Varieties of confirmation bias. In J. R. Busemeyer, R. Hastie, & D. L. Medin, eds., *Decision making from the perspective of cognitive psychology,* vol. 32: *The psychology of learning and motivation,* pp. 385–418. New York: Academic Press; Nickerson, R. S. (1998). Confirmation bias: A ubiquitous phenomenon in many guises. *Review of General Psychology, 2,* 175–220.

27. Klayman (1995), *supra* note 26, p. 386.

28. See Revlin, R., Leirer, V., Yopp, H., & Yopp, R. (1980). The belief-bias effect in formal reasoning: The influence of knowledge on logic. *Memory & Cognition, 8,* 584–592.

29. See Edwards, K., & Smith, E. E. (1996). A disconfirmation bias in the evaluation of arguments. *Journal of Personality and Social Psychology, 71,* 5–24.

30. Ibid.

31. Koehler, J. J. (1993). The influence of prior beliefs on scientific judgments of evidence quality. *Organizational Behavior and Human Decision Processes, 56,* 28–55; Mahoney, M. J. (1977). Publication prejudices: An experimental study of confirmatory bias in the peer review system. *Cognitive Therapy and Research, 1,* 161–175.

32. Darley, J. M., & Gross, P. H. (1983). A hypothesis-confirming bias in labeling effects. *Journal of Personality and Social Psychology, 44,* 20–33.

33. Hirt, E. R., & Markman, K. D. (1995). Multiple explanation: A consider-an-alternative strategy for debiasing judgments. *Journal of Personality and Social Psychology, 69,* 1069–1086 (study 3).

34. Attributed to French philosopher Emile Chartier (1868–1961).

35. Cohen, C. E. (1981). Person categories and social perception: Testing some boundaries of the processing effect of prior knowledge. *Journal of Personality and Social Psychology, 40,* 441–452.

36. Edwards & Smith (1996), *supra* note 29.

37. Greenhoot, A. F., Semb, G., Colombo, J., & Schreiber, T. (2004). Prior beliefs and methodological concepts in scientific reasoning. *Applied Cognitive Psychology, 18,* 203–221.

38. Fraser-Mackenzie, P. A. F., & Dror, I. E. (2009). Selective information sampling: Cognitive coherence in evaluation of a novel item. *Judgment and Decision Making, 4,* 307–316.

39. Kempton, J., Alani, A., & Chapman, K. (2002). Potential effects of the confirmation bias in house condition surveys. *Structural Survey, 20,* 6–12.

40. Wallsten, T. S. (1981). Physician and medical student bias in evaluating diagnostic information. *Medical Decision Making, 1,* 145–164. Another study found that 71 percent of medical students and residents converged on diagnoses that were tentatively presented to them, while fewer than 10 percent endorsed

nonsuggested yet plausible alternative ones. Leblanc, V. R., Brooks, L. R., & Norman, G. R. (2002). Believing is seeing: The influence of a diagnostic hypothesis on the interpretation of clinical features. *Academic Medicine, 77(10),* supp. See also Pines, J. M. (2005). Profiles in patient safety: Confirmation bias in emergency medicine. *Academic Emergency Medicine, 13,* 90–94.

41. Graber, M. L., Franklin, N., & Gordon, R. (2005). Diagnostic error in internal medicine. *Archives of Internal Medicine, 165,* 1493–1499.

42. Psychotherapists described an interviewee presented as a job applicant in neutral terms, such as "attractive and conventional looking" and "candid and innovative." When the same interviewee was presented as a patient, he was described as "dependent, passive-aggressive" and a "tight, defensive person, conflicted over homosexuality." The reported differences were stark for the two groups of analytic therapists, but less so among behavior therapists. Langer, E. J., & Abelson, R. P. (1974). A patient by any other name . . . : Clinician group difference in labeling bias. *Journal of Consulting and Clinical Psychology, 42,* 4–9.

43. Ben-Shakhar, G., Bar-Hilel, M., Bilu, Y., & Shefler, G. (1998). Seek and ye shall find: Test results are what you hypothesize they are. *Journal of Behavioral Decision Making, 11,* 235–249.

44. Ask, K., & Granhag, P. A. (2007a). Motivational bias in criminal investigators' judgments of witness reliability. *Journal of Applied Social Psychology, 37,* 561–591; Ask, K., Rebelius, A., & Granhag, P. A. (2008). The "elasticity" of criminal evidence: A moderator of investigator bias. *Applied Cognitive Psychology, 22,* 1245–1259.

45. No differences were found between seasoned and relatively inexperienced analysts. Kerstholt, J. H., & Eikelbloom, A. R. (2007). Effects of prior interpretation on situation assessment in crime analysis. *Journal of Behavioral Decision Making, 20,* 455–465.

46. Unbeknownst to these experts, they had previously analyzed the same pairs of prints in a real-life case and determined them to be a positive match. The researchers informed them (incorrectly) that the prints were a nonmatch. This misinformation appears to have had a strong impact on all but one of the experts tested. Of the five experts, three changed their judgments to nonmatches, and one changed to "cannot decide." Dror, I. E., Charlton, D., & Péron, A. E. (2006). Contextual information renders experts vulnerable to making erroneous identifications. *Forensic Science International, 156,* 74–78.

47. For informative discussions of tunnel vision in police investigations, see Martine, D. L. (2002). The police role in wrongful convictions: An international comparative study. In Saundra D. Westervelt & John A. Humphrey, eds., *Wrongfully convicted: Perspectives on failed justice,* pp. 77–95. New Brunswick, NJ: Rutgers University Press; Findley, K. A., & Scott, M. S. (2006). The multiple dimensions of tunnel vision in criminal cases. *Wisconsin Law Review,* 291–397;

and Risinger, M. D., Saks, M. J., Thompson, W. C., & Rosenthal, R. (2002). The *Daubert/Kumho* implications of observer effects in forensic science: Hidden problems of expectation and suggestion. *California Law Review, 90,* 1–56.

48. This is true for both the United States and the United Kingdom. National Research Council (2004), *supra* note 4, p. 74; Bayley, D. H. (2005). What do the police do? In T. Newburn, ed., *Policing: Key readings,* p. 145. Portland, OR: Willan Publishing; Bayley, D. H. (1994). *Police for the future,* p. 27. New York: Oxford University Press.

49. See, e.g., Lord, C. G., Ross, L., & Lepper, M. R. (1979). Biased assimilation and attitude polarization: The effects of prior theories on subsequently considered evidence. *Journal of Personality and Social Psychology, 37,* 2098–2109; Edwards & Smith (1996), *supra* note 29.

50. Findings to this effect were made with police personnel in Canada, Australia, France, the United Kingdom, and the United States. See Perrott, S. B., & Taylor, D. M. (1995). Attitudinal differences between police constables and their supervisors: Potential influences of personality, work environment, and occupational role. *Criminal Justice and Behavior, 22,* 326–339; Wortley, R. K., & Homel, R. J. (1995). Police prejudice as a function of training and outgroup contact: A longitudinal investigation. *Law and Human Behavior, 19,* 305–317; Furnham, A., & Alison, L. (1994). Theories of crime, attitudes to punishment and juror bias amongst police, offenders and the general public. *Personality and Individual Differences, 17,* 35–48; Sidanius, J., Liu, J. H., Shaw, J. S., & Pratto, F. (1994). Social dominance orientation, hierarchy attenuators and hierarchy enhancers: Social dominance theory and the criminal justice system. *Journal of Applied Social Psychology, 24,* 338–366. An experiment comparing Swedish experienced criminal investigators to students found that the former were more prone to interpret mixed evidence as inculpating of the focal suspect. Ask, K., & Granhag, P. A. (2005). Motivational sources of confirmation bias in criminal investigations: The need for cognitive closure. *Journal of Investigative Psychology and Offender Profiling, 2,* 43–63.

51. The confirmation bias thus fits the category of *mental contamination;* see Wilson, T. D., & Brekke, N. (1994). Mental contamination and mental correction: Unwanted influences on judgments and evaluations. *Psychological Bulletin, 116,* 117–142.

52. Jay Koehler found that although scientists' evaluations of research were biased by its compatibility with their own beliefs, they denied and deplored any such influence. See Koehler (1993), *supra* note 31.

53. See, e.g., Ask, Rebelius, & Granhag (2008), *supra* note 44; Dror, I. E., & Charlton, D. (2006). Why experts make errors. *Journal of Forensic Identification, 56,* 600–616.

54. See Weinreb, L. L. (1977). *Denial of justice,* chap. 2. New York: Free Press.

55. Cole, S. A. (2005). More than zero: Accounting for error in latent finger-print identification. *Journal of Criminal Law & Criminology, 95,* 985–1078; Giannelli, P. C. (1997). The abuse of scientific evidence in criminal cases: The need for independent crime laboratories. *Virginia Journal of Social Policy & the Law, 4,* 439–478.

56. Comment on Rule 3.8 of Model Rules of Professional Conduct. American Bar Association. See also *Berger v. United States,* 295 U.S. 78, 88 (1935); Weinreb (1977), *supra* note 54, chap. 3.

57. The theoretical foundation of the research on motivated reasoning was formulated by Ziva Kunda. See Kunda, Z. (1990). The case for motivated reasoning. *Psychological Bulletin, 108,* 480–498, p. 480.

58. Ditto, P. H., Munro, G. D., Apanovitch, A. M., Scepansky, J. A., & Lockhart, L. K. (2003). Spontaneous skepticism: The interplay of motivation and expectation in responses to favorable and unfavorable medical diagnoses. *Personality and Social Psychology Bulletin, 29,* 1120–1132.

59. Wyer, R. S., & Frey, D. (1983). The effects of feedback about self and others on the recall and judgments of feedback-relevant information. *Journal of Experimental Social Psychology, 19,* 540–559.

60. Munro, G. D., Ditto, P. H., Lockhart, L. K., Fagerlin, A., Gready, M., & Peterson, E. (2002). Biased assimilation of sociopolitical arguments: Evaluating the 1996 U.S. presidential debate. *Basic and Applied Social Psychology, 24,* 15–26.

61. Hastorf, A. H., & Cantril, H. (1954). They saw a game: A case study. *Journal of Abnormal and Social Psychology, 49,* 129–134.

62. Boiney, L. G., Kennedy, J., & Nye, P. (1997). Instrumental bias in motivated reasoning: More when more is needed. *Organizational Behavior and Human Decision Processes, 72,* 1–24.

63. Brownstein, A. L., Read, S. J., & Simon, D. (2004). Effects of individual expertise and task importance on pre-decision reevaluation of alternatives. *Personality and Social Psychology Bulletin, 30,* 819–904.

64. See, e.g., Larwood, L., & Whittaker, W. (1977). Managerial myopia: Self-serving biases in organizational planning. *Journal of Applied Psychology, 62,* 194–198; Risucci, D. A., Tortolani, A. J., & Ward, R. J. (1989). Ratings of surgical residents by self, supervisors and peers. *Surgery, Gynecology and Obstetrics, 169(6),* 519–526; Bass, B. M., & Yammarino, F. J. (1991). Congruence of self and others' leadership ratings of naval officers for understanding successful performance. *Applied Psychology, 40,* 437–454.

65. This study used a quasi-criminal setting, in which a university student was being investigated for academic misconduct. Simon, D., Stenstrom, D., & Read, S. J. (2008). *On the Objectivity of Investigations: An Experiment.* Paper presented at Conference for Empirical Legal Studies, Cornell Law School, September 9–10.

66. The adversarial distrust was manifested by the perception of the other investigator as less objective and more distrusting than they viewed themselves. Ibid.

67. Charlton, D., Fraser-Mackenzie, P., & Dror, I. E. (2010). Emotional experiences and motivating factors associated with fingerprint analysis. *Journal of Forensics Sciences, 55,* 385–393.

68. The war metaphor generates an aura of legitimacy and a network of entailments that provide a license for special lines of action. Lakoff, G., & Johnson, M. (1980). *Metaphors we live by.* Chicago: University of Chicago Press.

69. Klockers, C. B. (1985). *The idea of police.* Beverly Hills, CA: Sage Publications; Stenross, B., & Kleinman, S. (2003). The highs and lows of emotional labor: Detectives' encounters with criminals and victims. In M. R. Pogrebin, ed., *Qualitative approaches to criminal justice: Perspectives from the field,* pp. 107–115. Thousand Oaks, CA: Sage Publications; Charlton, Fraser-Mackenzie, & Dror (2010), *supra* note 67.

An illustration of the intensity of conviction in the noble cause was provided by Dean Bowman, the prosecutor who obtained the conviction of Darryl Hunt in the second trial: "The most rewarding thing about being a prosecutor is that you . . . know that you're doing the right thing or you're doing your best to do the right thing, and that you have a moral conviction that no matter what the odds are against you, that the truth will come out. You have to just trudge on, and you somehow know it will, and believe it will, and you move toward that. And I think, in doing that, you become very passionate about that, no matter what the obstacles are, if you believe that to be the truth, then it will prevail. And I found that it does." Interview with Dean Bowman, in *The trials of Darryl Hunt* (2005). Think Film, produced and directed by Ricki Stern and Anne Sundberg. Darryl Hunt was exonerated by DNA and released after spending eighteen and a half years in prison. http://www.innocenceproject.org/Content/Darryl _Hunt.php.

70. The official standards of reporting crime data to the FBI require that the suspect be arrested, charged with the crime, and turned over to the courts for prosecution. Federal Bureau of Investigation (2010). *Uniform crime reporting handbook.* http://www.fbi.gov/about-us/cjis/ucr/crime-in-the.u.s/2010/crime-in -the.u.s.-2010/methodology. In investigators' day-to-day practical terms, arresting the suspect can suffice. See Skolnick (1966), *supra* note 6, pp. 167–173; Waegel (1981), *supra* note 6.

71. See statement of chief of police Joseph Masten, in Stern & Sundberg (2005), *supra* note 69. Recall that Hunt was exonerated by DNA and released after spending eighteen and a half years in prison.

72. See Wilson, O. W. (1962). *Police planning,* p. 3. Springfield, IL: Charles C. Thomas; Skolnick (1966), *supra* note 6, chap. 8.

73. See Skolnick (1966), *supra* note 6; Waegel (1981), *supra* note 6.

74. In the New York Police Department, low clearance rates have been used to scold and embarrass precinct commanders in front of their peers and subordinates. Rashbaum, William K. (2010). Retired officers raise questions on crime data. *New York Times,* February 6. http://www.nytimes.com/2010/02/07/nyregion/07crime.html?scp=1&sq=Retired%20officers%20raise%20questions%20on%20crime%20data&st=cse.

75. Waegel (1981), *supra* note 6.

76. Rashbaum (2010), *supra* note 74; Baker, A. (2010). Former commander recalls pressures to alter reports. *New York Times,* February 7. http://www.nytimes.com/2010/02/08/nyregion/08captain.html; Rayman, G. (2010). The NYPD tapes: Inside Bed-Stuy's 81st precinct. *The Village Voice,* May 4, 2010; Davies, N. (2003). Fiddling the figures: Police cheats who distort force records. *The Guardian,* July 11. http://www.guardian.co.uk/uk/2003/jul/11/ukcrime.prisonsandprobation1.

77. The study estimated that some 30 percent of cleared crimes were solved on-scene, and 50 percent were solved on the basis of an initial identification made by the patrol officers. Detectives were involved in the remaining 20 percent, though a majority of these cases were solved by information volunteered by witnesses or by mundane tracking of information that could be done by clerical personnel. Petersilia, J. (1977). The investigative function. In P. W. Greenwood, J. M. Chaiken, & J. Petersilia, eds., *The criminal investigation process.* Lexington, MA: D. C. Heath. See also Waegel (1981), *supra* note 6; Stenross & Kleinman (2003), *supra* note 69. See also National Research Council (2004), *supra* note 4, pp. 74, 227–228.

In the United Kingdom, it has been estimated that some 70 percent of homicide cases can be considered "self-solvers." Innes, M. (2002). The "process structures" of police homicide investigations. *British Journal of Criminology, 42,* 669–688. In some jurisdictions in the United States, investigators call easy cases "dunkers." Manning (2006), *supra* note 7.

78. Bayley (2005), *supra* note 48, p. 145; Eck, J. (1992). *Solving crimes: The investigation of burglary and robbery.* Washington, DC: Police Executive Research Foundation.

79. National Research Council (2004), *supra* note 4, p. 74; Tilley, N., Robinson, A., & Burrows, J. (2007). The investigation of high volume crime. In T. Newburn, T. Williamson, & A. Wright, eds., *Handbook of criminal investigation,* pp. 226–254. Portland, OR: Willan Publishing.

80. Innes (2003), *supra* note 5, p. 15.

81. Joseph McCarthy, who prosecuted the Walter Snyder case (discussed in Chapter 4), explained: "And in a rape case, there is often a bonding between the victim and the prosecutor, and the investigator. They are going through a bad time. The psychology is that you're the last line of defense between them and the guy's getting out on the street." Dwyer, J., Neufeld, P., & Scheck, B. (2000). *Actual innocence: Five days to execution and other dispatches from the wrong-*

fully convicted, p. 238. New York: Doubleday. After spending thirteen years on a homicide case, a California homicide detective described a close relationship with the victim's mother: "She's part of my family and I am part of hers." Therolf, G. (2007). A "bitter joy" at murder arrests; After 13 years, Placentia police say new DNA evidence ties two cousins to the stabbing death of a Cal State Fullerton student. *Los Angeles Times,* July 7. http://www.latimes.com/news/local/la-me-torrez7jul07,1,2429489.story?coll=la-headlines-california.

82. On the relationship among these emotional reactions, see Kahneman, D., & Sunstein, C. R. (2005). Cognitive psychology of moral intuitions. In J. P. Changeux, A. R. Damasio, W. Singer, & Y. Christen, eds., *Neurobiology of human values,* pp. 91–105. Berlin: Springer.

83. Lerner, J. S., Goldberg, J. H., & Tetlock, P. E. (1998). Sober second thought: The effects of accountability, anger, and authoritarianism on attributions of responsibility. *Personality and Social Psychology Bulletin, 24,* 563–574; Goldberg, J. H., Lerner, J. S., & Tetlock, P. E. (1999). Rage and reason: The psychology of the intuitive prosecutor. *European Journal of Social Psychology, 29,* 781–795; Quigley, B. M., & Tedeschi, J. T. (1996). Mediating effects of blame attributions on feelings of anger. *Personality and Social Psychology Bulletin, 22,* 1280–1288. Anger was also found to mediate judgments of blame in apportioning responsibility for accidents. Feigenson, N., Park, J., & Salovey, P. (2001). The role of emotions in comparative negligence judgments. *Journal of Applied Social Psychology, 31,* 576–603. Heightened states of anger increase attributions of fault to human conduct rather than to situational conditions. Keltner, D., Ellsworth, P. C., & Edwards, K. (1993). Beyond simple pessimism: Effects of sadness and anger on social perception. *Journal of Personality and Social Psychology, 64,* 740–752.

84. For example, arousal of anger increased participants' tendency to believe an allegation that a Hispanic person behaved violently and that a student athlete cheated on an exam. Bodenhausen, G. V., Sheppard, L. A., & Kramer, G. P. (1994). Negative affect and social judgment: The differential impact of anger and sadness. *European Journal of Social Psychology, 24,* 45–62.

85. Ferguson, T. J., & Rule, B. G. (1983). An attributional perspective on anger and aggression. In R. G. Geen & E. I. Donnerstein, eds., *Aggression: Theoretical and empirical reviews,* vol. 1, pp. 41–74. New York: Academic Press.

86. Mackie, D. M., Devos, Thierry, & Smith E. R. (2000). Intergroup emotions: Explaining offensive action tendencies in an intergroup context. *Journal of Personality and Social Psychology, 79,* 602–616.

87. Dror, I. E., Péron, A. E., Hind, S. L., & Charlton, D. (2005). When emotions get the better of us: The effect of contextual top-down processing on matching fingerprints. *Applied Cognitive Psychology, 19,* 799–809.

88. The arousal of sadness had no such effect. Ask, K., & Granhag, P. A. (2007b). Hot cognition in investigative judgments: The differential influence of anger and sadness. *Law and Human Behavior, 31,* 537–551.

89. Tajfel, H., & Turner, J. (1979). An integrative theory of intergroup conflict. In W. G. Austin & S. Worchel, eds., *The Social psychology of intergroup relations,* pp. 33–47. Belmont, CA: Wadsworth; Abrams, D., & Hogg, M. A. (1990). *Social identity theory: Constructive and critical advances.* New York: Springer-Verlag; Abrams, D. (1999). Social identity, social cognition, and the self: The flexibility and stability of self-categorization. In D. Abrams, & M. A. Hogg, eds., *Social identity and social cognition,* pp. 197–229. Malden, MA: Blackwell.

90. For a review of experimental work, see Brewer, M. B. (1979). In-group bias in the minimal intergroup situation: A cognitive-motivational analysis. *Psychological Bulletin, 86,* 307–324. Recent research emphasizes the importance of morality in in-group evaluations. Leach, C. W., Ellemers, N., & Barreto, M. (2007). Group virtue: The importance of morality (vs. competence and sociability) in the positive evaluation of in-groups. *Journal of Personality and Social Psychology, 93,* 234–249. For anthropological illustrations, see Brewer, M. B., & Campbell, D. T. (1976). *Ethnocentrism and intergroup attitudes: East African evidence.* Beverly Hills, CA: Sage Publications; Phalet, K., & Poppe, E. (1997). Competence and morality dimensions of national and ethnic stereotypes: A study in six eastern-European countries. *European Journal of Social Psychology, 27,* 703–723.

91. As mentioned above, law enforcement personnel tend to hold attitudes associated with the position of *law and order.* See, e.g., Perrott & Taylor (1995), *supra* note 50; Wortley & Homel (1995), *supra* note 50; Furnham & Alison (1994), *supra* note 50; Sidanius et al. (1994), *supra* note 50.

92. White, K. M., Hogg, M. A., & Terry, D. J. (2002). Improving attitude-behavior correspondence through exposure to normative support from a salient ingroup. *Basic and Applied Social Psychology, 24,* 91–103.

93. Back, K. W. (1951). Influence through social communication. *Journal of Abnormal and Social Psychology, 46,* 9–23; Swann, W. B., Jr., Gómez, Á., Seyle, D. C., Morales, J. F., & Huici, C. (2009). Identity fusion: The interplay of personal and social identities in extreme group behavior. *Journal of Personality and Social Psychology, 96,* 995–1011. For a review of members' deference to the group norm, see Roccas, S., Sagiv, L., Schwartz, S., Halevy, N., & Eidelson, R. (2008). Toward a unifying model of identification with groups: Integrating theoretical perspectives. *Personality and Social Psychology Review, 12,* 280–306.

94. Dwyer, Neufeld, & Scheck (2000), *supra* note 81, p. 238. On the case of Walter Snyder, see Chapter 4.

95. Kerschreiter, R., Schulz-Hardt, S., Mojzisch, A., & Frey, D. (2008). Biased information search in homogeneous groups: Confidence as a moderator for the effect of anticipated task requirements. *Personality and Social Psychology Bulletin, 34,* 679–691.

96. Schulz-Hardt, S., Frey, D., Lüthgens, C., & Moscovici, S. (2000). Biased information search in group decision making. *Journal of Personality and Social Psychology, 78,* 655–669.

97. Rydell, R. J., Mackie, D. M., Maitner, A. T., Claypool, H. M., Ryan, M. J., & Smith, E. R. (2008). Arousal, processing, and risk taking: Consequences of intergroup anger. *Personality and Social Psychology Bulletin, 34,* 1141–1152.

98. As described by Irving Janis, groupthink encompasses illusions of invulnerability, collective rationalization, belief in the inherent morality of the group, stereotypes of out-groups, pressure on dissenters, self-censorship, illusions of unanimity, and self-appointed mind-guards. On the basis of historical case studies, Janis demonstrated that groupthink mindsets result in poor decisions. Janis, I. L. (1972). *Victims of groupthink.* Boston: Houghton Mifflin; Janis, I. L. (1982). *Groupthink: Psychological studies of policy decisions and fiascoes,* 2nd ed.. Boston: Houghton Mifflin.

99. The discrepancy between individual and group behavior has been labeled the *discontinuity effect.* Insko, C. A., & Schopler, J. (1998). Differential distrust of groups and individuals. In C. Sedikides, J. Schopler, & C. A. Insko, eds., *Intergroup cognition and intergroup behavior,* pp. 75–107. Mahwah, NJ: Lawrence Erlbaum.

100. See Johnston, K. L., & White, K. M. (2003). Binge-drinking: A test of the role of group norms in the theory of planned behaviour. *Psychology & Health, 18,* 63–77.

101. Jaffe, Y., Shapir, N., & Yinon, Y. (1981). Aggression and its escalation. *Journal of Cross-Cultural Psychology, 12,* 21–36; Jaffe, Y., & Yinon, Y. (1979). Retaliatory aggression in individuals and groups. *European Journal of Social Psychology, 9,* 177–186.

102. Meier, B. P., & Hinsz, V. B. (2004). A comparison of human aggression committed by groups and individuals: An interindividual-intergroup discontinuity. *Journal of Experimental Social Psychology, 40,* 551–559.

103. Jaffe, Shapir, & Yinon (1981), *supra* note 101.

104. Milgram, S. (1974). *Obedience to authority: An experimental view,* experiment 18, pp. 121–122. New York: Harper & Row.

105. Valdesolo, P., & DeSteno, D. (2007). Moral hypocrisy: Social groups and the flexibility of virtue. *Psychological Science, 18,* 689–690. For a real-life example, see Moser, K. (2010). San Francisco DA says office didn't know about problems at scandal-ridden crime lab, *The Recorder,* April 27. http://www.law .com/jsp/article.jsp?id=1202453216864&San_Francisco_DA_Says_Office_Didnt _Know_About_Problems_at_ScandalRidden_Crime_Lab.

106. Baumeister, R. F., & Leary, M. F. (1995). The need to belong: Desire for interpersonal attachments as a fundamental human motive. *Psychological Bulletin, 117,* 497–529.

107. For example, people hold in high regard traits such as "creative" and "bright," and disapprove of traits such as "lazy" and "incompetent." Alicke, M. D. (1985). Global self-evaluation as determined by the desirability and controllability of trait adjectives. *Journal of Personality and Social Psychology, 49,* 1621–1630.

108. For the need to be seen as fair, see Loewenstein, G., Issacharoff, S., Camerer, C., & Babcock, L. (1993). Self-serving assessments of fairness and pretrial bargaining. *Journal of Legal Studies, 22,* 135–159.

109. Aronson, E. (1969). The theory of cognitive dissonance: A current perspective. In L. Berkowitz, ed., *Advances in experimental social psychology,* vol. 4, pp. 1–34. San Diego: Academic Press; Aronson, E. (1992). The return of the repressed: Dissonance theory makes a comeback. *Psychological Inquiry, 3,* 303–311.

110. As suggested by Alicke (1985), *supra* note 107, some of the traits that are associated with good investigative work are also those that people assign themselves most strongly, such as "perceptive," "level headed," and "reliable." See also Aronson (1969), *supra* note 109.

111. See, e.g., Staw, B. M., & Fox, F. V. (1977). Escalation: The determinants of commitment to a chosen course of action. *Human Relations, 30,* 431–450; Garland, H., & Conlon, D. E. (1998). Too close to quit: The role of project completion in maintaining commitment. *Journal of Applied Social Psychology, 28,* 2025–2048.

112. The distortion of one's prior choices bears a resemblance to cognitive dissonance theory. See Festinger, L. (1957). *A theory of cognitive dissonance.* Evanston, IL: Row, Peterson; Harmon-Jones, E., & Mills, J., eds. (1999). *Cognitive dissonance: Progress on a pivotal theory in social psychology.* Washington, DC: American Psychological Association. The reference to cognitive dissonance theory was proposed in Bazerman, M. H., Giuliano, T., & Appelman, A. (1984). Escalation of commitment in individual and group decision making. *Organizational Behavior & Human Performance, 33,* 141–152.

113. This discrepancy is indicated by a preference for retroactive information that speaks to the decision already made, rather than prospective information about the decision to be made. See Beeler, J. D., & Hunton, J. E. (1997). The influence of compensation method and disclosure level on information search strategy and escalation of commitment. *Journal of Behavioral Decision Making, 10,* 77–91; Conlon, E. J., & Parks, J. M. (1987). Information requests in the context of escalation. *Journal of Applied Psychology, 72,* 344–350.

114. For example, when rating employees whom they originally hired, managers tend to inflate the ratings of their effectiveness, likelihood of improvement, and potential for promotion. See Schoorman, F. D. (1988). Escalation bias in performance appraisals: An unintended consequence of supervisor participation in hiring decisions. *Journal of Applied Psychology, 73,* 58–62; Bazerman, M. H., Beekun, R. I., & Schoorman, F. D. (1982). Performance evaluation in a dynamic context: A laboratory study of the impact of a prior commitment to the ratee. *Journal of Applied Psychology, 67,* 873–876; Slaughter, J. E., & Greguras, G. J. (2008). Bias in performance ratings: Clarifying the role of positive versus negative escalation. *Human Performance, 21,* 414–426.

115. Specifically, players picked high in the draft were given more game time and retained longer than players picked lower in the draft. Staw, B. M., & Hoang, H. (1995). Sunk costs in the NBA: Why draft order affects playing time and survival in professional basketball. *Administrative Science Quarterly, 40,* 474–494.

116. Staw, B. M., Barsade, S. G., & Koput, K. W. (1997). Escalation at the credit window: A longitudinal study of bank executives' recognition and write-off of problem loans. *Journal of Applied Psychology, 82,* 130–142.

117. One study found that season ticket holders who paid full price for the subscription attended more performances than did subscribers who bought it at a discount. Arkes, H. R., & Blumer, C. (1985). The psychology of sunk cost. *Organizational Behavior and Human Decision Processes, 35,* 124–140 (study 2).

118. Schoorman (1988), *supra* note 114.

119. O'Brien, B. (2009). Prime suspect: An examination of factors that aggravate and counteract confirmation bias in criminal investigations. *Psychology, Public Policy, and Law, 15,* 315–334.

120. Staw & Fox (1977), *supra* note 111; Bobocel, D. R., & Meyer, J. P. (1994). Escalating commitment to a failing course of action: Separating the roles of choice and justification. *Journal of Applied Psychology, 79,* 360–363; Whyte, G. (1993). Escalating commitment in individual and group decision making: A prospect theory approach. *Organizational Behavior and Human Decision Processes, 54,* 430–455.

121. Harrison, P. D., & Harrell, A. (1993). Impact of "adverse selection" on managers' project evaluation decisions. *Academy of Management Journal, 36,* 635–643. See also Simonson, I., & Nye, P. (1992). The effect of accountability on susceptibility to decision errors. *Organizational Behavior and Human Decision Processes, 51,* 416–446 (study 6).

122. Staw & Fox (1977), *supra* note 111.

123. Zhang, L., & Baumeister, R. F. (2006). Your money or your self-esteem: Threatened egotism promotes costly entrapment in losing endeavors. *Personality and Social Psychology Bulletin, 32,* 881–893; Harrison & Harrell (1993), *supra* note 121.

124. Beeler & Hunton (1997), *supra* note 113; Bobocel & Meyer (1994), *supra* note 120.

125. Garland & Conlon (1998), *supra* note 111; Moon, H. (2001). Looking forward and looking back: Integrating completion and sunk-cost effects within an escalation-of-commitment progress decision. *Journal of Applied Psychology, 86,* 104–113; Boehne, D. M., & Paese, P. W. (2000). Deciding whether to complete or terminate an unfinished project: A strong test of the project completion hypothesis. *Organizational Behavior and Human Decision Processes, 81,* 178–194.

126. Greitemeyer, T., Schulz-Hardt, S., & Frey, D. (2009). The effects of authentic and contrived dissent on escalation of commitment in group decision making. *European Journal of Social Psychology, 39,* 639–647; Bazerman, Giuliano, & Appelman (1984), *supra* note 112.

127. See, e.g., Whyte (1993), *supra* note 120.

128. Marques, J., Abrams, D., & Serôdio, R. G. (2001). Being better by being right: Subjective group dynamics and derogation of in-group deviants when generic norms are undermined. *Journal of Personality and Social Psychology, 81,* 436–447; Cota, A. A., Evans, C. R., Dion, K. L., Kilik, L., et al. (1995). The structure of group cohesion. *Personality and Social Psychology Bulletin, 21,* 572–580.

129. Jaffe & Yinon (1979), *supra* note 101.

130. Schachter, S. (1951). Deviation, rejection, and communication. *Journal of Abnormal and Social Psychology, 46,* 190–207. This is not to say that groups are always perfectly harmonious or egalitarian. Even when they are engaged in intergroup conflict, groups have internal stratification, hierarchical divisions, and even rivalry. Wit, A. P., & Kerr, N. L. (2002). "Me versus just us versus us all" categorization and cooperation in nested social dilemmas. *Journal of Personality and Social Psychology, 83,* 616–637. For the most part, though, these differences are tucked away within the groups, and tend not to be observable from across the intergroup divide.

131. See Blockars, C. B., Ikkovic, S. K., & Haberfeld, M. R. (2006). *Enhancing police integrity.* Dordrecht: Springer; Savitz, L. (1970). The dimensions of police loyalty. *American Behavioral Scientist, 13,* 693–704; Westley, W. A. (1970). *Violence and the police: A sociological study of law, custom, and morality.* Cambridge, MA: MIT Press. Selection to a detective unit usually entails a commitment to the team. One must prove oneself to be loyal, a team player. Loyalty affects retention and promotion in the units. See Manning (2006), *supra* note 7. The case of Richard Ceballos provides an example of group cohesion against a prosecutor who broke ranks. See *Garcetti v. Ceballos,* 547 U.S. 410 (2006).

132. For example, after the suspects in the Ford Heights case were charged with this high-profile murder, the Chicago police ignored witnesses who provided them with the correct evidence. Protess, D., & Warden, R. (1998). *A promise of justice,* chaps. 12, 14. New York: Hyperion.

133. The lead character in the Chinese film *King of Masks* (directed by Minglun Wei, 1996) captures this intuition: "The lightest breeze can blow you into jail, but the strongest ox cannot pull you out."

134. For prosecutorial resistance to admit investigative or prosecutorial errors, see Medwed, D. (2004). The zeal deal: Prosecutorial resistance to postconviction claims of innocence. *Boston University Law Review, 84,* 125–183.

135. Against the advice of his lawyer Scott Borthwick (who worked on the case pro bono), James Ochoa pleaded guilty to the crime. He was subsequently exonerated after the biological evidence from the crime scene was matched to a

man who was imprisoned at the time for similar crimes. Reza, H. G. (2006). Innocent man grabs his freedom and leaves town. *Los Angeles Times,* November 2. See also Moxely, R. S. (2005). The case of the dog that couldn't sniff straight. *OC Weekly,* November 5; Innocence Project, profile, James Ochoa. http://www .innocenceproject.org/Content/James_Ochoa.php.

136. See Garrett, B. L. (2011). *Convicting the innocent: Where criminal prosecutions go wrong,* pp. 100–102. Cambridge, MA: Harvard University Press.

137. Cooper, C. L., & Grimley, P. J. (1983). Stress among police detectives. *Journal of Occupational Medicine, 25,* 534–540; Wright, A. (2007). Ethics and corruption. In T. Newburn, T. Williamson, & A. Wright, eds., *Handbook of criminal investigation,* pp. 586–609, p. 605. Portland, OR: Willan Publishing.

138. Investigative dilemmas have been described as ethical "minefields." Wright (2007), *supra* note 137, p. 605.

139. On the tendency to discount the significance of future events, see Ainslie, G., & Haslam, N. (1992). Hyperbolic discounting. In G. Loewenstein & J. Elster, eds., *Choice over time,* pp. 57–92. New York: Russell Sage Foundation. It has also been shown that events that are far in the future are typically represented more abstractly whereas proximate events are seen to be more concrete and detailed. Trope, Y., & Liberman, N. (2003). Temporal construal. *Psychological Review, 110,* 403–421.

140. For a review of the literature, see Dunning, D., Heath, C., & Suls, J. M. (2004). Flawed self-assessment: Implications for health, education, and the workplace. *Psychological Science in the Public Interest, 5,* 69–106.

141. See Ramsey, R. J., & Frank, J. (2007). Wrongful conviction: Perceptions of criminal justice professionals regarding the frequency of wrongful conviction and the extent of system errors. *Crime & Delinquency, 53,* 436–470; Zalman, M., Smith, B., & Kiser, A. (2008). Officials' estimates of the incidence of "actual innocence" convictions. *Justice Quarterly, 25,* 72–100.

142. See Leo, R. A. (2008). *Police interrogation and American justice.* Cambridge, MA: Harvard University Press. A number of English criminologists depict *case construction* as a set of biased practices that include prejudicial decision making and manipulation of the facts in order to achieve strong cases for the prosecution. See, e.g., McConville, M., Sanders, M., & Leng, R. (1991). *The case for the prosecution: Police suspects and the construction of criminality.* London: Routledge. For discussions, see Innes (2003), *supra* note 5, pp. 214–216; Bayley (1994), *supra* note 48, p. 27. For opposite views, see Smith, D. J. (1997). Case construction and the goals of criminal process. *British Journal of Criminology, 37,* 319–346.

143. *Johnson v. United States,* 333 U.S. 10, 13–14 (1948).

144. See National Academy of Science (2009). *Strengthening forensic science in the United States: A path forward.* Washington, DC: National Academies

Press; Garrett, B. L., & Neufeld, P. J. (2009). Invalid forensic science testimony and wrongful convictions. *Virginia Law Review, 95,* 1–97; Mnookin, J. L. (2010). The Courts, the NAS, and the Future of Forensic Science. *Brooklyn Law Review, 75,* 1209–1275; Giannelli (1997), *supra* note 55.

145. Anecdotal evidence suggests that high-profile crimes are particularly susceptible to adversarial pressures, and thus to guilt-prone error. Notable examples include the conviction of five youths for the notorious assault on the Central Park jogger (see Saulny, S. [2002]. Convictions and charges voided in '89 Central Park jogger attack. *New York Times,* December 20. http://www.nytimes.com /2002/12/20/nyregion/convictions-and-charges-voided-in-89-central-park-jogger -attack.html); the indictment of three members of the Duke University lacrosse team on sexual assault and kidnapping charges (Wilson D., & and Barstow, D. [2007]. All charges dropped in Duke case. *New York Times,* April 12. http:// www.nytimes.com/2007/04/12/us/12duke.html); the relentless pursuit of Steven Hatfill, the army scientist who was suspected of being responsible for the deadly anthrax attacks in 2001 (Shane, S., & Lichtblau, E. [2008]. New details on F.B.I.'s false start in anthrax case. *New York Times,* November 25. http://www.nytimes .com/2008/11/26/washington/26anthrax.html?_r=1); the prolonged arrest of Wen Ho Lee, mistakenly suspected of spying for China (F.B.I. faulted in nuclear secrets investigation. *New York Times,* December 13, 2001. http://www.nytimes.com /2001/12/13/us/fbi-faulted-in-nuclear-secrets-investigation.html); the overturned conviction of members of the alleged Al Qaeda "sleeper operational combat cell" in Detroit (Hakim, D., & Lichtblau, E. [2004]. After convictions, the undoing of a U.S. terror prosecution. *New York Times,* October 7. http://www.nytimes.com /2004/10/07/national/07detroit.html); the false confession obtained from Abdallah Higazzi, implicating himself in the terrorist attacks on the World Trade Center's Twin Towers on September 11 (Dwyer, J. [2007]. Roots of false confession: Spotlight is now on the F.B.I. *New York Times,* October 31. http://www.nytimes .com/2007/10/31/nyregion/31about.html?ref=abdallahhigazy); and the prosecution of Alaska senator Ted Stevens (Lewis, N. A. [2009]. Tables turned on prosecution in Stevens case. *New York Times,* April 7. http://www.nytimes.com/2009/04 /08/us/politics/08stevens.html).

146. As mentioned in Chapter 1, police misconduct was observed in almost half of DNA exoneration cases, and prosecutorial misconduct was found in 45 percent of cases. False or misleading forensic testimony was given in about one-quarter of the cases.

147. The term *testilying* was coined by officers who were involved in committing perjury. Commission to Investigate Allegations of Police Corruption and the Anti-Corruption Practices of the Police Department, Milton Mollen, Chair, July 7, 1994, at 36. See also Slobogin, C. (1996). Testilying: Police perjury and what to do about it. *Colorado Law Review, 67,* 1037–1060. Renowned criminologist Jerome Skolnick observes that for the police, "lying is a routine way of

managing legal impediments—whether to protect fellow officers or to compensate for what [the officer] views as limitations the courts have placed on his capacity to deal with criminals." Skolnick, J. H. (1982). Deception by police. *Criminal Justice Ethics,* Summer/Fall, 40–54.

148. Diane Vaughn's study of NASA activities leading up to the crash of the Challenger shuttle reveal such a culture shift. Working under extreme pressure, NASA scientists and engineers progressively deviated from the standard operating procedures, and gradually generated a culture that normalized faulty practices. Without engaging in willful misconduct, these practices led to deeply flawed decision making. Vaughn, D. (1996). *The Challenger launch decision: Risky technology, culture, and deviance at NASA.* Chicago: University of Chicago Press.

149. For the strengthening of the police officers' attitudes over time, see Wortley & Homel (1995), *supra* note 50; Gatto, J., Dambrun, M., Kerbrat, C., & De Olivera, P. (2010). Prejudice in the police: On the processes underlying the effects of selection and group socialization. *European Journal of Social Psychology, 40,* 252–269; Perrott & Taylor (1995), *supra* note 50.

150. According to this count, the prosecution's case contained 139 evidence items and the defense's case 199. Kadane, J. B., & Schum, D. A. (1996). *A probabilistic analysis of the Sacco and Vanzetti case,* pp. 80, 286–337. New York: John Wiley & Sons.

151. The term *mental model* is used here in the broad sense of a structured representation. See Markman, A. B. (1999). *Knowledge representation.* Mahwah, NJ: Lawrence Erlbaum.

152. For experimental results, see Holyoak, K. J., & Simon, D. (1999). Bidirectional reasoning in decision making by constraint satisfaction. *Journal of Experimental Psychology: General, 128,* 3–31; Simon, D., Pham, L. B., Le, Q. A., & Holyoak, K. J. (2001). The emergence of coherence over the course of decision making. *Journal of Experimental Psychology: Learning, Memory, and Cognition, 27,* 1250–1260; Simon, D., Snow, C. J., & Read, S. J. (2004). The redux of cognitive consistency theories: Evidence judgments by constraint satisfaction. *Journal of Personality and Social Psychology, 86,* 814–837; Simon, D., Krawczyk, D. C., & Holyoak, K. J. (2004). Construction of preferences by constraint satisfaction. *Psychological Science, 15,* 331–336; Simon, D., Krawczyk, D. C., Bleicher, A., & Holyoak, K. J. (2008). The transience of constructed preferences. *Journal of Behavioral Decision Making, 21,* 1–14; Glöckner, A., & Betsch, T. (2008). Multiple-reason decision making based on automatic processing. *Journal of Experimental Psychology: Learning, Memory, and Cognition, 34,* 1055–1075; Glöckner, A., Betsch, T., & Schindler, N. (2010). Coherence shifts in probabilistic inference tasks. *Journal of Behavioral Decision Making, 23,* 439–462.

For reviews of the coherence effect, see Simon, D., & Holyoak, K. J. (2002). Structural dynamics of cognition: From consistency theories to constraint satisfaction. *Personality and Social Psychology Review, 6,* 283–294; Simon, D.

(2004). A third view of the black box: Cognitive coherence in legal decision making. *University of Chicago Law Review, 71, 511–586.*

For overviews of the underlying cognitive architecture, see Read, S. J., Vanman, E. J., & Miller, L. C. (1997). Connectionism, parallel constraint satisfaction processes, and Gestalt principles: (Re)introducing cognitive dynamics to social psychology. *Personality and Social Psychology Review, 1, 26–53;* Thagard, P. (2000). *Coherence in thought and action.* Cambridge, MA: MIT Press.

153. See Holyoak & Simon (1999), *supra* note 152, studies 2, 3.

154. Simon et al. (2001), *supra* note 152.

155. Simon, Snow, & Read (2004), *supra* note 152.

156. See Simon, Stenstrom, & Read (2008), *supra* note 65.

157. Ask & Granhag (2007a), *supra* note 44.

158. Simon, Stenstrom, & Read (2008), *supra* note 65.

159. By the same token, providing information that placed the defendant far from the scene led to more exculpatory evaluations of the rest of the evidence. Simon, Snow, & Read (2004), *supra* note 152, study 3. The effect of adding one piece of evidence on all the other evidence items was observed also in Holyoak & Simon (1999), *supra* note 152, study 3; Simon, Krawczyk, & Holyoak (2004), *supra* note 152, study 2.

160. Holyoak & Simon (1999), *supra* note 152, study 3.

161. Moreover, learning of a confession caused witnesses to change the responses they had given at a lineup conducted two days earlier. Hasel, L. E., & Kassin, S. M. (2009). On the presumption of evidentiary independence: Can confessions corrupt eyewitness identifications? *Psychological Science, 20, 122–126.*

162. Wells, G. L., & Bradfield, A. L. (1998). "Good, you identified the suspect": Feedback to eyewitnesses distorts their reports of the witnessing experience. *Journal of Applied Psychology, 83, 360–376;* Wells, G. L., Olson, E. A., & Charman, S. D. (2003). Distorted retrospective eyewitness reports as functions of feedback and delay. *Journal of Experimental Psychology: Applied, 9, 42–52.*

163. Likewise, simulated investigators rated a facial composite image to be more similar to the suspect when told that he had been identified by eyewitnesses. Lower similarity ratings were given when the investigators were told that the witnesses had not identified the suspect and when they were given no information about the witnesses' identification. In reality, the facial composite was not based at all on the suspect. Charman, S. D., Gregory, A. H., & Carlucci, M. (2009). Exploring the diagnostic utility of facial composites: Beliefs of guilt can bias perceived similarity between composite and suspect. *Journal of Experimental Psychology: Applied, 15, 76–90.*

164. Elaad, E., Ginton, A., & Ben-Shakhar, G. (1994). The effects of prior expectations and outcome knowledge on polygraph examiners' decisions. *Journal of Behavioral Decision Making, 7, 279–292.*

165. Unbeknownst to the participants, they had previously analyzed those very prints in a real-life case. The results showed that almost half of the experts were misled by the information, reaching conclusions that were opposite to their own prior judgments. Of the twelve relevant cases (where the matches were not easy, and where incorrect information was suggested), three judgments were reversed. Notably, experts reversed their previous findings also in two of the twelve difficult cases that contained no extraneous information. Dror & Charlton (2006), *supra* note 53.

166. Bruner, J. S., Goodnow, J. J., & Austin, G. A. (1956). *A study of thinking*. New York: Wiley. The positive test strategies was intuited also by Francis Bacon: "it is the peculiar and perpetual error of the human intellect to be more moved and excited by affirmatives than be negatives" (Bacon, F. [1844]. *Novum organum or true suggestions for the interpretation of nature*, p. 21. London: William Pickering).

167. A similar strategy, the *hypothesis-preservation strategy*, involves asking questions that are likely to lead to the conclusion that the working hypothesis is true. For reviews, see Klayman, J., & Ha, Y. W. (1987). Confirmation, disconfirmation, and information hypothesis testing. *Psychological Review, 94,* 211–228; Nickerson (1998), *supra* note 26.

168. Wason, P. C., & Johnson-Laird, P. N. (1972). *Psychology of reasoning: Structure and content*. Cambridge, MA: Harvard University Press.

169. Klayman (1995), *supra note* 26, p. 399. According to Jonathan Baron, the phenomenon can be described in the following terms: "To test a hypothesis, think of a result that would be found if the hypothesis were true and then look for that result (and do not worry about other hypotheses that might yield the same result)." Baron has labeled this the *congruence heuristic*. Baron, J. (2000). *Thinking and deciding*, p. 162. New York: Cambridge University Press.

The research has identified two information-gathering strategies that people use when testing hypotheses in making social judgments: a *diagnostic strategy* asks questions whose answers permit the greatest distinction between the focal hypothesis and its alternatives. A *confirmation strategy* tends to rely on questions that confirm the hypothesis without much regard to their diagnosticity. Skov, R. B., & Sherman, S. J. (1986). Information-gathering processes: Diagnosticity, hypothesis-confirmatory strategies, and perceived hypothesis confirmation. *Journal of Experimental Social Psychology, 22,* 93–121.

170. Snyder, M., & Swann, W. B. (1978). Hypothesis testing processes in social interaction. *Journal of Personality and Social Psychology, 36,* 1202–1212.

171. Kassin, S. M., Goldstein, C. C., & Savitsky, K. (2003). Behavioral confirmation in the interrogation room: On the dangers of presuming guilt. *Law and Human Behavior, 27,* 187–203.

172. Selective exposure was one of the central themes in Leon Festinger's cognitive dissonance theory. Festinger (1957), *supra* note 112, chaps. 6, 7. See

also Frey, D. (1986). Recent research on selective exposure to information. In L. Berkowitz, ed., *Advances in experimental social psychology,* vol. 19, pp. 41–80. New York: Academic Press; Snyder & Swann (1978), *supra* note 170; Jonas, E., Schulz-Hardt, S., Frey, D., & Thelen, N. (2001). Confirmation bias in sequential information search after preliminary decisions: An expansion of dissonance theoretical research on selective exposure to information. *Journal of Personality and Social Psychology, 80,* 557–571.

173. Selective exposure was observed also during the Senate's Watergate hearings of 1973, which were followed more by supporters of the Democratic Party than by Republicans. Sweeney, P. D., & Gruber, K. L. (1984). Selective exposure: Voter information preferences and the Watergate affair. *Journal of Personality and Social Psychology, 46,* 1208–1221.

174. Ehrlich, D., Guttman, I., Schönbach, P., & Mills, J. (1957). Postdecision exposure to relevant information. *Journal of Abnormal and Social Psychology, 54,* 98–102.

175. Holton, B., & Pyszczynski, T. (1989). Biased information search in the interpersonal domain. *Personality and Social Psychology Bulletin, 15,* 42–51.

176. Fischer, P., Jonas, E., Frey, D., & Schulz-Hardt, S. (2005). Selective exposure to information: The impact of information limits. *European Journal of Social Psychology, 35,* 469–492.

177. Kunda, Z. & Sinclair, L. (1999). Motivated reasoning with stereotypes: Activation, application, and inhibition. *Psychological Inquiry, 10,* 12–22.

178. A study of lay people's judgments of judicial decisions found that when the participants agree with the outcome of the court's decision, they are indifferent to the type of reasoning offered by the court. When they disagree with the outcome, they react differently to different modes of reasoning. Simon, D., & Scurich, N. (2011). Lay judgments of judicial decision making. *Journal of Empirical Legal Studies, 8,* 709–727.

179. Edwards & Smith (1996), *supra* note 29. Similar findings were made by political scientists Taber, C. S., & Lodge, M. (2006). Motivated skepticism in the evaluation of political beliefs. *American Journal of Political Science, 50,* 755–769.

180. Wyer & Frey (1983), *supra* note 59. For similar findings, see Pyszczynski, T., Greenberg, J., & Holt, K. (1985). Maintaining consistency between self-serving beliefs and available data: A bias in information evaluation. *Personality and Social Psychology Bulletin, 11,* 179–190.

181. Ditto et al. (2003), *supra* note 58.

182. The small but indisputable flaw was noticed by 71 percent of the reviewers who disagreed with the study's results, but by only 25 percent of the reviewers who agreed with them. Mahoney (1977), *supra* note 31.

183. This mechanism is also labeled *biased assimilation;* Lord, Ross, & Lepper (1979), *supra* note 49.

184. Duncan, B. L. (1976). Differential social perception and attribution of intergroup violence: Testing the lower limits of stereotyping of blacks. *Journal of Personality and Social Psychology, 34,* 590–598; Cohen (1981), *supra* note 35.

185. Munro et al. (2002), *supra* note 60.

186. Hastorf & Cantril (1954), *supra* note 61.

187. Brownstein, Read, & Simon (2004), *supra* note 63.

188. Dror, Charlton, & Péron (2006), *supra* note 46; Dror & Charlton (2006), *supra* note 53.

189. Shaklee, H., & Fischhoff, B. (1982). Strategies of information search in causal analysis. *Memory & Cognition, 10,* 520–530; Saad, G., & Russo, J. E. (1996). Stopping criteria in sequential choice. *Organizational Behavior and Human Decision Processes, 67,* 258–270.

190. Ditto, P. H., & Lopez, D. F. (1992). Motivated skepticism: Use of differential decision criteria for preferred and nonpreferred conclusions. *Journal of Personality and Social Psychology, 63,* 568–584.

191. McGonigle, S., & and Emily, J. (2008). A blind faith in eyewitnesses: 18 of 19 local cases overturned by DNA relied heavily on unreliable testimony. *Dallas Morning News,* October 12, p. 1A.

192. For reviews, see Lerner, J. S., & Tetlock, P. E. (1999). Accounting for the effects of accountability. *Psychological Bulletin, 125,* 255–275; Tetlock, P. E. (2002). Social functionalist frameworks for judgment and choice: Intuitive politicians, theologians, and prosecutors. *Psychological Review, 109,* 451–471.

193. Tetlock, P. E., & Boettger, R. (1989). Accountability: A social magnifier of the dilution effect. *Journal of Personality and Social Psychology, 57,* 388–398; Lerner & Tetlock (1999), *supra* note 192; Simonson & Nye (1992), *supra* note 121.

194. Wogalter, M. S., Malpass, R. S., & Mcquiston, D. E. (2004). A national survey of police on preparation and conduct of identification lineups. *Psychology, Crime & Law, 10,* 69–82.

195. In jurisdictions that have recently undergone a reform of identification procedures, 23 percent of officers videotape the procedures. Wise, R. A., Safer, M. A., & Maro, C. M. (2011). What U.S. law enforcement officers know and believe about eyewitness interviews and identification procedures. *Applied Cognitive Psychology, 25,* 488–500.

196. Incomplete records were mentioned in *Coleman v. Alabama,* 399 U.S. 1 (1970); *Gilbert v. California,* 388 U.S. 263 (1967); *Neil v. Biggers,* 409 U.S. 188 (1972); *Simmons v. United States,* 390 U.S. 377 (1968); *Stovall v. Denno,* 388 U.S. 263 (1967); and *United States v. Ash,* 413 U.S. 300 (1973).

197. Warren, A. R., & Woodall, C. E. (1999). The reliability of hearsay testimony: How well do interviewers recall their interviews with children? *Psychology, Public Policy, and Law, 5,* 355–371. The latter finding was observed also in a study in which mothers were asked about a conversation they had had some days earlier with their children. Only one of every six questions asked was recalled.

Bruck, M., Ceci, S. J., & Francoeur, E. (1999). The accuracy of mothers' memories of conversations with their preschool children. *Journal of Experimental Psychology: Applied, 5,* 89–106.

198. This study compared the notes taken with audio-tape recordings of the interviews. Lamb, M. E., Orbach, Y., Sternberg, K. J., Hershkowitz, I., & Horowitz, D. (2000). Accuracy of investigators' verbatim notes of their forensic interviews with alleged child abuse victims. *Law and Human Behavior, 24,* 699–708.

199. Gregory, A. H., Schreiber-Compo, N., Vertefeuille, L., & Zambrusky, G. (2011). A comparison of US police interviewers' notes with their subsequent reports. *Journal of Investigative Psychology and Offender Profiling, 8,* 203–215.

200. Moreover, under certain circumstances, accountability can actually increase bias. The construct's darker side appears when conformity, rather than preemptive self-criticism, is deemed the better way to gain the intended audience's approval. For example, when asked to explain their positions on issues such as affirmative action, university tuition increases, and nuclear armament, participants expressed more liberal views to the liberal audience and more conservative views to the conservative audience. Tetlock, P. E., Skitka, L., & Boettger, R. (1989). Social and cognitive strategies for coping with accountability: Conformity, complexity, and bolstering. *Journal of Personality and Social Psychology, 57,* 632–640. A criminal investigator wanting to curry favor with a heavy-handed superior or an overambitious prosecutor will be more likely to reach conclusions that comport with those preferences.

201. The FBI report: Stacey, R. B. (2004). A report on the erroneous fingerprint individualization in the Madrid train bombing case. *Journal of Forensic Identification, 54,* 706. The DOJ report: Department of Justice, Office of the Inspector General of the Oversight and Review Division (2006a). *A review of the FBI's handling of the Brandon Mayfield case, Executive Summary.* Washington, DC. http://www.usdoj.gov/oig/special/s0601/exec.pdf.

202. E.g., *United States v. Llera Plaza,* 188 F. Supp. 2d 549 (E. D. Pa. 2002). See Cole (2005), *supra* note 55.

203. The official reports of the Mayfield investigation conclude that the error was not driven by Mayfield's religion. Department of Justice (2006a), *supra* note 201, p. 18. Yet it seems inconceivable that investigators would have overlooked the fact that this former military man had embraced Islam and maintained contacts with suspected and convicted terrorists. One of the examiners admitted that if the person identified had been someone without Islamic characteristics, like the "Maytag Repairman," the laboratory might have treated the identification with greater skepticism. Ibid., p. 12.

204. Kershaw, S. (2004). Spain and U.S. at odds on mistaken terror arrest. *New York Times,* June 5, p. A1. http://www.nytimes.com/2004/06/05/us/spain-and-us-at-odds-on-mistaken-terror-arrest.html?scp=1&sq=kershaw%20sarah%20spain%20us%20at%20odds&st=cse.

205. Ibid.

206. Stacey (2004), *supra* note 201.

207. Ibid. The DOJ report found no evidence that the investigators were influenced by high profile nature of the case. Department of Justice (2006a), *supra* note 201, p. 11.

208. Department of Justice (2006a), *supra* note 201, p. 8.

209. "Level 3" details include tiny individual pores, incipient dots between ridges, ridge edges, and small between-ridge details. These details are controversial because they are small, and their appearance is highly variable, even between different prints made by the same finger. Ibid.

210. Ibid.

211. The examiners explained away the apparent mismatch of this region on the basis of a "double touch" theory, an explanation that was flatly rejected by the experts advising the inquiries. Ibid., p. 9.

212. Ibid., p. 8.

213. Ibid., p. 12.

214. Ibid., p. 7.

215. Stacey (2004), *supra* note 201.

216. Department of Justice (2006a), *supra* note 201, p. 10.

217. "Points," or "minutiae," are places where the individual ridges in the fingerprint end or split.

218. Kershaw (2004), *supra* note 204.

219. Ibid., quoting Mr. Corrales.

220. Department of Justice (2006a), *supra* note 201, p. 11.

221. Kershaw (2004), *supra* note 204. The judge stated: "I have no affidavit from any Spanish authorities as to questioning the fingerprint. The only information I have is that after consulting with the FBI, that they agreed with the 100 percent identification." Cited in Department of Justice, Office of the Inspector General of the Oversight and Review Division (2006b). *A review of the FBI's handling of the Brandon Mayfield case,* p. 80. Washington, DC. http://www.justice.gov/oig/special/s0601/Chapter2.pdf) The DOJ report described the inaccuracies in the affidavits as a "regrettable inattention to detail" (ibid., p. 268). The conduct of the attorneys was outside the purview of the DOJ inquiry.

222. Kershaw (2004), *supra* note 204.

223. Ibid.

224. See, e.g., De Bono, E. (1968). *New think: The use of lateral thinking in the generation of new ideas.* New York: Basic Books.

225. Detectives are encouraged to continually challenge the meaning and reliability of any material they gather. National Centre for Police Excellence (2005). *Practice advice on core investigative doctrine,* p. 62. Cambourne, UK: Association of Chief Police Officers. The English statute governing police investigations

(PACE) requires that all reasonable inquiries, both indicating and challenging the responsibility of the suspect, ought to be undertaken and recorded.

226. Canadian courts have ordered police officers to take into account "all the information available." Officers are entitled to disregard evidence only if they find it to be unreliable. *Dix v. AG Canada,* 2002, para. 357.

227. Lord, C. G., Lepper, M. R., & Preston, E. (1984). Considering the opposite: A corrective strategy for social judgment. *Journal of Personality and Social Psychology, 47,* 1231–1243; Mussweiler, T., Strack, F., & Pfeiffer, T. (2000). Overcoming the inevitable anchoring effect: Considering the opposite compensates for selective accessibility. *Personality and Social Psychology Bulletin, 26,* 1142–1150. Some research indicates that debiasing can occur when one considers any other hypothesis, not only the opposite one. Hirt & Markman (1995), *supra* note 33.

228. Arkes, H. R. (1991). Costs and benefits of judgment errors: Implications for debiasing. *Psychological Bulletin, 110,* 486–498. See also Mussweiler, Strack, & Pfeiffer (2000), *supra* note 227.

229. For example, although the intervention succeeded in reducing students' beliefs in a random scenario they were asked to explain (the victory of a team in a random sporting event), it was unsuccessful in debiasing their beliefs when their motivation was implicated in the outcome (a victory of their own team). Markman & Hirt (2002), *supra* note 19, study 1.

230. See, e.g., Sanna, L. J., Schwarz, N., & Stocker, S. L. (2002). When debiasing backfires: Accessible content and accessibility experiences in debiasing hindsight. *Journal of Experimental Psychology: Learning, Memory, and Cognition, 28,* 497–502; Hirt & Markman (1995), *supra* note 33, study 3.

231. A similar intervention involves designating a *devil's advocate,* which assigns the responsibility to lodge a critique of the focal hypothesis, without necessarily offering a countertheory.

232. For a review of the literature and a meta-analysis, see Schwenk, C. R. (1990). Effects of devil's advocacy and dialectical inquiry on decision making: A meta-analysis. *Organizational Behavior and Human Decision Processes, 47,* 161–176.

233. Greitemeyer, Schulz-Hardt, & Frey (2009), *supra* note 126; Nemeth, C., Brown, K., & Rogers, J. (2001). Devil's advocate versus authentic dissent: Stimulating quantity and quality. *European Journal of Social Psychology, 31,* 707–720. See also Gunia, B. C., Sivanathan, N., & Galinsky, A. D. (2009). Vicarious entrapment: Your sunk costs, my escalation of commitment. *Journal of Experimental Social Psychology, 45,* 1238–1244.

234. Kerstholt & Eikelbloom (2007), *supra* note 45.

235. As observed by Jacqueline Hodgson, the investigative magistrates *(juges d'instruction)* often tend to verify the evidence that was gathered by the police before being appointed to the case. Hodgson, J. (2005). *French criminal justice:*

A comparative account of the investigation and prosecution of crime in France, p. 247. Oxford: Hart Publishing.

236. Schachter (1951), *supra* note 130; Nemeth, Brown, & Rogers (2001), *supra* note 233.

237. Nemeth, C. J., Connell, J. B., Rogers, J. D., & Brown, K. S. (2001). Improving decision making by means of dissent. *Journal of Applied Social Psychology, 31,* 48–58; Nemeth, Brown, & Rogers (2001), *supra* note 233.

238. See http://www.dallasda.com/. Tellingly, the front page of the Summer 2011 issue of the newsletter of Watkins's office, *The Justice Report,* carries the story of an exoneration of a man convicted for aggravated rape by the office in 1984: http://dallascounty.org/department/da/media/Summer2011.pdf.

239. The high rate of exonerations is made possible by the fact that Dallas County has traditionally kept evidence from closed cases, which has enabled the presentation of compelling evidence for post-conviction review, at least in some cases.

240. On innocence commissions, see Chapter 8.

241. As noted in Chapter 1, Lloyd Weinreb proposed the establishment of an "investigating magistracy" (Weinreb [1977], *supra* note 54, p. 119). George Thomas proposed that criminal investigations and pretrial procedures be overseen by a "screening magistrate": Thomas, G. C. III (2008). *The supreme court on trial: How the American justice system sacrifices innocent defendants,* pp. 193–227. Ann Arbor: University of Michigan Press. Keith Findley has suggested a system that blends the strengths of the adversarial and inquisitorial systems: Findley, K. A. (in press). Adversarial inquisitions: Rethinking the search for the truth. *New York Law Review.*

242. See Kassin, S. M. (1998). Eyewitness identification procedures: The fifth rule. *Law and Human Behavior, 22,* 649–653.

243. The well-known RAND study of police investigations found that many investigative records are incomplete and casually maintained. Police files covered between 26 percent and 45 percent of the evidentiary questions considered essential by prosecutors. The authors posited that poor recordkeeping results in higher case dismissal rates and weakening of the prosecutors' plea-bargaining position. Greenwood, P. W., Chaiken, J. M., Petersilia, J., & Prusoff, L. L. (1975). *The criminal investigation process, Part III.* Santa Monica, CA: RAND. Likewise, experienced Canadian police officers concede that their note-taking habits result in case dismissals. Yuille, J. C. (1984). Research and teaching with police: A Canadian example. *International Review of Applied Psychology, 33,* 5–23.

3. "Officer, That's Him!"

1. Of the tellers shown a photospread that contained the photo of the suspect, 48 percent identified him correctly and 52 percent either identified an

innocent filler or stated incorrectly that the suspect was not in the lineup. Of those shown a photospread that contained only photos of innocent fillers, 63 percent stated correctly that the target was not present. Pigott, M. A., Brigham, J. C., & Bothwell, R. K. (1990). A field study on the relationship between quality of eyewitnesses' descriptions and identification accuracy. *Journal of Police Science and Administration, 17,* 84–88.

2. Goldstein, A. G., Chance, J. E., & Schneller, G. R. (1989). Frequency of eyewitness identification in criminal cases: A survey of prosecutors. *Bulletin of the Psychonomic Society, 27,* 71–74.

3. Identifications can also be based on clothing, jewelry, gait, physical features, voice, and the like.

4. Cutler, B. L., & Penrod, S. D. (1995). *Mistaken identification: The eyewitness, psychology, and the law.* New York: Cambridge University Press.

5. Cases reviewed by Valentine and colleagues, covering 640 witnesses who participated in 314 identification procedures, found rates of 41 percent identifications of the suspect, 39 percent no-choice decisions, and 21 percent foil identifications. See Valentine, T., Pickering, A., & Darling, S. (2003). Characteristics of eyewitness identification that predict the outcome of real lineups. *Applied Cognitive Psychology, 17,* 969–993. Wright and McDaid examined identifications involving 1,569 witnesses in 623 identification procedures, and found corresponding rates of 39 percent, 41 percent, and 20 percent. Wright, D. B., & McDaid, A. T. (1996). Comparing system and estimator variables using data from real line-ups. *Applied Cognitive Psychology, 10,* 75–84. A smaller data set of 134 identification procedures revealed marginally better rates of correct identifications, but similar rates of identification of innocent foils (58 percent, 21 percent, and 21 percent). See Wright, D. B., & Skagerberg, E. M. (2007). Postidentification feedback affects real eyewitnesses. *Psychological Science, 18,* 172–178.

6. These data are taken only from the live lineups, of which there were fifty-eight in this study. Unfortunately, in showups and photo lineups, police records do not distinguish between no-choices and identifications of innocent fillers, so it is impossible to discern the exact ratio of false identifications. In total, this study covered 271 cases, involving 374 perpetrators and 623 identification procedures. Behrman, B. W., & Davey, S. L. (2001). Eyewitness identification in actual criminal cases: An archival analysis. *Law and Human Behavior, 25,* 475–491.

The true rate of accuracy in real-world cases is likely to be lower than the archival data would indicate. Given that police investigators do not always know with certainty who the perpetrator is (the "ground truth"), picking out the police's suspect does not mean that the identification is necessarily correct. Knowledge of ground truth is one of the distinct advantages of laboratory research.

7. Clark, S. E., Howell, R. T., & Davey, S. L. (2008). Regularities in eyewitness identification. *Law and Human Behavior, 32,* 198–218.

8. The other half (52 percent) indicate correctly that the target is not present, or respond "don't know" (ibid.). As discussed later, high rates of false choices can be obtained in target-absent lineups, using simultaneous designs with "biased" instructions. The share of foil choices in target-absent lineups can reach as high as 95 percent. See, e.g., Wells, G. L., & Bradfield, A. L. (1998). "Good, you identified the suspect": Feedback to eyewitnesses distorts their reports of the witnessing experience. *Journal of Applied Psychology, 83,* 360–376; Brewer, N., & Wells, G. L. (2006). The confidence-accuracy relationship in eyewitness identification: Effects of lineup instructions, foil similarity, and target-absent base rates. *Journal of Experimental Psychology: Applied, 12,* 11–30.

9. In the laboratory experiments, the share of correct choosers (46 percent) out of all choosers (a total of 69 percent) amounts to two-thirds of the choosers. The accuracy rate in the available naturalistic data is 69 percent; the share of correct choosers (45 percent) out of all choosers (65 percent).

In reality, the risk to innocent people is lower than the ratio of false picks because not every mistaken choice at the lineup poses a risk of implicating an innocent person. Typically, the police have a particular suspect in mind, and all the fillers are supposed to be beyond suspicion. Thus, a choice of any person other than the target should cast a doubt over the witness's memory without imposing any risk to the chosen filler. Still, the odds are that one in five mistaken fillers will be the suspect, and that places him in a precarious situation. These odds pertain to lineups that follow best-practice procedures and are conducted under ideal conditions. As discussed throughout this chapter, numerous features of real-life lineups can induce the witness to pick out the person suspected by the police and thus increase the odds of a false conviction.

10. Of the 46 percent who pick the target correctly in the target-present lineups, 19 percent reject the lineup when he is absent and 27 percent pick innocent fillers. These data are taken from the analysis of ninety-four studies summarized in Clark, Howell, & Davey (2008), *supra* note 7 (table 2). This finding has been labeled the *target-to-foils shift*. A stricter measure of this phenomenon is provided by a small set of studies that compares target-present lineups with identical target-absent lineups that do not replace the absent target with an additional foil (the *removal without replacement* experimental design). These studies find that four-fifths of the equivalent number of people who correctly identify the target when he is present pick an innocent foil when he is not there. In three studies with a total of almost 400 participants, 44 percent of the participants in the target-present lineup correctly picked the target. In the target-absent lineups, only one-fifth of the equivalent 44 percent declined to choose anyone, as they should have, whereas four-fifths picked an innocent foil. These data come from a study reported in Wells, G. L. (1993). What do we know about eyewitness identification? *American Psychologist, 48,* 561; and Clark, S. E., & Davey, S. L. (2005). The target-to-foils shift in simultaneous and sequential lineups.

Law and Human Behavior, 29, 151–172. More troubling findings were obtained in a study that used computer-generated images of faces: 100 percent of the witnesses in the target-absent lineups picked innocent foils. Flowe, H. D., & Ebbesen, E. B. (2007). The effect of lineup member similarity on recognition accuracy in simultaneous and sequential lineups. *Law and Human Behavior, 31,* 33–52. All data are reported for simultaneous lineups only, which is the most prevalent kind of lineup conducted in the United States today.

11. See Wallace, D. B., & Penrod, S. D. (in progress). The decomposition and recomposition of eyewitness identifications: Eyewitness reliability, guessing and lineup bias; and Penrod, S. D. (2003). Eyewitness identification evidence: How well are witnesses and police performing? *Criminal Justice Magazine,* Spring, 36–47, 54. I thank Steven Penrod and Steven Clark for helpful discussions of these matters.

12. Edwin Borchard found that twenty-nine of sixty-five mistaken convictions involved a false identification. Borchard, E. M. (1932). *Convicting the innocent.* Garden City, NY: Garden City Publishing. See also Frank, J., & Frank, B. (1957). *Not guilty.* Garden City, NY: Doubleday; Gross, S. R. (1987). Loss of innocence: Eyewitness identification and proof of guilt. *Journal of Legal Studies, 16,* 395–453.

13. Gross, S. R., Jacoby, K., Matheson, D. J., Montgomery, N., & Patil, S. (2005). Exonerations in the United States 1989 through 2003. *Journal of Criminal Law & Criminology, 95,* 523–560; Garrett, B. L. (2011). *Convicting the innocent: Where criminal prosecutions go wrong.* Cambridge, MA: Harvard University Press; Innocence Project (2010). 250 exonerated, too many wrongfully convicted. http://www.innocenceproject.org/news/250.php. The heavy contribution of misidentifications to the DNA exoneration cases is due to the fact that most DNA exonerations are for crimes of rape, which typically rely on biological evidence.

14. Brown, S. C., & Craik, F. I. M. (2000). Encoding and retrieval of information. In E. Tulving & F. I. M. Craik, eds., *The Oxford handbook of memory,* pp. 93–107. New York: Oxford University Press.

15. For an evolutionary explanation of human memory, see Nairne, J. S., & Pandeirada, J. N (2008). Adaptive memory: Remembering with a Stone-Age brain. *Current Directions in Psychological Science, 17,* 239–243.

16. See Hasel, L. E., & Kassin, S. M. (2009). On the presumption of evidentiary independence: Can confessions corrupt eyewitness identifications? *Psychological Science, 20,* 122–126; and Smith, A. K., & Hasel, L. A. (2011). "I must have been mistaken": How information about an alibi can corrupt eyewitness identification decisions. Paper presented at the annual meeting of the American Psychology-Law Society, Miami, FL, March 3–6.

17. A good way to demonstrate the phenomenon is to present your participants a clip that contains a target person, and ask them to pick him out from a

lineup. For a publically available set of materials, see http://www.psychology .iastate.edu/~glwells/theeyewitnesstest.html. Given that this test is a target-absent lineup, all choices are necessarily incorrect.

18. Davis, D., Loftus, E. F., Vanous, S., & Cucciare, M. (2008). "Unconscious transference" can be an instance of "change blindness." *Applied Cognitive Psychology, 22,* 605–623.

19. Trial transcript, *State v. Cotton,* No. 257A85 (Alamance Co. Super. Ct., January 7, 1985), pp. 108–109.

20. Ibid., pp. 89, 343.

21. Lindsay, D. S., Read D. J., & Sharma K. (1998). Accuracy and confidence in person identification: The relationship is strong when witnessing conditions vary widely. *Psychological Science, 9,* 215–218.

22. Wells, G. (1978). Applied eyewitness-testimony research: System variables and estimator variables. *Journal of Personality and Social Psychology, 36,* 1546–1557. Wells's typology distinguished between "system variables" and "estimator variables." The category *incident factors* used here overlaps to a large degree with Wells's estimation variables, but it focuses more on their psychological effects and places less emphasis on their potential to assist in estimating the accuracy of identifications ex post facto.

23. For example, the contaminating effect of exposure to visual stimuli was found to be stronger when it was presented seven days after the original events as compared to just twenty minutes later. Jenkins, F., & Davies, G. (1985). Contamination of facial memory through exposure to misleading composite pictures. *Journal of Applied Psychology, 70,* 164–176.

24. Schacter, D. L. (1996). *The seven sins of memory: How the mind forgets and remembers.* New York: Houghton Mifflin, chap. 4; Mitchell, K. J., & Johnson, M. K. (2000). Source monitoring: Attributing mental experiences. In E. Tulving & F. I. M. Craik, eds., *The Oxford handbook of memory,* pp. 179–195. New York: Oxford University Press.

25. Megreya, A. M., & Burton, A. M. (2008). Matching faces to photographs: Poor performance in eyewitness memory (without the memory). *Journal of Experimental Psychology: Applied, 14(4),* 364–372.

26. Before the conversation, the pedestrians had a clear view of the confederate as they walked toward each other from a distance of about 20 meters. In these studies, which lasted 2–5 minutes, the two confederates wore different clothing, differed in height by 5 centimeters, and their voices were clearly distinguishable. Simons, D. J., & Levin, D. T. (1998). Failure to detect changes to people during a real-world interaction. *Psychonomic Bulletin & Review, 5,* 644–649. Video scenes from this experiment can be found on the first author's webpage at http://viscog.beckman.uiuc.edu/djs_lab/demos.html.

27. In this study, three-quarters of participants failed to detect the change, even though the two confederates had a different color and style of hair, distinct

facial features, and different voices. Levin, D. T., Simons, D. J., Angelone, B. L., & Chabris, C. F. (2002). Memory for centrally attended changing objects in an incidental real-world change detection paradigm. *British Journal of Psychology, 93,* 289–302. Low detection rates were found in studies in which actors were switched between two scenes of a video clip. In eight different video clips, the actors were substituted between scenes with other actors who wore different clothes and had noticeable other differences, such as different hair styles. Across the eight studies, only one-third of participants noticed the changes. Simons, D. J., & Levin, D. T. (1997). Change blindness. *Trends in Cognitive Sciences, 1,* 261–267.

28. Davis et al. (2008), *supra* note 18.

29. Johansson, P., Hall, L., Sikström, S., & Olsson, A. (2005). Failure to detect mismatches between intention and outcome in a simple decision task. *Science, 310,* 116–119.

30. Nisbett, R. E., & Wilson, T. D. (1977). Telling more than we can know: Verbal reports on mental processes. *Psychological Review, 84,* 231–259.

31. Wagenaar, W. A., & Van der Schrier J. H. (1996). Face recognition as a function of distance and illumination: A practical tool for use in the courtroom. *Psychology, Crime & Law, 2,* 321–332; De Jong, M., Wagenaar, W. A., Wolters, G., & Verstijnen, I. M. (2005). Familiar face recognition as a function of distance and illumination: A practical tool for use in the courtroom. *Psychology, Crime & Law, 2,* 87–97.

32. This field study did not find the pronounced change at the 15 meter range. Lindsay, R. C. L., Semmler, C., Weber, N., Brewer, N., & Lindsay, M. R. (2008). How variations in distance affect eyewitness reports and identification accuracy. *Law and Human Behavior, 32(6),* 526–535.

33. Trial transcript, *supra* note 19, p. 155.

34. Radvansky, G. A., Carlson-Radvansky, L. A., & Irwin, D. E. (1995). Uncertainty in estimating distances from memory. *Memory & Cognition, 23,* 596–606; Wiest, W. M., & Bell, B. (1985). Stevens's exponent for psychophysical scaling of perceived, remembered, and inferred distance. *Psychological Bulletin, 98,* 457–470.

35. Lindsay et al. (2008), *supra* note 32.

36. See Wells, G. L., & Quinlivan, D. S. (2009). Suggestive eyewitness identification procedures and the Supreme Court's reliability test in light of eyewitness science: 30 years later. *Law and Human Behavior, 33,* 1–24.

37. In this study, 95 percent of participants who were shown a video clip that contained a clear exposure of the perpetrator for forty-five seconds identified the perpetrator correctly, whereas the rate was only 29 percent for those who were shown a clip containing twelve seconds of clear exposure. In target-absent lineups, as many as 41 percent of those who watched the long clip and 90 percent of those who watched the short clip picked a filler. Memon, A., Hope, L., &

Bull, R. (2003). Exposure duration: Effects on eyewitness accuracy and confidence. *British Journal of Psychology, 94,* 339–354.

Lindsay, Read, & Sharma (1998), *supra* note 21, found that reducing the duration from three minutes to ten seconds cut the overall level of identification accuracy by almost half (from 86 percent to 44 percent).

38. Cutler, B. L., Penrod, S. D., & Martens, T. K. (1987). The reliability of eyewitness identification: The role of system and estimator variables. *Law and Human Behavior, 11,* 233–258.

39. Loftus, E. E., Schooler, J. W., Boone, S. M., & Kline, D. (1987). Time went by so slowly: Overestimation of event duration by males and females. *Applied Cognitive Psychology, 1,* 3–13.

40. Shorter time estimates (sixty-seven seconds on average) were recorded when the tellers were asked to assess the duration of the interaction by timing their mental reconstruction of the event with a stopwatch. Pigott, Brigham, & Bothwell (1990), *supra* note 1. See also Pedersen, A. C. I., & Wright, D. B. (2002). Do differences in event descriptions cause different duration estimates? *Applied Cognitive Psychology, 16,* 769–783.

41. For a meta-analysis, see Deffenbacher, K. A., Bornstein, B. H., Penrod, S. D., & McGorty, E. K. (2004). A meta-analytic review of the effects of high stress on eyewitness memory. *Law and Human Behavior, 28,* 687–706.

42. This program prepares soldiers from elite combat units for the experiences of captivity and torture. The study revealed 68 percent overall correct identifications in the low-stress interrogations and 32 percent in the high-stress condition. The rate of choosing innocent foils was 30 percent and 59 percent, respectively. Morgan, C. A., III, Hazlett, G., Doran, A., Garrett, S., Hoyt, G., Thomas, P., Baranoski, M., & Southwick, S. M. (2004). Accuracy of eyewitness memory for persons encountered during exposure to highly intense stress. *International Journal of Law and Psychiatry, 27,* 265–279.

43. The Horror Labyrinth is a maze that is designed to create a frightening experience for the visitors. This study found that among participants who reported low levels of anxiety, three-quarters correctly identified the target and about 20 percent identified a foil. Among participants who reported high levels of anxiety, fewer than one-fifth identified the target correctly, and just over half identified a foil. Valentine, T., & Mesout, J. (2009). Eyewitness identification under stress in the London Dungeon. *Applied Cognitive Psychology, 23,* 151–161.

44. Peters, D. P. (1988). Eyewitness memory and arousal in a natural setting. In M. M. Gruneberg, P. E. Morris, & R. N. Sykes, eds., *Practical aspects of memory: Current research and issues,* vol. 1, pp. 89–94. Chichester, UK: John Wiley & Sons.

45. Trial transcript, *supra* note 19, p. 241.

46. A meta-analysis revealed that the presence of a weapon had a significant but moderate effect of reducing identification accuracy. A more substantial effect was

found on witnesses' recall for event evidence. See Steblay, N. M. (1992). A meta-analytic review of the weapon focus effect. *Law and Human Behavior, 16,* 413–424. In the study of 640 real-life identifications by the London Metropolitan Police, no significant weapon effect was observed. However, only a fraction of those cases involved guns, which is the habitual weapon of choice in the (mostly American) laboratory studies. Valentine, Pickering, & Darling (2003), *supra* note 5.

47. The distraction appears to be caused by the fact that weapons are both unusual objects and threatening objects. See Hope, L., & Wright, D. (2007). Beyond unusual? Examining the role of attention in the weapon focus effect. *Applied Cognitive Psychology, 21(7),* 951–961.

48. Loftus, E. F., Loftus, G. R., & Messo, J. (1987). Some facts about "weapon focus." *Law and Human Behavior, 11,* 55–62.

49. For some time following the bombing, the FBI conducted a nationwide manhunt for a second person, dubbed John Doe 2. The second perpetrator was described in great detail by two witnesses who worked at the garage where McVeigh picked up the rental truck on the afternoon of April 17, two days before the bombing. A sketch based on the descriptions was shown extensively in the national media, but no such person was ever found, and it is generally believed that he did not exist. The likely explanation of this mystery stems from the fact that one day after McVeigh's visit, two men with no connection to the bombing were seen at the same garage, around the same time of day, as they inspected a van, just as McVeigh had done the day before. One of these men bore a general resemblance to McVeigh. It appears that the witnesses mistakenly associated the second man with McVeigh. Memon, A., & Wright, D. B. (1999). Eyewitness testimony and the Oklahoma bombing. *The Psychologist, 12,* 292–205. For a classical case, see Loftus, E. F. (1979). *Eyewitness testimony.* Cambridge, MA: Harvard University Press, p. 142.

50. Mueller-Johnson, K., & Ceci, S. J. (2004). Memory and suggestibility in older adults: Live event participation and repeated interview. *Applied Cognitive Psychology, 18,* 1109–1127. For another study demonstrating the phenomenon, see Ross, D. F., Ceci, S. J., Dunning, D., & Toglia, M. (1994). Unconscious transference and mistaken identity: When a witness misidentifies a familiar but innocent person. *Journal of Applied Psychology, 79,* 918–930.

51. The bystanders were picked on average by 24 and 30 percent of the witnesses respectively, whereas 13 percent picked other foils. Davis et al. (2008), *supra* note 18.

52. In a field study resembling the bank teller study described above, convenience-store clerks of different ethnicities in El Paso, Texas, were asked to identify confederates of the three ethnicities with whom they previously interacted in the stores. The results manifested a cross-ethnicity bias: rates of accuracy were lower and rates of error higher for targets who were of a different ethnicity from the

clerks. Platz, S. J., & Hosch, H. M. (1988). Cross-racial/ethnic eyewitness identification: A field study. *Journal of Applied Social Psychology, 18,* 972–984.

53. Meissner, C. A., & Brigham, J. C. (2001). Thirty years of investigating the own-race bias in memory for faces: A meta-analytic review. *Psychology, Public Policy, and Law, 7,* 3–35.

54. See Wells, G. L., & Olson, E. A. (2001). The other-race effect in eyewitness identification: What do we do about it? *Psychology, Public Policy, and Law, 7,* 230–246. For an argument supporting social factors, see Doyle, J. M. (2001). Discounting the error costs: Cross-racial false alarms in the culture of contemporary criminal justice. *Psychology, Public Policy, and Law, 7,* 253–262.

55. Wright, D. B., Boyd, C. E., & Tredoux, C. G. (2003). Inter-racial contact and the own-race bias for face recognition in South Africa and England. *Applied Cognitive Psychology, 17(3),* 365–373. White basketball fans were found to be more accurate than nonfans in identifying black men. The likely explanation is that exposure to the mostly black professional basketball players makes fans more sensitive to facial differences in black men. Li, J. C., Dunning, D., & Malpass, R. S. (1998). Cross-racial identification among European-Americans: Basketball fandom and the contact hypothesis. Paper presented at the biennial meeting of the American Psychology-Law Society, Redondo Beach, CA, March.

56. Rhodes, M. G., & Anastasi, J. S. (in press). The own-age bias in face recognition: A meta-analytic and theoretical review. *Psychological Bulletin.*

57. Yarmey, A. D. (1992). Stereotypes and recognition memory for faces and voices of good guys and bad guys. *Applied Cognitive Psychology, 7,* 419–431.

58. Flowe, H. D., & Humphries, J. E. (2011). An examination of criminal face bias in a random sample of police lineups. *Applied Cognitive Psychology, 25,* 265–273. At the same time, faces that resemble stereotypical criminals are recognized more easily, and thus might be remembered better. See MacLin, O. H., & MacLin, M. K. (2004). The effect of criminality on face attractiveness, typicality, memorability and recognition. *North American Journal of Psychology, 6(1),* 145–154.

59. For difficulties in constructing a fair lineup for distinctive-looking people, see Brigham, J. C., Ready, D. J., & Spier, S. A. (1990). Standards for evaluating the fairness of photograph lineups. *Basic and Applied Psychology, 11,* 149–163. See Brigham, J. C., Meissner, C. A., & Wasserman, A. W. (1999). Applied issues in the construction and expert assessment of photo lineups. *Applied Cognitive Psychology, 13,* S73–S92. See also Doob, A. N., & Kirshenbaum, H. M. (1973). Bias in police lineups—Partial remembering. *Journal of Police Science and Administration, 1,* 287–293.

60. Wells, G. L., Charman, S. D., & Olson, E. A. (2005). Building face composites can harm lineup identification performance. *Journal of Experimental Psychology: Applied, 11,* 147–156. Findings of low resemblance have been made only with composites constructed by means of graphic kits and computerized systems. There has not been sufficient testing of composites made by sketch artists.

61. Farah, M. J., Wilson, K. D., Drain, M., & Tanaka, J. N. (1999). What is "special" about face perception? *Psychological Review, 105,* 482–498. See also Wells, Charman, & Olson (2005), *supra* note 60.

62. Of the participants who created the composite, 58 percent made no identification in a subsequent lineup, and 30 percent identified a filler. Of the participants who did not create a composite, 84 percent correctly identified the target, and only 6 percent identified a filler. This research suggests that the decreased performance is caused primarily by the actual construction of the composite, rather than by exposure to the image. Wells, Charman, & Olson (2005), *supra* note 60; Wells, G. L., & Hasel, L. E. (2007). Facial composite production by eyewitnesses. *Current Directions in Psychological Science, 16,* 6–10.

63. Trial transcript, *supra* note 19, p. 324; Interview with Jennifer Thompson, *What Jennifer Saw, Frontline* series, PBS (1997). http://www.pbs.org/wgbh /pages/frontline/shows/dna/interviews/thompson.html.

64. Both images are available on the *Frontline* website: http://www.pbs.org /wgbh/pages/frontline/shows/dna/.

65. Meissner, C. A., Sporer, S. L., & Schooler, J. W. (2007). Person descriptions as eyewitness evidence. In R. C. L. Lindsay, D. F. Ross, J. D. Read, & M. P. Toglia, eds., *Handbook of eyewitness psychology*, vol. 2: *Memory for people*, pp. 3–34. Mahwah, NJ: Lawrence Erlbaum.

66. The study included 2,299 witness descriptions given by 1,313 witnesses of 431 different robberies. van Koppen, P. J., & Lochun, S. K. (1997). Portraying perpetrators: The validity of offender descriptions by witnesses. *Law and Human Behavior, 21,* 661–685. For similar findings from a Swedish archive, see Fahsing, I. A., Ask, K., & Granhag, P. A. (2004). The man behind the mask: Accuracy and predictors of eyewitness offender descriptions. *Journal of Applied Psychology, 89,* 722–729.

67. Pigott, Brigham, & Bothwell (1990), *supra* note 1.

68. For a meta-analysis, see Meissner, C. A., Sporer, S. L., & Susa, K. J. (2008). A theoretical review and meta-analysis of the description-identification relationship in memory for faces. *European Journal of Cognitive Psychology, 20,* 414–455.

69. For example, one study found that the accuracy of identifications was higher (62 percent) when conducted immediately after viewing the target than in lineups conducted on average one month following the viewing (47 percent). Sauer, J., Brewer, N., Zweck, T., & Weber, N. (2010). The effect of retention interval on the confidence-accuracy relationship for eyewitness identification. *Law and Human Behavior, 34(4),* 337–347 (data for choosers only). For a discussion of the relatively rare exceptions, see Chapter 4.

70. Deffenbacher, K. A., Bornstein, B. H., McGorty, E. K., & Penrod, S. D. (2008). Forgetting the once-seen face: Estimating the strength of an eyewitness's memory representation. *Journal of Experimental Psychology: Applied, 14,* 139–

150. The decay function is strongly influenced by the amount of repetition of the memory: memories that are frequently repeated are retained longer. It must also be appreciated that frequent repetition can contribute to contamination of the memory.

71. Valentine, Pickering, & Darling (2003), *supra* note 5.

72. See Behrman & Davey (2001), *supra* note 6.

73. Read, J. D., Vokey, J. R., & Hannersley, R. (1990). Changing photos of faces: Effects of exposure duration and photo similarity on recognition and the accuracy-confidence relationship. *Journal of Experimental Psychology: Learning, Memory, and Cognition, 5,* 870–882.

74. One study found that participants who were shown the same filler in both the mugshot book and the subsequent lineup were more likely to pick him out than are participants who did not initially see him (30 percent vs. 20 percent), and are less likely to identify the perpetrator correctly (59 percent vs. 80 percent). Memon, A., Hope, L., Bartlett, J., & Bull, R. (2002). Eyewitness recognition errors: The effects of mugshot viewing and choosing in young and old adults. *Memory & Cognition, 30,* 1219–1227. Another study found that of the participants who chose a mistaken foil from the mugshot search, only 10 percent went on to choose the true target from the lineup. Of those who picked a wrong person at the lineup, some 70 percent chose the same foil that they had chosen in the mugshot search. Goodsell, C. A., Neuschatz, J. S., & Gronlund, S. D. (2009). Effects of mugshot commitment on lineup performance in young and older adults. *Applied Cognitive Psychology, 23(6),* 788–803. Another study found that only 33 percent of participants who picked someone out in the first procedure (all erroneously, since the culprit was not included) correctly identified the culprit in the subsequent lineup. The success rate was higher (69 percent) for those who were not shown the initial mugshots. Brigham, J. C., & Cairns, D. L. (1988). The effect of mugshot inspections on eyewitness identification accuracy. *Journal of Applied Social Psychology, 18,* 1394–1410. For similar results, see Dysart, J. E., Lindsay, R. C. L., Hammond, R., & Dupuis, P. (2001). Mug shot exposure prior to lineup identification: Interference, transference, and commitment effects. *Journal of Applied Psychology, 86,* 1280–1284; and Hinz, T., & Pezdek, K. (2001). The effect of exposure to multiple lineups on face identification accuracy. *Law and Human Behavior, 25(2),* 185–198.

75. Across studies, the rate of correct identifications following mugshot exposure dropped from 50 percent to 43 percent, whereas the rate of false identifications of innocent fillers climbed from 15 percent to 37 percent. Deffenbacher, K. A., Bornstein, B. H., & Penrod, S. D. (2006). Mugshot exposure effects: Retroactive interference, mugshot commitment, source confusion, and unconscious transference. *Law and Human Behavior, 30,* 287–307.

76. A study by Gorenstein and Ellsworth found that participants who mistakenly chose a filler in a first photo lineup were less likely to choose the perpetrator

from the second lineup, as compared with participants who did not see the first lineup (22 percent vs. 39 percent). Gorenstein, G. W., & Ellsworth, P. C. (1980). Effect of choosing an incorrect photograph on a later identification by an eyewitness. *Journal of Applied Psychology, 65,* 616–622.

77. Valentine, T., Davis, J. P., Memon, A., & Roberts, A. (in press). Live showups and their influence on a subsequent video line-up. *Applied Cognitive Psychology.*

78. Out of the sixty-six successive viewings, the rate of suspect identifications was 45 percent for first-time identifications and 62 percent for the second procedure. As many as 45 percent of the witnesses who failed to identify the suspect on the earlier occasion made a pick at the later procedure. In only 27 percent of the cases, witnesses failed to make an identification in the second procedure after doing so in the first procedure. This latter decrease would have been expected given memory decay over time. Behrman & Davey (2001), *supra* note 6.

79. A large meta-analysis reveals that a stronger memory for faces was reported at a subsequent point in time in only six of the fifty-three studies, and those effects were very weak. Deffenbacher et al. (2008), *supra* note 70.

80. Another possible explanation for the increment is that it is due to increased pressure and suggestion by detectives. Detectives tend to be more strongly motivated to close cases over time.

81. See Deffenbacher, Bornstein, & Penrod (2006), *supra* note 75. For more on the phenomenon of source monitoring, see Chapter 4.

82. In the meta-analysis by Deffenbacher, Bornstein, & Penrod (2006), *supra* note 75, the strongest biasing results were found in cases in which participants were induced to express openly some form of commitment to their prior identifications.

83. In fact lawyers were aware of this kind of bias well before any research was done on the topic. Defense arguments were made, and rejected, in *Simmons v. United States,* 320 U.S. 377 (1968).

84. Interview with Jennifer Thompson, *supra* note 63.

85. Trial transcript, *supra* note 19, p. 110.

86. Interview with Jennifer Thompson, *supra* note 63.

87. As many as 40 percent of witnesses who were exposed to misleading visual information chose a person who matched the erroneous descriptions. Jenkins & Davies (1985), *supra* note 23. Exposure to drawings of faces can cause *memory conjunction,* that is, the blending of features from different images into a single memory. Kroll, N. E. A., Knight, R. T., Metcalfe, J., Wolf, E. S., & Tulving, E. (1996). Cohesion failure as a source of memory illusions. *Journal of Memory and Language, 35,* 176–196.

88. Morgan, C. A., Southwick, S., Steffian, G., Hazlett, G., & Loftus, E. F. (in progress). Misinformation can influence memory for recently experienced, highly stressful events.

89. This suggestion resulted in a fivefold increase in the rate of choices of targets with mustaches. Loftus, E. F., & Greene, E. (1980). Warning: Even memory for faces may be contagious. *Law and Human Behavior, 4,* 323–334, study 2.

90. In a subsequent lineup that contained both the innocent mustache-bearing person and the true perpetrator, almost 90 percent of witnesses picked the former. Ibid.

91. See ibid., study 1 and pilot study, respectively.

92. Weingardt, K. R., Leonesio, R. J., & Loftus, E. F. (1995). Viewing eyewitness research from a metacognitive perspective. In J. Metcalfe & A. P. Shimamura, eds., *Metacognition: Knowing about memory,* pp. 175–184. Cambridge, MA: MIT Press.

93. For example, a survey performed by the Georgia Innocence Project found that 82 percent of Georgia's 355 law enforcement agencies have no written identification procedure standards. Turner, D. (2007). DNA test clears man after 27 years. Associated Press, December 11.

94. In the data from Sacramento County, 42 percent of the recorded procedures were showups (258 of the 615 procedures). Behrman & Davey (2001), *supra* note 6. A rate of 59 percent was reported in the 153 stranger identification procedures included in a sample of rape, robbery, and assault investigations conducted in San Diego County between 1991 and 2000. Flowe, H. D., Mehta, A., & Ebbesen, E. B. (2011). The role of eyewitness identification evidence in felony case dispositions. *Psychology, Public Policy, and Law, 17,* 140–159. A showup rate of 30 percent was reported in El Paso County, Texas. McQuiston, D., & Malpass, R. (2001). Eyewitness identifications in criminal cases: An archival study. Paper presented at the fourth biennial meeting of the Society for Applied Research in Memory and Cognition, Kingston, Ontario, Canada, June. In a sample from a northern California city, 77 percent of identification procedures were showups (172 out of 224). Gonzalez, R., Ellsworth, P. C., & Pembroke, M. (1993). Response biases in lineups and showups. *Journal of Personality and Social Psychology, 64,* 525–537.

95. A survey of lineup administrators in a representative sample of police departments nationwide (220 surveys returned) reveals that 27 percent of the procedures conducted were live, and 73 percent were photographic. Wogalter, M. S., Malpass, R. S., & McQuiston, D. E. (2004). A national survey of U.S. police on preparation and conduct of identification lineups. *Psychology, Crime & Law, 10,* 69–82.

96. The rate of live lineups in the sample of 283 investigations conducted in San Diego County during the years 1991–2000 appears to be between zero and 6 percent. Eighty-nine percent of the procedures were showups or photo arrays. Flowe, Mehta, & Ebbesen (2011), *supra* note 94. Of the 108 Virginia police departments surveyed, some 90 percent used photographic lineups and almost 60 percent used showups, whereas only about one-quarter used live lineups. See Gould, J. B. (2008). *The Innocence Commission: Preventing wrongful convictions and restoring the criminal justice system.* New York: NYU Press, p. 137.

97. A meta-analysis found that showups and lineups yield similar rates of correct identifications (41 and 43 percent, respectively), but showups yield considerably more false identifications (18 vs. 11 percent). Clark, S. E., & Godfrey, R. D. (2009). Eyewitness identification evidence and innocence risk. *Psychonomic Bulletin & Review, 16*, 22–42. For critical views of showups, see Wells, G. L., Small, M., Penrod, S., Malpass, R. S., Fulero, S. M., & Brimacombe, C. A. E. (1998). Eyewitness identification procedures: Recommendations for lineups and photospreads. [Also known as the White Paper]. *Law and Human Behavior, 22*, 603–647; Yarmey, A. D., Yarmey, M. J., & Yarmey, A. L. (1996). Accuracy of eyewitness identification in showups and lineups. *Law and Human Behavior, 20*, 459–477. For a more mixed evaluation, see Dysart, J. E., & Lindsay, R. C. L. (2007). Show-up identifications: Suggestive technique or reliable method? In R. C. L. Lindsay, D. F. Ross, J. D. Read, & M. P. Toglia, eds., *Handbook of eyewitness psychology*, vol. 2: *Memory for people,* pp. 137–153. Mahwah, NJ: Lawrence Erlbaum. Showups yielded relatively favorable results in the experiments by Gonzalez, Ellsworth, & Pembroke (1993), *supra* note 94.

98. The rate of choosing innocent suspects who resembled the perpetrator was 17 percent in lineups and 23 percent in showups. Steblay, N., Dysart, J., Fulero, S., & Lindsay, R. C. L. (2003). Eyewitness accuracy rates in police showup and lineup presentations: A meta-analytic comparison. *Law and Human Behavior, 27(5),* 523–540.

99. See Behrman & Davey (2001), *supra* note 6.

100. The problems with relative judgments were pointed out by Gary Wells. See Wells, G. L. (1984). The psychology of lineup identifications. *Journal of Applied Social Psychology, 14,* 89–103. There is also a concern that the mere comparison of images leads to an accentuation of the differences between them (a spreading apart), which results in a subjective inflation in the resemblance of the chosen image to the memorized perpetrator. See the discussion of the coherence effect in Chapters 2 and 6.

101. Steblay, N. K., Dysart, J. E., & Wells, G. L. (2011). Seventy-two tests of the sequential lineup superiority effect: A meta-analysis and policy discussion. *Psychology, Public Policy, and Law, 17(1),* 99–139 (data from Full Design Dataset, table 3). Clark & Godfrey (2009, *supra* note 97) observe that sequential procedures lead to an overall reduction in false identifications from 17 percent to 10 percent, and in correct identifications from 54 percent to 43 percent. It is possible that the advantages of the sequential procedure are most pronounced in lineups in which the target stands out from the fillers. Clark, Howell, & Davey (2008), *supra* note 7. Evidence supporting this effect has been observed in Carlson, C. A., Gronlund, S. D., & Clark, S. E. (2008). Lineup composition, suspect position, and the sequential lineup advantage. *Journal of Experimental Psychology: Applied, 14,* 118–128. See also McQuiston-Surrett, D., Malpass,

R. S., & Tredoux, C. G. (2006). Sequential vs. simultaneous lineups: A review of methods, data, and theory. *Psychology, Public Policy, and Law, 12,* 137–169.

102. This study, encompassing 497 real-life criminal cases, found that relative to simultaneous procedures, sequential procedures yielded fewer filler choices (12 percent vs. 18 percent) without causing a reduction in suspect choices (27 percent vs. 25.5 percent). These data have not yet been analyzed fully, nor have they been subjected to peer review. Wells, G. L., Steblay, N. K., & Dysart, J. E. (2011). A test of the simultaneous vs. sequential lineup methods: An initial report of the AJS National Eyewitness Identification Field Studies. *American Judicature Society.* http://www.ajs.org/wc/pdfs/EWID_PrintFriendly.pdf. It should be noted that in comparison to field data from the United Kingdom, this study obtained considerably lower rates of suspect identifications and correspondingly high rates of nonidentifications. For more field data supporting the advantages of sequential procedures, see Klobuchar, A., Steblay, N., & Caligiuri, H. (2006). Improving eyewitness identifications: Hennepin County's blind sequential lineup project. *Cardozo Public Law, Policy, and Ethics Journal, 4,* 381–413.

Lineup format was the subject of a field study performed by the Illinois state police, named the Mecklenburg Study. The study was conducted under the supervision of Ebbe Ebbesen, a prominent critic of eyewitness research. This study's findings challenged the superiority of sequential, double-blind procedures. See http://eyewitness.utep.edu/Documents/IllinoisPilotStudyOnEyewitnessID.pdf. The Mecklenburg Study has been widely discredited by a range of researchers, including a panel of prominent experimental psychologists who do not participate in the eyewitness debates. The panel concluded that the study was based on a confounded design that bears "devastating consequences for assessing the real world implications of this particular study." Schacter, D. L., Dawes, R. E., Jacoby, L. J., Kahneman, D., Lempert, R., Roediger, H. L., & Rosenthal, R. E. (2008). Policy forum: Studying eyewitness investigations in the field. *Law and Human Behavior, 32,* 3–5. Notably, the study has been criticized in retrospect also by its technical advisor Roy Malpass, see Ross, S. J., & Malpass, R. S. (2008). Moving forward: Response to "Studying eyewitness investigations in the field." *Law and Human Behavior, 32(1),* 16–21. For a critical review of the methodology used in the study, see Steblay, N. K. (2011). What we know now: The Evanston Illinois field lineups. *Law and Human Behavior, 35(1),* 1–12.

103. Lindsay, R. C. L., & Wells, G. L. (1980). What price justice? Exploring the relationship of lineup fairness to identification accuracy. *Law and Human Behavior, 4,* 303–313.

104. Leippe, M. R., Eisenstadt, D., Rauch, S. M., & Stambush, M. A. (2006). Effects of social-comparative memory feedback on eyewitnesses' identification confidence, suggestibility, and retrospective memory reports. *Basic and Applied Social Psychology, 28,* 201–220.

105. In the United Kingdom the legal requirement is eight or more. See PACE, Code D, Annex (a)2; Annex B(c)9 (1984). http://police.homeoffice.gov.uk/news -and-publications/publication/operational-policing/PACE_Chapter_D.pdf ?view=Binary.

106. For a discussion of the positive value of a certain degree of dissimilarity, or "propitious heterogeneity," see Wells, G. L., & Bradfield, A. L. (1999a). Measuring the goodness of lineups: Parameter estimation, question effects, and limits to the mock witness paradigm. *Applied Cognitive Psychology, 13,* S27–S39.

107. Using fillers who are appreciably dissimilar from the fillers more than doubles the rate of misidentification (49 percent, as compared to 21 percent when the foils are more similar). Clark & Godfrey (2009), *supra* note 97, table 5. At the same time, using dissimilar fillers results in a higher rate of correct identifications (72 percent vs. 62 percent for lineups with more similar fillers). In other words, having the suspect stick out relative to the fillers leads to more false and correct identifications.

108. For discussion of functional lineup size, see Wells, G. L., Leippe, M., & Ostrom, T. M. (1979). Guidelines for empirically assessing the fairness of a lineup. *Law and Human Behavior, 3,* 285–293. For discussion of effective lineup size, see Malpass, R. S. (1981). Effective size and defendant bias in eyewitness identification lineups. *Law and Human Behavior, 5,* 299–309.

To complicate matters further, the fairness of a lineup is sensitive also to the exact placement of the suspect relative to the foils. Research has shown that the suspect is more likely to be chosen when he is placed immediately adjacent to dissimilar foils than when he is placed near similar ones. One study found respective identification rates of 32 percent and 15 percent. This effect, however, was weakened when the verbal description was more detailed and accurate. Gonzalez, R., Davis, J., & Ellsworth, P. C. (1995). Who should stand next to the suspect? Problems in the assessment of lineup fairness. *Journal of Applied Psychology, 80,* 525–531.

109. Wells & Bradfield (1999a), *supra* note 106. Another study tested the lineup used in the case of *United States v. Mills,* in which the robber was described as being "black, male, short, full beard and thin but not skinny." Of the sixty mock witnesses who had never seen Mills or his photograph, Miles was chosen by 61 percent of the participants who made a choice. Wells, Leippe, & Ostrom (1979), *supra* note 108. In a study used in the Canadian case of *Regina v. Shatford,* researchers found that the suspect was chosen by more than half of participants, on the basis of the description alone. Doob & Kirshenbaum (1973), *supra* note 59. Since the lineups were forwarded to the researchers from (probably frustrated) defense attorneys, this was not a random sample of lineups used.

110. Buckout, R. (1974). Eyewitness testimony. *Scientific American,* 23–31.

111. Brigham, Meissner, & Wasserman (1999), *supra* note 59.

112. Lindsay, R. C., Wallbridge, H., & Drennan, D. (1987). Do the clothes make the man? An exploration of the effect of lineup attire on eyewitness identification accuracy. *Canadian Journal of Behavioural Science/Revue canadienne des sciences du comportement, 19(4),* 463–478.

113. Dysart, J. E., Lindsay, R. C. L., & Dupuis, P. R. (2006). Show-ups: The critical issue of clothing bias. *Applied Cognitive Psychology, 20(8),* 1009–1023.

114. This well-established finding has led researchers to label instructions that do not contain that notification "biased instructions." A meta-analysis found that the "unbiased" instruction decreases the rate of choosing in target-absent lineups from 60 percent to 35 percent (all choices are incorrect), but has no effect on the rate of the correct identifications when the target was present (53 and 55 percent, respectively). Overall, the instruction raised the rate of correct identifications from 44 to 56 percent. These data are derived from twenty-two studies with over 2,588 participants. Steblay, N. M. (1997). Social influence in eyewitness recall: A meta-analytic review of lineup instruction effects. *Law and Human Behavior, 21,* 283–297.

A more recent meta-analysis by Clark & Godfrey (2009) *supra* note 97, found only a weak improvement in reducing false identifications (from 10 percent to 7 percent). This meager change seems to be affected by the unusually low absolute values (10 percent) of false identifications in the "biased" condition (compare with the meta-analysis by Clark, Howell, & Davey 2008, *supra* note 7, which found an overall rate of false identifications of over 20 percent). In other words, any potential reductions in false identifications would probably be thwarted by a floor effect in these particular studies. Still, this data set does find that the "unbiased" instructions lead to a reduction in correct identifications from 56 percent to 50 percent.

115. Phillips, M. R., McAuliff, B. D., Kovera, M. B., & Cutler, B. L. (1999). Double-blind photoarray administration as a safeguard against investigator bias. *Journal of Applied Psychology, 84,* 940–951. Garrioch, L., & Brimacombe (née Luus), C. A. E. (2001). Lineup administrators' expectations: Their impact on eyewitness confidence. *Law and Human Behavior, 25,* 299–314.

116. See for example, Greathouse, S. M., & Kovera, M. B. (2009). Instruction bias and lineup presentation moderate the effects of administrator knowledge on eyewitness identification. *Law and Human Behavior, 33(1),* 70–82.

117. Ibid. This study found that the diagnosticity of lineups conducted by blind administrators was twice as high as lineups in which the administrator was aware of the identity of the suspect.

118. Haw, R. M., & Fisher, R. P. (2004). Effects of administrator-witness contact on eyewitness identification accuracy. *Journal of Applied Psychology, 89,* 1106–1112.

119. Douglass, A. B., Smith, C., & Fraser-Thill, R. (2005). A problem with double-blind photospread procedures: Photospread administrators use one

eyewitness's confidence to influence the identification of another eyewitness. *Law and Human Behavior, 29,* 543–562.

120. Smith & Hasel (2011), *supra* note 16.

121. Hasel & Kassin (2009), *supra* note 16.

122. Note that all these witnesses were wrong since the target was not present in the lineup. Skagerberg, E. M. (2007). Co-witness feedback in line-ups. *Applied Cognitive Psychology, 21,* 489–497. See also Luus, C. A. E., & Wells, G. L. (1994). The malleability of eyewitness confidence: Co-witness and perseverance effects. *Journal of Applied Psychology, 79,* 714–723.

123. In one study, positive feedback increased mean confidence from 49 percent to 68 percent. In another study, the confidence measured on a 7-point scale rose from 4.0 to 5.4. Bradfield, A. L., Wells, G. L., & Olson, E. A. (2002). The damaging effect of confirming feedback on the relation between eyewitness certainty and identification accuracy. *Journal of Applied Psychology, 87,* 112–120; Wells & Bradfield (1998), *supra* note 8.

Another study found that witnesses' confidence in their identification was boosted by positive feedback they received from the investigator at a pervious interview concerning the criminal event. Leippe et al. (2006), *supra* note 104.

124. Douglass A. B., & Steblay, N. M. (2006). Memory distortion in eyewitnesses: A meta-analysis of the post-identification feedback effect. *Applied Cognitive Psychology, 20,* 859–869.

125. Bradfield, Wells, & Olson (2002), *supra* note 123.

126. *Neil v. Biggers* 409 U.S. 198 (1972); *Manson v. Brathwaite* 432 U.S. 98 (1977). See Wells & Quinlivan (2009), *supra* note 36.

127. Wells & Bradfield (1998), *supra* note 8. It has been shown, however, that the effect can be moderated by instructing witnesses to think about various aspects of their memory before exposing them to the feedback. Wells, G. L., & Bradfield, A. L. (1999b). Distortions in eyewitnesses' recollections: Can the postidentification-feedback effect be moderated? *Psychological Science, 10,* 138–144.

128. The feedback led to a drop in the confidence of those who picked fillers to almost floor level (from 4.9 to 2.75 on a scale of 1–10), and to an increase for those who picked the suspect from 7.8 to almost ceiling level (8.6). Wright & Skagerberg (2007), *supra* note 5.

129. Interview with Jennifer Thompson, *supra* note 63.

130. Detective Lieutenant Kenneth Patenaude, an experienced trainer in identification procedures, has noted that the vast majority of police officers have never received formal training. Patenaude, K. (2006). Police identification procedures: A time for change. *Cardozo Public Law, Policy, and Ethics Journal, 4,* 415–419.

131. A survey of a national sample of police departments revealed that police training is indeed unstructured. Some three-quarters of the officers reported learning the task informally from other officers. Wogalter, Malpass, & McQuiston (2004), *supra* note 95.

132. Wise, R. A., Safer, M. A., & Maro, C. M. (2011). What U.S. law enforcement officers know and believe about eyewitness interviews and identification procedures. *Applied Cognitive Psychology, 25,* 488–500. The reported data aggregate responses from all responding officers.

133. Innocence Project, profile, Wilton Dedge. http://www.innocenceproject.org/Content/Wilton_Dedge.php. Kevin Byrd of Texas was identified by the crime victim in a grocery store nearly four months after the crime. Innocence Project, profile, Kevin Byrd. http://www.innocenceproject.org/Content/Kevin_Byrd.php. Harold Buntin of Indiana too was identified while shopping in a grocery store. The victim was legally blind in one eye and nearsighted in the other. Innocence Project, profile, Harold Buntin. http://www.innocenceproject.org/Content/Harold_Buntin.php.

134. Vincent Moto was spontaneously identified by the victim some five months after the crime while walking down the street with a young woman and child. Innocence Project, profile, Vincent Moto. http://www.innocenceproject.org/Content/Vincent_Moto.php.

135. Innocence Project, profile, Julius Ruffin. http://www.innocenceproject.org/Content/Julius_Ruffin.php.

136. David Gray was sentenced to sixty years' imprisonment for the rape and brutal stabbing of a fifty-three-year-old woman. Innocence Project, profile, David A. Gray. http://www.innocenceproject.org/Content/David_A_Gray.php.

137. Innocence Project, profile, Julius Ruffin, *supra* note 135.

138. Innocence Project, profile, Charles Chatman. http://www.innocenceproject.org/Content/Charles_Chatman.php.

139. Innocence Project, profile, Keith E. Turner. http://www.innocenceproject.org/Content/Keith_E_Turner.php.

140. Innocence Project, profile, William Gregory. http://www.innocenceproject.org/Content/William_Gregory.php.

141. Innocence Project, profile, Brian Piszczek. http://www.innocenceproject.org/Content/Brian_Piszczek.php; Innocence Project, profile, Michael Mercer. http://www.innocenceproject.org/Content/Michael_Mercer.php.

142. The two children who testified against Kirk Bloodsworth actually failed to pick him out at a photographic lineup, and proceeded to pick innocent fillers at the live lineup. Weeks later, after Bloodsworth was shown on television news in police custody, the children's mothers informed police that the children had actually identified Bloodsworth at the live lineup but were afraid to announce their choice. The children testified in court that Bloodsworth was the man they saw, and one of them identified him in court. Bloodsworth was convicted and sentenced to death. In 1993 he was exonerated on the basis of a DNA test. Dwyer, J., Neufeld, P., & Scheck, B. (2000). *Actual innocence: Five days to execution and other dispatches from the wrongfully convicted,* chap. 11. New York: Doubleday; Junkin, T. (2004). *Bloodsworth: The true story of the first death row*

inmate exonerated by DNA. Chapel Hill, NC: Algonquin Books. For a similar occurrence, see Zerwick, P. (2007), Murder, race, justice: The state vs. Darryl Hunt. *Winston-Salem Journal,* November 16.

143. Armand Villasana was exonerated following a conviction, but before being sentenced. In all, he spent two years incarcerated while the process played itself out. Innocence Project, profile, Armand Villasana. http://www.innocence project.org/Content/Armand_Villasana.php.

144. Innocence Project, profile, Brandon Moon. http://www.innocenceproject .org/Content/222.php.

145. Hall, M. (2008). The exonerated: The 37 men in these pages spent 525 years in prison for crimes they didn't commit—then came the hard part: freedom. *Texas Monthly, 36(11),* 148. On the case of David Pope, see Innocence Project, profile, David Shawn Pope. http://www.innocenceproject.org/Content/David _Shawn_Pope.php.

146. Innocence Project, profile, Johnny Briscoe. http://www.innocenceproject .org/Content/Johnny_Briscoe.php.

147. For a review of the Steven Avery case, see Findley, K. A., & Scott, M. S. (2006). The multiple dimensions of tunnel vision in criminal cases. *Wisconsin Law Review,* 291–397.

148. Carlos Lavernia. http://www.law.northwestern.edu/wrongfulconvictions/ exonerations/txLaverniaSummary.html.

149. Innocence Project, profile, James Ochoa. http://www.innocenceproject .org/Content/James_Ochoa.php.

150. Innocence Project, profile, Thomas Doswell. http://www.innocenceproject .org/Content/Thomas_Doswell.php.

151. Innocence Project, profile, Michael Green. http://www.innocenceproject .org/Content/Michael_Green.php.

152. Innocence Project, profile, Alejandro Dominguez. http://www.inno cenceproject.org/Content/Alejandro_Dominguez.php.

153. Before being exposed to the poster, the key witness failed to identify Herman Atkins. Innocence Project, profile, Herman Atkins. http://www.innocence project.org/Content/Herman_Atkins.php.

154. Innocence Project, profile, Johnnie Lindsey. http://www.innocenceproject .org/Content/Johnnie_Lindsey.php.

155. Innocence Project, profile, Habib Wahir Abdal. http://www.innocence project.org/Content/Habib_Wahir_Abdal.php.

156. Innocence Project, profile, Albert Johnson. http://www.innocenceproject .org/Content/Albert_Johnson.php.

157. The identification of Thomas McGowan was also plagued by serious suggestion. Innocence Project, profile, Thomas McGowan. http://www.innocence project.org/Content/Thomas_McGowan.php.

158. Innocence Project, profile, Peter Rose. http://innocenceproject.org/Content /Peter_Rose.php.

159. Innocence Project, profile, Antonio Beaver. http://www.innocenceproject
.org/Content/DNA_Proves_Antonio_Beavers_Innocence_in_St_Louis_Carjacking
_10_Years_After_Conviction_Based_on_Victims_Misidentification.php.

160. Innocence Project, profile, Kevin Byrd, *supra* note 133. The victim first described her assailant as a white man with "honey brown color."

161. Innocence Project, profile, Alejandro Dominguez, *supra* note 152.

162. Innocence Project, profile, Marvin Mitchell. http://www.innocence
project.org/Content/Marvin_Mitchell.php.

163. Innocence Project, profile, Luis Diaz. http://www.innocenceproject.org
/Content/Luis_Diaz.php.

164. See Rutenberg, S. (2006). Anatomy of a miscarriage of justice: The wrongful conviction of Peter J. Rose. *Golden Gate University Law Review, 37,* 7–37; Innocence Project, profile, Peter Rose, *supra* note 158; Dwyer, Neufeld, & Scheck (2000), *supra* note 142, pp. 45–77; Innocence Project, profile, Walter Snyder. http://www.innocenceproject.org/Content/Walter_Snyder.php. See also the cases of Larry Fuller and Ronnie Taylor: Innocence Project, profile, Larry Fuller. http://www.innocenceproject.org/Content/Larry_Fuller.php; Innocence Project, profile, Ronald Gene Taylor. http://www.innocenceproject.org/Content /Ronald_Gene_Taylor.php.

165. See cases of Travis Hayes, Ryan Matthews, and Brandon Moon: Innocence Project, profile, Travis Hayes. http://www.innocenceproject.org/Content /Travis_Hayes.php; Innocence Project, profile, Ryan Matthews. http://www .innocenceproject.org/Content/Ryan_Matthews.php; and Innocence Project, profile, Brandon Moon, *supra* note 144.

166. Innocence Project, profile, Gilbert Alejandro. http://www.innocence
project.org/Content/Gilbert_Alejandro.php.

167. Innocence Project, profile, Terry Chalmers. http://www.innocenceproject
.org/Content/Terry_Chalmers.php.

168. Innocence Project, profile, Larry Mayes. http://www.innocenceproject
.org/Content/Larry_Mayes.php. The witness in the case of Jeffrey Pierce of Oklahoma failed to identify him in the original lineup, but identified him at a lineup that was conducted months later. Innocence Project, profile, Jeffery Pierce. http://www.innocenceproject.org/Content/Jeffrey_Pierce.php.

169. Innocence Project, profile, Calvin Johnson. http://www.innocenceproject
.org/Content/Calvin_Johnson.php.

170. For a compelling analysis of the case of William O'Dell Harris, see Castelle, G., & Loftus, E. F. (2002). Misinformation and wrongful convictions. In S. D. Westervelt & J. A. Humphrey, eds., *Wrongfully convicted: Perspectives on failed justice,* pp. 17–35. New Brunswick, NJ: Rutgers University Press; Innocence Project, profile, William O'Dell Harris. http://www.innocenceproject.org /Content/William_ODell_Harris.php.

171. On the case of Walter Snyder, see Dwyer, Neufeld, & Scheck (2000), *supra* note 142, pp. 45–77; Innocence Project, profile, Walter Snyder, *supra* note 164.

172. Innocence Project, profile, Robert Clark. http://www.innocenceproject .org/Content/Robert_Clark.php.

173. Innocence Project, profile, Arvin McGee. http://www.innocenceproject .org/Content/Arvin_McGee.php.

174. Innocence Project, profile, Clark McMillan. http://www.innocence project.org/Content/Clark_McMillan.php.

175. Innocence Project, profile, Luis Diaz, *supra* note 163.

176. Dwyer, Neufeld, & Scheck (2000), *supra* note 142, chap. 11; Junkin (2004), *supra* note 142.

177. E.g., Innocence Project, profile, Brandon Moon, *supra* note 144; Innocence Project, profile, Dennis Maher. http://www.innocenceproject.org/Content /Dennis_Maher.php; Innocence Project, profile, Clark McMillan, *supra* note 174.

178. Innocence Project, profile, Dennis Maher, *supra* note 177; Innocence Project, profile, Anthony Robinson. http://www.innocenceproject.org/Content /Anthony_Robinson.php. The perpetrator was also said to have a mustache, which Robinson did not have.

179. Innocence Project, profile, Thomas McGowan, *supra* note 157.

180. Innocence Project, profile, Ronnie Bullock. http://www.innocenceproject .org/Content/Ronnie_Bullock.php.

181. Anthony Capozzi: Son's arrest leads mother on a 22-year journey of faith (2007). *USA Today,* May 13. http://www.usatoday.com/news/nation/2007 -05-13-mothers-faith_N.htm. Capozzi, who suffered from schizophrenia, was subsequently identified by three victims.

182. Innocence Project, profile, Anthony Powell. http://www.innocenceproject .org/Content/Anthony_Powell.php.

183. Innocence Project, profile, Ronnie Taylor, *supra* note 164.

184. Innocence Project, profile, James Curtis Giles. http://www.innocence project.org/Content/James_Curtis_Giles.php.

185. Innocence Project, profile, Gregory Wallis. http://www.innocenceproject .org/Content/Gregory_Wallis.php.

186. Turtle, J., Lindsay, R. C. L., & Wells, G. L. (2003). Best practice recommendations for eyewitness evidence procedures: New ideas for the oldest way to solve a case. *Canadian Journal of Police and Security Services, 1,* 5–18.

187. These ex-post assessments are what Gary Wells has labeled estimations. See Wells (1978), *supra* note 22.

188. One study found accuracy levels of 87 percent for identifications that took less than 10 seconds, and about 50 percent for decisions that took more than 12 seconds. Dunning, D., & Perretta, S. (2002). Automaticity and eyewitness accuracy: A 10- to 12-second rule for distinguishing accurate from inaccurate positive identifications. *Journal of Applied Psychology, 87(5),* 951–962. Another study found accuracy levels of 70 percent for identifications that took

less than 15 seconds, and 43 percent for decisions that took longer than that. Choices that took more than 30 seconds were no more than 18 percent accurate. Smith, S. M., Lindsay, R. C. L., & Pryke, S. (2000). Postdictors of eyewitness errors: Can false identifications be diagnosed? *Journal of Applied Psychology, 85(4),* 542–550. Yet another time study found boundaries ranging from 5 to 29 seconds. Weber, N., Brewer, N., Wells, G. L., Semmler, C., & Keast, A. (2004). Eyewitness identification accuracy and response latency: The unruly 10–12-Second Rule. *Journal of Experimental Psychology: Applied, 10(3),* 139–147.

189. The accuracy rates were 88 percent for choices made within 10 seconds and accompanied by high confidence, and 54 percent for slow and low-confidence choices. Choices were considered confident for levels above 90 percent and low for levels under 80 percent. Weber, N., Brewer, N., Wells, G. L., Semmler, C., & Keast, A. (2004). Eyewitness identification accuracy and response latency: The unruly 10–12-second Rule. *Journal of Experimental Psychology: Applied, 10,* 139–147.

190. The rate of accuracy was 97 percent for witnesses who decided within 6 seconds and were more than 90 percent confident, as compared with 32 percent for witnesses who were slower and less confident. About one-third of the witnesses could not be classified in either of these categories. Sauerland, M., & Sporer, S. L. (2009). Fast and confident: Postdicting eyewitness identification accuracy in a field study. *Journal of Experimental Psychology: Applied, 15(1),* 46–62.

191. Heeding this caution is particularly difficult given that this dilemma typically arises when the police have a suspect at hand, with no alternative sources of evidence. Distrusting the identification often means that the crime will go unpunished.

192. The report was written by six prominent researchers with an eye toward law enforcement agencies. The document is restrained and cautious, and is manifestly sensitive to the concerns of its intended audience. The report made four recommendations: requiring double-blind administration, improved lineup instructions, fair lineup composition, and immediate recording of confidence statements. The report also endorsed, but did not formally adopt as recommendations the use of sequential presentation and the videotaping of lineups. Wells et al. (1998), *supra* note 97.

193. The *Guide* contains recommendations concerning the inclusion of only one suspect in the lineup, fair lineup composition, improved lineup instructions, immediate recording of confidence statements, and the preserving records of the procedures. The *Guide* mentions, but does not go as far as recommending, double-blind administration, sequential presentation, and videotaping of lineups. U.S. Department of Justice, National Institute of Justice (1999). *Eyewitness evidence: A guide for law enforcement.* http://www.ncjrs.gov/pdffiles1/nij/178240 .pdf. The *Guide* was written by a working group commissioned by then Attorney General Janet Reno. The group consisted of six eyewitness researchers, sixteen

law enforcement personnel, six prosecutors, and four defense attorneys. For the researchers' account of the working group experience and the *Guide*, see Wells, G. L., Malpass, R. S., Lindsay, R. C. L., Fisher, R. P., Turtle, J. W., & Fulero, S. M. (2000). From the lab to the police station: A successful application of eyewitness research. *American Psychologist, 55(6)*, 581–598.

194. Reforms of lineup procedures have been put into effect in some ten states, including North Carolina, New Jersey, Rhode Island, Vermont, and Delaware. See Innocence Project, http://www.innocenceproject.org/news/LawView5.php.

195. To counter the effects of the over-inclination to choose, suspects should not be placed in a lineup based on flimsy suspicions, such as a vague resemblance to the perpetrator, or being seen a few blocks from the crime scene. Gary Wells has proposed a threshold of "reasonable suspicion." Wells, G. L. (2006). Eyewitness identifications: Systemic reform. *Wisconsin Law Review*, 615–643.

196. It should be noted that there are tensions among some of the recommendations. For example, the recommendation to hold the procedure as early as possible could be in conflict with the recommendation not to conduct a lineup before the police have a substantial suspicion about a particular person. Balancing these recommendations would require nuanced judgment by police detectives.

Some recommendations are contingent on the implementation of other ones. For example, the double blind recommendation is vital for sequential procedures. Nonblind sequential procedures are likely to have deleterious effects in that they increase the danger of administrator suggestion. When the targets are presented sequentially, that is, alone, there are more opportunities for a leak or suggestion from the administrator.

197. Recall that blinding the administrator to the suspect's identity decreases the rate of false identifications (from 24 percent to 12 percent) and of correct identifications (from 56 percent to 43 percent). Clark, S. E. (under review). Trade-off in correct and false identifications: Protecting the innocent is not free.

198. Recall that laboratory studies show that sequential procedures lower the rate of false identifications in target-absent lineups (32 percent vs. 54 percent for simultaneous lineups), and to a lesser degree they also reduce correct identifications in target-present lineups (44 percent vs. 52 percent). Steblay, Dysart, & Wells (2011), *supra* note 101. The recent field data, however, show no decrease in correct identifications in sequential as compared to simultaneous lineups (presumably, these were mostly target present procedures). Wells, Steblay, & Dysart (2011), *supra* note 102.

199. See data discussed in note 10.

200. Lampinen, J. M., Judges, D. P., Odegard, T. N., & Hamilton, S. (2005). The reactions of mock jurors to the Department of Justice guidelines for the collection and preservation of eyewitness evidence. *Basic and Applied Social Psychology, 27*, 155–162.

201. E.g., Wells et al. (2000), *supra* note 193.

202. One such program, called PC_Eyewitness, has been developed mostly for research purposes by a group of researchers from the University of Northern Iowa. MacLin, O. H., Meissner, C. A., & Zimmerman, L. A. (2005). PC_Eyewitness: A computerized framework for the administration and practical application of research in eyewitness psychology. *Behavior Research Methods, 37,* 324–334; MacLin, O. H., Zimmerman, L. A., & Malpass, R. S. (2005). PC_Eyewitness and the sequential superiority effect: Computer-based lineup administration. *Law and Human Behavior, 29,* 303–321.

203. See Wells, Steblay, & Dysart (2011), *supra* note 102.

204. On the procedures currently conducted in the United Kingdom, see Valentine, T., Hughes, C., & Munro, R. (2009). Recent developments in eyewitness identification procedures in the United Kingdom. In R. Bull, T. Valentine, & T. Williamson, eds., *Handbook of psychology of investigative interviewing: Current developments and future directions,* pp. 221–240. Chichester, UK: Wiley-Blackwell.

205. Valentine, T., & Heaton, P. (1999). An evaluation of the fairness of police line-ups and video identifications. *Applied Cognitive Psychology, 13,* S59–S72. While the lineups would ideally be conducted with video images, still photographs should be used where video lineups are not feasible, and if necessary for mugshot searches. The videos should consist of full body and head shots from multiple angles, as well as voice recordings.

206. On the logistical problems involved in conducting lineups in the United Kingdom, see Roberts, A. (2004). The problem of mistaken identification: Some observations on process. *International Journal of Evidence & Proof, 8,* 100–119.

207. As far as constitutional protections are concerned, there is little doubt that the police are permitted to film a suspect who has been arrested. The Supreme Court ruled in *United States v. Wade* (1967) that the right against self-incrimination does not protect an accused from participating in identification procedures. On the basis of Supreme Court dicta, there is reason to believe that it would be permissible to detain a suspect temporarily for the purpose of filming him solely on the basis of a reasonable suspicion. *Hayes v. Florida,* 470 U.S. 811 (1985).

4. "Officer, That's What Happened"

1. In the psychological literature, event memory falls into the category of *episodic memory,* which is defined as memories of personal experiences that can be remembered as occurring at a particular time and a particular place. Recollections of falling off a bicycle and receiving a letter of acceptance to college are examples of episodic memory. Episodic memory must be distinguished from semantic memory and working memory. *Semantic memory* contains the person's massive body of general knowledge: knowing the meaning of the word *spoon*

and that Shakespeare's *Hamlet* took place in Denmark. *Working memory* enables people to retain limited amounts of information for brief periods. Working memory stores information to facilitate other cognitive processing, such as following a conversation or observing an ongoing occurrence.

2. For the case of Ryan Matthews and Travis Hayes, see *Louisiana v. Hayes,* 806 So.2d 816, 01–736 (La. App. 5 Cir. 12/26/01); Innocence Project, profile, Ryan Matthews. http://www.innocenceproject.org/Content/Ryan_Matthews.php. The two men were exonerated on the basis of a DNA test that matched the ski mask used in the crime to another person.

3. *State v. Cotton,* No. 257A85 Alamance Co. Super. Ct., January 7, 1985, trial transcript, pp. 360, 371.

4. On the case of Clarence Elkins, see 2000 Ohio App. LEXIS 4670; Innocence Project, profile, Clarence Elkins. http://innocenceproject.org/Content/Clarence_Elkins.php.

5. Innocence Project, profile, Glen Woodall. http://www.innocenceproject.org/Content/Glen_Woodall.php.

6. Innocence Project, profile, Dwayne Scruggs. http://www.innocenceproject.org/Content/Dwayne_Scruggs.php.

7. Innocence Project, profile, Ben Salazar. http://www.innocenceproject.org/Content/Ben_Salazar.php; Tharp, G. W. R. (2006). DNA frees man jailed 18 years. *Dallas Morning News,* March 21.

8. Innocence Project, profile, Eduardo Velasquez. http://www.innocenceproject.org/Content/Eduardo_Velasquez.php.

9. See the cases of Ryan Matthews above, and Edward Honaker below.

10. Innocence Project, profile, David Shawn Pope. http://www.innocenceproject.org/Content/David_Shawn_Pope.php.

11. Innocence Project, profile, Donte Booker. http://www.innocenceproject.org/Content/Donte_Booker.php.

12. Innocence Project, profile, Leonard McSherry. http://www.innocenceproject.org/Content/Leonard_McSherry.php.

13. In neither of the victim's first two reports given to the police was there any mention of a basement or of oil. Rather, on the day of the crime, the victim stated that he "had a strong body odor and the odor of alcohol on his breath." The next day she described to the detective "a musky odor, a combination of sweat and alcohol and possibly cigarette smoke." Snyder was sentenced to forty-five years in prison but was exonerated by a DNA test after serving six and a half years. On the case of Walter Snyder, see Dwyer, J., Neufeld, P., & Scheck, B. (2000). *Actual innocence: Five days to execution and other dispatches from the wrongfully convicted,* pp. 45–77. New York: Doubleday; Innocence Project, profile, Walter Snyder. http://www.innocenceproject.org/Content/Walter_Snyder.php.

14. Innocence Project, profile, Clark McMillan. http://www.innocenceproject.org/Content/Clark_McMillan.php.

15. See trial transcript, *Commonwealth of Virginia v. Edward William Honaker,* No. CR1977 (Nelson Co. Cir. Ct. February 6, 1985). See also Gould, J. B. (2008). *The Innocence Commission: Preventing wrongful convictions and restoring the criminal justice system,* p. 104. New York: NYU Press; Innocence Project, profile, Edward Honaker. http://innocenceproject.org/Content/Edward_Honaker.php.

16. In these studies, the accuracy rate was found to be 82 percent when using standard interview techniques and 85 percent when using the Cognitive Interview protocol. Köhnken, G., Milne, R., Memon, A., & Bull, R. (1999). The cognitive interview: A meta-analysis. *Psychology, Crime & Law, 5,* 3–27. A Swedish study testing the memories of witnesses to a filmed kidnapping found an accuracy rate of 65 percent. Granhag, P. A., Strömwall, L. A., & Allwood, C. M. (2000). Effects of reiteration, hindsight bias, and memory on realism in eyewitness confidence. *Applied Cognitive Psychology, 14,* 397–420.

17. A study with English police trainees yielded average rates of 68 percent. Yuille, J. C., Davies, G., Gibling, F., Marxsen, D., & Porter, S. (1994). Eyewitness memory of police trainees for realistic role plays. *Journal of Applied Psychology, 79,* 931–936. The study with Scottish police officers yielded average accuracy rates of 82 percent. Hulse, L. M., & Memon, A. (2006). Fatal impact? The effects of emotional arousal and weapon presence on police officers' memories for a simulated crime. *Legal and Criminological Psychology, 11,* 313–325.

18. The memories of twenty-one people who witnessed a shootout on a Vancouver street were found to be slightly over 80 percent accurate. In the original police interview, the rate of accuracy was 82 percent, and in an interview conducted by the researchers some months later, it was 81 percent. Yuille, J. C., & Cutshall, J. L. (1986). A case study of eyewitness memory of a crime. *Journal of Applied Psychology, 71,* 291–301. The same researchers found somewhat higher rates of accuracy in two shooting incidents (92 percent) and a series of bank robberies (90 percent). Cutshall, J., & Yuille, J. C. (1988). Field studies of eyewitness memory of actual crimes. In D. C. Raskin, ed., *Psychological methods in criminal investigation and evidence,* pp. 97–124. New York: Springer.

Similar accuracy was found by Swedish researchers who studied memories of fifty-eight people who had witnessed twenty-two bank robberies in Stockholm. The rate of accuracy for witnesses who were the actual victims of the robberies was 81 percent. The accuracy of bystanders and other employees who were not personally targeted by the robbers were 62 percent and 72 percent, respectively. Christianson, S. A., & Hübinette, B. (1993). Hands up! A study of witnesses' emotional reactions and memories associated with bank robberies. *Applied Cognitive Psychology, 7,* 365–379. Even higher accuracy rates were reported in a Scottish study that examined the memories of witnesses to criminal assaults that were captured on closed-circuit video cameras (CCTV). No fewer than 96 percent of the classifiable details reported by nine assault victims and ten bystanders were found to match the CCTV footage. Woolnough, P. S., & MacLeod, M. (2001). Watching the birdie watching you: Eyewitness memory for actions using CCTV recordings of actual crimes. *Applied Cognitive Psychology, 15,* 395–411.

19. For a series of studies focusing on memory quantity (though not completeness), see Koriat, A., & Goldsmith, M. (1996). Monitoring and control processes in the strategic regulation of memory accuracy. *Psychological Review, 103,* 490–517.

20. One study measured participants' memories of a three-minute police training video depicting a bank robbery, and found that they remembered 25 percent of the 154 possible details depicted in the scene. The memory test was conducted two days after viewing the video. Gilbert, J. A. E., & Fisher, R. P. (2006). The effects of varied retrieval cues on reminiscence in eyewitness memory. *Applied Cognitive Psychology, 20,* 723–739. In a study that measured memory for a 1.5-minute movie sequence of a homicide, participants were found to remember 15–30 percent of the forty-five depicted details. Bornstein, B. H., Liebel, L. M., & Scarberry, N. C. (1998). Repeated testing in eyewitness memory: A means to improve recall of a negative emotional event. *Applied Cognitive Psychology, 12,* 119–131. In one of these studies, witnesses recalled 15 percent of the details of the crime scene under daylight lighting conditions, but only 5 percent under nighttime conditions. The rate was better for details concerning the perpetrator and the victim (27 and 31 percent, respectively under daylight illumination and 6 percent for both types of memories under nighttime illumination). Yarmey, A. D. (1986). Verbal, visual, and voice identification of a rape suspect under different levels of illumination. *Journal of Applied Psychology, 71,* 363–370.

Other studies measured memory for larger segments of the events, revealing average rates of completeness of 47, 42, and 31 percent, respectively in the following studies: Scrivner, E., & Safer, M. A. (1988). Eyewitnesses show hypermnesia for details about a violent event. *Journal of Applied Psychology, 73,* 371–377; Turtle, J. W., & Yuille, J. C. (1994). Lost but not forgotten details: Repeated eyewitness recall leads to reminiscence but not hypermnesia. *Journal of Applied Psychology, 79,* 260–271; and Vidmar, N., & Laird, N. M. (1983). Adversary social roles: Their effects on witnesses' communication of evidence and the assessments of adjudicators. *Journal of Personality and Social Psychology, 44,* 888–898. In the study of Scottish police officers conducted in a crime simulator, the average rate of memorized details was 51 percent. Hulse & Memon (2006), *supra* note 17.

It must be acknowledged that setting the boundaries for the definition of what constitutes an identifiable "detail" is a nebulous task. Any given scene can be broken down into an infinite number of minute details: not just whether the perpetrator wore a hat, but also its color, shape, logo, rim design, type of stitching, color of thread, etc. Needless to mention, people cannot be expected to perceive and encode every such detail. For practical purposes, it is best to focus on the level of detail that can could make a difference to a criminal investigation.

21. A survey of English police officers revealed that witnesses' spontaneous memories often fall short of satisfying investigative needs. In response to the question "How often do witnesses remember as much as you want?," 51 percent of officers responded "rarely." Forty percent responded "usually," with only 8 percent responding "almost always," and zero responding "always." Kebbell, M. R., & Milne, R. (1998). Police officers' perceptions of eyewitness performance in forensic investigations. *Journal of Social Psychology, 138,* 323–330.

22. In this study, participants who identified a perpetrator correctly (57 percent of the sample) responded correctly to 6.4 of the 11 questions about the crime scene environment, whereas participants who picked an innocent filler (32 percent) responded correctly to 8.5 questions. The remaining 18 percent were weak on both counts, in that they picked no one, and correctly remembered only 5.1 details. Wells, G. L., & Leippe, M. R. (1981). How do triers of fact infer the accuracy of eyewitness identifications? Using memory for peripheral detail can be misleading. *Journal of Applied Psychology, 66,* 682–687.

23. See the discussion below on the phenomenon of *reminiscence.*

24. For a summary of the research, see Ley, P. (1979). Memory for medical information. *British Journal of Social and Clinical Psychology, 18,* 245–255. Another study found that patients recalled only 61 percent of the information correctly. Bertakis, K. D. (1977). The communication of information from physician to patient: A method for increasing patient retention and satisfaction. *Journal of Family Practice, 5,* 217–222. A simple intervention increased the rate of accuracy to 83 percent.

25. A large study ($N=1,751$) found that even among chronically ill patients, a majority failed to recall elements of potentially important medical advice. Kravitz, R. L., Hays, R. D., Sherbourne, C. D., DiMatteo, M. R., Rogers, W. H., Ordway, L., & Greenfield, S. (1993). Recall of recommendations and adherence to advice among patients with chronic medical conditions. *Archives of Internal Medicine, 153(16),* 1869–1878.

26. On average, participants recalled only 51 percent of the relevant medical information they kept in their diaries over a period of three months. Two months later, the level of recall dropped to 39 percent. Cohen, G., & Java, R. (1995). Memory for medical history: Accuracy of recall. *Applied Cognitive Psychology, 9,* 273–288.

27. Schacter, D. L. (1996). *Searching for memory.* New York: Basic Books.

28. Schmechel, R. S., O'Toole, T. P., Easterly, C., & Loftus, E. F. (2006). Beyond the kin? Testing jurors' understanding of eyewitness reliability evidence. *Jurimetrics, 46,* 177–214.

29. Wise, R. A., Safer, M. A., & Maro, C. M. (2011). What U.S. law enforcement officers know and believe about eyewitness interviews and identification procedures. *Applied Cognitive Psychology, 25,* 488–500.

30. Yuille, J. C. (1984). Research and teaching with police: A Canadian example. *International Review of Applied Psychology, 33,* 5–23.

31. The survey was completed by 159 officers, with a mean length of police service of twelve years. Kebbell & Milne (1998), *supra* note 21.

32. Mitchell, K. J., & Johnson, M. K. (2000). Source monitoring: Attributing mental experiences. In E. Tulving & F. I. M. Craik, eds., *The Oxford handbook of memory,* pp. 179–195. New York: Oxford University Press.

33. Bartlett, F. C. (1932). *Remembering: A study in experimental and social psychology.* Cambridge: Cambridge University Press.

34. The constructive nature of memory was demonstrated also in the events surrounding the famous testimony given by John Dean to the Senate committee investigating the Watergate affair in June 1973. The former counsel to President Nixon provided the committee with a 245-page account of his memories and testified about them extensively. Dean was lauded for the acuity of his memory and was even dubbed by observers as "the human tape recorder." Important parts of Dean's testimony pertained to conversations he had had with Nixon in the Oval Office as they schemed about ways to thwart the probe into Nixon's involvement. Soon after Dean's testimony, the committee discovered that all conversations held in the Oval Office had been surreptitiously recorded. The recordings offer an opportunity to measure objectively the accuracy of Dean's memories. The tapes show that at the gist level, Dean's testimony was correct, in that Nixon was indeed involved in the cover-up. However, at the level of specific details, the much-heralded testimony was far from accurate. Dean was wrong about a number of details and verbatim statements that he recalled. The recollections of two pivotal conversations with the president demonstrate the intrusion of Dean's hopes and aspirations, as he reported making statements that he never made (though probably wished he had) and attributed statements to Nixon that the president never made (mostly praise for Dean). Dean also committed source monitoring errors by placing certain statements in the wrong conversation. See Neisser, U. (1981). John Dean's memory: A case study. *Cognition, 9,* 1–22.

35. Brainerd, C. J., & Reyna, V. F. (1990). Gist is the grist: Fuzzy-trace theory and the new intuitionism. *Developmental Review, 10,* 3–47; Brainerd, C. J., & Reyna, V. F. (2002). Fuzzy-trace theory and false memory. *Current Directions in Psychological Science, 11,* 164–169.

36. *Source monitoring theory* posits that memories entail judgments about their origins. Memory judgments are of three kinds: discriminating internally generated information from externally derived information (reality monitoring), discriminating between two external memory sources (source monitoring), and discriminating between two internal sources of memory (internal source monitoring). Johnson, M. K., Hashtroudi, S., & Lindsay, D. S. (1993). Source monitoring. *Psychological Bulletin, 114,* 3–28.

37. Johnson, M. K. (1997). Source monitoring and memory distortion. *Philosophical Transactions of the Royal Society B: Biological Sciences, 352,* 1733–1745.

38. Kroll, N. E. A., Knight, R. T., Metcalfe, J., Wolf, E. S., & Tulving, E. (1996). Cohesion failure as a source of memory illusions. *Journal of Memory and Language, 35,* 176–196; Brown, S. C., & Craik, F. I. M. (2000). Encoding and retrieval of information. In E. Tulving & F. I. M. Craik, eds., *The Oxford handbook of memory,* pp. 93–107. New York: Oxford University Press. This process has also be labeled *cohesion;* see Moscovitch, M. (1994). Memory and working with memory: Evaluation of a component process model and comparisons with other models. In D. L. Schacter & E. Tulving, eds., *Memory systems,* pp. 269–310. Cambridge, MA: MIT Press.

39. The video depicts a group of people passing a basketball around. Participants are instructed to count the number of times the ball is passed. About twenty seconds into the clip, a person dressed in a full-body black gorilla suit steps into the middle of the scene, turns to face the camera, thumps its chest, and walks away. Some 40 percent of pariciapants fail to notice the gorilla. Simons, D. J., & Chabris, C. F. (2000). Gorillas in our midst: sustained inattentional blindness for dynamic events. *Perception, 28,* 1059–1074.

40. For example, employees at a large manufacturing company recalled considerably more details in remembering what they had done the day before than what they had done a week earlier. Eldridge, M. A., Barnard, P. J., & Bekerian, D. A. (1994). Autobiographical memory and daily schemas at work. *Memory 2,* 51–74. Many studies show that delaying the first interview results in memory reports that contain less correct information and more incorrect information. For one example, see Tuckey, M. R., & Brewer, N. (2003). The influence of schemas, stimulus ambiguity, and interview schedule on eyewitness memory over time. *Journal of Experimental Psychology: Applied, 9,* 101–118.

41. The meta-analysis included 210 published studies. Rubin, D. C., & Wenzel, A. E. (1996). One hundred years of forgetting: A quantitative description of retention. *Psychological Review, 103,* 734–760.

42. Bornstein, Liebel, & Scarberry (1998, *supra* note 20) found overall increases of about 20 percent over the three tests, and Dunning and Stern (1992) found about a 10 percent increase. Dunning, D., & Stern, L. B. (1992). Examining the generality of eyewitness hypermnesia: A close look at time delay and question type. *Applied Cognitive Psychology, 6,* 643–657.

43. The strongest findings were made by Gilbert & Fisher (2006, *supra* note 20), who found increases of 30 percent when using standard interview techniques and 50 percent increases when varying the retrieval cues.

44. For forensic purposes, the moderate gains in reminiscence are largely swamped by the overall incompleteness of memory accounts. Recall that witnesses' memory for forensically relevant event details is limited. An optimistic

net reminiscence gain of 20 percent would push an initial memory that is 25 percent complete to a completeness level of 30 percent. That, however, leaves big memory gaps.

45. Whether the offsetting between reminiscence and forgetting produces a net memory gain *(hypermnesia)* or a net loss depends on the particular circumstances of the study. For conflicting results, see Dunning & Stern (1992), *supra* note 42, and Turtle & Yuille (1994), *supra* note 20.

46. Rubin & Wenzel (1996), *supra* note 41.

47. Flashbulb memories were taken to have an "almost perceptual quality." Brown, R., & Kulik, J. (1977). Flashbulb memories. *Cognition, 5,* 73.

48. Some studies found superior performance for flashbulb memories. E.g., Neisser, U., Winograd, E., Bergman, E. T., Schreiber, C. A., Palmer, S. E., & Weldon, M. S. (1996). Remembering the earthquake: Direct experience vs. hearing the news. *Memory, 4,* 337–357; Tinti, C., Schmidt, S., Sotgiu, I., Testa, S., & Curci, A. (in press). The role of importance/consequentiality appraisal in flashbulb memory formation: The case of the death of Pope John Paul II. *Applied Cognitive Psychology.* Other studies have failed to find the effect. E.g., Schmolck, H., Buffalo, E. A., & Squire, L. R. (2000). Memory distortions develop over time: Recollections of the O. J. Simpson trial verdict after 15 and 32 months. *Psychological Science, 11,* 39–45; Talarico, J. M., & Rubin, D. C. (2003). Confidence, not consistency, characterizes flashbulb memories. *Psychological Science, 14,* 455–461; Talarico, J. M., & Rubin, D. C. (2007). Flashbulb memories are special after all; in phenomenology, not accuracy. *Applied Cognitive Psychology, 21,* 557–578.

49. The studies typically test for memories of personal circumstances such as the respondents' location when hearing about the event for the first time, the activity interrupted by the news, the source of the news, their own emotional reactions, the emotional reactions of others, and the like. In most criminal investigations, these types of details are unlikely to help in identifying the perpetrator or determining his level of culpability.

50. Talarico & Rubin (2003), *supra* note 48; Talarico & Rubin (2007), *supra* note 48. High confidence was reported also in the study about the O. J. Simpson verdict by Schmolck, Buffalo, & Squire (2000), *supra* note 48; Conway, A. R. A., Skitka, L. J., Hemmerich, J. A., & Kershaw, T. C. (2009). Flashbulb memory for 11 September 2001. *Applied Cognitive Psychology, 23,* 605–623.

51. In one study, participants were asked to recall facts that were not included in the film they saw, such as the color of a dog that did not actually appear in the scene. Despite the option to respond "don't know," about one-third of the responses contained affirmative answers, which were naturally wrong. Hastie, R., Landsman, R., & Loftus, E. F. (1978). Eyewitness testimony: The dangers of guessing. *Jurimetrics, 19,* 1–8. In a study that tracked people's memories for facts surrounding the O. J. Simpson verdict, the rate of "don't remember" responses decreased threefold between fifteen and thirty months from the

event. Thus, as respondents' memories grew weaker, they were more prone to report affirmative memories, which were largely incorrect. The rate of accurate answers dropped from 38 percent to 20 percent over the corresponding period. Schmolck, Buffalo, & Squire (2000), *supra* note 48.

52. Recall from Chapter 3 that participants in a Canadian field study underestimated the distances to a target person by about one-third, and when they used ranges to describe their estimations the true distances fell outside the estimated ranges in more than half of the cases. Lindsay, R. C. L., Semmler, C., Weber, N., Brewer, N., & Lindsay, M. R. (2008). How variations in distance affect eyewitness reports and identification accuracy. *Law and Human Behavior, 32(6)*, 526–535. See also Radvansky, G. A., Carlson-Radvansky, L. A., & Irwin, D. E. (1995). Uncertainty in estimating distances from memory. *Memory & Cognition, 23*, 596–606; Wiest, W. M., & Bell, B. (1985). Stevens's exponent for psychophysical scaling of perceived, remembered, and inferred distance. *Psychological Bulletin, 98*, 457–470.

53. Pedersen, A. C. I., & Wright, D. B. (2002). Do differences in event descriptions cause different duration estimates? *Applied Cognitive Psychology, 16*, 769–783; Loftus, E. F., Schooler, J. W., Boone, S. M., & Kline, D. (1987). Time went by so slowly: Overestimation of event duration by males and females. *Applied Cognitive Psychology, 1*, 3–13.

54. In one study, speed estimations of a car traveling at 12 miles per hour ranged from 10 to 50 miles per hour. Marshall, J. (1969). *Law and psychology in conflict*. New York: Anchor Books. Cited in Loftus, E. F., & Palmer, J. C. (1974). Reconstruction of automobile destruction: An example of the interaction between language and memory. *Journal of Verbal Learning and Verbal Behavior, 13*, 585–589.

55. In the study of the Vancouver gun store incident, witnesses provided a total of twenty-three metric descriptions of the people involved. These descriptions were only 50 percent accurate, that is, no better than chance. Yuille & Cutshall (1986), *supra* note 18.

56. Allport, G. W. (1954). *The nature of prejudice*. Garden City, NY: Doubleday/Anchor. In a classic study by Duncan, white people interpreted an ambiguous shove by a black man as a violent act more so than a similar shove by a white man. Duncan, B. L. (1976). Differential social perception and attribution of intergroup violence: Testing the lower limits of stereotyping of Blacks. *Journal of Personality and Social Psychology, 34*, 590–598.

57. For example, sports fans judge events on the field in a way that favors their team. Hastrof, A. H., & Cantril, H. (1954). They saw a game: A case study. *Journal of Abnormal and Social Psychology, 49*, 129–134. Motivated perception has been demonstrated in how people interpret ambiguous visual images. Balcetis, E., & Dunning, D. (2006). See what you want to see: Motivational influences on visual perception. *Journal of Personality and Social Psychology, 91*, 612–625.

Motivations have also been found to affect judgments of physical properties, such as the steepness of hills. Proffitt, D. R., Creem, S. H., & Zosh, W. (2001). Seeing mountains in mole hills: Geographical slant perception. *Psychological Science, 12,* 418–423. People also interpret events in conformance with their political preferences. Fischle, M. (2000). Mass response to the Lewinsky scandal: Motivated reasoning or Bayesian updating? *Political Psychology, 21,* 135–159.

58. Johnson, M. K., Bransford, J. D., & Solomon, S. K. (1973). Memory for tacit implications of sentences. *Journal of Experimental Psychology, 98,* 203–205.

59. The rate of false recall for forty-eight sentences of this type was .73. Chan, J. C. K., & McDermott, K. B. (2006). Remembering pragmatic inferences. *Applied Cognitive Psychology, 20,* 633–639. See also McDermott, K. B., & Chan, J. C. (2006). Effects of repetition on memory for pragmatic inferences. *Memory & Cognition, 34,* 1273–1284. For early experimentation, see Brewer, W. F. (1977). Memory for the pragmatic implications of sentences. *Memory & Cognition, 5,* 673–678.

60. Bransford, J. D., & Franks, J. J. (1971). The abstraction of linguistic ideas. *Cognitive Psychology, 2,* 331–350. Again, while these statements were plausible inferences, they were not actually observed by the participants.

61. Carli, L. L. (1999). Cognitive reconstruction, hindsight, and reactions to victims and perpetrators. *Personality and Social Psychology Bulletin, 25,* 966–99.

62. In these studies, one participant's description of a picture of a scene in a subway train was told and retold through a chain of six or seven participants who had not seen the picture. The picture depicted a well-dressed black man wearing a suit and tie, facing an apparently working-class white man. The white man seemed somewhat aggressive, and he was holding a large and exposed razor blade by his side. In some 50 percent of the groups, by the time the story had circled the group, it was distorted in a way that reversed the roles of the two men so that the black man was said to be wielding the blade. Some of the distortions were accompanied by detailed accounts of the black man's aggression toward the white man. Allport, G. W., & Postman, L. J. (1947). *The psychology of rumor.* New York: Henry Holt. See also Fyock, J., & Stangor, C. (1994). The role of memory biases in stereotype maintenance. *British Journal of Social Psychology, 33,* 331–343. For research demonstrating the effect of gender stereotypes on memory, see MacRae, C. N., Schloerscheidt, A. M., Bodenhausen, G. V., & Milne, A. B. (2002). Creating memory illusions: Expectancy-based processing and the generation of false memories. *Memory, 10,* 63–80. For other evidence of stereotype intrusions into memory, see Sherman, J. W., Groom, C. J., Ehrenberg, K., & Klauer, K. C. (2003). Bearing false witness under pressure: Implicit and explicit components of stereotype-driven memory distortions. *Social Cognition, 21,* 213–246; Sherman, J. W., & Bessenoff, G. R. (1999). Stereotypes as source-monitoring cues: On the interaction between episodic and semantic memory. *Psychological Science, 10,* 106–110.

63. Cohen, C. E. (1981). Person categories and social perception: Testing some boundaries of the processing effects of prior knowledge. *Journal of Personality and Social Psychology, 40,* 441–452.

64. Nake, M., Itsukushima, Y., & Itoh, Y. (1996). Eyewitness testimony after three months: A field study on memory for an incident in everyday life. *Japanese Psychological Research, 38,* 14–24.

65. O'Brien, B. (2009). Prime suspect: An examination of factors that aggravate and counteract confirmation bias in criminal investigations. *Psychology, Public Policy, and Law, 15,* 315–334.

66. One study found that after choosing a certain job candidate over another, decision makers' memories were distorted in a way that supports the choice they made. Specifically, participants attributed a greater number of positive features to the chosen candidate and a greater number of negative features to the rejected one. Mather, M., Shafir, E., & Johnson, M. K. (2000). Misremembrance of options past: Source monitoring and choice. *Psychological Science, 11,* 132–138. College students who were steered to make skewed predictions of the outcome of sporting events subsequently recalled the information about the teams as consistent with the biasing task. Markman, K. D., & Hirt, E. R. (2002). Social prediction and the "allegiance bias." *Social Cognition, 20,* 58–86; Hirt, E. R., & Sherman, S. J. (1985). The role of prior knowledge in explaining hypothetical events. *Journal of Experimental Social Psychology, 21,* 519–543. See also Bodenhausen, G. V., & Wyer, R. S. (1985). Effects of stereotypes on decision making and information-processing strategies. *Journal of Personality and Social Psychology, 48,* 267–282.

67. Crombag, H. M., Wagenaar, W. A., & van Koppen, P. J. (1996). Crashing memories and the problem of "source monitoring." *Applied Cognitive Psychology, 10,* 95–104.

68. One might take issue with the classification of crashing memories as spontaneous false memories. The first study included an implicit suggestion of the existence of the films, as Crombag and colleagues asked, "Did you see the television film of the moment the plane hit the apartment building?" Crombag, Wagenaar, & van Koppen (1996), *supra* note 67. Later studies, however, obtained similar results absent any such suggestion. Smeets, T., Jelicic, M., Peters, M. J. V., Candel, I., Horselenberg, R., & Merckelbach, H. (2006). "Of course I remember seeing that film": How ambiguous questions generate crashing memories. *Applied Cognitive Psychology, 20,* 779–789; Jelicic, M., Smeets, T., Peters, M. J. V., Candel, I., Horselenberg, R., & Merckelbach, H. (2006). Assassination of a controversial politician: Remembering details from another non-existent film. *Applied Cognitive Psychology, 20(5),* 591–596.

69. The assassination of controversial politician Pim Fortuyn was not captured on film. Still, 27–63 percent of the respondents reported seeing it on TV. Jelicic et al. (2006), *supra* note 68; Smeets et al. (2006), *supra* note 68.

70. Forty-four percent of the English sample claimed to have viewed the film. Ost, J., Vrij, A., Costall, A., & Bull, R. (2002). Crashing memories and reality monitoring: Distinguishing between perceptions, imaginations, and "false memories." *Applied Cognitive Psychology, 16,* 125–134.

71. A similar error occurs when participants remember items that are composed of a mixture of features of a witnessed item and unfamiliar features (e.g., remembering the word *blackboard*). Reinitz, M. T., Morrissey, J., & Demb, J. (1994). Role of attention in face encoding. *Journal of Experimental Psychology: Learning, Memory, and Cognition, 20,* 161–168.

72. Lindsay, D. S., Allen, B. P., Chan, J. C. K., & Dahl, L. C. (2004). Eyewitness suggestibility and source similarity: Intrusions of details from one event into memory reports of another event. *Journal of Memory and Language, 50,* 96–111.

73. Odegard, T. N., & Lampinen, J. M. (2004). Memory conjunction errors for autobiographical events: More than just familiarity. *Memory, 12,* 288–300.

74. Participants were told either to perform certain actions (e.g., to break a toothpick) or just to imagine performing them. A memory test conducted two weeks later showed some confusion between actions taken and actions imagined. Goff, L. M., & Roediger, H. L. (1998). Imagination inflation for action events: Repeated imaginings lead to illusory recollections. *Memory & Cognition, 26,* 20–33.

75. Overall, the exposure to misleading information reduced the rate of accuracy from 75 percent to 41 percent. Loftus, E. F., Miller, D. G., & Burns, H. J. (1978). Semantic integration of verbal information into a visual memory. *Journal of Experimental Psychology: Human Learning and Memory, 4,* 19–31.

76. In contrast, among participants who received no suggestion of a barn, less than 3 percent reported having seen one. Loftus, E. F. (1975). Leading questions and the eyewitness report. *Cognitive Psychology, 7,* 560–572.

77. The mean responses for the five verbs "smashed," "collided," "bumped," "hit," and "contacted" were 41, 39, 38, 34, and 32 miles per hour respectively. Loftus & Palmer (1974), *supra* note 54.

78. E.g., Smith, V. L., & Ellsworth, P. C. (1987). The social psychology of eyewitness accuracy: Misleading questions and communicator expertise. *Journal of Applied Psychology, 72,* 294–300.

79. For a review, see Davis, D., & Loftus, E. F. (2007). Internal and external sources of misinformation in adult witness memory. In M. P. Toglia, J. D. Read, D. F. Ross, & R. C. L. Lindsay, eds., *Handbook of eyewitness psychology,* vol. 1: *Memory for events,* pp. 195–237. Mahwah, NJ: Lawrence Erlbaum. See also Paterson, H. M., & Kemp, R. I. (2006b). Comparing methods of encountering post-event information: The power of co-witness suggestion. *Applied Cognitive Psychology, 20,* 1083–1099.

80. Seventy-three percent of participants were misled by a narrative that mentioned that the object in the background of a kitchen scene was a blender

rather than a coffeemaker. Likewise, describing a bystander's shirt color as blue rather than orange led 85 percent of participants to misremember the color they saw. Wright, D. B., & Stroud, J. N. (1998). Memory quality and misinformation for peripheral and central objects. *Legal and Criminological Psychology, 3,* 273–286.

81. Heath, W. P., & Erickson, J. R. (1998). Memory for central and peripheral actions and props after varied post-event presentation. *Legal and Criminological Psychology, 3,* 321–346. Another study found that false memories for suggested peripheral details were more than three times higher than for suggested central details. Dalton, A. L., & Daneman, M. (2006). Social suggestibility to central and peripheral misinformation. *Memory, 14,* 486–501.

82. In the first study of its kind, 29 percent of participants reported memories of the false event. Loftus, E. F., & Pickrell, J. E. (1995). The formation of false memories. *Psychiatric Annals, 25,* 720–725.

83. In these studies, conducted by New Zealand researchers, participants were shown doctored photographs of themselves as children between the ages of four and eight, riding with a family member in a hot-air balloon. As confirmed with their parents, the ride never occurred. None of the participants recalled the ride spontaneously; they were encouraged to imagine the ride and were asked to think of it a few minutes each night. By the third interview, conducted a few days later, half of the participants reported some recollection of the ride. Wade, K. A., Garry, M., Read, J. D., & Lindsay, S. (2002). A picture is worth a thousand lies: Using false photographs to create false childhood memories. *Psychonomic Bulletin & Review, 9,* 597–603. An even higher rate of false recollections was obtained by giving a written narrative describing the event. Garry, M., & Wade, K. A. (2005). Actually, a picture is worth less than 45 words: Narratives produce more false memories than photographs do. *Psychonomic Bulletin & Review, 12,* 359–366. For similar results, see Garry, M., & Gerrie, M. P. (2005). When photographs create false memories. *Current Directions in Psychological Science, 14,* 321–325.

84. After three interviews, an average of 37 percent of participants reported false memories on a number of scenarios that included being saved by a lifeguard and finding a shark's tooth while walking on the beach. Heaps, C. M., & Nash, M. (2001). Comparing recollective experience in true and false autobiographical memories. *Journal of Experimental Psychology: Learning, Memory, and Cognition, 27,* 920–930.

85. An average of 40 percent of participants recalled memories of undergoing medical procedures that never occurred. Mazzoni, G., & Memon, A. (2003). Imagination can create false autobiographical memories. *Psychological Science, 14,* 186–188.

86. Twenty-six percent of participants reported complete memories for the false event, and another 30 percent exhibited a partial false memory. Porter, S.,

Yuille, J. C., & Lehman, D. R. (1999). The nature of real, implanted, and fabricated memories for emotional childhood events: Implications for the recovered memory debate. *Law and Human Behavior, 23, 517–537.*

87. By the third interview, 37 percent of participants recalled experiencing this event. Hyman, I. E., & Pentland, J. (1996). The role of mental imagery in the creation of false childhood memories. *Journal of Memory and Language, 35, 101–117.* In other studies, participants came to endorse false memories of being in a grocery store when the fire extinguisher sprinkler system went on. Hyman, I. E., Husband, T. H., & Billings, F. J. (1995). False memories of childhood experiences. *Applied Cognitive Psychology, 9, 181–197.*

88. In these studies, one-fourth of participants reported memories of meeting Bugs. Grinely, M. J. (2002). Effects of advertising on semantic and episodic memory. Master's thesis, University of Washington, cited in Loftus, E. F. (2003). Make-believe memories. *American Psychologist,* November, 867–873.

89. Johnson, Hashtroudi, & Lindsay (1993), *supra* note 36.

90. Various measures have been used to distinguish between true and false memories, most notably the Memory Characteristics Questionnaire (MCQ). See Johnson, M. K., Foley, M. A., Suengas, A. G., & Raye, C. L. (1988). Phenomenal characteristics of memories for perceived and imagined autobiographical events. *Journal of Experimental Psychology: General, 117, 371–376.*

91. Porter and colleagues found that implanted memories were less vivid and coherent, and held with less confidence than real memories. Porter, Yuille, & Lehman (1999), *supra* note 86. In the study about memories of knocking over the bowl of punch at a wedding, confidence for true memories was 5.6 on a scale of 1–7, but only 3 for false memories. Hyman & Pentland (1996), *supra* note 87. In the hot-air balloon-ride study, the mean confidence for true events was 91 percent, but only 44 percent for the false memory of the balloon ride. Wade et al. (2002), *supra* note 83. See also Loftus & Pickrell (1995), *supra* note 82.

In some studies, false memories were reported as based on a vague sense of familiarity, rather than on a distinct recollection of witnessing the event. For example, see MacRae et al. (2002), *supra* note 62.

92. Some studies have found that false memories are reported with levels of confidence comparable to true memories. In a study of people's memories for the events of September 11, 2001, the confidence of people who responded in error was higher than for the people who responded correctly. Pezdek, K. (2003). Event memory and autobiographical memory for the events of September, 11, 2001. *Applied Cognitive Psychology, 17, 1033–1045.* In a study by Schmolck, Buffalo, & Squire (2000, *supra* note 48), 61 percent of the participants whose recollections were grossly inaccurate gave confidence ratings of 4 or 5 on a scale of 1–5. Roediger & McDermott (1995) found no difference in the level of confidence for true and false memories. Roediger, H. L., & McDermott, K. B. (1995). Creating false memories: Remembering words not presented in

lists. *Journal of Experimental Psychology: Learning, Memory, and Cognition, 21,* 803–814. In one study, participants were actually more confident in erroneous memories than in true memories. Bransford & Franks (1971), *supra* note 60.

Some studies found that participants reporting false memories were as likely as participants reporting true memories to state that they "remembered" actually encountering the information, as opposed to merely "knowing" the information more generally. Chan & McDermott (2006), *supra* note 59. Similar findings were made by Roediger & McDermott (1995), *supra* note 92, and Odegard & Lampinen (2004), *supra* note 73.

In the crashing memory studies by Smeets et al. (2006, *supra* note 68), and Ost et al. (2002, *supra* note 70), the Memory Characteristics Questionnaire (MCQ) did not help distinguish between those who reported having seen the film and those who did not, or between those who provided details of the fictitious event and those who did not.

93. Mitchell & Johnson (2000), *supra* note 32.

94. In one study, false memories appeared initially to have been distinguishable from the true memories, but the differences were mostly washed away following successive interviews. Heaps & Nash (2001), *supra* note 84.

95. Eldridge, Barnard, & Bekerian (1994), *supra* note 40.

96. One-third of participants who were asked how fast the cars were going when they "smashed" into each other reported seeing broken glass. The rate was considerably lower for participants who were cued with the other verbs, such as "hit." The probability of reporting broken glass was not mediated entirely by participants' estimation of the speed, which means that the false memory was caused also by the semantic content of the word "smash." Loftus & Palmer (1974), *supra* note 54.

97. Crombag, Wagenaar, & van Koppen (1996), *supra* note 67.

98. For example, an excerpt from one participant's reported memory: "I was really scared that we were going to fly away and be stuck up in the air. And my dad was laughing but I was really mad at him because I just wanted to get out. I was really, really scared. Um, and it was cold and the wind was blowing in my face and there were quite a few people around." Garry & Wade (2005), *supra* note 83, p. 363.

99. Mazzoni & Memon (2003), *supra* note 85.

100. Hyman, Husband, & Billings (1995), *supra* note 87.

101. Grinely (2002), *supra* note 88; presentation by Elizabeth Loftus at conference "Off The Witness Stand: Using Psychology in the Practice of Justice," John Jay College of Criminal Justice, New York, March 3, 2007.

102. False memories have also been found to comport with temporal schemas, also known as *scripts,* which is the person's expectations with regard to sequences of events. Greenberg, M. S., Westcott, D. R., & Bailey, S. E. (1998).

When believing is seeing: The effect of scripts on eyewitness memory. *Law and Human Behavior, 22,* 685–694.

103. See Eldridge, Barnard, & Bekerian (1994), *supra* note 40; Loftus & Palmer (1974), *supra* note 54.

104. Johnson, M. K., Nolde, S. F., & De Leonardis, D. M. (1996). Emotional focus and source monitoring. *Journal of Memory and Language, 35,* 135–156; Lyle, K. B., & Johnson, M. K. (2006). Importing perceived features into false memories. *Memory, 14(2),* 197–213.

105. Given that the balloons have no means of self-propulsion, they float in the moving block of air, which means that there is no motion between the riders and the air that surrounds them.

106. For a study testing a number of viewing conditions, see Tuckey & Brewer (2003), *supra* note 40.

107. A study using fMRI found a positive relationship between amygdala activation and memory accuracy, especially for high levels of emotional intensity. Amygdala activity is believed to cause both heightened arousal at encoding and heightened consolidation postencoding. Canli, T., Zhao, Z., Brewer, J., Gabrieli, J. D., & Cahill, L. (2000). Event-related activation in the human amygdala associates with later memory for individual emotional response. *Journal of Neuroscience, 20,* RC99. Other research shows that the amygdala influences memory by means of hormone secretion. Cahill, L., & McGaugh, J. L. (1998). Mechanisms of emotional arousal and lasting declarative memory. *Trends in Neurosciences, 21,* 294–299.

108. The advantage in memory accuracy of the participants who encountered the arousing situation was 72 percent versus 63 percent, but the average number of details was 38 percent versus 51 percent. Yuille et al. (1994), *supra* note 17.

109. Hulse & Memon (2006), *supra* note 17.

110. Bornstein, Liebel, & Scarberry (1998), *supra* note 20.

111. Safer, M. A., Christianson, S. Å., Autry, M. W., & Österlund, K. (1998). Tunnel memory for traumatic events. *Applied Cognitive Psychology, 12,* 99–117. Another interpretation offered is that emotional arousal per se tends to strengthen memory, while stress weakens it. Deffenbacher, K. A., Bornstein, B. H., Penrod, S. D., & McGorty, E. K. (2004). A meta-analytic review of the effects of high stress on eyewitness memory. *Law and Human Behavior, 28,* 687–706. For a similar view, see Schacter, D. L. (2001). *The seven sins of memory: How the mind forgets and remembers,* p. 162. Boston: Houghton Mifflin. For a theoretical account of the findings, see Mather, M. (2007). Emotional arousal and memory binding: An object-based framework. *Perspective on Psychological Science, 2,* 33–52.

112. Mather (2007), *supra* note 111, p. 45.

113. According to the many different testimonies, either before or after the shooting, Booth uttered a statement, but witnesses could not agree on what he

stated. Sixteen witnesses remembered him stating either the motto of the state flag of Virginia, "Sic semper tyrannis" (Thus always to tyrants), or the words "The South is avenged," and four recalled him stating both. Gopnik, A. (2007). Annals of biography: Angles and ages. *New Yorker,* May 28, 30–37. See also Good, T. S., ed. (1995). *We saw Lincoln shot: One hundred eyewitness accounts.* Jackson: University Press of Mississippi.

114. Memory disintegration can be reduced by means of repeated questioning about an event, a process known as true memory inoculation. Reyna, V. F., & Lloyd, F. (1997). Theories of false memory in children and adults. *Learning and Individual Differences, 9,* 95–123.

115. On memory fluency, see Jacoby, L. L., & Dallas, M. (1981). On the relationship between autobiographical memory and perceptual learning. *Journal of Experimental Psychology: General, 110,* 306–340.

116. Following the earthquake of 1989 in the Bay area, T-shirts appeared stating, "Thank you for not sharing your earthquake experience." Neisser et al. (1996), *supra* note 48.

117. For example, telling a story in order to elicit sympathy or telling a story to entertain an audience results in opposite effects on the narrative. Marsh, E. J., & Tversky, B. (2004). Spinning the stories of our lives. *Applied Cognitive Psychology, 18,* 491–503.

118. Participants read a story of a murder and were instructed to retell it in a manner that made a certain suspect look guilty. As expected, these stories were narrated in a way that supported that proposition. More importantly, a subsequent recall test revealed that the participants' memories contained more inculpating and fewer exculpating facts. Tversky, B., & Marsh, E. J. (2000). Biased retellings of events yield biased memories. *Cognitive Psychology, 40,* 1–38.

119. Higgins, E. T., & Rholes, W. S. (1978). "Saying is believing": Effects of message modification on memory and liking for the person described. *Journal of Experimental Social Psychology, 14,* 363–378.

120. Marsh, E. J. (2007). Retelling is not the same as recalling. *Current Directions in Psychological Science, 16,* 16–20.

121. For discussions of memory for conversations and its forensic significance, see Davis, D., & Friedman, R. D. (2007). Memory for conversation: The orphan child of witness memory researchers. In R. C. L. Lindsay, D. F. Ross, J. D. Read, & M. P. Toglia, eds., *Handbook of eyewitness psychology,* vol. 2: *Memory for people,* pp. 3–52. Mahwah, NJ: Lawrence Erlbaum; Duke, S. B., Lee, A. S., & Pager, C. K. (2007). A picture's worth a thousand words: Conversational versus eyewitness testimony in criminal convictions. *American Criminal Law Review, 44,* 1–52.

122. See Bransford, J. D., & Johnson, M. K. (1972). Contextual prerequisites for understanding: Some investigations of comprehension and recall. *Journal of Verbal Learning and Verbal Behavior, 11,* 717–726.

123. Kent, G. G., Davis, J. D., & Shapiro, D. A. (1978). Resources required in the construction and reconstruction of conversation. *Journal of Personality and Social Psychology, 36,* 13–22.

124. These findings were obtained in a test conducted minutes after the exposure to the stimulus. Four days later, the number of recalled items decreased to 9.3 and 0.05, respectively. Campos, L., & Alonso-Quecuty, M. L. (2006). Remembering a criminal conversation: Beyond eyewitness testimony. *Memory, 14,* 27–36.

125. Sachs, J. S. (1967). Recognition memory for syntactic and semantic aspects of connected discourse. *Perception & Psychophysics, 2,* 437–442.

126. Mothers recalled about 66 percent of the primary events discussed but only 5 percent of the statements actually uttered. They recalled only 16 percent of the statements they themselves had uttered. Bruck, M., Ceci, S. J., & Francoeur, E. (1999). The accuracy of mothers' memories of conversations with their preschool children. *Journal of Experimental Psychology: Applied, 5,* 89–106.

127. Parks, T. E. (1997). False memories of having said the unsaid: Some new demonstrations. *Applied Cognitive Psychology, 11,* 485–494.

128. For a discussion of the conflicting memories, see Gopnik (2007), *supra* note 113.

129. Brewer, W. F. (1988). Memory for randomly-selected autobiographical events. In U. Neisser & E. Winograd, eds., *Remembering reconsidered: Ecological and traditional approaches to the study of memory,* pp. 21–90. New York: Cambridge University Press.

130. Gibbons, J. A., & Thompson, C. P. (2001). Using a calendar in event dating. *Applied Cognitive Psychology, 15,* 33–44.

131. Odegard & Lampinen (2004), *supra* note 73.

132. In the interview conducted four to five months after the Vancouver shooting incident, ten of the thirteen witnesses failed to recall the month of the incident, and only six recalled the day of the week. See Yuille & Cutshall (1986), *supra* note 18. For more examples, see Hyman, I. E., & Loftus, E. F. (1998). Errors in autobiographical memory. *Clinical Psychology Review, 18,* 933–947.

133. One study found that some 63 percent of the participants made at least one sequencing error with regard to the six central events that occurred on September 11, 2001. Altman, E. M. (2003). Reconstructing the serial order of events: A case study of September 11, 2001. *Applied Cognitive Psychology, 17,* 1067–1080.

134. Another type of memory content that warrants specific attention is memory for automobiles. Preliminary research on car lineups indicates that people display low levels of accuracy in identifying automobiles. In one study, only 24 percent of participants correctly identified a target car from a ten-car sequential lineup. Villegas, A. B., Sharps, M. J., Satterthwaite, B., & Chisholm, S. (2005). Eyewitness memory for vehicles. *Forensic Examiner, 14,* 24–28.

135. Respondents accurately remembered 79 percent of their A grades but only 29 percent of their D grades. Errors in the upward direction were more than four times as many as downward errors. Bahrick, H. P., Hall., L. K., & Berger, S. A. (1996). Accuracy and distortion in memory for high school grades. *Psychological Science, 7,* 265–271.

136. Bahrick, H. P., Hall, L. K., & Dunlosky, J. (1993). Reconstructive processing of memory content for high versus low test scores and grades. *Applied Cognitive Psychology, 7,* 1–10. Secondary analyses of the data show that the findings are driven primarily by ego-enhancing motives rather than by aptitude limitations of the low-performing students.

137. Mather, Shafir, & Johnson (2000), *supra* note 66.

138. See Hastrof & Cantril (1954), *supra* note 57; Balcetis & Dunning (2006), *supra* note 57; Proffitt, Creem, & Zosh (2001), *supra* note 57.

139. Memories influenced by other people are also known as *transactive memory*. Wegner, D. M., Erber, R., & Raymond, P. (1991). Transactive memory in close relationships. *Journal of Personality and Social Psychology, 61,* 923–929.

140. A vast majority (86 percent) of respondents reported discussing the event with cowitnesses. Almost two-thirds reported having talked about the event immediately, and one-fifth talked about it later the same day. Paterson, H. M., & Kemp, R. I. (2006a). Co-witness talk: A survey of eyewitness discussion. *Psychology, Crime & Law, 12,* 181–191.

141. Allwood, C. M., Knutsson, J., & Granhag, P. A. (2006). Eyewitnesses under influence: How feedback affects the realism in confidence judgments. *Psychology, Crime & Law, 12,* 25–38.

142. Participants were paired to discuss an ambiguous event with other participants who saw the same event filmed from a different perspective and thus contained some different facts. Only one of the versions depicted the protagonist stealing money from an unattended purse. Following a discussion, memory tests revealed that some 70 percent of participants reported seeing details that were seen on their partner's video but not on theirs. Of the participants who were not shown the theft, 60 percent reported seeing the protagonist steal the money. Gabbert, F., Memon, A., & Allan, K. (2003). Memory conformity: Can eyewitnesses influence each other's memories for an event? *Applied Cognitive Psychology, 17,* 533–543. See also Valentine, T., & Maras, K. (2011). The effect of cross-examination on the accuracy of adult eyewitness testimony. *Applied Cognitive Psychology, 25,* 554–561.

143. Participants who were showed a film depicting a crime committed by a single perpetrator were paired to discuss the event with participants who were shown the same crime being perpetrated by two people. When participants were initially tested alone, the rate of correct memories of that fact was 97 percent. After the discussion however, fifteen of the twenty pairs agreed on a shared version:

about half reported seeing an accomplice, and the other half reported seeing none. Wright, D. B., Self, G., & Justice, C. (2000). Memory conformity: Exploring misinformation effects when presented by another person. *British Journal of Psychology, 91,* 189–202.

144. Gabbert, F., Memon, A., Allan, K., & Wright, D. B. (2004). Say it to my face: Examining the effects of socially encountered misinformation. *Legal and Criminological Psychology, 9,* 215–227.

145. Participants' memories for a simulated criminal event were found to have been influenced by responses given by a putative cowitness (actually a confederate). The accuracy rates in the two experiments were 30–35 percent when the cowitness responded incorrectly, as compared to 65–70 percent when he or she responded correctly, and 57–58 percent when there was no response from the cowitness. The influences of cowitnesses were found to affect people's memories even when tested alone, at a later date. Shaw, J. S., Garven, S., & Wood, J. M. (1997). Cowitness information can have immediate effects on eyewitness memory reports. *Law and Human Behavior, 21,* 503–523.

146. Wright, D. B., Mathews, S. A., & Skagerberg, E. M. (2005). Social recognition memory: The effect of other people's responses for previously seen and unseen items. *Journal of Experimental Psychology: Applied, 11,* 200–209.

147. As discussed in Chapter 3, the transference error that generated the futile search for John Doe 2 was first reported by only one witness, Tom Kessinger. As the investigation progressed, the second witness, Eldon Elliott, came to provide the same (erroneous) statement. Memon, A., & Wright, D. B. (1999). Eyewitness testimony and the Oklahoma bombing. *The Psychologist, 12,* 292–205.

148. See, e.g., Fisher, R. P., & Geiselman R. E. (1992). *Memory-enhancing techniques in investigative interviewing: The Cognitive Interview.* Springfield, IL: C. C. Thomas.

149. Ron Fisher and his colleagues found that interviews conducted by robbery detectives in Florida contained frequent interruptions, overreliance on short specific questions, inappropriately sequenced questions, poorly phrased questions, distractions, judgmental comments, and more. Fisher, R. P., Geiselman, R. E., & Raymond, D. S. (1987). Critical analysis of police interview techniques. *Journal of Police Science and Administration, 15,* 177–185. A recent review of interviews conducted by detectives in south Florida revealed similar patterns of inadequate interviewing. Fisher, R. P., & Schreiber, N. (2007). Interview protocols to improve eyewitness memory. In M. P. Toglia, J. D. Read, D. F. Ross, & R. C. L. Lindsay, eds., *Handbook of eyewitness psychology,* vol. 1: *Memory for events,* pp. 53–80. Mahwah, NJ: Lawrence Erlbaum.

150. In interviews conducted by five samples of English policemen prior to training, 67–80 percent of the questions were closed-ended, 13–16 percent were leading, and only 3–5 percent were open-ended. George, R., & Clifford, B. (1992). Making the most of witnesses. *Policing, 8,* 185–198.

151. In the Canadian police study, the interviewers spoke 35 percent of the time, and they asked almost four questions per minute, two-thirds of which were closed-ended and about 7 percent of which were leading. Wright, A. M., & Alison, L. (2004). Questioning sequences in Canadian police interviews: Constructing and confirming the course of events? *Psychology, Crime & Law, 10,* 137–154; Snook, B., & Keating, K. (2011). A field study of adult witness interviewing practices in a Canadian police organization. *Legal and Criminological Psychology, 16,* 160–172.

152. German police interviews contained more closed-ended questions than open-ended ones (twenty-nine vs. six per interview), allowing only 7 percent of the witness's testimony for free narrative. Berresheim, A., & Webber, A. (2003). Structured witness interviewing and its effectiveness (in German). *Kriminalistik, 57,* 757–771, cited in Fisher & Schreiber (2007), *supra* note 149.

153. Norwegian officers were found to talk about 50 percent of the time, often firing bursts of closed-ended and yes/no questions. Myklebust, T., & Alison, L. J. (2000). The current state of police interviews with children in Norway: How discrepant are they from models based on current issues in memory and communication? *Psychology, Crime & Law, 6,* 331–351.

154. Loftus (1975), *supra* note 76; Smith & Ellsworth (1987), *supra* note 78.

155. Henkel, L. A., & Mather, M. (2007). Memory attributions for choices: How beliefs shape our memories. *Journal of Memory and Language, 57,* 163–176.

156. These interviews were performed prior to training in the Cognitive Interview method. George & Clifford (1992), *supra* note 150.

157. Yuille (1984), *supra* note 30.

158. Berliner, L., & Lieb, R. (2001). Child sexual abuse investigations: Testing documentation methods. Olympia: Washington State Institute for Public Policy, doc. no. 01-01-4102.

159. Warren, A. R., Woodall, C. E., Thomas, M., Nunno, M., Keeney, J. M., Larson, S. M., & Stadfeld, J. A. (1999). Assessing the effectiveness of a training program for interviewing child witnesses. *Applied Developmental Science, 3,* 128–135. The effect of leading and suggestive questioning is coupled with the general tendency to respond in the affirmative. Kunda, Z., Fong, G. T., Sanitioso, R., & Reber, E. (1993). Directional questions direct self-conceptions. *Journal of Experimental Social Psychology, 29,* 63–86. It is unlikely that this finding will hold when the responder has a strong opinion or stake in the question.

160. For example, in the hot-air balloon studies, participants were presented with real photographs of themselves at an early age, falsely implanted into a photograph of a hot-air balloon basket. Other participants were presented with narrative accounts of the false event. Garry & Wade (2005), *supra* note 83. It should be acknowledged that props that do not contain misleading information can be advantageous.

161. *State v. Cotton,* trial transcript, *supra* note 3, pp. 191–192.

162. In one study, the rate of false memories reported after three suggestive interviews was found to be about five times higher than after the first one. Zaragoza, M. S., & Mitchell, K. J. (1996). Repeated exposure to suggestion and the creation of false memories. *Psychological Science, 7,* 294–300.

163. Garry & Wade (2005), *supra* note 83; Garry & Gerrie (2005), *supra* note 83.

164. Hyman & Pentland (1996), *supra* note 87.

165. Shaw, J. S. (1996). Increases in eyewitness confidence resulting from postevent questioning. *Journal of Experimental Psychology: Applied, 2,* 126–146; Shaw, J. S., & McClure, K. A. (1996). Repeated postevent questioning can lead to elevated levels of eyewitness confidence. *Law and Human Behavior, 20,* 629–653.

166. In one of Loftus's early studies, the suggestive effect of the intrusion was strongest when the information was introduced long after the event rather than immediately after it. Loftus, Miller, & Burns (1978), *supra* note 75.

167. Fisher, R. P. (1995). Interviewing victims and witnesses of crime. *Psychology, Public Policy, and Law, 1,* 732–764.

168. Studies in the implanted memory paradigm routinely exhort participants to expend effort during retrieval. The hot-air balloon-ride study showed that participants who reported spending more time working at remembering the false event were more likely to experience a false memory. Garry & Wade (2005), *supra* note 83.

169. Nilsson, L. G. (1987). Motivated memory: Dissociation between performance data and subjective reports. *Psychological Research, 49,* 183–188; Shaw, J. S., & Zerr, T. K. (2003). Extra effort during memory retrieval may be associated with increases in eyewitness confidence. *Law and Human Behavior, 27,* 315–329; Koriat & Goldsmith (1996), *supra* note 19.

170. Asking witnesses to describe a ring that was allegedly depicted being taken by a burglar in a video clip increased memories for that ring, even though the witnesses never saw the burglar take any jewelry. Drivdahl, S. B., & Zaragoza, M. S. (2001). The role of perceptual elaboration and individual differences in the creation of false memories for suggested events. *Applied Cognitive Psychology, 15,* 265–281.

171. Drivdahl, S. B., Zaragoza, M. S., & Learned, D. M. (in press). The role of emotional elaboration in the creation of false memories. *Applied Cognitive Psychology, 23,* 13–35.

172. Zaragoza, M. S., Payment, K. E., Ackil, J. K., Drivdahl, S. B., & Beck, M. (2001). Interviewing witnesses: Forced confabulation and confirmatory feedback increase false memories. *Psychological Science, 12,* 473–477; Pezdek, K., Sperry, K., & Owens, S. M. (2007). Interviewing witnesses: The effect of forced confabulation on event memory. *Law and Human Behavior, 31,*

463–478. Similar distortions were observed in memory tests that followed an instruction to drum up a false description of a real fact. On a subsequent memory test, as many as 27 percent of the incorrect descriptive details originated in the confabulated descriptions. Pickel, K. L. (2004). When a lie becomes the truth: The effects of self-generated misinformation on eyewitness memory. *Memory, 12*, 14–26. The contaminating effect of guessing was observed also in Hastie, Landsman, & Loftus (1978), *supra* note 51.

173. The rate of false memories was 37 percent for participants instructed to imagine the event, as compared to 12 percent of participants instructed to "think about the event." Hyman & Pentland (1996), *supra* note 87. Instructions to imagine the event were included in other implanted memory studies. E.g., Garry & Wade (2005), *supra* note 83; Wade et al. (2002), *supra* note 83.

It is possible that the imaginability of an event contributes to the prospect of its being falsely recalled. In the study concerning Princess Diana's car crash, 44 percent of respondents claimed to have seen the nonexisting video of the car crash, but only 10 percent of respondents in a pilot study reported having seen the princess's funeral. Ost et al. (2002), *supra* note 70.

174. This treatment increased the rate of false memories from 26 percent to 51 percent. Hanba, J. M., & Zaragoza, M. S. (2007). Interviewer feedback in repeated interviews involving forced confabulation. *Applied Cognitive Psychology, 21*, 433–455.

175. Pezdek, Sperry, & Owens (2007), *supra* note 172.

176. The more times participants were instructed to imagine performing an act, the more likely they were to report that they had actually performed it. Goff & Roediger (1998), *supra* note 74.

177. Blagrove, M., & Akehurst, L. (2000). Effects of sleep loss on confidence-accuracy relationships for reasoning and eyewitness memory. *Journal of Experimental Psychology: Applied, 6*, 59–73.

178. Assefi, S. L., & Garry, M. (2003). Absolute memory distortions: Alcohol placebos influence the misinformation effect. *Psychological Science, 14*, 77–80.

179. Participants who scored higher on a measure of acquiescence were more likely to report suggested false information. Acquiescence is operationalized by the degree to which people respond affirmatively to contradictory statements. Eisen, M. L., Morgan, D. Y., & Mickes, L. (2002). Individual differences in eyewitness memory and suggestibility: Examining relations between acquiescence, dissociation, and resistance to misleading information. *Personality and Individual Differences, 33*, 553–572. A similar measure of compliance was found to be related to participants' reports of (highly unlikely) childhood memories from less than two years of age. Malinoski, P. T., & Lynn, S. J. (1999). The plasticity of early memory reports: Social pressure, hypnotizability, compliance, and interrogative suggestibility. *International Journal of Clinical and Experimental Hypnosis, 47*, 320–345.

180. Fantasy proneness was found to be positively correlated with suggestibility in a Canadian study that induced participants to report impossible memories from their crib, one day after birth. Spanos, N. P., Burgess, C. A., Burgess, M. F., Samuels, C., & Blois, W. O. (1999). Creating false memories of infancy with hypnotic and non-hypnotic procedures. *Applied Cognitive Psychology, 13,* 201–218. Fantasy proneness was found to be positively related to reports of remembering the nonexistent images in one of the Dutch studies of crashing memories described above. Jelicic et al. (2006), *supra* note 68.

181. Granhag, Strömwall, & Allwood (2000), *supra* note 16. This study found that witnesses were better calibrated when asked to measure their memories in terms of frequencies, that is, an overall assessment of how many of the forty-five questions they answered correctly. Shaw & McClure (1996), *supra* note 165, found that witnesses who reported very high levels of confidence (a rating of 6 on a 1–7 scale) were only 55 percent accurate, and witnesses who reported maximal confidence were only about 80 percent accurate.

182. Tomes, J. L., & Katz, A. N. (2000). Confidence-accuracy relations for real and suggested events. *Memory, 8,* 273–283.

183. Overconfidence was even more pronounced for assessments of memory under nighttime illumination: the witnesses recalled only 5 percent of the details, but believed that they recalled 65 percent. Yarmey (1986), *supra* note 20.

184. Shaw (1996), *supra* note 165; Shaw & McClure (1996), *supra* note 165.

185. Hastie, Landsman, & Loftus (1978), *supra* note 51.

186. Garry, M., & Polaschek, D. L. (2000). Imagination and memory. *Current Directions in Psychological Science, 9,* 6–10; Garry, M., Manning, C. G., Loftus, E. F., & Sherman, S. J. (1996). Imagination inflation: Imagining a childhood event inflates confidence that it occurred. *Psychonomic Bulletin & Review, 3,* 208–214.

187. Garry et al. (1996), *supra* note 186; Goff & Roediger (1998), *supra* note 74.

188. Hanba & Zaragoza (2007), *supra* note 174. By the same token, confidence can be decreased, disconfirming cowitness memories and negative feedback from the interviewer. See also Zaragoza et al. (2001), *supra* note 172; Allwood, Knutsson, & Granhag (2006), *supra* note 141.

189. Allwood, Knutsson, & Granhag (2006), supra note 141.

190. Shaw & Zerr (2003), *supra* note 169.

191. Leippe, M. R., Eisenstadt, D., Rauch, S. M., & Stambush, M. A. (2006). Effects of social-comparative memory feedback on eyewitnesses' identification confidence, suggestibility, and retrospective memory reports. *Basic and Applied Social Psychology, 28,* 201–220. In one of the conditions, positive feedback was found to improve the accuracy of witnesses on the subsequent identification task, but the results are somewhat mixed.

192. Bayen, U. J., Nakamura, G. V., Dupuis, S. E., & Yang, C. (2000). The use of schematic knowledge about sources in source monitoring. *Memory & Cognition, 28,* 480–500.

193. Mather, M., Johnson, M. K., & De Leonardis, D. M. (1999). Stereotype reliance in source monitoring: Age differences and neuropsychological test correlates. *Cognitive Neuropsychology, 16,* 437–458.

194. Johnson, Hashtroudi, & Lindsay (1993), *supra* note 36, p. 4.

195. Sacchi, D. L. M., Agnoli, F., & Loftus, E. F. (2007). Changing history: Doctored photographs affect memory for past public events. *Applied Cognitive Psychology, 21,* 1005–1022.

196. Garry, M., Strange, D., Bernstein, D. M., & Kinzett, T. (2007). Photographs can distort memory for the news. *Applied Cognitive Psychology, 21,* 995–1004.

197. Koriat & Goldsmith (1996), *supra* note 19.

198. Echterhoff, G., Higgins, E. T., Kopietz, R., & Groll, S. (2008). How communication goals determine when audience tuning biases memory. *Journal of Experimental Psychology: General, 137,* 3–21.

199. Roper, R., & Shewan, D. (2002). Compliance and eyewitness testimony: Do eyewitnesses comply with misleading "expert pressure" during investigative interviewing? *Legal and Criminological Psychology, 7,* 155–163.

200. Providing witnesses with a negative (fictitious) assessment of their memory led to a doubling of false memories in a subsequent interview. Leippe et al. (2006), *supra* note 191.

201. Ibid.

202. Inducing participants to report memories from the age of two years old was facilitated by informing them (incorrectly) that research shows that everyone can retrieve those memories if they try hard enough. Malinoski & Lynn (1999), *supra* note 179. Strong expectations were used also to induce participants to report (impossible) memories from their hospital crib one day after their birth. Spanos et al. (1999), *supra* note 180.

203. Smith & Ellsworth (1987), *supra* note 78, found the rate of error due to postevent misinformation twice as high when the source of the suggestion was perceived to be knowledgeable as when the source of the suggestion was perceived to have little knowledge (41 percent vs. 18 percent).

204. The technique is based on three basic psychological principles: attending to the witness's cognitive task of memory retrieval, fostering a positive social dynamic with the witness, and facilitating a communicative environment. The first principle, concerning memory and general cognition, leads to the following prescriptions: interviewers should reinstate the context of the event; interviewers should minimize overloading the witness by asking fewer, shorter, and non-interruptive questions; interviewers should tailor the questions to the specific

witness's mental and cultural capabilities; interviewers should vary the retrieval cues by asking about the event from different perspectives; interviewers should monitor the witness's metacognition by instructing her to respond "don't know" rather than guess; interviewers should refrain from applying social pressure; interviewers should refrain from encouraging answers about uncertain facts; and interviewers should minimize the possibility of memory contamination by means of postevent information. The social dynamics principle suggests that interviewers should develop a positive and meaningful rapport with the witness and invite the witness to take an active and even a leading role in the conversation. The communication principle promotes extensive and detailed responses, allowing witnesses to choose their means of expressing their memories. Fisher & Geiselman (1992), *supra* note 148. For a review, see Fisher & Schreiber (2007), *supra* note 149.

205. A meta-analysis of fifty-five comparisons between the Cognitive Interview and other protocols, involving 2,447 participants, demonstrated a substantial increase in recalled details by the Cognitive Interview compared to the results obtained from the standard interview. No difference was found in accuracy rates (85 percent and 82 percent, respectively). This means that the Cognitive Interview increases the level of both accurate and inaccurate details. Köhnken et al. (1999), *supra* note 16.

206. On difficulties with the implementation of and training for the protocol, see Dando, C., Wilcock, R., & Milne, R. (2008). The Cognitive Interview: Inexperienced police officers' perceptions of their witness/victim interviewing practices. *Legal and Criminological Psychology, 13,* 59–70.

5. "Just Admit It, You're Guilty"

1. *Chambers v. Florida,* 309 U.S. 227, 237–238 (1940). See also *Miranda v. Arizona,* 384 U.S. 436, 507 (1966).

2. The Supreme Court has ordered that the proper criterion for admissibility of confessions is whether they were "freely self-determined." *Rogers v. Richmond,* 365 U.S. 534, 544–545 (1961).

3. *Miranda v. Arizona,* 384 U.S. 436 (1966).

4. See Kassin, S. M., Leo, R. A., Meissner, C. A., Richman, K. D., Colwell, L. H., Leach, A. M., & La Fon, D. (2007). Police interviewing and interrogation: A self-report survey of police practices and beliefs. *Law and Human Behavior, 31(4),* 381–400; Thomas, G. C. (1996). Plain talk about the *Miranda* empirical debate: A "steady-state" theory of confessions. *UCLA Law Review, 43,* 933–959.

5. The teens' innocence was revealed in 2002, when Matias Reyes, a convicted serial rapist, confessed to having committed the crime alone. Reyes's guilt was confirmed by a DNA match. As in many other cases, the confessions were corroborated by forensic evidence later found to be flawed. For an in-depth

analysis of the case, see Barnes, S. (2011). *The Central Park Five: A chronicle of a city wilding.* New York: Knopf.

6. See Snyder, L., McQuillian, P., Murphy, W. L., & Joselson, R. (2007). Report on the conviction of Jeffrey Deskovic. http://www.westchesterda.net /Jeffrey%20Deskovic%20Comm%20Rpt.pdf. This report, commissioned by the district attorney of Westchester County, was prepared by a committee of four legal professionals, which included two retired judges.

7. Innocence Project, profile, Joseph White. http://www.innocenceproject .org/Content/Joseph_White.php.

8. Drizin, S. A., & Leo, R. A. (2004). The problem of false confessions in the post-DNA world. *North Carolina Law Review, 82,* 891–1007. One-quarter of the DNA exonerees were convicted on the basis of their confessions. Innocence Project, False confessions. http://www.innocenceproject.org/understand /False-Confessions.php.

9. Drizin & Leo (2004), *supra* note 8.

10. On the typology of false confessions, see Wrightsman, L. S., & Kassin, S. M. (2003). *Confessions in the courtroom.* Newbury Park, CA: Sage Publications.

11. The survey included 1,828 officers from ten police agencies from across the country. Of these officers, 54 percent reported having received instruction on the Reid method. Reppucci, N. D., Meyer, J., & Kostelnik, J. (2010). Custodial interrogation of juveniles: Results of a national survey of police. In G. D. Lassiter & C. A. Meissner, eds., *Police interrogations and false confessions: Current research, practice, and policy recommendations,* pp. 67–80. Washington, DC: American Psychological Association.

12. Inbau, F. E., Reid, J. E., Buckley, J. P., & Jayne, B. C. (2001). *Criminal interrogation and confessions.* 4th ed. Sudbury, MA: Jones and Bartlett. A fifth edition of the book is expected to be published in 2012. For a brief overview of the method, see Buckley, J. P. (2006). The Reid Technique of Interviewing and Interrogation. In T. Williamson, ed., *Investigative interviewing: Rights, research, and regulation,* pp. 190–206. Portland, OR: Willan.

13. See http://www.reid.com/r_about.html.

14. The website cites a survey of Minnesota and Alaska law enforcement investigators trained by John E. Reid & Associates. According to this survey, 3,153 (99.4 percent) of their 3,162 confessions were admitted by the courts. http://www.reid.com/r_about.html.

15. Quoted in Kassin, S. M., & Gudjonsson, G. H. (2004). The psychology of confessions: A review of the literature and issues. *Psychological Science in the Public Interest, 5(2),* 36. This confidence is not shared by police forces in other countries. For example, a publication of the New Zealand police states: "There is no typical non-verbal behaviour which is associated with deception. Despite this, research has found that people (including both interviewers and interviewees) often hold stereotypical views about non-verbal behaviour which are incorrect.

Thus, conclusions based solely on someone's behaviour in the interview room are not reliable." Schollum, M. (2005). *Investigative interviewing: The literature,* p. 4. Wellington, NZ: Office of the Commissioner of Police.

16. http://www.reid.com/services/r_behavior.html.

17. Zuckerman, M., DePaulo, B. M., & Rosenthal, R. (1981). Verbal and nonverbal communication of deception. In L. Berkowitz, ed., *Advances in experimental social psychology.* vol. 4, pp. 1–59. New York: Academic Press.

18. DePaulo, B. M., Lindsay, J. J., Malone, B. E., Muhlenbruck, L., Charlton, K., & Cooper, H. (2003). Cues to deception. *Psychological Bulletin, 129,* 74–118.

19. In a follow-up study conducted with 2,500 people in sixty-three countries, gaze aversion was cited by 72 percent of the respondents, again, more than any other cue. Global Deception Research Team (2006). A world of lies. *Journal of Cross-Cultural Psychology, 37,* 60–74.

20. Einav, S., & Hood, B. M. (2008). Tell-tale eyes: Children's attribution of gaze aversion as a lying cue. *Developmental Psychology, 44,* 1655–1667.

21. Two visual cues—pupil dilation and chin raise—were found to be positively related to deceit, but they were measured in only four studies each. DePaulo et al. (2003), *supra* note 18.

22. For example, most people associate deceit with increased arm and leg movements, while the research shows that these movements are actually inhibited during deceit. Akehurst, L., Köhnken, G., Vrij, A., & Bull, R. (1996). Lay persons' and police officers' beliefs regarding deceptive behaviour. *Applied Cognitive Psychology, 10,* 461–471.

23. Some cues are interpreted by different people to indicate opposite conclusions. For example, one study found that whereas two-thirds of people believe that people tend to inhibit hand and finger movement while telling lies, the other third believe the opposite. Vrij, A. (2008). *Detecting lies and deceit: Pitfalls and opportunities.* 2nd ed. New York: John Wiley & Sons.

24. Bond, C. F., Jr., & DePaulo, B. M. (2006). Accuracy of deception judgments. *Personality and Social Psychology Review, 10,* 214–234.

25. A meta-analysis shows that differences in performance among individuals are no different from what would be expected by chance, and that the highest levels of accuracy do not differ from what a stochastic mechanism would predict. When it comes to telling lies, individual differences are pronounced. Bond, C. F., Jr., & DePaulo, B. M. (2008). Individual differences in judging deception: Accuracy and bias. *Psychological Bulletin, 134,* 477–492.

26. In this study, the witness was actually telling a lie. Granhag, P. A., & Strömwall, L. A. (2000). Effects of preconceptions on deception detection and new answers to why lie-catchers often fail. *Psychology, Crime & Law, 6,* 197–218.

27. Vrij (2008), *supra* note 23.

28. The confidence-accuracy relationship was found to be minute ($r = .04$) and not statistically significant. Across the studies, the correlations ranged from –.20

to .26. DePaulo, B. M., Charlton, K., Cooper, H., Lindsay, J. J., & Muhlenbruck, L. (1997). The accuracy-confidence correlation in the detection of deception. *Personality and Social Psychology Review, 1,* 346–357.

29. For the most part, these participants were offered monetary rewards for success.

30. The standardized difference measure (or *d* value) of voice pitch was 0.59, which is considered medium). DePaulo et al. (2003), *supra* note 18. In a meta-analysis by Sporer and Schwandt, the mean weighted *r* effect size for voice pitch was 0.52, while the other three significant cues (message duration, speech rate, and response latency) were between 0.1 and 0.2. Sporer, S. L., & Schwandt, B. (2006). Para-verbal indicators of deception: A meta-analytic synthesis. *Applied Cognitive Psychology, 20,* 421–446.

31. The effect size for gaze aversion, measured in standardized difference *(d),* was −0.15. DePaulo et al. (2003), *supra* note 18.

32. Bond & DePaulo (2006), *supra* note 24.

33. Deceit related to concealing a transgression revealed more nervousness $(d=.51)$, more blinking $(d=.38)$, a faster rate of speech $(d=.32)$, and less foot and leg movement $(d=-.24)$. DePaulo et al. (2003), *supra* note 18.

34. Ibid.

35. Akehurst et al. (1996), *supra* note 22; Colwell, L. H., Miller, H. A., Miller, R. S., & Lyons, P. M., Jr. (2006). US police officers' knowledge regarding behaviors indicative of deception: Implications for eradicating erroneous beliefs through training. *Psychology, Crime & Law, 12(5),* 489–503.

36. Gaze aversion was cited by 78 percent of the students tested and 73 percent of the professional lie catchers. Vrij, A., & Semin, G. R. (1996). Lie experts' beliefs about nonverbal indicators of deception. *Journal of Nonverbal Behavior, 20,* 65–80. Similar opinions were obtained by Zuckerman, M., Koestner, R., & Driver, R. (1981). Beliefs about cues associated with deception. *Journal of Nonverbal Behavior, 6,* 105–114.

37. Only 33 percent of prison inmates tested seemed to believe that gaze aversion is related to deceit. Vrij & Semin (1996), *supra* note 36. Prisoners' superior knowledge of deceit cues was confirmed in a Swedish study. Granhag, P. A., Andersson, L. O., Strömwall, L. A., & Hartwig, M. (2004). Imprisoned knowledge: Criminals' beliefs about deception. *Legal and Criminological Psychology, 9,* 103–119. Inmates have also been found to be somewhat more accurate than students in deceit detection accuracy (65 percent vs. 58 percent). The accuracy of inmates was superior in judging deceitful statements, but no better in judging truths. Hartwig, M., Granhag, P. A., Strömwall, L. A., & Andersson, L. O. (2004). Suspicious minds: Criminals' ability to detect deception. *Psychology, Crime & Law, 10,* 83–95.

38. See Bond & DePaulo (2006), *supra* note 24. A study conducted in the laboratory of Vrij, Mann, and others found accuracy levels of 46 percent (in the control

condition). Vrij, A., Mann, S. A., Fisher, R. P., Leal, S., Milne, R., & Bull, R. (2008). Increasing cognitive load to facilitate lie detection: The benefit of recalling an event in reverse order. *Law and Human Behavior, 32(3), 253–265.*

Somewhat better performance (around 65 percent accuracy) was found in a series of studies of English police officers judging criminals in real cases. O'Sullivan, M., Frank, M. G., Hurley, C. M., & Tiwana, J. (2009). Police lie detection accuracy: The effect of lie scenario. *Law and Human Behavior, 33(6), 530–538.* The calculation of the accuracy for criminals in the high-stakes condition was based on studies 5, 6, 7, 9, and 10 from table 1 and adjusted to include the findings of the unmentioned study. Vrij, A., & Mann, S. (2001a). Who killed my relative? Police officers' ability to detect real-life high-stake lies. *Psychology, Crime & Law, 7,* 119–132. An analysis by Vrij (2008), *supra* note 23, reaches similar findings (pp. 161, 166–167).

These findings are to some degree encouraging, but they suffer from methodological limitations. Five of the seven studies that fall into this category used the same set of materials, which contained clips of only fourteen suspects. By contrast, the study that relied on clips from a different group of suspects found accuracy rates no different from chance. In this study, Dutch police officers fared no better than chance level in detecting deceit by people who were concealing that they had actually murdered family members. The materials in this study contained eight suspects (Vrij & Mann 2001a).

More importantly, there is reason to question the task that was tested in these studies. The materials consisted of various subsamples from sixty-five clips that were culled from interviews with fourteen people whose guilt was reliably established. Although all suspects were guilty, some of the clips were of truthful statements and some were of deceitful statements. The task in these studies was to judge the veracity of the individual clips, not to determine whether the suspect was honest or deceitful, which is the forensically relevant issue. In fact, the instructions informed the participants that they could expect to see multiple clips of the same target, some of which could be truths and some could be lies (e.g., Mann, S., Vrij, A., & Bull, R. [2004]. Detecting true lies: Police officers' ability to detect suspects' lies. *Journal of Applied Psychology, 89,* 137–149, p. 140). It seems that this instruction effectively countered any distortion produced by global judgments of the suspect or the investigator bias (discussed later). The study by Vrij & Mann (2001a) was the only one in this category that tested police officers' ability to judge suspects (as opposed to individual clips), and it revealed poor performance.

39. One study that tested the motivation to catch the liar actually decreased detection accuracy (from 60 percent to 46 percent) while increasing confidence (data for no-feedback condition). Porter, S., McCabe, S., Woodworth, M., & Peace, K. A. (2007). Genius is 1% inspiration and 99% perspiration . . . or is it? An investigation of the impact of motivation and feedback on deception detection. *Legal and Criminological Psychology, 12(2), 297–309.*

40. Blair, J. P. Levine, T. R., & Shaw, A. S. (2010). Content in context improves deception detection accuracy. *Human Communication Research, 36,* 423–442.

41. On the effect of suspicion on judgments of deceit, see Toris, C., & DePaulo, B. M. (1984). Effects of actual deception and suspiciousness of deception on interpersonal perceptions. *Journal of Personality and Social Psychology, 47(5),* 1063–1073; Bond, C. F., Jr., & Fahey, W. E. (1987). False suspicion and the misperception of deceit. *British Journal of Social Psychology, 26(1),* 41–46.

42. See Meissner, C. A., & Kassin, S. M. (2004). "You're guilty, so just confess!" Cognitive and behavioral confirmation biases in the interrogation room. In G. D. Lassiter, ed., *Perspectives in law & psychology,* vol. 20: *Interrogations, confessions, and entrapment,* pp. 85–106. New York: Kluwer Academic/Plenum.

43. Levine, T. R., Asada, K. J. K., & Park, H. S. (2006). The lying chicken and the gaze avoidant egg: Eye contact, deception, and causal order. *Southern Communication Journal, 71(4),* 401–411.

44. Leo, R. A. (2008). *Police interrogation and American justice,* p. 97. Cambridge, MA: Harvard University Press.

45. Inbau et al. (2001), *supra* note 12, pp. 291–292.

46. See, e.g., Meissner, C. A., & Kassin, S. M. (2002). "She's guilty!" Investigator bias in judgments of truth and deception. *Law and Human Behavior, 26(5),* 469–480; Elaad, E. (2003). Effects of feedback on the overestimated capacity to detect lies and the underestimated ability to tell lies. *Applied Cognitive Psychology, 17(3),* 349–363. Surveyed police investigators assessed that they were correct in detecting deceit 77 percent of the time. Kassin et al. (2007), *supra* note 4.

47. See Bull, R., & Soukara, S. (2010). Four studies of what really happens in police interviews. In G. D. Lassiter & C. A. Meissner, eds., *Police interrogations and false confessions: Current research, practice, and policy recommendations,* pp. 81–95. Washington, DC: American Psychological Association.

48. The accuracy of judging lying suspects increased from 41 percent to 68 percent. Hartwig, M., Granhag, P. A., Strömwall, L. A., & Vrij, A. (2005). Detecting deception via strategic disclosure of evidence. *Law and Human Behavior, 29,* 469–484.

49. The accuracy of judgments of both lying and truthful suspects increased from 56 percent to 85 percent. Hartwig, M., Granhag, P. A., Strömwall, L. A., & Kronkvist, O. (2006). Strategic use of evidence during police interviews: When training to detect deception. *Law and Human Behavior, 30,* 603–619.

50. For example, police officers were more accurate at detecting deceit when suspects were asked to recount their story in reverse order. The accuracy rate was 53 percent for suspects asked to recount the story in reverse order, which was somewhat higher than the control condition (46 percent). See Vrij et al. (2008), *supra* note 38; Vrij, A., Fisher, R., Mann, S., & Leal, S. (2006). Detecting

deception by manipulating cognitive load. *Trends in Cognitive Sciences, 10(4)*, 141–142.

51. To be sure, people also lie to the police for reasons other than hiding their involvement in a particular crime. People may lie to cover up for someone else or to conceal some other deed (e.g., truancy, an extramarital affair). Ideally, these matters would be cleared up in the course of the interrogation.

52. Inbau et al. (2001), *supra* note 12, p. 130.

53. Ibid., p. 151. The authors state also that in response to the interrogator's accusation, "the guilty suspect probably will look at the floor or to the side as much as possible in order to avoid direct eye-to-eye contact" (p. 223).

54. Ibid., p. 223.

55. Ibid., p. 144.

56. Ibid., pp. 137, 135.

57. Ibid., pp. 136, 176.

58. Ibid., p. 176.

59. Ibid., pp. 179, 182, 174.

60. Ibid., pp. 129, 179.

61. Ibid., p. 159; Buckley (2006), *supra* note 12, p. 198.

62. Inbau et al. (2001), *supra* note 12, p. 223.

63. Ibid., p. 305.

64. Ibid., pp. 134–135.

65. Ibid., p. 136.

66. Ibid., p. 176. See also Horvath, F., Blair, J. P., & Buckley, J. B. (2008). The behavioural analysis interview: Clarifying the practice, theory and understanding of its use and effectiveness. *International Journal of Police & Management, 10,* 101–118.

67. Inbau et al. (2001), *supra* note 12, pp. 137–138.

68. Ibid., p. 139.

69. Buckley (2006), *supra* note 12, p. 192.

70. Inbau et al. (2001), *supra* note 12, p. 151. The investigator is left to figure out how to distinguish between "apprehension" and "concern," and how to determine whether a "casual manner is unrestrained."

71. Ibid., p. 308.

72. Ibid., p. 190. Elsewhere the textbook states only: "The investigator should have some basis for believing a suspect has not told the truth before confronting the suspect" (p. 8).

73. The authors provide only abstract advice: "The basis for this belief may be the suspect's behavior during an interview or inconsistencies with the suspect's account, physical evidence, or circumstantial evidence, coupled with behavior observations" (ibid., p. 8).

74. Ibid., p. 223.

75. Ibid., p. 181.

76. See, e.g., Hartwig, M., Granhag, P. A., & Strömwall, L. A. (2007). Guilty and innocent suspects' strategies during police interrogations. *Psychology, Crime & Law, 13(2)*, 213–227; Porter, S., Doucette, N. L., Woodworth, M., Earle, J., & MacNeil, B. (2008). Halfe the world knowes not how the other halfe lies: Investigation of verbal and non-verbal signs of deception exhibited by criminal offenders and non-offenders. *Legal and Criminological Psychology, 13(1)*, 27–38. See also Vrij (2008), *supra* note 23.

77. Ahern, E. C., Lyon, T. D., & Quas, J. A. (2011). Young children's emerging ability to make false statements. *Developmental Psychology, 47*, 61–66; Lewis, M. (1993). The development of deception. In M. Lewis & C. Saarni, eds., *Lying and deception in everyday life*, pp. 90–105. New York: Guilford Press; Talwar, V., Murphy, S. M., & Lee, K. (2007). White lie-telling in children for politeness purposes. *International Journal of Behavioral Development, 31*, 1–11.

78. See Gudjonsson, G. H. (1988). How to defeat the polygraph tests. In A. Gale, ed., *The polygraph test: Lies, truth and science*, pp. 126–136. Thousand Oaks, CA: Sage Publications; Rosenfeld, J. P., Soskins, M., Bosh, G., & Ryan, A. (2004). Simple, effective countermeasures to P300-based tests of detection of concealed information. *Psychophysiology, 41*, 205–219.

Given that Reid & Associates also offers courses in polygraph testing (http://www.reid.com/services/r_polygraph.html), it is hard to believe that the corporation is unfamiliar with the issue of countermeasures.

79. Elaad, E., & Ben-Shakhar, G. (2009). Countering countermeasures in the concealed information test using covert respiration measures. *Applied Psychophysiology and Biofeedback, 34(3)*, 197–208.

80. The company's website states: "Identifying countermeasures is a critical part of a competent examiner's training. In our office almost 25% of guilty suspects are identified primarily because of their use of countermeasures. . . . None of the software developed for this purpose is capable of identifying specific subject countermeasures." The Polygraph Technique Part II: Value during an investigation (Investigator Tips, September 2001). http://www.reid.com/educational_info/r_tips.html?serial=321090728120738.

81. Inbau et al. (2001), *supra* note 12, p. 158. Innocent suspects could feel anxious also because of concerns over not being able to afford a lawyer, missing work, having to face up to one's family, losing face within the community, and more.

82. Ibid.

83. Ibid., pp. 122–123.

84. Masip, L., Herrero, C., Garrido, E., & Barba, A. (2011). Is the behaviour analysis interview just common sense? *Applied Cognitive Psychology, 25*, 593–604; Masip, J., & Ces, C. (2011). Guilty and innocent suspects' self-reported strategies during an imagined police interview. Poster presented at the Fourth International Congress on Psychology and Law, Miami, FL, March 2–5.

85. The study examined sixty taped interviews of people who were suspected in real life by their employers of various workplace infractions, mostly theft. The interviews were conducted according to the BAI method by only five interviewers, all employees of the corporation, and those interviews were judged by four evaluators (who also appear to have been employed by the company). The study found that the evaluators correctly classified 78 percent of the truthful suspects and 66 percent of the deceptive ones, with 16 percent inconclusive judgments. Removing the inconclusive cases brought the rate of accuracy to 91 percent for truthful suspects and 80 percent for deceptive ones, which averages to 86 percent. Horvath, F., Jayne, B., & Buckley, J. (1994). Differentiation of truthful and deceptive criminal suspects in behavior analysis interviews. *Journal of Forensic Science, 39,* 793–807.

86. Ibid., p. 805. In those two cases, employees were accused of stealing money from their employers. It was revealed that the money was never actually received by the employer. The veracity of thirty-four of the suspects was said to be "established by a corroborated confession of the guilty suspect" (p. 797). Oddly, later on, the authors note that thirteen of the thirty-four suspects were actually truthful (p. 798). The veracity of the remaining suspects was based on a "factual analysis," that is, the researchers' subjective evaluation based on the suspects' biographical information, opportunity, motivation, and propensity to commit the act (p. 797). These judgments are a patently insufficient basis for scientific claims.

87. Blair, J. P., & McCamey, W. P. (2002). Detection of deception: An analysis of the Behavioral Analysis Interview technique. *Illinois Law Enforcement Executive Forum, 2,* 165–170. Note that this study finds a baseline accuracy of lie detection (before instruction in the BAI method) at 71 percent, which is quite unusual. The corporation claims that its findings were replicated also in the unpublished Master's thesis of Peter Blair. See Blair, J. P. (1997). The effect of training in assessing behavior symptoms of criminal suspects. University of Western Illinois (unpublished). For a critique of the study, see Vrij (2008), *supra* note 23, chap. 7.

88. Vrij, A., Mann, S., & Fisher, R. P. (2006). An empirical test of the Behaviour Analysis Interview. *Law and Human Behavior, 30(3),* 329–345.

89. Kassin, S. M., & Fong, C. T. (1999). "I'm innocent!" Effects of training on judgments of truth and deception in the interrogation room. *Law and Human Behavior, 23(5),* 499–516.

90. For example, honest suspects are expected to be more motivated to prove the investigator wrong (Inbau et al. 2001, *supra* note 12, p. 306), while deceptive suspects are said to be more prone to make declarations against their self-interest (p. 137) and they are more likely to behave in a friendly manner and to wink and smile at the investigator (pp. 129, 142).

91. In justifying the protocol's reliance on nonverbal cues, the authors note "hence the commonplace expressions 'Actions speak louder than words' and

'Look me straight in the eye if you're telling the truth'" (ibid., p. 143). In a rare nod to social science, the authors note (without citation): "according to various social studies, 70% of a message communicated between persons occurs at the nonverbal level" (ibid., p. 143).

92. See also Leo (2008), *supra* note 44, p. 98.

93. For the continued reliance of U.S. police officers on mistaken cues, notably gaze aversion, see Colwell et al. (2006), *supra* note 35.

94. Snyder et al. (2007), *supra* note 6.

95. See Kassin, S. M. (2008). Confession evidence: Commonsense myths and misconceptions. *Criminal Justice and Behavior, 35,* 1309–1322. Gary Gauger was not exonerated on the basis of a DNA test. He struck luck in 1997, when an unrelated federal investigation of a Milwaukee motorcycle gang caught two gang members on tape boasting about committing the double homicide. One of these men pleaded guilty to the murders, and the other was convicted of the crimes in 2000. See http://www.law.northwestern.edu/cwc/exonerations/ilGau gerSummary.html. On the Michael Crowe case, see Sauer, M., & Wilkens, J. (1999). Haunting questions: The Stephanie Crowe case, part 1: The night she was killed. *San Diego Union-Tribune,* May 11. http://ww.uniontrib.com/news /reports/crowe/crowe1.html.

96. Leo (2008), *supra* note 44, chap. 3.

97. Of the 125 false confessions studied by Drizin & Leo (2004, *supra* note 8), 81 percent were obtained in murder cases and 9 percent in rape cases.

98. Inbau et al. (2001), *supra* note 12, chap. 13.

99. For reviews of the research, see Kassin & Gudjonsson (2004), *supra* note 15, pp. 33–67; Kassin, S. M., Drizin, S. A., Grisso, T., Gudjonsson, G. H., Leo, R. A., & Redlich, A. D. (2010). Police-induced confessions: Risk factors and recommendations. *Law and Human Behavior, 34(1),* 3–38.

100. Kassin, S. M., Meissner, C. A., & Norwick, R. J. (2005). "I'd know a false confession if I saw one": A comparative study of college students and police investigators. *Law and Human Behavior, 29(2),* 211–227.

101. Leo's research is based on his examination of some 2,000 real-life interrogations. See Leo (2008), *supra* note 44; Leo, R. A. (1996). Inside the interrogation room. *Journal of Criminal Law & Criminology, 86,* 266–303; Ofshe, R., & Leo, R. A. (1997). The social psychology of police interrogation: The theory and classification of true and false confessions. *Studies in Law, Politics and Society, 16,* 189–251.

102. Braun, B. (2007). She's got a right to say the death penalty is wrong. *Star-Ledger* (Newark, NJ), November 19, p. 13. Byron Halsey explained that he did not actually write the confession; "I signed what the cops wrote." Halsey was released from prison after serving nineteen years of a life sentence. See Innocence Project, profile, Byron Halsey. http://www.innocenceproject.org/Content /Byron_Halsey.php.

In a prison study conducted in Iceland, 12 percent of inmates stated that they had falsely confessed to the police at one point or another. The most frequent reason given for the confessions was a desire to escape the pressure of the investigation. Sigurdsson, J. F., & Gudjonsson, G. H. (1996). The psychological characteristics of "false confessors": A study among Icelandic prison inmates and juvenile offenders. *Personality and Individual Differences, 20(3),* 321–329.

103. *Bram v. United States,* 168 U.S. 532, 543–43 (1897).

104. See Kassin & Gudjonsson (2004), *supra* note 15.

105. In *Frazier v. Cupp,* 394 U.S. 731 (1969), the Court condoned falsely informing the defendant that his accomplice had confessed to having jointly committing the murder. In *Oregon v. Mathiason,* 429 U.S. 492 (1977), the Court condoned lying about finding the suspect's fingerprints at the scene of the crime.

106. Drizin & Leo (2004), *supra* note 8.

107. Referring to the threat of execution, Sacia implored his fellow legislators: "Don't take that tool from law enforcement." Long, R., & Wilson, T. (2010). Death penalty ban passes Illinois House on second try. *Chicago Tribune,* January 6. http://newsblogs.chicagotribune.com/clout_st/2011/01/death -penalty-ban-fails-by-one-vote-in-illinois-house.html.

108. Inbau et al. (2001), *supra* note 12, pp. 365–366. The manual also advises investigators to have the full confession witnessed by a second party.

109. Kassin, S. M., Goldstein, C. C., & Savitsky, K. (2003). Behavioral confirmation in the interrogation room: On the dangers of presuming guilt. *Law and Human Behavior, 27(2),* 187–203.

110. Kassin, S. M., & McNall, K. (1991). Police interrogations and confessions: Communicating promises and threats by pragmatic implication. *Law and Human Behavior, 15(3),* 233–251.

111. This study indicates that the minimization technique reduces the diagnosticity ratio of confession evidence (true confessions divided by false confessions) from 7.7 to 5.1. The study also found that issuing threats and promises increases the rate of confessions from guilty suspects by about half, while more than doubling the rate of confessions from innocent suspects. The combination of minimization and the "deal" resulted in a decrease in the diagnosticity ratio to 2.0. Russano, M. B., Meissner, C. A., Narchet, F. M., & Kassin, S. M. (2005). Investigating true and false confessions within a novel experimental paradigm. *Psychological Science, 16(6),* 481–486.

112. Of the innocent participants, 81 percent waived their rights to refuse the interrogation. The rate was only 36 percent among guilty participants. Kassin, S. M., & Norwick, R. J. (2004). Why people waive their *Miranda* rights: The power of innocence. *Law and Human Behavior, 28(2),* 211–221.

113. Kassin, S. M., & Kiechel, K. L. (1996). The social psychology of false confessions: Compliance, internalization, and confabulation. *Psychological Science, 7(3),* 125–128.

114. Horselenberg, R., Merckelbach, H., & Josephs, S. (2003). Individual differences and false confessions: A conceptual replication of Kassin and Kiechel (1996). *Psychology, Crime & Law, 9(1),* 1–8.

115. Perillo, J. T., & Kassin, S. (2011). Inside interrogation: The lie, the bluff, and false confessions. *Law and Human Behavior, 35,* 327–337.

116. 384 U.S. 436 (1966).

117. Schulhofer, S. (2006). *Miranda v. Arizona:* A modest but important legacy. In C. Steiker, ed., *Criminal procedure stories,* pp. 115–180. New York: Foundation Press.

118. The report by the National Research Council cites studies that find that the *Miranda* requirement curtailed the investigative function only minimally. National Research Council (2004). *Fairness and effectiveness in policing: The evidence,* ed. W. Skogan & K. Frydl, p. 256. Washington, DC: National Academies Press. One legal authority has stated that the *Miranda* decision "is a hoax." Slobogin, C. (2003). Toward taping. *Ohio State Journal of Criminal Law, 1,* 309.

119. See *supra* note 14.

120. Leo, R. A. (2001). Questioning the relevance of *Miranda* in the twenty-first century. *Michigan Law Review, 99,* 1000–1029. Claims to the contrary were made by Paul Cassell, a critic of the *Miranda* doctrine. See Cassell, P. G. (1996). *Miranda's* social costs: An empirical reassessment. *Northwestern University Law Review, 90,* 387–499; Cassell, P. G., & Hayman, B. S. (1996). Police interrogation in the 1990s: An empirical study of the effects of Miranda. *UCLA Law Review, 43,* 839–931. Cassell's work has been widely criticized. See, e.g., Schulhofer, S. J. (1996). *Miranda's* practical effect: Substantial benefits and vanishingly small social costs. *Northwestern University Law Review, 90,* 500–564; Thomas, G. C., & Leo, R. A. (2002). The effects of *Miranda v. Arizona:* "Embedded" in our national culture? *Crime and Justice: A Review of Research, 29(20),* 3–271.

121. This data point is substantiated by both surveys of law enforcement personnel (Kassin et al., 2007, *supra* note 4) and observational research (Leo 1996, *supra* note 101).

122. Leo (2008), *supra* note 44, chap. 4.

123. Dix, G. E. (1988). Federal constitutional confession law: The 1986 and 1987 Supreme Court terms. *Texas Law Review, 67,* 231–349, pp. 272–276.

124. For example, compare *Bram v. United States,* 168 U.S. 532 (1897), with *Colorado v. Connelley,* 479 U.S. 157 (1986).

125. *Missouri v. Seibert,* 542 U.S. 600, 608–609 (2004) (plurality opinion).

126. Inbau et al. (2001), *supra* note 12, p. 212; see also Buckley (2006), *supra* note 12, p. 198.

127. Buckley (2006), *supra* note 12, p. 201.

128. Leo (1996), *supra* note 101.

129. The duration of the interrogation was reported in forty-four of the false confession cases. See Drizin & Leo (2004), *supra* note 8. In contrast, 90 percent of all interrogations take less than two hours. Leo (1996), *supra* note 101.

130. For example, in the data set compiled by Sam Gross and his colleagues, 69 percent of the mentally ill or mentally retarded exonerees and 69 percent of the exonerees aged 12–15 were convicted on the basis of their false confessions. The ratio was only 8 percent for healthy adults. Gross, S. R., Jacoby, K., Matheson, D. J., Montgomery, N., & Patil, S. (2005). Exonerations in the United States 1989 through 2003. *Journal of Criminal Law & Criminology, 95, 523–560.* Among the DNA exonerees, eighteen of the thirty-one false confessors were either mentally retarded, under the age of eighteen, or both. Garrett, B. L. (2008). Judging innocence. *Columbia Law Review, 108,* 89.

131. Kassin, S. M. (2005). On the psychology of confessions: Does innocence put innocents at risk? *American Psychologist, 60(3),* 215–228.

132. Gilovich, T., Savitsky, K., & Medvec, V. H. (1998). The illusion of transparency: Biased assessments of others' ability to read one's emotional states. *Journal of Personality and Social Psychology, 75(2),* 332–346.

133. Leo (1996), *supra* note 101. Suspects with no criminal records are probably more likely to be innocent than suspects who have been convicted in the past.

134. Of the innocent participants, 81 percent waived their rights to refuse the interrogation. The rate was only 36 percent among guilty participants. Kassin & Norwick (2004), *supra* note 112.

135. On the weak empirical basis of the Reid method and the possibility that it results in false confessions, see Blair, J. P., & Kooi, B. (2004). The gap between training and research in the detection of deception. *International Journal of Police Science and Management, 6,* 77–83.

136. See the Police and Criminal Evidence Act (1984), Code of Practice for the Detention, Treatment, and Questioning of Persons by Police Officers (Code C).

137. The mnemonic PEACE stands for Planning and Preparation, Engage and Explain, obtain an Account, Closure, and Evaluation.

138. The principles also instruct that investigators are free to ask a wide range of questions in order to obtain material that may assist an investigation; investigators should recognize the positive impact of an early admission in the context of the criminal justice system; investigators are not bound to accept the first answer given; questioning is not unfair merely because it is persistent; and even when the right of silence is exercised by a suspect, investigators have a responsibility to put questions to them. National Policing Improvement Agency

(2009). National investigative interviewing strategy. http://www.npia.police.uk /en/docs/National_Investigative_Interviewing_Strategy_09.pdf.

139. Shepherd, E. (1993). *Aspects of police interviewing.* Leicester, UK: British Psychological Society. For a recent account, see Shepherd, E. (2007). *Investigative interviewing: The conversation management approach.* New York: Oxford University Press.

140. The analogy to Columbo was proposed by Ray Bull. Carey, B. (2009). Judging honesty by words, not fidgets. *New York Times,* May 9. http://www .nytimes.com/2009/05/12/science/12lying.html?_r=2&emc=eta1.

141. See Meissner, C. A., Russano, M. B., & Narchet, F. M. (2010). The importance of a laboratory science for improving the diagnostic value of confession evidence. In G. D. Lassiter & C. A. Meissner, eds., *Police interrogations and false confessions: Current research, practice, and policy recommendations,* pp. 111–126. Washington, DC: American Psychological Association.

142. Other drawbacks included lack of preparation, failure to establish relevant facts, general ineptitude, poor technique, undue repetitiveness, and persistent and labored questioning. See Milne, R., Shaw, G., & Bull, R. (2007). Investigative interviewing: The role of research. In D. Carson, R. Milne, F. Pakes, & K. Shalev, eds., *Applying psychology to criminal justice,* pp. 65–80. Chichester, UK: Wiley.

143. Griffiths, A., & Milne, B. (2006). Will it all end in tiers? Police interviews with suspects in Britain. In T. Williamson, ed., *Investigative interviewing: Rights, research, and regulation,* pp. 167–189. Portland, OR: Willan.

144. Bull & Soukara (2010), *supra* note 47.

145. Clarke, C., Milne, R., & Bull, R. (2011). Interviewing suspects of crime: The impact of PEACE training, supervision and the presence of a legal advisor. *Journal of Investigative Psychology and Offender Profiling, 8,* 149–162.

146. New Zealand Police (2005). Investigative interviewing: The literature. https://admin.police.govt.nz/resources/2005/investigative-interviewing/index.html.

147. Fahsing, I. A., & Rachlew, A. (2009). Investigative interviewing in the Nordic region. In T. Williamson, B. Milne, & S. P. Savage, eds., *International developments in investigative interviewing,* pp. 39–65. Portland, OR: Willan.

148. Ibid.

149. See Kassin, S. M., Appleby, S. C., & Perillo, J. T. (2010). Interviewing suspects: Practice, science, and future directions. *Legal and Criminological Psychology, 15(1),* 39–55.

150. See, e.g., American Bar Association. (2004). Resolution 8A—Videotaping custodial interrogations. Approved February 9, 2004, Midyear 2004 Meeting; Cassell (1996), *supra* note 120; Kassin et al. (2010), *supra* note 99; Leo (2008), *supra* note 44; Slobogin (2003), *supra* note 118.

151. See Sullivan, T. P. (2008). Recording federal custodial interviews. *American Criminal Law Review, 45,* 1297–1345.

152. Eighty-one percent of the 574 American police officers and 57 Canadian customs officials who participated in a survey opined that interrogations ought to be recorded in full. Kassin et al. (2007), *supra* note 4.

153. Research on taping interrogations has found that focusing the video camera exclusively on the suspect inflates the perceived voluntariness of the suspect's statements, which results in unwarranted trust in coerced confessions. See Lassiter, D. G., Ware, L. J., Ratcliff, J. J., & Irvin, C. R. (2009). Evidence of the camera perspective bias in authentic videotaped interrogations: Implications for emerging reform in the criminal justice system. *Legal and Criminal Psychology, 14,* 157–170. For a review and recommendations to minimize this phenomenon, see Lassiter, G. D., Ware, L. J., Lindberg, M. J., & Ratcliff, J. J. (2010). Videotaping custodial interrogations: Toward a scientifically based policy. In G. D. Lassiter & C. A. Meissner, eds., *Decade of behavior/Science conference grant. Police interrogations and false confessions: Current research, practice, and policy recommendations,* pp. 143–160. Washington DC: American Psychological Association.

6. "We Find the Defendant Guilty"

1. *Wainwright v. Sykes,* 433 U.S. 72, 90 (1977).

2. *Herrera v. Collins,* 506 U.S. 390, 416 (1993).

3. White, J. B. (1999). *From expectation to experience: Essays on law and legal education,* p. 108. Ann Arbor: University of Michigan Press; Burns, R. P. (2009). *The death of the American trial.* Chicago: University of Chicago Press.

4. This imagery has been suggested by proponents and critics of the trial alike. See Shepard, R. T. (2006). Brennan Lecture: The new role of state supreme courts as engines of court reform. *New York University Law Review, 81,* 1535–1552, p. 1543; and Foucault, M. (1994). *Ethics: Subjectivity and truth.* Ed. P. Rabinow. Trans. R. Hurley et al. New York: New Press.

5. For a rich discussion of the rationalist tradition of adjudication, see Twining, W. (1990). *Rethinking evidence,* pp. 32–91. Chicago: Northwestern University Press. This tradition dates back to Jeremy Bentham and can be traced through the writings of James Fitzjames Stephen, James Bradley Thayer, John Wigmore, and Lon Fuller. Fuller described adjudication as "a device which gives formal and institutional expression to the influence of reasoned argument in human affairs. As such it assumes a burden of rationality not borne by any other form of social ordering." Fuller, L. (1978). The forms and limits of adjudication. *Harvard Law Review, 92,* 353–409, p. 360. This theme is echoed regularly by the Supreme Court. See, e.g., *Taylor v. Kentucky,* 436 U.S. 478, 485 (1978).

A model of adjudication based on the rationalist tradition does not imply that jurors evaluate evidence by means of formal mathematical models, such as Bayes's Theorem. Rather, it assumes that the process is performed in a generally rational manner and free of systematic biases. See Hastie, R. (1993). Algebraic models of juror decision processes. In R. Hastie, ed., *Inside the juror: The psychology of juror decision making*, pp. 84–115. New York: Cambridge University Press.

6. E.g., Abramson, J. (2000). *We the jury: The jury system and the ideal of democracy.* Cambridge, MA: Harvard University Press; Vidmar, N., & Hans, V. P. (2007). *American juries: The verdict.* New York: Prometheus Books; Burns, R. P. (1999). *A theory of the trial.* Princeton, NJ: Princeton University Press.

7. *District Attorney's Office v. Osborne*, 129 S.Ct. 2308, 2323 n. 10 (2009).

8. E.g., *Herrera*, 506 U.S. at 420 (O'Connor, J., concurring). A central tenet of this process is that the litigating parties ought to be permitted to present the fact finder with the accounts that best serve their respective interests. This clash of partisan accounts is deemed the best route to reaching correct judicial decisions. See Damaška, M. R. (1985). *The faces of justice and state authority: A comparative approach to the legal process.* New Haven, CT: Yale University Press; Landsman, S. (1988). *Readings on adversarial justice: The American approach to adjudication.* St. Paul, MN: West.

9. *Crawford v. Washington*, 541 U.S. 36, 50 (2004).

10. *Lilly v. Virginia*, 527 U.S. 116, 124 (1999); *Watkins v. Sowders*, 449 U.S. 341, 349 (1980).

11. *Duncan v. Louisiana*, 391 U.S. 145 (1968).

12. *McCleskey v. Kemp*, 481 U.S. 279, 313 (1987).

13. *Watkins v. Sauders*, 449 U.S. 341, 347 (1981).

14. *Parker v. Randolph*, 442 U.S. 62, 73 (1979).

15. "It is part of our adversary system that we accept at trial much evidence that has strong elements of untrustworthiness." *Manson v. Brathwaite*, 438 U.S. 98, 113 (1977).

16. "A fundamental premise of our criminal trial system is that 'the *jury* is the lie detector.' Determining the weight and credibility of witness testimony, therefore, has long been held to be the 'part of every case [that] belongs to the jury, who are presumed to be fitted for it by their natural intelligence and their practical knowledge of men and the ways of men' " (citations omitted). *United States v. Scheffer*, 523 U.S. 303, 313 (1997).

17. "An instruction directing the jury to consider a codefendant's extrajudicial statement only against its source has been found sufficient to avoid offending the confrontation right of the implicated defendant in numerous decisions of this Court." *Parker v. Randolph*, 442 U.S. 62, 73 (1979).

18. *Gregg v. Georgia*, 428 U.S. 153 (1976); *McCleskey v. Kemp*, 481 U.S. 279 (1987).

19. "Due process means a jury capable and willing to decide the case solely on the evidence before it." *Smith v. Phillips*, 455 U.S. 209, 217 (1982).

20. Recall that this book deals mostly with difficult cases, which pose substantial factual questions pertaining to the defendant's guilt. The foregoing discussion

hardly applies to crimes that are easily solved by the police and readily decided by juries.

21. For example, federal magistrate judges did not perform better than lay subjects in tasks involving anchoring effects, the hindsight bias, and the egocentric bias, but did better in tasks involving framing effects and the representativeness heuristic. Judges have been found to perform better on the Cognitive Reflection Task (which tests people's ability to override erroneous intuitive judgments) than did undergraduate students at some colleges, but worse than students from four elite universities. Guthrie, C., Rachlinksi J. J., & Wistrich, A. J. (2001). Inside the judicial mind. *Cornell Law Review, 86,* 777–830; Guthrie, C., Rachlinksi J. J., & Wistrich, A. J. (2007). Blinking on the bench: How judges decide cases. *Cornell Law Review, 93,* 1–44. Bankruptcy judges were found to be susceptible to anchoring and framing effects, but appeared uninfluenced by the omission bias and some emotional factors. Rachlinksi, J. J., Guthrie, C., & Wistrich, A. J. (2006a). Inside the bankruptcy judge's mind. *Boston University Law Review, 86,* 1227–1265. Like lay people, judges' evaluations of the voluntariness of confessions were found to be biased by the perspective of the camera. Lassiter, G. D., Diamond, S. S., Schmidt, H. C., & Elek, J. K. (2007). Evaluating videotaped confessions: Expertise provides no defense against the camera-perspective effect. *Psychological Science, 18(3),* 224–226. As mentioned in Chapter 7, judges performed rather poorly when it came to ignoring evidence that they had themselves determined to be inadmissible. Wistrich, A. J., Guthrie, C., & Rachlinski, J. J. (2005). Can judges ignore inadmissible information? The difficulty of deliberately disregarding. *University of Pennsylvania Law Review, 153,* 1251–1345. As discussed below, under some conditions judges, like lay people, fail to follow the dictates of the law. See Rachlinksi, J. J., Guthrie, C., & Wistrich, A. J. (2006b), *infra* note 122.

22. Interview with Jennifer Thompson, "Lying Eyes," American Justice Series, A&E Entertainment. See also Thompson-Cannino, J., Cotton, R., & Torneo, E. (2009). *Picking cotton,* p. 46. New York: St. Martin's Press.

23. See, e.g., Hewstone, M., Rubin, M., & Willis, H. (2002). Intergroup bias. *Annual Review of Psychology, 53,* 575–604.

24. Thompson-Cannino, Cotton, & Torneo (2009), *supra* note 22, pp. 46, 71.

25. Thompson recounts: "We were all very, very pleased, very happy that Ronald was going away forever." Interview with Jennifer Thompson, *CNN Newsnight* with Aaron Brown, "A Look at DNA Evidence," May 17, 2005. See also Thompson-Cannino, Cotton, & Torneo (2009), *supra* note 22, p. 71.

26. For example, manipulating people's motivation to persuade others to participate in a blood drive yielded higher rates of donation. Anderson, C. A. (1983). Motivational and performance deficits in interpersonal settings: The effect of attributional style. *Journal of Personality and Social Psychology, 45,* 1136–1147.

27. See Frankel, M. E. (1978). *Partisan justice.* New York: Hill & Wang.

28. American Law Institute (2000). *Official comment to Section 116 of the American Law Institute's Restatement of the Law Third: The law governing lawyers.* St. Paul, MN: American Law Institute.

29. Sheppard, B. H., & Vidmar, N. (1980). Adversary pretrial procedures and testimonial evidence: Effects of lawyer's role and Machiavellianism. *Journal of Personality and Social Psychology, 39,* 320–332.

30. In this study, prosecution witnesses were subjected to a cross-examination by a defense attorney and then testified in a simulated trial. Some witnesses were forewarned that the defense attorney was going to "act very antagonistically towards you" and "do her utmost to discredit your testimony in the eyes of the jury." They were also instructed to rehearse their testimony. Overall, adding this information increased conviction rates from 31 percent to 51 percent. The confidence of witnesses who had identified the wrong person increased from 3.8 to 6.1 (on a 7-point scale), and the corresponding conviction rates increased from 28 to 61 percent. Wells, G. L., Ferguson, T. J., & Lindsay, R. C. L. (1981). The tractability of eyewitness confidence and its implications for triers of fact. *Journal of Applied Psychology, 66,* 688–696.

31. Vidmar, N., & Laird, N. M. (1983). Adversary social roles: Their effects on witnesses' communication of evidence and the assessments of adjudicators. *Journal of Personality and Social Psychology, 44,* 888–898. This finding is qualified somewhat by the fact that although the assignment influenced the evaluations of the testimony by third parties, the witnesses' own assessment of the evidence revealed no such bias.

32. Garrett, B. L. (2011). *Convicting the innocent: Where criminal prosecutions go wrong.* Cambridge, MA: Harvard University Press.

33. Ibid.

34. As the Court stated in the *Miranda* opinion, "Privacy results in secrecy and this in turn results in a gap in our knowledge as to what in fact goes on." *Miranda v. Arizona,* 384 U.S. 436, 448 (1966).

35. About half of the eyewitness identification cases that have reached the Court were based on incomplete records of the identification procedures.

36. See the discussion in Chapter 2.

37. Schmechel, R. S., O'Toole, T. P., Easterly, C., & Loftus, E. F. (2006). Beyond the kin? Testing jurors' understanding of eyewitness reliability evidence. *Jurimetrics, 46,* 177–214.

38. Levin, D. T., Momen, N., Drivdahl, S. B., & Simons, D. J. (2000). Change blindness blindness: The metacognitive error of overestimating change-detection ability. *Visual Cognition, 7,* 397–412.

39. Harley, E. M., Carlsen, K. A., & Loftus, G. R. (2004). The "saw-it-all-along" effect: Demonstrations of visual hindsight bias. *Journal of Experimental Psychology: Learning, Memory, and Cognition, 30,* 960–968.

40. For these and other estimation studies, see Wells, G. L. (1984). The adequacy of human intuition for judging testimony. In G. L. Wells & E. F. Loftus, eds., *Eyewitness testimony: Psychological perspectives,* pp. 256–272. New York: Cambridge University Press. Although most estimation studies show a consistent pattern of overestimation, one study found both over- and underestimation. Yarmey, A. D. (2004). Eyewitness recall and photo identification: A field experiment. *Psychology, Crime & Law, 10,* 53–68.

41. Brigham, J. C., & Bothwell, R. K. (1983). The ability of prospective jurors to estimate the accuracy of eyewitness identifications. *Law and Human Behavior, 7,* 19–30.

42. In this study, students who witnessed a staged theft played the role of witnesses. Their testimony was videotaped as they were examined and cross-examined by experienced crown prosecutors, defense attorneys, and law students. That testimony was later assessed by other students playing the role of jurors. Lindsay, R. C. L., Wells, G. L., & O'Connor, F. J. (1989). Mock-juror belief of accurate and inaccurate eyewitnesses: A replication and extension. *Law and Human Behavior, 13,* 333–339.

43. Wells, G. L., Lindsay, R. C., & Ferguson, T. J. (1979). Accuracy, confidence, and juror perceptions in eyewitness identification. *Journal of Applied Psychology, 64,* 440–448.

44. Lindsay, R. C. L., Wells, G. L., & Rumpel, C. M. (1981). Can people detect eyewitness-identification accuracy within and across situations? *Journal of Applied Psychology, 66,* 79–89.

45. In this study, 70 percent of the accurate witnesses were believed by the participants, whereas only 33 percent of the inaccurate witnesses were believed. Ibid.

46. Simulated jurors believed 68 percent of accurate witnesses and 70 percent of inaccurate witnesses. Lindsay, Wells, & O'Connor (1989), *supra* note 42.

47. Wells, Lindsay, & Ferguson (1979, *supra* note 43) found that 86 percent of simulated jurors believed the identification by witnesses who were actually incorrect and 76 percent believed identifications by accurate witnesses (data for nonleading questioning condition). Similarly, Wells, Lindsay, and Tousignant found belief rates of 64 percent for inaccurate witnesses and 59 percent for accurate witnesses. Wells, G. L., Lindsay, R. C., & Tousignant, J. P. (1980). Effects of expert psychological advice on human performance in judging the validity of eyewitness testimony. *Law and Human Behavior, 4(4),* 275–285 (data for tests without expert testimony). More recently, Reardon and Fisher found belief rates of 59 percent and 52 percent, respectively. Reardon, M. C., & Fisher, R. P. (2011). Effect of viewing the interview and identification process on juror perceptions of eyewitness accuracy. *Applied Cognitive Psychology, 25,* 68–77; and email communication from Margaret Reardon, September 24, 2010 (data from jurors in the control condition).

48. See Garrett (2011), *supra* note 32, p. 315, note 43.

49. Lindsay, D. S., Read, D. J., & Sharma, K. (1998). Accuracy and confidence in person identification: The relationship is strong when witnessing conditions vary widely. *Psychological Science, 9*, 215–218.

50. Deffenbacher, K. A., & Loftus, E. F. (1982). Do jurors share a common understanding concerning eyewitness behavior? *Law and Human Behavior, 6*, 15–30.

51. All four items where there was agreement concerned *incident* factors, that is, factors that are related to the viewing of the perpetrator by the witness. There was no agreement on any *system* factors, which pertain to the investigative procedures conducted by the police. Benton, T. R., Ross, D. F., Bradshaw, E., Thomas, W. N., & Bradshaw, G. S. (2006). Eyewitness memory is still not common sense: Comparing jurors, judges and law enforcement to eyewitness experts. *Applied Cognitive Psychology, 20*, 115–129. People's lack of familiarity with system factors was most apparent in a study that asked respondents to generate their own list of factors that they believed influence identification accuracy. Only 1 percent of the spontaneously generated factors pertained to system factors. Shaw, J. S., III, Garcia, L. A., & McClure, K. A. (1999). A law perspective on the accuracy of eyewitness testimony. *Journal of Applied Social Psychology, 29*, 52–71.

The insensitivity of jurors to system factors means that jurors are unlikely to discount the reliance on identifications that were obtained from poorly conducted lineup procedures. This gives the police less of an incentive to conduct lineups properly.

52. A majority of respondents did, however, appreciate the problematic nature of showups. Schmechel et al. (2006), *supra* note 37.

53. The study tested groups of students and jury-eligible citizens. The nine factors included three incident factors (e.g., whether the perpetrator wore a disguise and whether he carried a gun) and six system factors (e.g., the time delay before the lineup was conducted and the number of fillers in the lineup). The witness confidence was manipulated to be either 80 percent confident or 100 percent confident. Cutler, B. L., Penrod, S. D., & Stuve, T. E. (1988). Juror decision making in eyewitness identification cases. *Law and Human Behavior, 12*, 41–55; Cutler, B. L., Penrod, S. D., & Dexter, H. R. (1990). Juror sensitivity to eyewitness identification evidence. *Law and Human Behavior, 14*, 185–191.

54. Lindsay, R. C. L., Lim, R., Marando, L., & Cully, D. (1986). Mock-juror evaluations of eyewitness testimony: A test of metamemory hypotheses. *Journal of Applied Social Psychology, 16*, 447–459.

55. In this study, the rate of convictions was unaffected by whether the black suspect was identified by a white or a black witness. Abshire, J., & Bornstein, B. H. (2003). Juror sensitivity to the cross-race effect. *Law and Human Behavior, 27*, 471–480.

56. In an estimation study, participants made similar predictions of filler choices in target-absent conditions in which the witness was given biased and unbiased lineup instructions (16 percent and 18 percent), while the actual rate of filler choices was 78 percent and 33 percent, respectively. See Wells (1984), *supra* note 40.

57. Devenport, J. L., Stinson, V., Cutler, B. L., & Kravitz, D. A. (2002). How effective are the cross-examination and expert testimony safeguards? Jurors' perceptions of the suggestiveness and fairness of biased lineup procedures. *Journal of Applied Psychology, 87,* 1042–1054.

58. Lindsay, Wells, & Rumpel (1981), *supra* note 44.

59. All cases used the same vignette that described a burglary followed by a sexual assault, with certain variations in the witnessing conditions and in the lineup procedures. This study was part of the *Jurors' Beliefs Survey,* which tested a wide range of lay people's beliefs, knowledge, and opinions regarding the criminal justice system. The survey sample consisted of some 650 respondents, half of whom were from a general sample of Internet users and half were college students. Simon, D., Stenstrom, D., & Read, S. J. (2008). Jurors' background knowledge and beliefs. Paper presented at American Psychology-Law Society annual conference, Jacksonville, FL, March 6–8.

60. In this scenario, the victim got two glances at her attacker, under conditions of relatively dim light. One week after the attack, the victim failed to identify her attacker from a live lineup. Three months later, in the courtroom, she managed to identify the defendant. Ibid.

61. Wells, G. L., & Bradfield, A. L. (1998). "Good, you identified the suspect": Feedback to eyewitnesses distorts their reports of the witnessing experience. *Journal of Applied Psychology, 83,* 360–376.

62. Lindsay, Wells, & O'Connor (1989), *supra* note 42.

63. The rate of belief was 63 percent for confident witnesses but only 32 percent for witnesses who expressed low confidence. Lindsay, R. C. L. (1994). Expectations of eyewitness performance: Jurors' verdicts do not follow from their beliefs. In D. F. Ross, J. D. Read, & M. Toglia, eds., *Adult eyewitness testimony: Current trends and development,* pp. 362–384. New York: Cambridge University Press.

64. The rates of belief for witnesses who claimed to be completely certain and somewhat uncertain were 83 percent and 28 percent, respectively. Wells (1984), *supra* note 40.

65. Culhane, S. E., & Hosch, H. M. (2004). An alibi witness' influence on mock jurors' verdicts. *Journal of Applied Social Psychology, 34,* 1604–1616.

66. Simon, D. (2011). The coherence effect: Blending cold and hot cognitions by constraint satisfaction. Paper presented at the Max Planck Institute for Research on Collective Goods, Bonn, Germany, July 6.

67. One study found that manipulating the viewing conditions affected judgments of nonconfident witnesses (47 percent, 54 percent, and 76 percent for the three respective viewing conditions), but not identifications made by confident ones (76 percent, 76 percent, and 78 percent). Lindsay, Wells, & Rumpel (1981), *supra* note 44.

68. Leippe, M. R., & Eisenstadt, D. (2007). Eyewitness confidence and the confidence-accuracy relationship in memory for people. In R. C. L. Lindsay, D. F. Ross, J. D. Read, & M. P. Toglia, eds., *Handbook of eyewitness psychology*, vol. 2: *Memory for people,* pp. 377–425. Mahwah, NJ: Lawrence Erlbaum; Sporer, S. L., Penrod, S., Read, D., & Cutler, B. (1995). Choosing, confidence, and accuracy: A meta-analysis of the confidence-accuracy relation in eyewitness identification studies. *Psychological Bulletin, 118,* 315–327. This correlation pertains to witnesses who actually choose someone at the lineup. The relationship is weaker for witnesses who fail to pick out any target. This result does not diminish the practical value of the relationship because witnesses who do not pick out a suspect rarely testify at trial.

69. Brewer, N., & Wells, G. L. (2006). The confidence-accuracy relationship in eyewitness identification: Effects of lineup instructions, foil similarity, and target-absent base rates. *Journal of Experimental Psychology: Applied, 12,* 11–30.

70. Douglass, A. B., Neuschatz, J. S., Imrich, J., & Wilkinson, M. (2010). Does post-identification feedback affect evaluations of eyewitness testimony and identification procedures? *Law and Human Behavior, 34,* 282–294.

71. Wells & Seelau view in-court identifications as a mere formality. Wells, G. L., & Seelau, E. P. (1995). Eyewitness identification: Psychological research and legal policy on lineups. *Psychology, Public Policy, and Law, 1,* 765–791. John Wigmore stated that they were "of little testimonial force." Wigmore, J. H. (1940). *A treatise on the Anglo-American system of evidence in trials at common law,* 3rd ed., vol. 4, p. 208. Boston: Little, Brown.

72. See Nash, R. A., & Wade, K. A. (2009). Innocent but proven guilty: Eliciting internalized false confessions using doctored-video evidence. *Applied Cognitive Psychology, 23,* 624–637; Gabbert, F., Memon, A., Allan, K., & Wright, D. B. (2004). Say it to my face: Examining the effects of socially encountered misinformation. *Legal and Criminological Psychology, 9,* 215–227.

73. Simon, Stenstrom, & Read (2008), *supra* note 59.

74. Innocence Project, profile, Dean Cage. http://www.innocenceproject.org /Content/Dean_Cage.php.

75. Innocence Project, profile, Robert Clark. http://www.innocenceproject .org/Content/Robert_Clark.php.

76. For the case of Willie O. "Pete" Williams, see Torpy, B., & Rankin, B. (2007). Group: DNA clears man in 1985 rape. *Atlanta Journal-Constitution,* January 20. http://www.ajc.com/metro/content/metro/atlanta/stories/2007/01

/19/0120bmetinnocent.html; Innocence Project, profile, Willie Williams. http://www.innocenceproject.org/Content/Willie_Williams.php.

77. Possley, M. (2006). DNA results clear prisoner: Crime lab failed to do testing earlier. *Chicago Tribune,* November 23, p. B1. On the case of Marlon Pendleton, see Innocence Project, profile, Marlon Pendleton. http://www.innocenceproject.org/Content/Marlon_Pendleton.php.

78. For a rare treatment of this issue, see Mandery, E. (1996). Due process considerations of in-court identifications. *Albany Law Review, 60,* 389–424.

79. Pointing to the person sitting at the defense table is no better a test of the witness's memory than testing a spelling-bee contestant while showing him the word spelled out on a placard. To be sure, showing the word does not mean that the contestant did not know how to spell it correctly. That is the very problem with the design of this contest—it is, at best, nondiagnostic of the contestant's capabilities. In-court identifications are no more diagnostic of witnesses' memories.

80. For examples, see *People v. Patterson,* 88 Ill. App. 3d 168, 176 (1980); *People v. Monroe,* 925 P.2d 767 (Colo. 1996).

81. *United States v. Wade,* 388 U.S. 218, 224 (1967).

82. *United States v. Ash,* 413 U.S. 300 (1973). For similar decisions, see *United States v. Kimball,* 73 F.3d 269 (10 Cir. 1995); *Smith v. State,* 553 N.E.2d 832 (Ind. 1990).

83. *Miles v. U.S.,* 483 A.2d 649 (D.C. 1984).

84. *State v. Taylor,* 200 W. Va. 661 (1997); *State v. McCall,* 139 Ariz. 147 (1983).

85. A Florida court went so far as to permit the prosecution to present evidence of an in-court identification, even though the witness failed to identify her perpetrator in the courtroom. This "reverse" in-court identification was based on the witness's testimony that the defendant kept staring at her during the hearing, that is, on his putative recognition of her. *Hazen v. State,* 700 So. 2d 1207 (Fla. 1997), cited in Sobel., N. R. (1981). *Eyewitness identification: Legal and practical problems,* 2nd ed., §3:11. New York: Clark Boardman Company.

On occasion, courts limit the excesses. For example, a federal court of appeals disallowed an in-court identification after the prosecutor pointed to the defendant sitting at the defense table and asked the witness: "Is [the defendant] in the courtroom? Is he over at this table?" *United States v. Warf,* 529 F.2d 1170 (5th Cir. 1976). The foregoing cases are cited to describe the breadth of the doctrine. None of the defendants in these cases has been found to be innocent.

86. Appellate courts have generally rejected challenges to the constitutionality of the practice and have ruled that it is soundly within the trial court's discretion. *United States v. Brown,* 699 F.2d 585 (2d Cir. 1983); *United States v. Dixon,* 201 F.3d 1223, 1229 (9th Cir. 2000).

87. The lawyer also engaged in other conduct that was considered unethical, such as informing the clerk that the defendant was not going to be sworn in before the commencement of the trial and failing to correct the record once the

misidentification was made. *Illinois v. Simac,* 161 Ill. 2d. 297 (1994). For other cases involving substitution see *United States v. Sabater,* 830 F.2d 7 (2d Cir. 1987); *People v. Gow,* 382 N.E.2d 673 (Ill. App. Ct. 1978).

88. In dissent, Justice Nickels noted correctly that defense attorneys are under no obligation to provide prosecution witnesses with suggestive identification settings. *Illinois v. Simac,* 161 Ill. 2d. 297 (1994).

89. See, e.g., Hanba, J. M., & Zaragoza, M. S. (2007). Interviewer feedback in repeated interviews involving forced confabulation. *Applied Cognitive Psychology, 21,* 433–455; Schooler, J. W., Gerhard, D., & Loftus, E. F. (1986). Qualities of the unreal. *Journal of Experimental Psychology: Learning, Memory, and Cognition, 12,* 171–181.

90. Other aspects of vividness have been tested less frequently. These include the witness's rate of pauses, hesitations, and response latency. Hanba & Zaragoza (2007), *supra* note 89. Other aspects include the number of "don't know" answers, verbal hedges, and hesitations. Leippe, M. R., Manion, A. P., & Romanczyk, A. (1992). Eyewitness persuasion: How and how well do fact finders judge the accuracy of adults' and children's memory reports? *Journal of Personality and Social Psychology, 63(2),* 181–197. The vividness of memory is closely related to the concept of memory *fluency.* See Shaw, J. S. (1996). Increases in eyewitness confidence resulting from postevent questioning. *Journal of Experimental Psychology: Applied, 2,* 126–146. People use the richness-of-detail cue also for monitoring the source of their own memories. See Johnson, M. K., Bush, J. G., & Mitchell, K. J. (1998). Interpersonal reality monitoring: Judging the sources of other people's memories. *Social Cognition, 16,* 199–224.

91. The detailed testimony was found to be more believable (54 vs. 44, on a believability scale of 0–100), and to result in higher conviction rates (29 percent vs. 11 percent). Bell, B. E., & Loftus, E. F. (1988). Degree of detail of eyewitness testimony and mock juror judgments. *Journal of Applied Social Psychology, 18,* 1171–1192; Bell, B. E., & Loftus, E. F. (1985). Vivid persuasion in the courtroom. *Journal of Personality Assessment, 49,* 659–664; Keogh, L., & Markham, R. (1998). Judgements of other people's memory reports: Differences in reports as a function of imagery vividness. *Applied Cognitive Psychology, 12,* 159–171. Another study found no such effect. Pickel, K. L. (1993). Evaluation and integration of eyewitness reports. *Law and Human Behavior, 17,* 569–595.

92. Brewer, N., Potter, R., Fisher, R. P., Bond, N., & Luszcz, M. A. (1999). Beliefs and data on the relationship between consistency and accuracy of eyewitness testimony. *Applied Cognitive Psychology, 13,* 297–313.

93. One study found that inconsistent testimony reduced the level of guilty verdicts from 53 percent to 7 percent. Brewer, N., & Hupfeld, R. M. (2004). Effects of testimonial inconsistencies and witness group identity on mock-juror judgments. *Journal of Applied Social Psychology, 34,* 493–513. Prosecution witnesses who provided inconsistent testimony about a robbery were found to be

less effective than those who provided consistent testimony, resulting in conviction rates of 20 percent and 69 percent, respectively. Berman, G. L., Narby, D. J., & Cutler, B. L. (1995). Effects of inconsistent eyewitness statements on mock-jurors' evaluations of the eyewitness, perceptions of defendant culpability and verdicts. *Law and Human Behavior, 19,* 79–88; Berman, G. L., & Cutler, B. L. (1996). Effects of inconsistencies in eyewitness testimony on mock-juror decision making. *Journal of Applied Psychology, 81,* 170–177. In another study, however, inconsistencies were not found to have an effect on observers' judgments (at least not with adult witnesses). Leippe, M. R., & Romanczyk, A. (1989). Reactions to child (versus adult) eyewitnesses: The influence of jurors' preconceptions and witness behavior. *Law and Human Behavior, 13,* 103–132.

94. Brewer et al. (1999), *supra* note 92.

95. Highly confident prosecution testimony resulted in higher assessments of guilt (57 percent vs. 32 percent) and a higher conviction rate (39 percent vs. 9 percent). The confidence manipulation swamped any effects from the consistency of the witnesses' story. Brewer, N., & Burke, A. (2002). Effects of testimonial inconsistencies and eyewitness confidence on mock-juror judgments. *Law and Human Behavior, 26,* 353–364.

96. See Leippe, Manion, & Romanczyk (1992), *supra* note 90; Pickel (1993); and Whitley, B. E., & Greenberg, M. S. (1986). The role of eyewitness confidence in juror perceptions of credibility. *Journal of Applied Social Psychology, 16,* 387–409.

97. It is theoretically possible that there are other accuracy cues that have not been identified by researchers, though it is not very likely that powerful cues have been completely overlooked.

98. Brewer et al. (1999), *supra* note 92; Gilbert, J. A. E., & Fisher, R. P. (2006). The effects of varied retrieval cues on reminiscence in eyewitness memory. *Applied Cognitive Psychology, 20,* 723–739.

99. One study found a negative correlation of −.21 between the number of memorized peripheral details and the accuracy of identifications of the perpetrator. Cutler, B. L., Penrod, S. D., & Martens, T. K. (1987). The reliability of eyewitness identification: The role of system and estimator variables. *Law and Human Behavior, 11,* 233–258. A field study conducted in Tokyo found no relationship between memory for the event and identification accuracy. Nake, M., Itsukushima, Y., & Itoh, Y. (1996). Eyewitness testimony after three months: A field study on memory for an incident in everyday life. *Japanese Psychological Research, 38,* 14–24. See also Wells, G. L., & Leippe, M. R. (1981). How do triers of fact infer the accuracy of eyewitness identifications? Using memory for peripheral detail can be misleading. *Journal of Applied Psychology, 66,* 682–687. This negative relationship could be explained by the limited cognitive resources. The attention paid to peripheral details comes at the expense of attending to other facets of the event.

100. Brewer et al. (1999), *supra* note 92. See Gilbert & Fisher (2006), *supra* note 98.

101. Granhag, P. A., Strömwall, L. A., & Allwood, C. M. (2000). Effects of reiteration, hindsight bias, and memory on realism in eyewitness confidence. *Applied Cognitive Psychology, 14,* 397–420.

102. Tomes, J. L., & Katz, A. N. (2000). Confidence-accuracy relations for real and suggested events. *Memory, 8,* 273–283.

103. Tomes & Katz (ibid.) reported an average confidence-accuracy relationship of about 0.61. Leippe, Manion, & Romanczyk (1992, *supra* note 90) observed a correlation as high as 0.5, but it was significant in only one of three tests. Another study found overall weak to nonexistent relationships. Shaw, J. S., & McClure, K. A. (1996). Repeated postevent questioning can lead to elevated levels of eyewitness confidence. *Law and Human Behavior, 20,* 629–653. Shaw and Zerr observed values ranging between zero and 0.4. Shaw, J. S., & Zerr, T. K. (2003). Extra effort during memory retrieval may be associated with increases in eyewitness confidence. *Law and Human Behavior, 27,* 315–329. Brewer et al. (1999, *supra* note 92) found no confidence-accuracy relationship at all.

104. Leippe, Manion, & Romanczyk (1992), *supra* note 90.

105. One study (Hanba & Zaragoza 2007, *supra* note 89) found that repetition of memory tests accompanied with false feedback boosted the consistency of false memories up to 100 percent.

106. See Fisher, R. P., Brewer, N., & Mitchell, G. (2009). The relation between consistency and accuracy of eyewitness testimony: Legal versus cognitive explanations. In R. Bull, T. Valentine, & T. Williamson, eds., *Handbook of psychology of investigative interviewing: Current developments and future directions,* pp. 121–136. Chichester, UK: Wiley-Blackwell.

107. Tomes & Katz (2000), *supra* note 102.

108. Shaw & Zerr (2003), *supra* note 103.

109. *Parker v. Randolph,* 442 U.S. 62, 72 (1979).

110. *People v. Schader,* 62 Cal. 2d 716, 731 (1965).

111. For example, an Illinois youth confessed to committing a double murder in the uptown neighborhood of Chicago. Prosecutors pursued the case even though police records showed that the defendant had been in jail at the time of the murders. Criticizing the police records, the prosecutor argued: "Paperwork is not foolproof . . . But I'll tell you what is foolproof. And what is foolproof are the defendant's own words." Mills, S., Possley, M., & Armstrong, K. (2001). When jail is no alibi in murders: New evidence undercuts state case. *Chicago Tribune,* December 19.

112. To enter a confession before a jury, the prosecution need only show that it was made voluntarily by the deferential standard of preponderance of the evidence. *Lego v. Twomey,* 404 U.S. 477 (1972).

113. Of the 60 false confessors included in the first study, 23 were released before the decision, 7 pled guilty, 8 were acquitted at trial, and 22 were convicted. Leo, R. A., & Ofshe, R. J. (1998). The consequences of false confessions: Deprivations of liberty and miscarriages of justice in the age of psychological interrogation. *Journal of Criminal Law & Criminality, 88,* 429–496. The second study contained confessions by 125 suspects, of whom 74 were released pretrial, 14 pled guilty, 7 were acquitted at trial, and 30 were convicted. Drizin, S. A., & Leo, R. A. (2004). The problem of false confessions in the post-DNA world. *North Carolina Law Review, 82,* 891–1007. These data, however, are possibly incomplete in that acquittals might have been underrepresented in these data sets.

114. Snyder, L., McQuillian, P., Murphy, W. L., & Joselson, R. (2007). Report on the conviction of Jeffrey Deskovic. http://www.westchesterda.net/Jeffrey %20Deskovic%20Comm%20Rpt.pdf.

115. Barnes, S. (2011). *The Central Park Five: A chronicle of a city wilding.* New York: Knopf.

116. Innocence Project, profile, Joseph White. http://www.innocenceproject .org/Content/Joseph_White.php.

117. Innocence Project, profile, Nathaniel Hatchett. http://www.innocence project.org/Content/Nathaniel_Hatchett.php.

118. Blandón-Gitlin, I., Sperry, K., & Leo, R. (2011). Jurors believe interrogation tactics are not likely to elicit false confessions: Will expert witness testimony inform them otherwise? *Psychology, Crime & Law, 17,* 239–260.

119. Costanzo, M., Shaked-Schroer, N., & Vinson, K. (2010). Juror beliefs about police interrogations, false confessions, and expert testimony. *Journal of Empirical Legal Studies, 7,* 231–247.

120. See Henkel, L. A., Coffman, K. A. J., & Dailey, E. M. (2008). A survey of people's attitudes and beliefs about false confessions. *Behavioral Sciences and the Law, 26,* 555–584; Kassin, S. A. (1997). The psychology of confession evidence. *American Psychologist, 52,* 221–233. See also Leo, R. A., & Liu, B. (2009). What do potential jurors know about police interrogation and techniques and false confessions? *Behavioral Sciences and the Law, 27,* 381–399.

121. The rate of conviction was found to be almost identical when the judge ruled that the confession was admissible and when he ruled it inadmissible and ordered the jurors to ignore it (50 percent vs. 44 percent). These rates were considerably higher than when no confession was presented (19 percent). Kassin, S. M., & Sukel, H. (1997). Coerced confessions and the jury: An experimental test of the "harmless error" rule. *Law and Human Behavior, 21,* 27–46 (data taken from study 2, collapsed over the four confession conditions; high-pressure condition only). Low sensitivity to coercive techniques was found by Blandón-Gitlin, Sperry, & Leo (2011), *supra* note 118. For similar results, see study 3 of Kassin, S. M., & McNall, K. (1991). Police interrogations and confessions: Communicating promises and threats by pragmatic implication. *Law and Hu-*

man Behavior, 15, 233–251; Kassin, S. M., & Wrightsman, L. S. (1981). Coerced confessions, judicial instruction, and mock juror verdicts. *Journal of Applied Social Psychology, 11*, 489–506.

122. A study of federal and state judges found that evidence of police coercion appears to have eliminated any reliance on the confession in an armed robbery case (30 percent vs. 28 percent conviction rates; comparing no confession with coercive confession), but failed to do so in a murder case (increasing the rate from 24 to 44 percent). Rachlinksi, J. J., Guthrie, C., & Wistrich, A. J. (2006b). Context effects in judicial decision making. Paper presented at the fourth annual Conference on Empirical Legal Studies, University of Southern California, November 20–21, 2009. Available at Social ScienceResearch Network, http://ssrn.com/abstract=1443596.

123. The *Jurors' Beliefs Survey* found that people believe that knowledge of nonpublic facts is a strong indicator of the confessor's involvement in the crime. The mode and median responses to this question were both 9, on a scale of 1–11. Simon, Stenstrom, & Read (2008), *supra* note 59.

124. Interrogation manuals instruct detectives that, in addition to a detailed description of the crime, the narratives ought to contain trivial details. Inbau, F. E., Reid, J. E., Buckley, J. P., & Jayne, B. C. (2004). *Criminal interrogation and confessions,* 4th ed. Sudbury, MA: Jones and Bartlett.

125. Garrett (2011), *supra* note 32.

126. *Commonwealth of Pennsylvania v. Bruce Godschalk,* 00934-87, Montgomery County, Jury Trial, May 27, 1987, pp. 22–23.

127. Garrett (2011), *supra* note 32, p. 20. For analyses of other cases, see Leo, R. A. (2008). *Police interrogation and American justice.* Cambridge, MA: Harvard University Press.

128. Absent any record of the interrogation, it is hard to tell whether detectives deliberately feed the information to defendants or merely mention it unwittingly.

129. Garrett (2011), *supra* note 32. In the case of Bruce Godschalk, the detective insisted at trial: "Never did I offer anything to him." Leo (2008), *supra* note 127, p. 184.

130. For example, when asked if he was confessing freely, Bruce Godschalk responded, "On my own free will," and when asked if he had been treated well by the police he replied, "Very well." *Commonwealth of Pennsylvania v. Bruce Godschalk,* 00934-87, Montgomery County, Jury Trial, May 27, 1987, pp. 133, 126–127. Recall that Godschalk also apologized to the victims for "what I've done to these two nice women" (pp. 138–139).

131. For a useful taxonomy of alibi evidence, see Olson, E. A., & Wells, G. L. (2004). What makes a good alibi? A proposed taxonomy. *Law and Human Behavior, 28*, 157–176.

132. See Garret (2011), *supra* note 32 (data from the 207 trials for which the transcript could be located).

133. Ibid. For example, an Oklahoma man was convicted primarily on the basis of an identification by an eleven-year-old girl despite the fact that eleven witnesses placed him in Dallas at the time of the crime. On the case of Tim Durham, see Dwyer, J., Neufeld, P., & Scheck, B. (2000). *Actual innocence: Five days to execution and other dispatches from the wrongfully convicted,* pp. 213–222. New York: Doubleday. Another Oklahoma man was convicted even though two coworkers testified at trial that he was at lunch with them when the rape occurred. See "Under the Microscope," *60 Minutes,* February 11, 2009. http://www.cbsnews.com/stories/2001/05/08/60II/main290046.shtml. On the case of Jeffrey Pierce, see Innocence Project, profile, http://www.innocenceproject.org/Content/Jeffrey_Pierce.php. Steven Avery, a Wisconsin man, was convicted mostly on the basis of an eyewitness identification, even though sixteen alibi witnesses testified that he was elsewhere at the time. In 2007, following his release, Avery was convicted of a brutal murder in an unrelated case. On the case of Steven Avery, see http://www.law.northwestern.edu/wrongfulconvictions/exonerations/wiAverySSummary.html.

134. The increase, however, was not statistically significant. McAllister, H. A., & Bregman, N. J. (1989). Juror underutilization of eyewitness nonidentifications: A test of the disconfirmed expectancy explanation. *Journal of Applied Social Psychology, 19,* 20–29.

135. Olson & Wells (2004), *supra* note 131. The case of Juan Catalan is illustrative of the difficulties of proving an alibi. Catalan, a Los Angeles man, was facing capital charges after being identified by an eyewitness as having committed a murder of a witness in another case. Catalan insisted that at the time of the crime he was watching a baseball game at Dodger Stadium with his daughter. Investigators dismissed his ticket stubs as proof of his alibi. His lawyer searched the footage of the sports TV coverage of the game but failed to spot Catalan. By coincidence, an HBO TV crew happened to be at the stadium that day to film an episode of Larry David's show *Curb Your Enthusiasm.* Catalan was seen in the footage, sitting with his daughter in their designated seats, eating hotdogs at the time the murder was committed. Sweetingham, L. (2004). "Enthusiasm" saves defendant wrongly accused in murder case. CNN, June 7. http://www.cnn.com/2004/LAW/06/07/larry.david/index.html.

136. Burke, T. M., & Turtle, J. W. (2004). Alibi evidence in criminal investigations and trials: Psychological and legal factors. *Canadian Journal of Police & Security Services, 1,* 286–294. James Earl Giles of Texas was convicted of aggravated rape on the basis of the victim's identification and an informant's tip, even though he produced phone records and restaurant receipts showing that he could not have been present at the crime scene. Bustillo, M. (2007). Texas men's innocence puts a county on trial. *Los Angeles Times,* April 9. http://www.latimes.com/news/nationworld/nation/la-na-exonerate9apr09,1,265991.story. Giles was exonerated on the basis of a DNA test while on parole, some twenty-five years after his conviction.

137. Olson & Wells (2004), *supra* note 131.

138. In one study, corroboration by a stranger reduced the conviction rate from 60 percent to 27 percent while the alibi corroborated by a brother-in-law was no different from baseline (57 percent). Lindsay et al. (1986), *supra* note 54. Other studies found that corroboration by the defendant's girlfriend did not significantly reduce the conviction rate (45 percent vs. 35 percent), but the neighbor's testimony did (17 percent). Culhane & Hosch (2004), *supra* note 65; Olson & Wells (2004), *supra* note 131. The corroboration provided by the daughter of Juan Catalan discussed above did little to make the detectives believe his alibi.

139. Of the 300 jury-eligible undergraduate students, 75 percent admitted that they would lie to provide a false alibi for their sibling; 63 percent said the same for their best friend. Only 4 percent would do the same for strangers. Hosch, H. M., Culhane, S. E., & Hawley, L. R. (2003). Effects of an alibi witness' relationship to the defendant on mock jurors' judgments. *Law and Human Behavior, 35,* 127–142.

140. Burke & Turtle (2004), *supra* note 136.

141. This was the case, for example, in the cases of Charles Chatman, Brian Piszczek, and Steven Philips. See Innocence Project, profiles, http://www.innocenceproject.org/Content/Charles_Chatman.php, http://www.innocenceproject.org/Content/Brian_Piszczek.php, and http://www.innocenceproject.org/Content/Steven_Phillips.php.

142. Transcript of interview with jury member Dallas Fry in *What Jennifer Saw, Frontline* series, produced and directed by Ben Loeterman, PBS (1997). http://www.pbs.org/wgbh/pages/frontline/shows/dna/.

143. See Montagne, R. (2009). Family of man cleared by DNA still seeks justice, *NPR morning edition,* February 5. On the case of Timothy Cole, who died in prison prior to his exoneration, see Innocence Project, profile, Timothy Cole. http://www.innocenceproject.org/Content/Timothy_Cole.php.

144. *United States v. Scheffer,* 523 U.S. 303, 313 (1997).

145. For example, the Massachusetts jury instructions read: "Often it may not be *what* a witness says, but *how* he says it that might give you a clue whether or not to accept his version of an event as believable. You may consider a witness's appearance and demeanor on the witness stand, his frankness or lack of frankness in testifying, whether his testimony is reasonable or unreasonable, probable or improbable." The Massachusetts Court System (2010). *Criminal Jury Instructions,* Instruction 2.260.

146. Black, H. C. (1990). *Black's law dictionary,* 6th ed. St. Paul, MN: West.

147. Notably, the effect of deceit on voice pitch amounts to a change of just a few Hertz, which is imperceptible to the naked ear. Vrij, A. (2008). *Detecting lies and deceit: Pitfalls and* opportunities, 2nd ed., p. 55. New York: John Wiley.

148. DePaulo, B. M., Lindsay, J. J., Malone, B. E., Muhlenbruck, L., Charlton, K., & Cooper, H. (2003). Cues to deception. *Psychological Bulletin, 129,* 74–118.

149. Bond, C. F., Jr., & DePaulo, B. M. (2006). Accuracy of deception judgments. *Personality and Social Psychology Review, 10,* 214–234.

150. Granhag, P. A., & Strömwall, L. A. (2002). Repeated interrogations: Verbal and non-verbal cues to deception. *Applied Cognitive Psychology, 16,* 243–257.

151. Granhag, P. A., & Strömwall, L. A. (2000). Effects of preconceptions on deception detection and new answers to why lie-catchers often fail. *Psychology, Crime & Law, 6(3),* 197–218.

152. O'Sullivan, M. (2003). The fundamental attribution error in detecting deception: The boy-who-cried-wolf effect. *Personality and Social Psychology Bulletin, 29,* 1316–1327.

153. A meta-analysis of 18 studies found the confidence-accuracy relationship to be minute and not statistically significant ($r = .04$). Across the studies, the correlations ranged from –.20 to .26. DePaulo, B. M., Charlton, K., Cooper, H., Lindsay, J. J., & Muhlenbruck, L. (1997). The accuracy-confidence correlation in the detection of deception. *Personality and Social Psychology Review, 1,* 346–357.

154. Frank, M. G., Paolantonio, N., Feeley, T. H., & Servoss, T. J. (2004). Individual and small group accuracy in judging truthful and deceptive communication. *Group Decision and Negotiation, 13,* 45–59; Park, E. S., Levine, T. R., Harms, C. M., & Ferrara, M. H. (2002). Group and individual accuracy in deception detection. *Communication Research Reports, 19,* 99–106.

155. The Court has stated that only the courtroom fact finder can "be aware of the variations in demeanor and tone of voice that bear so heavily on the listener's understanding and belief in what is said." *Anderson v. Bessemer City,* 470 U.S. 564, 575 (1985).

156. See, e.g., Kassin, S. M., Meissner, C. A., & Norwick, R. J. (2005). "I'd know a false confession if I saw one": A comparative study of college students and police investigators. *Law and Human Behavior, 29(2),* 211–227; DePaulo, B. M., Lassiter, G. D., & Stone, J. I. (1982). Attentional determinants of success at detecting deception and truth. *Personality and Social Psychology Bulletin, 8(2),* 273–279.

157. Indeed, some DNA exonerees were convicted at trial after turning down plea offers. See, e.g., Zerwick, P. (2007). Murder, race, justice: The State vs. Darryl Hunt, part 6. *Winston-Salem Journal,* November 27; Vertuno, J. (2009). Judge clears dead Texas man of rape conviction. *Austin American-Statesman,* February 7.

158. See Gregory, W. L., Mowen, J. C., & Linder, D. E. (1978). Social psychology and plea bargaining: Applications, methodology, and theory. *Journal of*

Personality and Social Psychology, 36, 1521–1530; Tor, A., Gazal-Eyal, O., & Garcia, S. M. (2010). Fairness and the willingness to accept plea bargain offers. *Journal of Legal Studies, 7,* 97–116.

159. In some instances, such as murder charges and third-strike prosecutions, prosecutors might not offer a plea deal and defendants might be inclined to proceed to trial even in the face of strong inculpating evidence.

160. The *liberation hypothesis* suggests that jurors tend to insert their values and beliefs into their verdicts only when the case is close. Kalven, H., & Zeisel, H. (1966). *The American jury.* Boston: Little, Brown. The particular sensitivity of close cases has been replicated in both naturalistic and experimental data, e.g., Devine, D. J., Buddenbaum, J. Houp, S., Studebaker, N., & Stolle, D. P. (2009). Strength of evidence, extraevidentiary influence, and the Liberation Hypothesis: Data from the field. *Law and Human Behavior, 33,* 136–148; Brewer & Hupfeld (2004), *supra* note 93; Johnson, J. D., Whitestone, E., Jackson, L. A., & Gatto, L. (1995). Justice is still not colorblind: Differential racial effects of exposure to inadmissible evidence. *Personality and Social Psychology Bulletin, 21,* 893–898.

161. These conditions can also be a source of stress for jurors. Bornstein, B. H., Miller, M. K., Nemeth, R. J., Page, G. L., & Musil, S. (2005). Juror reactions to jury duty: Perceptions of the system and potential stressors. *Behavioral Sciences & the Law, 23,* 321–346. Jury service can also be traumatizing. Robertson, N., Davies, G., & Nettleingham, A. (2009). Vicarious traumatisation as a consequence of jury service. *Howard Journal of Criminal Justice, 48,* 1–12.

162. Green, M. C., & Brock, T. C. (2002). In the mind's eye: Transportation-imagery model of narrative persuasion. In M. C. Green, J. J. Strange, & T. C. Brock, eds., *Narrative impact: Social and cognitive foundations,* pp. 315–342. Mahwah, NJ: Lawrence Erlbaum.

163. Of the possible stories that could plausibly be constructed from the trial evidence, jurors tend to adopt the strongest narrative, as determined by its coverage of the known facts, internal consistency, correspondence with background knowledge, and expectations of the world, as well as the familiarity of its narrative structure. For a review, see Pennington, N., & Hastie, R. (1993). The story model for juror decision making. In R. Hastie, ed., *Inside the juror: The psychology of juror decision making,* pp. 192–221. New York: Cambridge University Press. The story model was preceded by Bennett, W. L., & Feldman, M. S. (1981). *Reconstructing reality in the courtroom: Justice and judgment in American culture.* New Brunswick, NJ: Rutgers University Press. See also Wagenaar, W. A., van Koppen, P. J., & Crombag, H. F. M. (1993). *Anchored narratives: The psychology of criminal evidence.* New York: St. Martin's Press.

164. This is not to say that the story model is entirely a construct of persuasion. Pennington & Hastie's (1993, *supra* note 163) research demonstrates that

people apply the story format intrapersonally, as an adaptive cognitive tool to enable the handling of complex evidence sets. The point, rather, is that storytelling serves also as a persuasive device.

165. Petty, R. E., & Cacioppo, J. (1986). *Communication and persuasion: Central and peripheral routes to attitude change.* New York: Springer-Verlag; Chaiken, S., Liberman, A., & Eagly, A. H. (1989). Heuristic and systematic information processing within and beyond the persuasion context. In J. S. Uleman & J. A. Bargh, eds., *Unintended thought,* pp. 212–252. New York: Guilford Press; Chen, S., & Chaiken, S. (1999). The heuristic-systematic model in its broader context. In S. Chaiken & Y. Trope, eds., *Dual-process theories in social psychology,* pp. 73–96. New York: Guilford Press.

This dual-process model of persuasion is consistent with the familiar distinction between two general types of cognitive processing. The loose assortment of processes dubbed *System I* is typically holistic, associationistic, crude, and superficial. The processes are often driven by emotion, motivation, affect, effort-minimization, and closure-seeking. *System II* processing is purportedly analytical, thorough, and rational. Gilbert, D. T. (1989). Thinking lightly about others: Automatic components of the social inference process. In J. S. Uleman & J. A. Bargh, eds., *Unintended thought,* pp. 189–211. New York: Guilford Press; Epstein S. (1994). Integration of the cognitive and psychodynamic unconscious. *American Psychologist, 49,* 709–724; Sloman, S. A. (1996). The empirical case for two systems of reasoning. *Psychological Bulletin, 119,* 3–22; Stanovich, K. E. (1999). *Who is rational? Studies of individual differences in reasoning.* Mahwah, NJ: Lawrence Erlbaum.

Although the precise relationship between the two systems is disputed, the correct view seems to be that the two systems are not so distinct or independent of each other. In particular, *System I* processing can play a decisive role in *System II* processing. Evans, J. St. B. T. (2008). Dual-processing accounts of reasoning, judgment, and social cognition. *Annual Review of Psychology, 59,* 255–278. In other words, analytic thinking is susceptible to being skewed by superficial heuristic processing.

166. Crano, W. D., & Prislin, R. (2006). Attitudes and persuasion. *Annual Review of Psychology, 57,* 345–374.

167. Sopory, P., & Dillard, J. P. (2002). The persuasive effects of metaphor: A meta-analysis. *Human Communication Research, 28,* 382–419.

168. Gibbs, R. W., Jr., & Izett, C. D. (2005). Irony as persuasive communication. In H. L. Colston & A. N. Katz, eds., *Figurative language comprehension: Social and cultural influences,* pp. 131–151. Mahwah, NJ: Lawrence Erlbaum.

169. Roskos-Ewoldsen, D. R. (2003). What is the role of rhetorical questions in persuasion?. In J. Bryant, D. Roskos-Ewoldsen, & J. Cantor, eds., *Communication and emotion: Essays in honor of Dolf Zillmann,* pp. 297–321. Mahwah, NJ: Lawrence Erlbaum.

170. Hobbs, P. (2007). Lawyers' use of humor as persuasion. *Humor: International Journal of Humor Research, 20,* 123–156.

171. Kaplan, M. F., & Miller, L. E. (1978). Reducing the effects of juror bias. *Journal of Personality and Social Psychology, 36,* 1443–1455.

172. Wood, W. (2000). Attitude change: Persuasion and social influence. *Annual Review of Psychology, 51,* 539–570.

173. Petty, R. E., Wegener, D. T., & Fabrigar, L. R. (1997). Attitudes and attitude change. *Annual Review of Psychology, 48,* 609–647.

174. Petty, R. E., Briñol, P., & Tormala, Z. L. (2002). Thought confidence as a determinant of persuasion: The self-validation hypothesis. *Journal of Personality and Social Psychology, 82,* 722–741.

175. Borgida, E., & Nisbett, R. E. (1977). The differential impact of abstract vs. concrete information on decisions. *Journal of Applied Social Psychology, 7,* 258–271. In a study testing judgments of a tort case, jurors were about twice as likely to find for the plaintiff when the defense's expert witness presented scientific data as when the witness presented anecdotes (59 percent vs. 31 percent). Bornstein, B. H. (2004). The impact of different types of expert scientific testimony on mock jurors' liability verdicts. *Psychology, Crime & Law, 10,* 429–446.

176. In a simulated tort case, jurors awarded higher damages for a bodily injury when it was depicted in color photographs than when it was depicted in black-and-white photographs or in text form. Whalen, D. H., & Blanchard, F. A. (1982). Effects of photographic evidence on mock juror judgement. *Journal of Applied Social Psychology, 12,* 30–41.

177. Evans, K. (1994). *The common sense rule of trial advocacy.* St. Paul, MN: West.

178. Haydock, R., & Sonsteng, J. (2004). *Trial: Advocacy before judges, jurors, and arbitrators,* 3rd ed., pp. 18–19. St. Paul, MN: West Thompson.

179. These titles are published by the National Institute for Trial Advocacy. NITA is a well-regarded, 501(c)(3) charitable organization, whose primary mission is to "promote justice through effective and ethical advocacy."

180. For example, workshops in the group therapy technique of psychodrama have been designed for lawyers. Proponents of the program contend that it could help in persuading juries. Garrison, J. (2006). Lawyers learn to share their pain with jurors. *Los Angeles Times,* November 25.

181. American Society of Trial Consultants (2011). *The Jury Expert: The Art and Science of Litigation Advocacy, 23(5).* http://www.thejuryexpert.com/wp-content/uploads/TheJuryExpertSeptember2011.pdf.

182. Jurors are instructed to that effect. For example, the California pattern instructions state: "You must use only the evidence that is presented in the courtroom." Judicial Council of California (2010). *Criminal jury instructions,* p. 104. http://www.courts.ca.gov/partners/documents/calcrim_juryins.pdf.

183. A long-standing finding in cognitive psychology is that people do not always settle for the information they receive. As part of the ubiquitous drive to make sense of the world, people tend to *go beyond the information given*. Bruner, J. S. (1957). Going beyond the information given. In J. S. Bruner, E. Brunswik, L. Festinger, F. Heider, K. F. Muenzinger, C. E. Osgood, & D. Rapaport, eds., *Contemporary approaches to cognition,* pp. 41–69. Cambridge, MA: Harvard University Press.

184. A thorny problem arises when the extra-evidential information is factually true. Such instances actually increase accuracy, though they tend to violate the rule that rendered the evidence inadmissible in the first place.

185. Moran, G., & Cutler, B. L. (1991). The prejudicial impact of pretrial publicity. *Journal of Applied Social Psychology, 21,* 345–367; Nietzel, M. T., & Dillehay, R. C. (1983). Psychologists as consultants for changes of venue: The use of public opinion surveys. *Law and Human Behavior, 7,* 309–335.

186. Devine et al. (2009), *supra* note 160.

187. The DNA test that exculpated Robert Miller also identified the true perpetrator. Dwyer, Neufeld, & Scheck (2000), *supra* note 133; Innocence Project, profile, Robert Miller. http://www.innocenceproject.org/Content/Robert _Miller.php.

188. Sue, S., Smith, R. E., & Gilbert, R. (1974). Biasing effects of pretrial publicity on judicial decisions. *Journal of Criminal Justice, 2,* 163–171.

189. Kerr, N. L., Niedermeier, K. E., & Kaplan, M. F. (1999). Bias in jurors vs. bias in juries: New evidence from the SDS perspective. *Organizational Behavior and Human Decision Processes, 80,* 70–86.

190. Hope, L., Memon, A., & McGeorge, P. (2004). Understanding pretrial publicity: Predecisional distortion of evidence by mock jurors. *Journal of Experimental Psychology: Applied, 10,* 111–119.

191. Ruva, C., McEvoy, C., & Bryant, J. B. (2007). Effects of pre-trial publicity and jury deliberation on juror bias and source memory errors. *Applied Cognitive Psychology, 21,* 45–67; Ruva, C. L., & McEvoy, C. (2008). Negative and positive pretrial publicity affect juror memory and decision making. *Journal of Experimental Psychology: Applied, 14,* 226–235.

192. Steblay, N. M., Besirevic, J., Fulero, S. M., & Jimenez-Lorente, B. (1999). The effects of pretrial publicity on juror verdicts: A meta-analytic review. *Law and Human Behavior, 23,* 219–235. The effects are strongest for studies conducted under more realistic conditions.

193. Ogloff, J. R. P., & Vidmar, N. (1994). The impact of pretrial publicity on jurors: A study to compare the relative effects of television and print media in a child sex abuse case. *Law and Human Behavior, 18,* 507–525.

194. Ruva, McEvoy, & Bryant (2007), *supra* note 191. On the issue of source monitoring, see Chapter 4.

195. See, e.g., Judicial Council of California (2010). Instruction 101: "Do not let bias, sympathy, prejudice, or public opinion influence your decision." Judicial Council of California (2010), *supra* note 182.

196. Douglas, K. S., Lyon, D. R., & Ogloff, J. R. P. (1997). The impact of graphic photographic evidence on mock jurors' decisions in a murder trial: Probative or prejudicial? *Law and Human Behavior, 21,* 485–501.

197. In one study, exposure to gruesome evidence increased the conviction rate from 14 percent to 34 percent. Bright, D. A., & Goodman-Delahunty, J. (2004). The influence of gruesome verbal evidence on mock juror verdicts. *Psychiatry, Psychology and Law, 11,* 154–166. See also Bright, D. A., & Goodman-Delahunty, J. (2006). Gruesome evidence and emotion: Anger, blame, and jury decision-making. *Law and Human Behavior, 30,* 183–202. Other studies, however, have provided only partial support for the effect of gruesome evidence. See Kassin, S. M., & Garfield, D. A. (1991). Blood and guts: General and trial-specific effects of videotaped crime scenes on mock jurors. *Journal of Applied Social Psychology, 21,* 1459–1472.

198. Anger can play a legitimate role in sentencing decisions. Various homicide statutes recognize heinousness as a factor that can aggravate a homicide to a first-degree murder, and even to a capital murder.

199. See Federal Rule of Evidence 403.

200. Closing argument of the prosecutor Dean Bowman in Hunt's second trial. Quoted in Zerwick (2007), *supra* note 157. Darryl Hunt was exonerated based on a DNA test after serving more than eighteen years in prison.

201. Weinstein, H. (2006). Freed man gives lesson on false confessions: An ex-inmate tells a state panel how Texas police coerced him into admitting to murder. *Los Angeles Times,* June 21. Ochoa was convicted and sentenced to life in prison. He was freed eleven years later on the basis of a DNA test. On the case of Christopher Ochoa, see Innocence Project, profile, Christopher Ochoa. http://www.innocenceproject.org/Content/Christopher_Ochoa.php.

202. The victim in the trial of Brian Piszczek wept while she recounted the details of the brutal assault that she endured. Piszczek recalls: "I looked at the jury . . . and a couple of the ladies' mouths dropped. I could read their minds. They were thinking, 'You horrible, filthy man you.'" Suspect convicted on faulty memory. (1995). *Houston Chronicle,* February 13, p. A4. Piszczek was released from prison based on a DNA test after serving three years in prison.

203. See, e.g., Damasio, A. R. (1994). *Descartes' error: Emotion, reason, and the human brain.* New York: Putnam; Loewenstein, G., & Lerner, J. S. (2003). The role of affect in decision making. In R. J. Davidson, K. R. Scherer, & H. H. Goldsmith, eds., *Handbook of affective sciences,* pp. 619–642. Oxford: Oxford University Press.

For example, portraying the defendant in a libel suit in a positive light (a benevolent country doctor) resulted in more verdicts in his favor than when he was portrayed as a Wall Street shark (78 percent vs. 28 percent). See Holyoak, K. J., & Simon, D. (1999). Bidirectional reasoning in decision making by constraint satisfaction. *Journal of Experimental Psychology: General, 128,* 3–31, study 3. Recall that witnesses who were judged to be friendly, likable, and attractive were also more likely to be believed. O'Sullivan (2003), *supra* note 152.

204. See, e.g., Otto, A. L., Penrod, S. D., & Dexter, H. R. (1994). The biasing impact of pretrial publicity on juror judgments. *Law and Human Behavior, 18,* 453–869.

205. Paynter, B. (1986). Man convicted of rape; voice print evidence given. *Dallas Morning News,* February 8, p. A39. On the case of David Pope, who served fifteen years in prison before being exonerated on the basis of a DNA test, see Innocence Project, profile. http://www.innocenceproject.org/Content/David_Shawn_Pope.php.

206. For illustration of discrimination in employment, see Bertrand, M., & Mullainathan, S. (2004). Are Emily and Brendan more employable than Lakisha and Jamal? *American Economic Review, 94,* 991–1014. For examples of discrimination in organ transplants and car purchasing, see Ayres, I. (2001). *Pervasive prejudice? Unconventional evidence of race and gender discrimination.* Chicago: University of Chicago Press.

207. Jones, C. S., & Kaplan, M. F. (2003). The effects of racially stereotypical crimes on juror decision-making and information-processing strategies. *Basic and Applied Social Psychology, 25,* 1–13; Gordon, R. A., Bindrim, T. A., McNicholas, M. L., & Walden, T. L. (1988). Perceptions of blue-collar and white-collar crime: The effect of defendant race on simulated juror decisions. *Journal of Social Psychology, 128,* 191–197; Gordon, R. A. (1990). Attributions for blue-collar and white-collar crime: The effects of subject and defendant race on simulated juror decisions. *Journal of Applied Social Psychology, 20,* 971–983. Stereotype effects were observed in judgments of white defendants accused of molestation and black defendants accused of assault. Bodenhausen, G. V. (1990). Second-guessing the jury: Stereotypic and hindsight biases in perceptions of court cases. *Journal of Applied Social Psychology, 20,* 1112–1121.

Prejudicial effects have also been found when the race of the defendant coincided with a race-neutral case feature, such as inadmissible incriminating evidence. See Johnson et al. (1995), *supra* note 160. In other words, putatively race-neutral factors were employed to reach racially discriminatory results.

208. Garrett, B. (2008). Judging innocence. *Columbia Law Review, 108,* 55–142, p. 96. These data pertain to the first 200 DNA exonerees.

209. Of the 194,000 rapes reported by white victims in 2006, the race of the offender was known in 83 percent of the reports. Of these instances, 17 percent were perpetrated by black men. U.S. Department of Justice, Bureau of Justice

Statistics (2008). *Criminal victimization in the United States,* table 42. http://bjs.ojp.usdoj.gov/content/pub/pdf/cvus08.pdf.

210. Innocence Project (2007). 200 exonerated: Too many wrongfully convicted, 20–21. http://www.innocenceproject.org/200/ip_200.pdf.

211. For laboratory findings, see Blair, I. V., Judd, C. M., Sadler, M. S., & Jenkins, C. (2002). The role of Afrocentric features in person perception: Judging by features and categories. *Journal of Personality and Social Psychology, 83,* 5–25; Blair, I. V., Chapleau, K. M., & Judd, C. M. (2005). The use of Afrocentric features as cues for judgment in the presence of diagnostic information. *European Journal of Social Psychology, 35,* 59–68.

212. A study of a sample of 216 Florida convicted inmates revealed that those whose appearance was 1 standard deviation above the group mean measure of Afrocentric features received sentences that were seven to eight months longer than inmates with 1 standard deviation below the mean. Blair, I. V., Judd, C. M., & Chapleau, K. M. (2004). The influence of Afrocentric facial features in criminal sentencing. *Psychological Science, 15,* 674–679.

213. Among the forty-four Philadelphia cases in which black defendants were convicted for capital murder of a white victim, 24 percent of defendants classified as having low Afrocentric features were sentenced to death, whereas the rate was 57 percent for defendants who had a strong stereotypical look. Eberhardt, J. L., Davies, P. G., Purdie-Vaughns, V. J., & Johnson, S. L. (2006). Looking deathworthy: Perceived stereotypicality of black defendants predicts capital-sentencing outcomes. *Psychological Science, 17,* 383–386.

214. Simon, D., Snow, C. J., & Read, S. J. (2004). The redux of cognitive consistency theories: Evidence judgments by constraint satisfaction. *Journal of Personality and Social Psychology, 86,* 814–837; Glöckner, A., & Engel, C. (under review). Can we trust intuitive jurors? Standards of proof and the probative value of evidence in coherence based reasoning.

Recall that similar results were observed in the decision of a noncriminal legal case (Holyoak & Simon 1999, *supra* note 203), as well as in nonlegal decisions; see Simon, D., Krawczyk, D. C., & Holyoak, K. J. (2004). Construction of preferences by constraint satisfaction. *Psychological Science, 15,* 331–336; Simon, D., Krawczyk, D. C., Bleicher, A., & Holyoak, K. J. (2008). The transience of constructed preferences. *Journal of Behavioral Decision Making, 21,* 1–14; Glöckner, A., & Betsch, T. (2008). Multiple-reason decision making based on automatic processing. *Journal of Experimental Psychology: Learning, Memory, and Cognition, 34,* 1055–1075; Glöckner, A., Betsch, T., & Schindler, N. (2010). Coherence shifts in probabilistic inference tasks. *Journal of Behavioral Decision Making, 23,* 439–462.

215. In the experiments simulating a criminal case, more than half of the confidence ratings were 8 or above and only 15 percent were under 6 (on a scale of 1–11). Simon, Snow, & Read (2004), *supra* note 214. In another study,

three-quarters of participants rated their confidence at a level or 4 or 5, on a scale of 1–5. Holyoak & Simon (1999), *supra* note 203.

216. See Simon, Snow, & Read (2004), *supra* note 214, p. 821.

217. As discussed in Chapter 7, there is good reason to view the psychological construct that underlies the beyond a reasonable doubt standard as a measure of the fact finder's confidence.

218. This effect is unlikely to have any practical effect on the verdict when the juror is leaning toward acquittal. Given the asymmetric standard of proof in criminal trials, a juror who is inclined to acquit must do so regardless of the strength of that leaning.

219. This accumulation resulted in seemingly illogical inferences, such as greater trust in the eyewitness's identification, and weaker belief in the defendant's explanation for the source of the money found on him. By the same token, providing information that placed the defendant far from the crime scene resulted in more exculpatory interpretations of all the other evidence items. Simon, Snow, & Read (2004), *supra* note 214, study 3.

220. Holyoak & Simon (1999), supra note 203, study 3.

221. Bell & Loftus (1988), *supra* note 91; Bell, B. E., & Loftus, E. F. (1989). Trivial persuasion in the courtroom: The power of (a few) minor details. *Journal of Personality and Social Psychology, 56,* 669–679.

222. Borckardt, J. J., Sprohge, E., & Nash, M. (2003). Effects of the inclusion and refutation of peripheral details on eyewitness credibility. *Journal of Applied Social Psychology, 33,* 2187–2197.

223. Smith, B. C., Penrod, S. D., Otto, A. L., & Park, R. C. (1996). Jurors' use of probabilistic evidence. *Law and Human Behavior, 20,* 49–82. See also McKenzie, C. R. M., Lee, S. M., & Chen, K. K. (2002). When negative evidence increases confidence: Changes in belief after hearing two sides of a dispute. *Journal of Behavioral Decision Making, 15,* 1–18.

224. Charman, S. D., Gregory, A. H., & Carlucci, M. (2009). Exploring the diagnostic utility of facial composites: Beliefs of guilt can bias perceived similarity between composite and suspect. *Journal of Experimental Psychology: Applied, 15,* 76–90 (study 2).

225. Lagnado, D. A., & Harvey, N. (2008). The impact of discredited evidence. *Psychonomic Bulletin & Review, 15,* 1166–1173.

226. To be sure, at times the information that is being excluded is factually accurate. In those instances, the exposure to the inadmissible information is likely to increase the accuracy of the verdict.

227. Hope, Memon, & McGeorge (2004), *supra* note 190.

228. Kassin, S. M., & Sommers, S. R. (1997). Inadmissible testimony, instructions to disregard, and the jury: Substantive versus procedural considerations. *Personality and Social Psychology Bulletin, 23,* 1046–1054.

229. Greene, E., & Dodge, M. (1995). The influence of prior record evidence on juror decision making. *Law and Human Behavior, 19,* 67–78; Hans, V. P., & Doob, A. N. (1976). Section 12 of the Canada Evidence Act and the deliberation of simulated juries. *Criminal Law Quarterly, 18,* 253–253. Exposing jurors to incriminating pretrial publicity in a murder trial also led them to rate the prosecutor more favorably and the defense attorney more negatively, while exposure to publicity that was favorable to the defendant resulted in opposite assessments. Ruva & McEvoy (2008), *supra* note 191.

230. An initial study indicated that a debiasing intervention could reduce the coherence effect by about one-half (see Simon, D. [2004]. A third view of the black box: Cognitive coherence in legal decision making. *University of Chicago Law Review, 71,* 511–586, pp. 569–574), though that finding was not replicated in subsequent (unpublished) experiments.

231. This research has been confined mostly to eyewitness identification testimony. See Cutler, B. L., Penrod, S. D., & Dexter, H. R. (1989). The eyewitness, the expert psychologist, and the jury. *Law and Human Behavior, 13(3),* 311–332; Devenport et al. (2002), *supra* note 57. For a review, see Leippe, M. R. (1995). The case for expert testimony about eyewitness memory. *Psychology, Public Policy, and Law, 1,* 909–959. For a critical view of the research, see Martire, K. A., & Kemp, R. I. (2011). Can experts help jurors to evaluate eyewitness evidence? A review of eyewitness expert effects. *Legal and Criminological Psychology, 16(1),* 24–36. More research on this issue would be most welcome.

232. For a discussion of the admissibility of expert testimony across jurisdictions, see Schmechel et al. (2006), *supra* note 37.

233. To be sure, identifications should not be barred for minute flaws in the procedure. Delineating the appropriate boundaries for exclusion is beyond the scope of this discussion, though suffice it to say that the courts should not have admitted the identifications that were the subject of the landmark cases *Neil v. Biggers* (409 U.S. 188 [1972]) and *Manson v. Brathwaite* (432 U.S., 98 [1977]), not to mention the numerous grossly suggestive procedures described in Chapter 3 ("Lineups in the Wild"). There is little reason to expect the exclusion of identifications obtained by lineups conducted according to the recommendations listed in Chapter 3. Computerized lineups should be even more immune to exclusion.

234. For more on these recommendations and the research that underlies them, see Leo, R. A., Drizin, S. A., Neufeld, P. J., Hall, B. R., & Vatner, A. (2006). Bringing reliability back in: False confessions and legal safeguards in the twenty-first century. *Wisconsin Law Review, (2),* 479–538. For a discussion of the courts' backing away from examination of the reliability of confessions, see Dix, G. E. (1988). Federal constitutional confession law: The 1986 and 1987 Supreme Court terms. *Texas Law Review, 67,* 231–349, pp. 272–276.

This principle is mandated by law in the United Kingdom. Section 76 of the Police and Criminal Evidence Act (1984) instructs that a confession should not be admitted when it "was or may have been obtained" by means of oppression of the suspect or under circumstances that were "likely . . . to render [the confession] unreliable." This presumptive inadmissibility can be overcome only if the prosecution proves to the court beyond a reasonable doubt that the confession was not obtained in such a manner.

7. "Bolting Out the Truth"

1. The Sixth Amendment reads in part: "In all criminal prosecutions, the accused shall enjoy the right to . . . be confronted with the witnesses against him . . . and to have the Assistance of Counsel for his defence."

2. Matthew Hale, quoted in Langbein, J. H. (2003). *The origins of adversary criminal trial,* p. 234. New York: Oxford University Press.

3. Wigmore, J. H. (1974). *Evidence in trials at common law,* vol. 5, p. 32 (J. H. Chadbourn, Rev.). Boston: Little, Brown and Co. See, e.g., *Lilly v. Virginia,* 527 U.S. 116, 124 (1999); *Watkins v. Sowders,* 449 U.S. 341, 349 (1981).

4. See Underwager, R., & Wakefield, H. (1996). Responding to improper and abusive impeachment efforts. *American Journal of Forensic Psychology, 14,* 5–23.

5. This oft-repeated maxim is listed as one of the Ten Commandments of cross-examination. See Younger, I. (1976). *The art of cross-examination,* p. 23. Chicago: American Bar Association.

6. On the case of *Brady v. Maryland* (373 U.S. 83, 87 [1963]) and its progeny, see Medwed, D. S. (2010). Brady's bunch of flaws. *Washington & Lee Law Review, 67,* 1533–1567; Sundby, S. E. (2002). Fallen superheroes and constitutional mirages: The tale of *Brady v. Maryland. McGeorge Law Review, 33,* 643–663.

7. For findings of backfiring effects against accusers, see Rucker, D. D., & Petty, R. E. (2003). Effects of accusations on the accuser: The moderating role of accuser culpability. *Personality and Social Psychology Bulletin, 29,* 1259–1271.

8. A study found that innuendo inserted by the defense attorney during cross-examination had a negative impact on jurors' evaluations of the testimony of an expert witness, but not of the victim. Kassin, S. M., Williams, L. N., & Saunders, C. L. (1990). Dirty tricks of cross-examination: The influence of conjectural evidence on the jury. *Law and Human Behavior, 14,* 373–384.

9. Frank, J. (1949). *Courts on trial.* Princeton, NJ: Princeton University Press; Frankel, M. E. (1978). *Partisan justice.* New York: Hill & Wang.

10. Freedman, M. H. (1966). Professional responsibility of the criminal defense lawyer: The three hardest questions. *Michigan Law Review, 64,* 1469–1484.

11. Valentine, T., & Maras, K. (2011). The effect of cross-examination on the accuracy of adult eyewitness testimony. *Applied Cognitive Psychology, 25,* 554–561.

12. Kebbell, M. R., & Johnson, S. D. (2000). Lawyers' questioning: The effect of confusing questions on witness confidence and accuracy. *Law and Human Behavior, 24,* 629–641; Perry, N. W., McAuliff, B. D., Tam, P., & Claycomb, L. (1995). When lawyers question children: Is justice served? *Law and Human Behavior, 19,* 609–629. The latter experiment found that convoluted questions had adverse effects on subjects in four age groups ranging from kindergarten to college.

13. Wheatcroft, J. M., Wagstaff, G. F., & Kebbell, M. R. (2004). The influence of courtroom questioning style on actual and perceived eyewitness confidence and accuracy. *Legal and Criminological Psychology, 9,* 83–101.

14. On the accuracy-confidence relationship, see discussions in Chapter 6.

15. Evans, K. (1994). *The common sense rules of trial advocacy.* St. Paul, MN: West Publishing.

16. Wells, G. L., Ferguson, T. J., & Lindsay, R. C. L. (1981). The tractability of eyewitness confidence and its implications for triers of fact. *Journal of Applied Psychology, 66,* 688–696.

17. Cross-examination has the capacity to assist the adjudicative process when it is used for less ambitious goals. The measure affords the cross-examining party an opportunity to use the witness to introduce additional information or alternative explanations from those proposed by the opposite party. In this capacity, the measure provides the fact finder with a richer set of evidence, even when it does not serve its primary function of undermining unreliable testimony.

18. As the Supreme Court stated in *Taylor v. Louisiana* (419 U.S. 522, 530 [1975]), juries embody "the commonsense judgment of the community" as a check against prosecutorial excesses and "in preference to the professional or perhaps over-conditioned or biased response of a judge."

19. The principle *nullum crimen sine lege* states that conduct does not constitute a crime unless it has previously been declared to be so by the law.

20. On jury nullification, see Marder, N. S. (1999). The myth of the nullifying jury. *Northwestern Law Review, 93,* 877–959; Vidmar, N., & Hans, V. P. (2007). *American juries: The verdict.* New York: Prometheus Books.

21. A failure to follow jury instructions does not necessarily compromise the factual accuracy of the decision. In some instances—such as when the rules of evidence mandate keeping a piece of accurate evidence out of court—failure to follow the instruction could actually increase the accuracy of the verdict.

22. *Parker v. Randolph,* 442 U.S. 62, 73 (1979). To support this belief, the Court has offered the circular argument that if jurors did not follow instructions, "it would be pointless for a trial court to instruct a jury, and even more pointless

for an appellate court to reverse a criminal conviction because the jury was improperly instructed." See also *Greer v. Miller*, 483 U.S. 756, 767 (1987).

23. For example, a large postdeliberation study of instruction comprehension found levels of accuracy around 30 percent. Hastie, R., Penrod, S. D., & Pennington, N. (1983). *Inside the jury.* Cambridge, MA: Harvard University Press. Comprehension levels on insanity defense instructions were found to range from 15 percent to 43 percent correct. Ogloff, J. R. (1991). A comparison of insanity defense standards on juror decision making. *Law and Human Behavior, 15,* 509–531. For a review of the research, see Lieberman, J. D., & Sales, B. D. (1997). What social science teaches us about the jury instruction process. *Psychology, Public Policy, and Law, 3,* 589–644.

24. See, e.g., Strawn, D. U., & Buchanan, R. W. (1976). Jury confusion: A threat to justice. *Judicature, 59,* 478–483; Buchanan, R. W., Pryor, B., Taylor, K. P., & Strawn, D. U. (1978). Legal communication: An investigation of juror comprehension of pattern instructions. *Communication Monographs, 26,* 31–35.

25. For example, a study of Michigan jurors found that instruction increased correct responses on procedural rules, but not on definitions of crimes. In this study, the level of comprehension was shy of 50 percent on both types of instructions. Reifman, A., Gusick, S. M., & Ellsworth, P. C. (1992). Real jurors' understanding of the law in real cases. *Law and Human Behavior, 16,* 539–554.

26. For example, Michigan jurors' responses barely reached chance level on instructions pertaining to the use of evidence for limited purposes and the definition of specific intent. Kramer, G., & Koenig, D. (1990). Do jurors understand criminal jury instructions? Analyzing the results of the Michigan juror comprehension project. *University of Michigan Journal of Law Reform, 23,* 401–437.

27. Thomas, C. (2010). *Are juries fair?* Ministry of Justice Research Series 1/10. http://www.justice.gov.uk/downloads/publications/research-and-analysis /moj-research/are-juries-fair-research.pdf.

28. In the Washington sample, participants applied the instructions correctly 60 percent of the time. Severance, L. J., & Loftus, E. F. (1982). Improving the ability of jurors to comprehend and apply criminal jury instructions. *Law & Society Review, 17,* 153–198; Buchanan et al. (1978), *supra* note 24.

29. Nonetheless, respondents relied on the wording of the definitions to justify their decisions. Spackman, M. P., Belcher, J. C., Calapp, J. W., & Taylor, A. (2002). An analysis of the effects of subjective and objective instruction forms on mock-juries' murder/manslaughter distinctions. *Law and Human Behavior, 26,* 605–623.

30. A study by Dan Kahan found no difference in conviction rates among three different crime definitions (ranging from 53 percent to 55 percent). Minor differences were observed with two unconventional instructions (rates of 62 percent and 65 percent). Kahan, D. (2010). Culture, cognition, and consent:

Who perceives what, and why, in "acquaintance rape" cases. *University of Pennsylvania Law Review, 158,* 729–813.

31. Ogloff (1991), *supra* note 23.

32. See Kassin, S. M., & Sommers, S. R. (1997). Inadmissible testimony, instructions to disregard, and the jury: Substantive versus procedural considerations. *Personality and Social Psychology Bulletin, 23,* 1046–1054. See also Finkel, N. J. (1995). *Commonsense justice: Jurors' notions of the law.* Cambridge, MA: Harvard University Press; Robinson, P., & Darley, J. (1995). *Justice, liability, and blame.* Boulder, CO: Westview Press.

33. Smith, V. L. (1991). Prototypes in the courtroom: Lay representations of legal concepts. *Journal of Personality and Social Psychology, 61,* 857–872; Smith, V. L. (1993). When prior knowledge and law collide: Helping jurors use the law. *Law and Human Behavior, 17,* 507–536.

34. Dhami, M. K. (2008). On measuring quantitative interpretations of reasonable doubt. *Journal of Experimental Psychology: Applied, 14,* 353–363.

35. As mentioned in Chapter 6, a study with federal and state judges observed that the judges were more likely to follow the law and ignore a confession obtained through an impermissibly coercive interrogation when the suspect was charged with a less serious offense than when the offense was more serious. Rachlinksi, J. J., Guthrie, C., & Wistrich, A. J. (2009). Context effects in judicial decision making. Paper presented at the fourth annual Conference on Empirical Legal Studies, University of Southern California, November 20–21, 2009. http://ssrn.com/abstract=1443596.

36. For a review of the research, see Wenzlaff, R. M., & Wegner, D. M. (2000). Thought suppression. *Annual Review of Psychology, 51,* 59–91. Indeed, in some jury simulations, issuing instructions to ignore evidence actually increased the impact of the impermissible evidence on the decision. Pickel, K. L. (1995). Inducing jurors to disregard inadmissible evidence: A legal explanation does not help. *Law and Human Behavior, 19,* 407–424; Wolf, S., & Montgomery, D. A. (1977). Effects of inadmissible evidence and level of judicial admonishment to disregard on the judgments of mock jurors. *Journal of Applied Social Psychology, 7,* 205–219.

37. Wright, R. A., Greenberg, J., & Brehm, S. S., eds. (2004). *Motivational analyses of social behavior: Building on Jack Brehm's contributions to psychology.* Mahwah, NJ: Lawrence Erlbaum.

38. Fischhoff, B. (1975). Hindsight is not equal to foresight: The effect of outcome knowledge on judgment under uncertainty. *Journal of Experimental Psychology: Human Perception and Performance, 1,* 288–299.

39. Anderson, C. A., Lepper, M. R., & Ross, L. (1980). Perseverance of social theories: The role of explanation in the persistence of discredited information. *Journal of Personality and Social Psychology, 39,* 1037–1049.

40. Recall that due to circuitous influences, the impermissible evidence can sway all the other evidence items and drive them toward a state of coherence with the corresponding conclusion. Even if people were capable of suppressing the specific item of inadmissible information, their decisions could still be affected by the permissible evidence that had shifted to cohere with that inadmissible information. See Chapters 2 and 6, and Simon, D. (2004). A third view of the black box: Cognitive coherence in legal decision making. *University of Chicago Law Review, 71,* 511–586.

41. Steblay, N., Hosch, H. M., Culhane, S. E., & McWethy, A. (2006). The impact on juror verdicts of judicial instruction to disregard inadmissible evidence: A meta-analysis. *Law and Human Behavior, 30,* 469–492.

42. Kassin & Sommers (1997), *supra* note 32.

43. Fein, S., McCloskey, A. L., & Tomlinson, T. M. (1997). Can the jury disregard that information? The use of suspicion to reduce the prejudicial effects of pretrial publicity and inadmissible testimony. *Personality and Social Psychology Bulletin, 23,* 1215–1226.

44. Admonitions were found to be ineffective when the evidence to be ignored contained a recording of the defendant's admission of guilt, provided key facts about an obscure homicide, or connected the defendant's gun to the crime. See Ruva, C. L., & McEvoy, C. (2008). Negative and positive pretrial publicity affect juror memory and decision making. *Journal of Experimental Psychology: Applied, 14,* 226–235; Fein, McCloskey, & Tomlinson (1997), *supra* note 43; Kassin, S. M., & Sukel, H. (1997). Coerced confessions and the jury: An experimental test of the "harmless error" rule. *Law and Human Behavior, 21,* 27–46; Sue, S., Smith, R. E., & Gilbert, R. (1974). Biasing effects of pretrial publicity on judicial decisions. *Journal of Criminal Justice, 2,* 163–171.

45. Kassin & Sommers (1997), *supra* note 32.

46. Sue, Smith, & Gilbert (1974), *supra* note 44.

47. Hunt, J. S., & Budesheim, T. L. (2004). How jurors use and misuse character evidence. *Journal of Applied Psychology, 89,* 347–361.

48. See Greene, E., & Loftus, E. F. (1985). When crimes are joined at trial. *Law and Human Behavior, 9,* 193–207.

49. For example, a simulated jury study found that merely suggesting that an expert witness's reputation was poorly regarded in the field had an adverse effect on his credibility. Even when the expert denied the conjecture, and even when the judge sustained an objection to the yet-unanswered question, jurors found the witness to be less competent, less persuasive, and less believable. Kassin, Williams, & Saunders (1990), *supra* note 8.

50. Instructions to ignore hearsay evidence—which can be seen as lying in the gray area of popular conceptions of justice—yields mixed results. Such instructions were unsuccessful in the study by Fein, McCloskey, & Tomlinson (1997), *supra* note 43, but generally successful in the study by Pickel (1995), *supra* note 36.

51. Wistrich, A. J., Guthrie, C., & Rachlinski, J. J. (2005). Can judges ignore inadmissible information? The difficulty of deliberately disregarding. *University of Pennsylvania Law Review, 153,* 1251–1345.

52. For example, informing the jury of the defendant's prior criminal history could help prove specific facts that are relevant to the current charge, and arguably serve as an indicator of the credibility of her testimony. At the same time, the ubiquitous tendency to stereotype and make unwarranted inferences about the defendant's propensity to commit crimes could prejudice her case, as judging the defendant by "who she is" rather than "what she did" can readily sway judgments of the likelihood of guilt.

53. Federal Rule of Evidence 404 (b) instructs that "Evidence of other crimes, wrongs, or acts is not admissible to prove the character of a person in order to show action in conformity herewith." The rule, however, contains exceptions that permit evidence of other crimes, wrongs, or acts for "other purposes, such as proof of motive, opportunity, intent, preparation, plan, knowledge, identity, or absence of mistake or accident." Moreover, Federal Rule of Evidence 609(a) instructs that under some conditions, evidence of prior convictions can be admitted for the purpose of attacking the credibility and character for truthfulness of a witness.

54. Federal Rule of Evidence 105.

55. For example, see Devine, P. G. (1989). Stereotypes and prejudice: Their automatic and controlled components. *Journal of Personality and Social Psychology, 56,* 5–18; Gilbert, D. T. (1998). Ordinary personology. In D. T. Gilbert, S. T. Fiske, & G. Lindzey, eds., *Handbook of social psychology,* 4th ed., vol. 2, pp. 89–150. New York: McGraw-Hill; Uleman, J. S., Saribay, S. A., & Gonzalez, C. M. (2008). Spontaneous inferences, implicit impressions, and implicit theories. *Annual Review of Psychology, 59,* 329–360.

56. Bargh, J. A. (1994). The four horsemen of automaticity: Awareness, intention, efficiency, and control in social cognition. In R. S. Wyer Jr. & T. K. Srull, eds., *Handbook of social cognition,* 2nd ed., vol. 1: *Basic processes,* pp. 1–40. Hillsdale, NJ: Lawrence Erlbaum.

57. Doob, A. N., & Kirshenbaum, H. M. (1972). Some empirical evidence of the effect of section 12 of the Canada Evidence Act upon the accused. *Criminal Law Quarterly, 15,* 88–96; Hans, V. P., & Doob, A. N. (1976). Section 12 of the Canada Evidence Act and the deliberation of simulated juries. *Criminal Law Quarterly, 18,* 253–253; Wissler, R. L., & Saks, M. J. (1985). On the inefficacy of limiting instructions: When jurors use prior conviction evidence to decide on guilt. *Law and Human Behavior, 9,* 37–48; Greene, E., & Dodge, M. (1995). The influence of prior record evidence on juror decision making. *Law and Human Behavior, 19,* 67–77.

Simulated jurors are somewhat more responsive to limiting instructions when the prior and current charges pertain to different crimes. See Wissler & Saks

(1985), *supra* note 57. The likely reason is that the intuitive assumptions of re-cidivism do not hold so strongly between different types of criminal behavior.

58. Steblay et al. (2006), *supra* note 41.

59. Compare Wissler & Saks (1985), *supra* note 57, with Tanford, S., & Cox, M. (1988). The effects of impeachment evidence and limiting instructions on individual and group decision making. *Law and Human Behavior, 12,* 477–497.

60. *Krulewitch v. United States,* 336 U.S. 440, 453 (1949).

61. *Nash v. United States,* 54 F.2d 1006, 1007 (1932).

62. *United States v. Grunewald,* 233 F.2d 556, 574 (1956).

63. *Sandez v. United States,* 239 F.2d 239, 248 (9th Cir. 1956).

64. *Dunn v. United States,* 307 F.2d 883, 886 (5th Cir. 1962).

65. As the Court explains, "We normally presume that a jury will follow an instruction to disregard inadmissible evidence inadvertently presented to it, unless there is an 'overwhelming probability' that the jury will be unable to follow the court's instructions . . . and a strong likelihood that the effect of the evidence would be 'devastating' to the defendant." *Greer v. Miller,* 483 U.S. 756, 767 (1987) (citations omitted); *Richardson v. Marsh,* 481 U.S. 200 (1987).

66. A meta-analysis showed that decisions to admit the contested evidence result in rates of conviction that are 50 percent higher than when the evidence is ruled inadmissible and followed by an instruction to ignore (74 percent vs. 46 percent). Steblay et al. (2006), *supra* note 41.

67. The following discussion does not purport to cover the vast range of psychological issues involved in the topic of capital punishment. It is confined to jurors' ability to comprehend and follow the sentencing instructions.

68. This ruling struck down all extant capital sentencing statutes and vacated the death sentences of some 600 people then inhabiting death row. Justice Stewart's plurality opinion found that in practice, death sentencing was performed "wantonly and freakishly," befalling only the "capriciously selected random handful." Receiving the punishment was not unlike "being struck by lightning." *Furman v. Georgia,* 408 U.S. 238, 309–310 (1972). Justice Brennan likened the arbitrariness to a "lottery system" (p. 293). Although most of the justices shunned the thorny issue of race, racial disparities were clearly on the justices' minds. Justice Douglas highlighted the death penalty's discriminative effect on black people, the poor, and the uneducated. For example, Douglas's opinion included data showing a disparity in the rate of commutations of death sentences (20 percent for whites and 12 percent for blacks) (p. 250). The discriminatory effects of the punishment were quite obvious. For example, in the forty years preceding the case, 405 black men had been executed for the crime of rape, whereas only 45 white people were executed for the same crime. Haney, C. (2005). *Death by design: Capital punishment as a social psychological system.* New York: Oxford University Press.

69. *Gregg v. Georgia,* 428 U.S. 153, 195 (1976). On the political environment that spurred the reinstatement of the death penalty statutes, see Banner, S. (2002). *The death penalty: An American history.* Cambridge, MA: Harvard University Press; Haney (2005), *supra* note 68.

70. *Gregg v. Georgia, supra* note 69, at 195.

71. *Lockett v. Ohio,* 438 U.S. 586 (1978). More recently, the Court has stated that jurors ought to be given the opportunity "to give meaningful consideration and effect to all mitigating evidence that might provide a basis for refusing to impose the death penalty." *Abdul-Kabir v. Quarterman,* 550 U.S. 233 (2007).

72. Correct or partially correct definitions were given for the term *aggravating* by 79 percent of the respondents, but by only 59 percent for the term *mitigating.* Haney, C., & Lynch, M. (1994). Comprehending life and death matters: A preliminary study of California's capital penalty instructions. *Law and Human Behavior, 18,* 411–436. See also Haney, C., & Lynch, M. (1997). Clarifying life and death matters: An analysis of instructional comprehension and penalty phase closing arguments. *Law and Human Behavior, 21,* 575–595.

73. Haney & Lynch (1994), *supra* note 72. The likely reason for the difficulty in comprehending the catchall mitigator is the relative unfamiliarity of the word *extenuate.*

74. Haney & Lynch (1997), *supra* note 72.

75. Even with the best instructions, lay people reach comprehension scores that are below 50 percent correct. Smith, A. E., & Haney, C. (2011). Getting to the point: Attempting to improve juror comprehension of capital penalty phase instructions. *Law and Human Behavior, 35,* 339–350. California's new pattern instructions, CALCRIM, were adopted by the Judicial Council in 2005 and came into effect in 2006. The primary innovation in these instructions is the use of psycholinguistic principles to simplify the language of the instructions. *Judicial Council of California Criminal Jury Instructions* (2011). New Providence, NJ: LexisNexis, Matthew Bender.

76. Wiener, R. L., Pritchard, C. C., & Weston, M. (1995). Comprehensibility of approved jury instructions in capital murder cases. *Journal of Applied Psychology, 80,* 455–467.

77. Wiener, R. L., Hurt, L. E., Thomas, S. L., Sadler, M. S., Bauer, C. A., & Sargent, T. M. (1998). The role of declarative and procedural knowledge in capital murder sentencing. *Journal of Applied Social Psychology, 28,* 124–144; Wiener, R. L., Rogers, M., Winter, R., Hurt, L., Hackney, A., Kadela, K., Seib, H., Rauch, S., Warren, L., & Morasco, B. (2004). Guided jury discretion in capital murder cases: The role of declarative and procedural knowledge. *Psychology, Public Policy, and Law, 10,* 516–576.

78. Only 40 percent of these respondents correctly understood the rule regarding the nonenumerated mitigating factors, and 33 percent miscomprehended the nonunanimity rule for mitigating factors. Diamond, S., & Levi, J. N. (1996).

Improving decisions on death by revising and testing jury instructions. *Judicature, 79,* 224–232.

79. The overall rate of correct responses in this study was 47.5 percent (for death-eligible respondents). Otto, C. W., Applegate, B. K., & Davis, R. K. (2007). Improving comprehension of capital sentencing instructions: Debunking juror misconceptions. *Crime & Delinquency, 53,* 502–517.

80. Frank, J., & Applegate, B. K. (1998). Assessing juror understanding of capital-sentencing instructions. *Crime & Delinquency, 44,* 412–433.

81. Correct responses ranged from 22 percent to 83 percent, with most values around 50 percent accuracy. Blankenship, M. B., Luginbuhl, J., Cullen, F. T., & Redick, W. (1997). Jurors' comprehension of sentencing instructions: A test of the death penalty process in Tennessee. *Justice Quarterly, 14,* 325–351.

82. Wiener, Pritchard, & Weston (1995), *supra* note 76; Wiener et al. (2004), *supra* note 77; Diamond & Levi (1996), *supra* note 78.

83. Lynch, M., & Haney, C. (2000). Discrimination and instructional comprehension: Guided discretion, racial bias, and the death penalty. *Law and Human Behavior, 24,* 337–358; Lynch, M., & Haney, C. (2009). Capital jury deliberation: Effects on death sentencing, comprehension, and discrimination. *Law and Human Behavior, 33,* 481–496.

84. The more serious problem caused by the policy of death qualification is that precluding people who object to the death penalty incidentally increases the likelihood that the jury will vote for conviction. See O'Neil, K. M., Patry, M. W., & Penrod, S. D. (2004). Exploring the effects of attitudes toward the death penalty on capital sentencing verdicts. *Psychology, Public Policy, and Law, 10,* 443–470; Butler, B. M., & Moran, G. (2002). The role of death qualification in venirepersons' evaluations of aggravating and mitigating circumstances in capital trials. *Law and Human Behavior, 26,* 175–184.

85. Of the jurors whose comprehension was in the lower half, 60 percent voted for the death sentence when the defendant was black, whereas only 41 percent voted the same when he was white. The disparity was even greater between black defendants charged with killing white victims (68 percent) and white defendants charged with killing black victims (36 percent). Lynch & Haney (2000), *supra* note 83.

86. While some 70 percent of the respondents believed that death was mandatory for repeat murderers, only about one-quarter shared the same position for murders that are generally perceived to be less condemnable. Bowers, W. J., Steiner, B. D., and Antonio, M. E. (2003). The capital sentencing decision: Guided discretion, reasoned moral judgment, or legal fiction. In J. R. Acker, R. M. Bohm, & C. S. Lanier, eds., *America's experiment with capital punishment: Reflections on the past, present, and future of the ultimate penal sanction,* 2nd ed., pp. 413–467. Durham, NC: Carolina Academic Press.

87. Some 30 percent of jurors who sat on South Carolina death penalty cases stated that the law requires imposition of a death sentence when they find that the defendant will be dangerous in the future. This erroneous belief is patently driven by people's preconceptions, because future dangerousness is not even mentioned in the instructions. Eisenberg, T., & Wells, M. T. (1993). Deadly confusion: Juror instructions in capital cases. *Cornell Law Review, 79,* 1–17.

88. The study also found strong disparities in the exercise of prosecutorial discretion: the death penalty was sought in 19 percent of cases in which a white man was charged with killing a black man, but in 70 percent of cases in which the races were reversed. A regression analysis showed that killing a white victim had roughly the same impact on the likelihood of receiving a death sentence as did aggravating factors that were officially prescribed, such as the defendant's serious prior criminal record or the fact that the death was perpetrated for the purpose of an armed robbery. Killing a white victim had three times the impact as killing a police officer. Baldus, D. C., Woodworth, G., & Pulaski, C. A. (1990). *Equal justice and the death penalty: A legal and empirical analysis.* Boston: Northeastern University Press.

See also Baldus, D. C., Pulaski, C., & Woodworth, G. (1983). Comparative review of death sentences: An empirical study of the Georgia experience. *Journal of Criminal Law & Criminology, 74,* 661–754; Baldus, D. C., Woodworth, G., Zuckerman, D., Weiner, N. A., & Broffitt, B. (1998). Race discrimination and the death penalty in the post-Furman era: An empirical and legal analysis with recent findings from Philadelphia. *Cornell Law Review, 83,* 1638–1770; Blume, J., Eisenberg, T., & Wells, M. T. (2004). Explaining death row's population and racial composition. *Journal of Empirical Legal Studies, 1,* 165–207.

89. The Court asserted that the jury's discretion is "controlled by clear and objective standards so as to produce non-discriminatory application." *McCleskey v. Kemp,* 481 U.S. 279, 302 (1987).

90. A study of capital sentencing in Philadelphia revealed that juries were twice as likely to sentence a black defendant to death as a nonblack defendant (24 percent vs. 12 percent). This study contained 338 sentencing decisions rendered between 1978 and 2000. Baldus, D. C., & Woodworth, G. (2003). Race discrimination in the administration of the death penalty: An overview of the empirical evidence with special emphasis on the post-1990 research. *Criminal Law Bulletin, 39,* 194–226. In Maryland, juries sentenced to death almost half of black defendants convicted of killing white victims but only one-third of white defendants convicted of killing black victims. Overall, taking the entire process into consideration, black defendants charged with killing white victims are 4.1 times more likely to receive a death sentence than when the races are reversed. Paternoster, R., Brame, R., Bacon, S., Ditchfield, A. (2004). Justice by

geography and race: The administration of the death penalty in Maryland, 1978–1999. *University of Maryland Law Journal of Race, Religion, Gender, 4,* 1–97. In New Jersey, the rate of death sentences awarded to killers of white victims was 1.7 times higher than for killers of black victims. Among all death-eligible cases, 12 percent resulted in death sentences for killing white victims but only 7 percent for killing black victims. Baime, D. S. (2005). Report to the New Jersey Supreme Court: Systemic Proportionality Review Project 2004–2005, Term 6 (December 15). http://www.judiciary.state.nj.us/pressrel/Baime2005Report12-16-05.pdf.

91. This review concluded that even after controlling for all legally relevant variables, differences remain in the likelihood of receiving the death penalty on the basis of the race of the victim. General Accounting Office (1990). *Death penalty sentencing: Research indicates pattern of racial disparities.* Washington, DC: General Accounting Office. For a summary of findings from seventeen states and the federal system, see Baldus & Woodworth (2003), *supra* note 90.

92. As some critics charge, the litigants' true objective in jury selection is not to attain a fair representation of the community or to maximize the chances for a fair trial in other ways. Rather, they use the process to stack the jury with people who they expect will vote in their favor.

93. *Smith v. Phillips,* 455 U.S. 209, 217 (1982).

94. A sizable body of research shows that many of our reasoning and decision-making processes are conducted without awareness. Bargh, J. A., & Morsella, E. (2008). The unconscious mind. *Perspectives on Psychological Science, 3,* 73–79. Studies show, for example, that participants are often unaware of changes in their attitudes that were precipitated by the experiment. Bem, D. J., & McConnell, H. K. (1970). Testing the self-perception explanation of dissonance phenomena: On the salience of premanipulation attitudes. *Journal of Personality and Social Psychology, 14,* 23–31; Goethals, G. R., & Reckman, R. F. (1973). The perception of consistency in attitudes. *Journal of Experimental Social Psychology, 9,* 491–501. For findings of unawareness of belief changes, see Holyoak, K. J., & Simon, D. (1999). Bidirectional reasoning in decision making by constraint satisfaction. *Journal of Experimental Psychology: General, 128,* 3–31, studies 2, 3.

95. Nisbett, R. E., & Wilson, T. D. (1977). Telling more than we can know: Verbal reports on mental processes. *Psychological Review, 84,* 231–259. Studies of decision making find that participants' reports of the weights they assign to decision factors are often substantially discrepant from the weights objectively derived from their decisions. Slovic, P., & Lichtenstein, S. (1971). Comparison of Bayesian and regression approaches to the study of information processing in judgment. *Organizational Behavior & Human Performance, 6,* 649–744; Latane, B., & Darley, J. M. (1970). *The unresponsive bystander: Why doesn't he help?* New York: Appleton-Century-Crofts.

96. The belief in one's introspective abilities has been labeled the *introspection illusion.* Pronin, E., Gilovich, T., & Ross, L. (2004). Objectivity in the eye of the beholder: Divergent perceptions of bias in self versus others. *Psychological Review, 111,* 781–799.

97. Nisbett & Wilson (1977), *supra* note 95.

98. For people's beliefs in their fairness, see Liebrand, W. B., Messick, D. M., & Wolters, F. J. (1986). Why we are fairer than others: A cross-cultural replication and extension. *Journal of Experimental Social Psychology, 22,* 590–604. The belief in one's objectivity is captured by a sense of *naïve realism,* which refers to the "unshakable conviction that he or she is somehow privy to an invariant, knowable, objective reality—a reality that others will also perceive faithfully, provided that they are reasonable and rational, a reality that others are apt to misperceive only to the extent that they (in contrast to oneself) view the world through a prism of self-interest, ideological bias, or personal perversity." Robinson, R. J., Keltner, D., Ward, A., & Ross, L. (1995). Actual versus assumed differences in construal: "Naive realism" in intergroup perception and conflict. *Journal of Personality and Social Psychology, 68,* 404–417, p. 405. See also Ross, L., & Ward, A. (1996). Naive realism in everyday life: Implications for social conflict and misunderstanding. In E. S. Reed, E. Turiel, and T. Brown, eds., *Values and knowledge,* pp. 103–135. Hillsdale, NJ: Lawrence Erlbaum.

99. Ehrlinger, J., Gilovich, T., & Ross, L. (2005). Peering into the bias blind spot: People's assessments of bias in themselves and others. *Personality and Social Psychology Bulletin, 31,* 680–692. For example, participants denied being biased when they overpredicted aggressive behavior of people with typical Afrocentric features. Blair, I. V., Chapleau, K. M., & Judd, C. M. (2005). The use of Afrocentric features as cues for judgment in the presence of diagnostic information. *European Journal of Social Psychology, 35,* 59–68. In refereeing social science research, scientists denied being influenced by their prior conceptions, even as they were swayed by them. Koehler, J. J. (1993). The influence of prior beliefs on scientific judgments of evidence quality. *Organizational Behavior and Human Decision Processes, 56,* 28–55. In a study of deceit detection that contained biasing information about the witness, only 1 participant out of 100 cited that information as a reason for her judgment. Granhag, P. A., & Strömwall, L. A. (2000). Effects of preconceptions on deception detection and new answers to why lie-catchers often fail. *Psychology, Crime & Law, 6,* 197–218. In a study simulating an investigation of a case of academic misconduct, participants deemed their judgments as highly objective even though they were swayed by their role assignment. Simon, D., Stenstrom, D., & Read, S. J. (2008a). On the objectivity of investigations: An experiment. Paper presented at the Conference on Empirical Legal Studies, Cornell University, September.

100. Pyszczynski, T., & Greenberg, J. (1987). Toward an integration of cognitive and motivational perspectives on social inference: A biased hypothesis-testing

model. In L. Berkowitz, ed., *Advances in experimental social psychology,* vol. 20, pp. 297–340. San Diego: Academic Press; Kunda, Z. (1990). The case for motivated reasoning. *Psychological Bulletin, 108,* 480–498; Pronin, Gilovich, & Ross (2004), *supra* note 96. One of the prominent and invariant features of biased processes is that they are deeply hidden beneath the level of conscious awareness. Wilson, T. D., & Brekke, N. (1994). Mental contamination and mental correction: Unwanted influences on judgments and evaluations. *Psychological Bulletin, 116,* 117–142.

101. Ogloff, J. R. P., & Vidmar, N. (1994). The impact of pretrial publicity on jurors: A study to compare the relative effects of television and print media in a child sex abuse case. *Law and Human Behavior, 18,* 507–525; Moran, G., & Cutler, B. L. (1991). The prejudicial impact of pretrial publicity. *Journal of Applied Social Psychology, 21,* 345–367; Sue, S., Smith, R. E., & Pedroza, G. (1975). Authoritarianism, pretrial publicity, and awareness of bias in simulated jurors. *Psychological Reports, 37,* 1299–1302.

102. Wissler & Saks (1985), *supra* note 57; Greene & Dodge (1995), *supra* note 57.

103. Douglas, K. S., Lyon, D. R., & Ogloff, J. R. P. (1997). The impact of graphic photographic evidence on mock jurors' decisions in a murder trial: Probative or prejudicial? *Law and Human Behavior, 21,* 485–501.

104. Kassin & Sukel (1997), *supra* note 44.

105. Even if such a response is insincere, these people appear to be driven by ulterior motives, which renders them unsuitable for the task.

106. *In re Winship,* 397 U.S. 358, 372 (1970).

107. Blackstone W. (1765). *Commentaries on the laws of England,* vol. 4, p. 358 (J. Chitty, ed., 1826). London: W. Walker.

108. *Bell v. Wolfish,* 441 U.S. 520 (1979). For an expansive view of the presumption of innocence, see Findley, K. A. (in press). Defining innocence. *Albany Law Review.* On the presumption's effect of expressingthe respect that society accords the freedoms and reputations of its members, see Tribe, L. H. (1971). Trial by mathematics: Precision and ritual in the legal process. *Harvard Law Review, 84,* 1329–1393, p. 1370.

109. For example, the Connecticut pattern jury instructions explain that at the beginning of the trial, the defendant "stood before you free of any bias, prejudice or burden arising from his position as the accused." 5 Conn. Prac., Criminal Jury Instructions §2.8 (3rd ed.).

110. Simon, D., Stenstrom, D., & Read, S. J. (2008b). Jurors' background knowledge and beliefs. Paper presented at American Psychology–Law Society annual conference, Jacksonville, FL, March 6–8.

111. Half of these respondents interpreted the charges as "strong evidence" of guilt. Saxton, B. (1998). How well do jurors understand jury instructions? A

field test using real juries and real trials in Wyoming. *Law and Water Law Review, 33,* 59–189.

112. Helgeson, V. S., & Shaver, K. G. (1990). Presumption of innocence: Congruence bias induced and overcome. *Journal of Applied Social Psychology, 20,* 276–302. See in particular study 3.

113. Ostrom, T. M., Werner, C., & Saks, M. J. (1978). An integration theory analysis of jurors' presumptions of guilt or innocence. *Journal of Personality and Social Psychology, 36,* 436–450.

114. Strawn & Buchanan (1976), *supra* note 24.

115. The accuracy of noninstructed jurors was even lower, a result suggesting that the instruction had a moderately positive impact on comprehension. Buchanan et al. (1978), *supra* note 24.

116. A majority of these jurors had recently served as jurors in a criminal trial. Reifman, Gusick, & Ellsworth (1992), *supra* note 25.

117. Some 20 percent of the respondents stated that once the state has made its case, it becomes the defendant's responsibility to provide proof that he did not commit the crime. Saxton (1998), *supra* note 111.

118. Strawn & Buchanan (1976), *supra* note 24.

119. Legal historian James Whitman argues that the term was not originally intended as a standard of proof, but as a mechanism for providing jurors with moral comfort in the exercise of their solemn task. As such, the standard is ill equipped to aid contemporary jurors in the quest for determining the truth. Whitman, J. Q. (2008). *The origins of reasonable doubt: Theological roots of the criminal trial.* New Haven, CT: Yale University Press.

120. For a minority view on this matter, see Laudan, L. (2004). Is reasonable doubt reasonable? *Legal Theory 9,* 295–331.

121. This issue has been a focal point in the debate between the "Bayesian" and "Bayesioskeptic" camps. Compare the following: Lempert, R. O., Gross, S. R., & Liebman, J. S. (2000). *A modern approach to evidence: Text, problems, transcripts and cases,* 3rd ed., pp. 228–239. St. Paul, MN: West Publishing; and Allen, R. J. (1997). Rationality, algorithms, and juridical proof: A preliminary inquiry. *International Journal of Evidence & Proof, 1,* 254–275.

122. In the seminal *In re Winship,* Justice Brennan explained that the standard of proof instructs the fact finder about "the degree of confidence he is expected to have in the correctness of his factual conclusions." 397 U.S. 358, 370 (1970). This conception is also consistent with the various definitions described later, such as "firmly convinced," "abiding conviction," and "near certitude."

123. For a minority view supporting the latter position, see Laudan (2004), *supra* note 120.

124. For example, in *People v. Malmenato* (14 Ill.2d 52, 61 [1958]), the Illinois Supreme Court stated: "Reasonable doubt is a term which needs no elaboration

and we have so frequently discussed the futility of attempting to define it that we might expect the practice to be discontinued."

125. Florida Standard Jury Instructions in Criminal Cases, 2.03.

126. See Solan, L. (1999). Refocusing the burden of proof in criminal cases: Some doubt about reasonable doubt. *Texas Law Review, 78,* 105–147.

127. See, for example, Connecticut pattern jury instruction 2.10: "If, based on your consideration of the evidence, you are firmly convinced that the defendant is guilty of the crime charged, you must find him guilty." 5 Conn. Prac., Criminal Jury Instructions §2.10 (3rd ed.). This version, recommended by the Federal Judicial Center, was also endorsed by Justice Ginsburg in *Victor v. Nebraska,* 511 U.S. 1, 25 (1994).

128. For example, the California pattern jury instruction instructs: "Proof beyond a reasonable doubt is proof that leaves you with an abiding conviction that the charge is true." *Judicial Council of California Criminal Jury Instructions,* CALCRIM, *supra* note 75, 220.

129. *Jackson v. Virginia,* 443 U.S. 307, 315 (1979).

130. The definition included "real tangible substantial basis," not "caprice and conjecture," not "give rise to a grave uncertainty," not "a mere possible doubt," "actual and substantial," "reasonable man can seriously entertain," not "an absolute or mathematical certainty," and "moral certainty." *Cage v. Louisiana,* 498 U.S. 39 (1990). The Court struck down the instruction, but not because of its potential to confuse jurors.

131. See, for example, Kerr, N. L., Atkin, R. S., Strasser, G., Meek, D., Holt, R. W., & Davis, J. H. (1976). Guilt beyond a reasonable doubt: Effects of concept definition and assigned decision rule on the judgments of mock jurors. *Journal of Personality and Social Psychology, 34,* 282–294 (finding an average assessment of 87 percent). Kassin & Sommers (1997, *supra* note 32) found a rate of 89 percent.

132. The value of 90 percent (or 91 percent) is frequently said to be derived from Blackstone's error ratio of 10:1. That inference is mistaken. To derive the standard of proof from the error ratio, one would need also to know the base rate of guilt among the prosecuted cases and the jury's diagnostic capabilities. See DeKay, M. L. (1996). The difference between Blackstone-like error ratios and probabilistic standards of proof. *Law and Social Inquiry, 21,* 95–132.

133. Greene & Dodge (1995), *supra* note 57.

134. Horowitz, I. A., & Kirkpatrick, L. C. (1996). A concept in search of a definition: The effects of reasonable doubt instructions on certainty of guilt standards and jury verdicts. *Law and Human Behavior, 20,* 671–670.

135. Kramer & Koenig (1990), *supra* note 26.

136. Ogloff, J. R. P. (1998). Jury instructions and the jury: A comparison of alternative strategies. Final Report. Vancouver, Canada: British Columbia Law Foundation. Summarized in Ogloff, J. R. P., & Rose, V. G. (2005). The compre-

hension of judicial instructions. In N. Brewer & K. D. Williams, eds., *Psychology and law: An empirical perspective*, pp. 407–444. New York: Guilford Press.

137. Zander, M. (2000). The criminal standard of proof: How sure is sure? *New Law Journal,* October 20, 1517–1519. Some 40 percent of a sample of German respondents stated a threshold of 95–99 percent. Glöckner, A., & Engel, C. (under review). Can we trust intuitive jurors? Standards of proof and the probative value of evidence in coherence based reasoning.

138. While legal observers tend to follow the classic error ratio of 10:1 proposed by Blackstone, lay people appear to be far less sensitive to false convictions. Only 66 percent of respondents indicated that a false conviction is worse than a false acquittal, with 30 percent of the respondents maintaining the opposite. Bechert, I., & Quandt, M. (2010). ISSP Data Report: Attitudes toward the role of government (data for U.S. respondents). http://www.ssoar.info/ssoar /files/2011/1535/gs%206%20-%20issp%20data%20report.pdf. In the *Jurors' Beliefs Survey* respondents were provided with a continuous scale that listed different ratios of false convictions to false acquittals and asked to indicate their preferred error ratio. The mode response was 1:1, that is, that the errors are equally bad. The median response was: "It is better to acquit one guilty person than convict one innocent person." Simon, Stenstrom, & Read (2008b), *supra* note 110.

The high thresholds provide another reason to doubt that jurors rely on probabilistic assessments in deciding cases. If jurors reach verdicts based on their strength of belief in the evidence, the unrealistic numeric thresholds they report would not necessarily impede on their performance.

139. In one study, the heightened standard reduced the rate of convictions by deliberating participants from 42 percent to 26 percent, a result that was marginally significant. No difference was observed for nondeliberating jurors. MacCoun, R. J., & Kerr, N. L. (1988). Asymmetric influence in mock jury deliberation: Jurors' bias for leniency. *Journal of Personality and Social Psychology, 54,* 21–33. Another study found a decrease from 65 percent to 48 percent for nondeliberating participants. To prevent a confound between the standard of proof and the presumption of innocence, the 293 jury-eligible participants were informed that this was an arbitration procedure, not a criminal trial. Simon, D., Snow, C. J., & Read, S. J. (unpublished data).

140. Glöckner & Engel (2011), *supra* note 137. These data compare the results of the conditions in which the procedure was described as an arbitration and the standard of proof was the preponderance of the evidence (study 1, treatments 3, 4, and study 2, treatment 4), with the conditions descried as a criminal procedure with the beyond a reasonable doubt standard (study 1, treatments 1, 2; and study 2, treatment 1). The latter conditions yielded conviction rates that were less than half of the former conditions (18 percent vs. 44 percent). In an early experiment, Lawrence Wrightsman and Saul Kassin found that presenting

jurors with the presumption of innocence and the beyond a reasonable doubt standard reduced conviction rates from 56 pecent to 35 percent (data for jurors who were given the instructions prior to the evidence). Kassin, S. M., & Wrightsman, L. S. (1979). On the requirements of proof: The timing of judicial instruction and mock juror verdicts. *Journal of Personality and Social Psychology*, *37(10)*, 1877–1887. This finding should be qualified due to the low number of participants.

141. As one would expect, when the evidence favoring the prosecution was described as strong (ratings of 6 and 7 on a 1–7 scale), the conviction rate was high: 97 percent of the juries convicted the defendants and 99 percent of the judges stated that they would have done the same. Sixty-one percent of the juries voted to convict, and 78 percent of the judges would have done the same when the evidence was deemed to be of medium strength (ratings of 3, 4, 5). Even more startling is the fact that 17 percent of the juries voted to convict when they deemed the evidence to be weak (ratings of 1, 2), and 27 percent of the judges would have convicted on the basis of that weak evidence (calculated from data in table 4, p. 186). Eisenberg, T., Hannaford-Agor, P. L., Hans, V. P., Waters, N. L., Munsterman, G. T., Schwab, S. J., & Wells, M. T. (2005). Judge-jury agreement in criminal cases: A partial replication of Kalven and Zeisel's *The American Jury. Journal of Empirical Studies, 2*, 171. For graphic presentations of the data, see figs. 1 and 2, pp. 188–189. Assuming that the evaluations of the evidence strength are reliable, these findings have troubling implications for the effect of the standard of proof.

A multistate field study of child maltreatment investigations found that while the thresholds for substantiating suspected child maltreatment vary from state to state, the actual decisions made in the various jurisdictions are unaffected by the formal standards. Levine, M. (1998). Do standards of proof affect decision making in child protection investigations? *Law and Human Behavior, 22*, 341–347.

142. Abramson, J. (2000). *We the jury: The jury system and the ideal of democracy.* Cambridge, MA: Harvard University Press; Vidmar & Hans (2007), *supra* note 20.

143. These data account for the 222 juries for which detailed data are available. These studies are summarized in Kerr, N. L., & MacCoun, R. J. (under review). Is the leniency bias really dead? Misinterpreting asymmetry effects in criminal jury deliberation (table 4, coding assumption 2). The following analyses will follow the suggestion of Kerr and MaCoun to split the "undecided" votes on the first ballot evenly between the guilty and not-guilty columns.

144. These data pertain to the nonhung juries. Sixteen of the trials ended with hung juries. In the ten cases in which the first ballots were split evenly, five ended with a conviction and five with an acquittal. This study, comprising 225 criminal cases conducted in Chicago and Brooklyn, was reported in Kalven, H., & Zeisel, H. (1966). *The American jury.* Boston: Little, Brown.

145. In this study, the rate of conviction was zero when there were four or fewer votes to convict on the first ballot, and 100 percent when there were eight or more votes to convict. The conviction rate was 57 percent when the first ballot had an even split or a majority of seven to five. These data exclude the eleven hung juries and were coded per Kerr & MacCoun (under review), *supra* note 143. These data underestimate the rate of conviction, since they pertain only to the votes on the most serious charge. Devine, D. J., Buddenbaum, J., Houp, S., Stolle, D. P. & Studebaker, N. (2007). Deliberation quality: A preliminary examination in criminal juries. *Journal of Empirical Legal Studies, 4*, 273–303.

146. In this study, the rate of conviction was zero when there were four or fewer votes to convict on the first ballot, and 94 percent when there were eight or more votes to convict. The conviction rate was 66 percent when the first ballot had an even split or a majority of seven to five. These data exclude the hung juries and were coded per Kerr & MacCoun (under review), *supra* note 143. Sandys, M., & Dillehay, R. C. (1995). First-ballot votes, predeliberation dispositions, and final verdicts in jury trials. *Law and Human Behavior, 19*, 175–195.

147. Hannaford-Agor, P. L., Hans, V. P., Mott, N. L., & Munsterman, G. T. (2002). Are hung juries a problem? National Center for State Courts. http://contentdm.ncsconline.org/cgi-bin/showfile.exe?CISOROOT=/juries&CISOPTR=27. In this study the rate of conviction was 4 percent when there were four or fewer votes to convict on the first ballot, and 94 percent when there were eight or more votes to convict. The conviction rate was 82 percent when the first ballot had an even split or a majority of seven to five. These data exclude the twenty-five hung juries and were coded by Kerr & MacCoun (under review, *supra* note 143).

148. There is some debate about the existence of a skew toward acquittals following deliberation, a phenomenon known as the leniency bias (see MacCoun & Kerr 1988, *supra* note 139) and recently labeled the asymmetry effects in jury deliberation (Kerr & MacCoun, under review, *supra* note 143). Compare the work of MacCoun and Kerr with Devine, D. J., Clayton, L. D., Dunford, B. B., Seying, R., & Pryce, J. (2001). Jury decision making: 45 years of empirical research on deliberating groups. *Psychology, Public Policy, and Law, 7*, 622–727 (table 6). Teasing the different theories apart is hindered by the sparsity of close votes on initial ballots: in the 222 cases studied, only one jury had an initial split of five jurors favoring conviction (it voted not guilty), and only four juries had an initial split of 6–6 (three of these juries voted guilty). See Kerr & MacCoun (under review), *supra* note 143 (table 4, coding assumption 2).

Hastie, Penrod, & Pennington (1983, *supra* note 23) found that juries are just as likely to shift toward severity as toward leniency (for juries governed by a unanimous decision rule). Mona Lynch and Craig Haney have tested the effects of deliberation in the context of death penalty sentencing, and found evidence of a *severity shift*, with deliberation increasing death sentences from 54 percent to 66 percent. Lynch & Haney (2009), *supra* note 83. Leniency and severity biases are likely to have the same effect on guilty and innocent defendants, and thus do not directly affect the diagnosticity of the adjudicative process.

149. These cases were part of the data set of 222 cases, as summarized by Kerr & MacCoun (under review, *supra* note 143) (table 4, coding assumption 2).

150. For a review, see Kerr, N. L., & Tindale, R. S. (2004). Group performance and decision making. *Annual Review of Psychology, 55,* 623–655.

151. For example, groups are found to outperform individuals in tasks of general knowledge and estimation of quantities. See Sniezek, J. A., & Henry, R. A. (1989). Accuracy and confidence in group judgment. *Organizational Behavior and Human Decision Processes, 43,* 1–28; Sniezek, J. A., & Henry, R. A. (1990). Revision, weighting, and commitment in consensus group judgment. *Organizational Behavior and Human Decision Processes, 45,* 66–84.

152. For example, a study that tested pairs of participants in solving math puzzles found that when both members were independently correct or independently wrong, joining forces did not affect their joint accuracy. The performance of mixed pairs was affected by the deliberation, in that the joint solution was determined mostly by the member who was more influential—typically, more confident—irrespective of his or her accuracy. Johnson, H. H., & Torcivia, J. M. (1967). Group and individual performance on a single-stage task as a function of distribution of individual performance. *Journal of Experimental Social Psychology, 3,* 266–273. In performing rule-induction problems, groups perform as well as their best members, but only under optimal conditions. If the information or time is limited, groups fail to meet that standard. Laughlin, P. R., VanderStoep, S. W., & Hollingshead, A. B. (1991). Collective versus individual induction: Recognition of truth, rejection of error, and collective information processing. *Journal of Personality and Social Psychology, 61,* 50–67.

153. For example, groups have been found to be more biased than individuals in the search for information. Schulz-Hardt, S., Frey, D., Lüthgens, C., & Moscovici, S. (2000). Biased information search in group decision making. *Journal of Personality and Social Psychology, 78,* 655–669. Brainstorming is an acute example of the discrepancy between the widespread belief in the superiority of groups and the empirical findings to the contrary. On the illusion of group productivity, see Pauhus, P. B., Dzindolet, M. T., Poletes, G., & Camacho, L. M. (1993). Perception of performance in group brainstorming: The illusion of group productivity. *Personality and Social Psychology Bulletin, 19,* 78–89; Nijstad, B. A., Stroebe, W., & Lodewijkx, H. F. M. (2006). The illusion of group productivity: A reduction of failures explanation. *European Journal of Social Psychology, 36,* 31–48.

154. See, e.g., Kerr, N. L., MacCoun, R. J., & Kramer, G. P. (1996). Bias in judgment: Comparing individuals and groups. *Psychological Review, 103,* 687–719; Kerr, N. L., Niedermeier, K. E., & Kaplan, M. F. (1999). Bias in jurors vs.

bias in juries: New evidence from the SDS perspective. *Organizational Behavior and Human Decision Processes, 80,* 70–86.

155. Deutsch, M., & Gerard, H. B. (1955). A study of normative and informational social influences upon individual judgment. *Journal of Abnormal and Social Psychology, 51,* 629–636. For a review, see Wood, W. (1999). Motives and modes of processing in the social influence of groups. In S. Chaiken & Y. Trope, eds., *Dual-process theories in social psychology,* pp. 547–570. New York: Guilford.

156. Studies of simulated jurors find that people remember about two-thirds of the relevant details presented at trial. Pritchard, M. E., & Keenan, J. M. (1999). Memory monitoring in mock jurors. *Journal of Experimental Psychology: Applied, 5,* 152–168; Pritchard, M. E., & Keenan, J. M. (2002). Does jury deliberation really improve jurors' memories? *Applied Cognitive Psychology, 16,* 589–601. In another study, jurors recalled about 60 percent of the evidence presented. See Hastie, Penrod, & Pennington (1983), *supra* note 23.

157. Ellsworth, P. C. (1989). Are twelve heads better than one? *Law & Contemporary Problems, 52,* 205–224. For similar findings, see Pritchard & Keenan (2002), *supra* note 156; Hastie, Penrod, & Pennington (1983), *supra* note 23.

158. This phenomenon is labeled *collaborative inhibition.* Weldon, M. S., & Bellinger, K. D. (1997). Collective memory: Collaborative and individual processes in remembering. *Journal of Experimental Psychology: Learning, Memory, and Cognition, 23,* 1160–1175. Collaborative inhibition increases with group size, and is likely to be substantial in groups of twelve. Basden, B. H., Basden, D. R., & Henry, S. (2000). Costs and benefits of collaborative remembering. *Applied Cognitive Psychology, 14,* 497–507. Groups have been found to have superior memory when tested with recognition tasks, which are less relevant to the jury setting. See, e.g., Hinsz, V. B. (1990). Cognitive and consensus processes in group recognition memory performance. *Journal of Personality and Social Psychology, 59,* 705–718.

159. For a review of the research, see Pritchard & Keenan (2002), *supra* note 156. Pritchard & Keenan found that group recall was better than recall by individuals by 3.4 percent.

160. Ellsworth (1989), *supra* note 157. Deliberation was found to be generally ineffective also by Severance & Loftus (1982), *supra* note 28.

161. Ogloff & Rose (2005), *supra* note 136.

162. Wiener et al. (2004), *supra* note 77.

163. Lynch & Haney (2009), *supra* note 83.

164. Diamond & Levi (1996), *supra* note 78.

165. One study found that deliberation reduced guilt ratings following a judge's admonition to disregard inadmissible evidence (5.7 to 4.4 on a scale of 1–9). Kerwin, J., & Shaffer, D. R. (1994). Mock jurors versus mock juries: The

role of deliberations in reactions to inadmissible testimony. *Personality and Social Psychology Bulletin, 20,* 153–162. Another study found that deliberation halved conviction rates given by admonished jurors. London, K., & Nunez, N. (2000). The effect of jury deliberations on jurors' propensity to disregard inadmissible evidence. *Journal of Applied Psychology, 85,* 932–939.

166. In one study, deliberation was found to reduce admonished jurors' conviction rates by a mere 5 percent. Hans & Doob (1976), *supra* note 57. Deliberation did not make a difference in a study that exposed jurors to pretrial publicity in a murder case. Ruva, C., McEvoy, C., & Bryant, J. B. (2007). Effects of pre-trial publicity and jury deliberation on juror bias and source memory errors. *Applied Cognitive Psychology, 21,* 45–67.

167. In a study simulating a child-molestation charge, jurors presented with inadmissible pretrial publicity were considerably more likely to convict the defendant following deliberation than prior to it (29 percent vs. 11 percent). This result was obtained where the evidence was ambiguous, which is the most forensically relevant type of situation. Kerr, Niedermeier, & Kaplan (1999), *supra* note 154. A large study found that pretrial publicity affected judgments only following deliberation, increasing convictions from 6 percent to 21 percent. Kramer, G. P., Kerr, N. L., & Carroll, J. S. (1990). Pretrial publicity, judicial remedies, and jury bias. *Law and Human Behavior, 14,* 409–438.

A limited number of deliberation studies included in the meta-analysis of pretrial publicity show that deliberation had no appreciable curative effect. Steblay, N. M., Besirevic, J., Fulero, S. M., & Jimenez-Lorente, B. (1999). The effects of pretrial publicity on juror verdicts: A meta-analytic review. *Law and Human Behavior, 23,* 219–235.

168. Compare Wright, E. F., & Wells, G. L. (1985). Does group discussion attenuate the dispositional bias? *Journal of Applied Social Psychology, 15,* 531–546; with Wittenbaum, G. M., & Stasser, G. (1995). The role of prior expectancy and group discussion in the attribution of attitudes. *Journal of Experimental Social Psychology, 31,* 82–105.

169. In one study, deliberation increased the accuracy rate from 56 percent to 60 percent. Groups were more suspicious and were more inclined to judge the statements as deceitful. Frank, M. G., Paolantonio, N., Feeley, T. H., & Servoss, T. J. (2004). Individual and small group accuracy in judging truthful and deceptive communication. *Group Decision and Negotiation, 13,* 45–59. In a second study, deliberation resulted in a non-significant increase in the rate of accuracy from 51.5 percent to 53 percent. Park, E. S., Levine, T. R., Harms, C. M., & Ferrara, M. H. (2002). Group and individual accuracy in deception detection. *Communication Research Reports, 19,* 99–106. The weak contribution of deliberation is likely due to the low level of individual performance in the task of deceit detection.

170. Some reduction in the coherence effect was observed for members of the minority who changed their minds following the deliberation. Fiedler, S., &

Glöckner, A. (in progress). Coherence shifts in groups: Information distortions in legal decisions after group deliberation.

171. Gigone, D., & Hastie, R. (1997). Proper analysis of the accuracy of group judgments. *Psychological Bulletin, 121,* 149–167.

172. For classic studies on social influence, see Asch, S. E. (1956). Studies of independence and conformity: I. A minority of one against a unanimous majority. *Psychological Monographs, 70,* 1–70.

173. Jury deliberation lacks discursive conventions that resemble the idealized forms of deliberative democracy. For example, Jürgen Habermas posits a discourse that aspires to be "public and inclusive, to grant equal communication rights for participants, to require sincerity and to diffuse any kind of force other than the forceless force of the better argument." Habermas, J. (1999). An author's reflections. *Denver University Law Review, 76,* 937–942 (p. 940).

174. These factors were combined to create a *Group Dynamics Index,* which predicted whether juries hung or reached a verdict. The index had a scale reliability of Cronbach's $\alpha = .91$. Hannaford-Agor et al. (2002), *supra* note 147.

175. Jurors were asked "If it were entirely up to you as a one-person jury, what would your verdict have been in this case?" Waters, N. L., & Hans, V. P. (2009). A jury of one: Opinion formation, conformity, and dissent on juries. *Journal of Empirical Legal Studies, 6,* 513–540. There is reason to believe that the true number of silent dissenters is even higher given that people are not inclined to admit to having defied their own conscience to appease others.

176. Tanford, S., & Penrod, S. (1986). Jury deliberations: Discussion content and influence processes in jury decision making. *Journal of Applied Social Psychology, 16,* 322–347; Park et al. (2002), *supra* note 169.

177. Ellsworth (1989), *supra* note 157; Pritchard & Keenan (1999), *supra* note 156; Pritchard & Keenan (2002), *supra* note 156. These findings of social influence are consistent with recent research on *social vigilantism,* an individual difference construct that corresponds to people's tendency to impress and propagate their beliefs onto others and to resist being persuaded in return. See Saucier, D. A., & Webster, R. J. (2010). Social vigilantism: Measuring individual differences in belief superiority and resistance to persuasion. *Personality and Social Psychology Bulletin, 36,* 19–32.

178. Hansen, K. L., Schaefer, E. G., & Lawless, J. J. (1993). Temporal patterns of normative, informational, and procedural-legal discussion in jury deliberations. *Basic and Applied Social Psychology, 14,* 33–46.

179. Smith, V. L., & Kassin, S. M. (1993). Effects of the dynamite charge on the deliberations of deadlocked mock juries. *Law and Human Behavior, 17,* 625–643; Kassin, S. M., Smith, V. L., & Tulloch, W. F. (1990). The dynamite charge: Effects on the perceptions and deliberation behavior of mock jurors. *Law and Human Behavior, 14,* 537–550.

180. Devine et al. (2007), *supra* note 145.

181. On the *white male dominance* phenomenon, see Bowers, W. J., Steiner, B. D., & Sandys, M. (2001). Death sentencing in black and white: An empirical analysis of the role of juror race and jury racial composition. *University of Pennsylvania Journal of Constitutional Law, 3,* 171–274.

182. Lynch & Haney (2009), *supra* note 83.

183. Hastie, Penrod, & Pennington (1983), *supra* note 23.

184. Hannaford-Agor et al. (2002), *supra* note 147.

185. One juror, who sat on a jury that convicted a person who was subsequently exonerated by DNA, reported that before the start of the deliberation, some of his fellow jurors pronounced: "He's guilty. He's guilty." Torpy, B., & Rankin, B. (2005). A crime, then a tragedy: Twists in rape case snared wrong man. *Atlanta Journal-Constitution,* December 11, p. A1. On the case of Robert Clark, see Innocence project, profile, Robert Clark. http://www.innocenceproject.org/Content/Robert_Clark.php.

186. For reviews, see Isenberg, D. J. (1986). Group polarization: A critical review and meta-analysis. *Journal of Personality and Social Psychology, 50,* 1141–1151; Sunstein, C. R. (2008). *Why groups go to extremes.* Washington, DC: American Enterprise Institute Press.

187. Sniezek & Henry (1990), *supra* note 151; Zarnoth, P., & Sniezek, J. A. (1997). The social influence of confidence in group decision making. *Journal of Experimental Social Psychology, 33,* 345–366.

188. Pritchard & Keenan (2002), *supra* note 156.

189. Ruva, McEvoy, & Bryant (2007), *supra* note 166.

190. Kaplan, M. F., & Miller, L. E. (1978). Reducing the effects of juror bias. *Journal of Personality and Social Psychology, 36,* 1443–1455.

191. One study found that deliberation increased the confidence of group members from 81 percent to 89 percent. Park et al. (2002), *supra* note 169. See also Frank et al. (2004), *supra* note 169.

192. Recall from Chapter 6 that the coherence effect should not affect the votes of jurors who are inclined to acquit. As a result of the asymmetric standard of proof, a juror leaning toward acquittal should vote to acquit regardless of the strength of that leaning.

193. Convictions for federal crimes are appealed to federal courts of appeal.

194. *Habeas corpus* proceedings are designed to provide convicted inmates and other people held in custody with a separate procedure for challenging the legality of their detention. Most commonly, *habeas* proceedings are initiated by convicted inmates to claim that their constitutional rights were violated in the course of the criminal process. See King, N. J., Hoffmann, J. L. (2011). *Habeas for the twenty-first century: Uses, abuses, and the future of the Great Writ.* Chicago: University of Chicago Press.

195. Garrett, B. L. (2011). *Convicting the innocent: Where criminal prosecutions go wrong,* chap 7. Cambridge, MA: Harvard University Press.

196. Ibid.

197. The five claims that received relief were based mostly on the procedural grounds of ineffective assistance of counsel with respect to the identification. Ibid.

198. Ibid.

199. Ibid.

200. *Arizona v. Youngblood,* 488 U.S. 51 (1988). See also Innocence Project, profile, Larry Youngblood. http://www.innocenceproject.org/Content/Larry _Youngblood.php.

201. Garrett (2011), *supra* note 195, chap. 7.

202. Every one of the DNA exonerations was matched with a randomly selected inmate convicted for the same crime, in the same state, in the same year. Ibid.

203. Ibid.

204. Ibid.

205. High expectations of accuracy were expressed by respondents in the *Jurors' Beliefs Survey.* In response to a question about the acceptable rate of wrongful convictions, the median response was 2 out of 1,000 convictions, while the mode response was zero. Simon, Stenstrom, & Read (2008b), *supra* note 110. A somewhat higher tolerance of error was observed in a smaller survey of 133 college students. These respondents stated that an acceptable rate of wrongful convictions was 5 percent, and of wrongful acquittals 8 percent. Arkes, H. R., & Mellers, B. A. (2002). Do juries meet our expectations? *Law and Human Behavior, 26,* 625–639.

206. The general, unreasoned, and obscured decision was described by an early observer as "the great procedural opiate." Sunderland, E. R. (1920). Verdicts, special and general. *Yale Law Journal, 29,* 253–267, p. 262.

Given the historical development of the common law's criminal justice process, its limited diagnosticity is not altogether surprising. As described by John Langbein, the English criminal process evolved piecemeal, as a series of ad hoc tactical measures intended to balance out the advantages of the opposing adversaries and to circumvent the disbursement of punishments that were discordant with prevailing public sentiment. These historical developments transpired with little concern for the system's capacity or propensity to ascertain truth. Langbein (2003), *supra* note 2, pp. 306–336.

It should be noted that the limited diagnosticity of the adjudicatory process is not limited to the criminal domain. Research of medical malpractice suits indicates that 9 percent of the cases in which plaintiffs win at trial are decided incorrectly. See Studdert, D. M., & Mello, M. M. (2007). When tort resolutions are "wrong": Predictors of discordant outcomes in medical malpractice litigation. *Journal of Legal Studies, 36,* 547–578. The rate of 9 percent pertains to cases where the correct outcome was rather certain. The rate is likely higher for close call cases.

207. See, e.g., Burns, R. P. (1999). *A theory of the trial,* pp. 153–154. Princeton, NJ: Princeton University Press; Vidmar & Hans (2007), *supra* note 20; Lempert, R. (1998). Why do juries get a bum rap? Reflections on the work of Valerie Hans. *DePaul Law Review, 48,* 453–462, p. 454. This observation is well established in the research. The rate of agreement between juries and judges was 78 percent in the classic study reported in Kalven & Zeisel (1966, *supra* note 144). A similar rate of 75 percent was observed in the study conducted by the National Center for State Courts that examined more than 300 felony trials. See Eisenberg et al. (2005), *supra* note 141.

208. Recall that the National Center for State Courts study indicates that both jurors and judges displayed a similar tendency of over-convicting defendants relative to their own estimation of the strength of the prosecution's evidence. Eisenberg et al. (2005), *supra* note 141.

209. Burns (1999), *supra* note 207, p. 143; Burns, R. P. (2009). *The death of the American trial.* Chicago: University of Chicago Press, p. 21; Vidmar & Hans (2007), *supra* note 20, pp. 339–340; Lempert (1998), *supra* note 207, p. 462. For experimental support of this assertion, see Visher, C. A. (1987). Juror decision making: The importance of evidence. *Law and Human Behavior, 11,* 1–17; Kassin, S., & Wrightsman, L. (1985). *The psychology of evidence and trial procedure.* Beverly Hills, CA: Sage Publications; De La Fuente, L., De La Fuente, E. I., & García, J. (2003). Effects of pretrial juror bias, strength of evidence and deliberation process on juror decisions: New validity evidence of the Juror Bias Scale scores. *Psychology, Crime & Law, 9,* 197–209.

210. The study by the National Center for State Courts found *beta* values of about 0.4 between juror verdicts and assessments of the strength of the prosecution's evidence. Garvey, S. P., Hannaford-Agor, P. L., Hans, V. P., Mott, N. L., Munsterman, G. T., & Wells, M. T. (2004). Juror first votes in criminal trials. *Journal of Empirical Studies, 1,* 371–398. These relationships refer to the strength of evidence as reported by the judges who sat on the cases. A study of 179 criminal jury trials conducted in Indianapolis found that the correlations of evidence strength and verdicts ranged from 0.4 to 0.6. Notably, only 30 percent of the variance in verdicts was explained by the strength of the evidence (Nagelkerke $R^2 = .30$). Devine et al. (2007), *supra* note 145. In this study, the strength of evidence was based on combined estimates from prosecutors, defense attorneys, and judges. More data on this relationship would be most welcome.

8. Toward Accuracy

1. See, e.g., Abramson, J. (2000). *We the jury: The jury system and the ideal of democracy.* Cambridge, MA: Harvard University Press; Vidmar, N., & Hans, V. P. (2007). *American juries: The verdict.* New York: Prometheus Books; Nesson, C. R. (1985). The evidence or the event? On judicial proof and the acceptability

of verdicts. *Harvard Law Review, 98,* 1357–1392; Foucault, M. (1997). Michel Foucault: Ethics, subjectivity and truth. In P. Rabinow, ed., *The essential works of Michel Foucault,* vol. 1: *1954–1984.* London: Allen Lane, Penguin Press.

2. As noted by Mirjan Damaška, the place of factual truth is contingent on the overall nature and objectives of the respective legal regime. Damaška, M. R. (1985). *The faces of justice and state authority: A comparative approach to the legal process.* New Haven, CT: Yale University Press.

3. On the principle of orality, see Honoré, T. (1981). The primacy of oral evidence? In *Crime, proof and punishment: Essays in memory of Sir Rupert Cross,* pp. 172–192. London: Butterworths.

4. E.g., *Teague v. Lane,* 489 U.S. 288 (1989); *Murray v. Carrier,* 477 U.S. 478 (1986).

5. LaFave, W. R., Israel, J. H., King, N. J., & Kerr, O. S. (2007). *Criminal procedure: West's criminal practice series* (3rd ed.), vol. 7, §1.4. St. Paul, MN: Thompson West; Damaška (1985), *supra* note 2.

6. *Lisenba v. California,* 314 U.S. 219, 236 (1941). See also *Colorado v. Connelly,* 479 U.S. 157, 167 (1986). Chief Justice Rehnquist explained: "The inquiry made by a court concerned with these matters is not whether the proponent of the evidence wins or loses his case on the merits, but whether the evidentiary Rules have been satisfied." *Bourjaily v. United States,* 483 U.S. 171, 175 (1987).

7. *Crawford v. Washington,* 541 U.S. 36, 61 (2004). The exception to this approach is the due process protection that the Court applies to eyewitness identifications obtained by suggestive procedures. See Wells, G. L., & Quinlivan, D. S. (2009). Suggestive eyewitness identification procedures and the Supreme Court's reliability test in light of eyewitness science: 30 years later. *Law and Human Behavior, 33,* 1–24.

8. See Thomas, G. C., III (2008). *The Supreme Court on trial: How the American justice system sacrifices innocent defendants.* Ann Arbor: University of Michigan Press; Stuntz, W. J. (1997). The uneasy relationship between criminal procedure and criminal justice. *Yale Law Journal, 107,* 1–76; Dripps, D. A. (2002). *About guilt and innocence: The origins, development, and future of constitutional criminal procedure.* Westport, CT: Praeger Publishers.

The preeminence of constitutional protections is epitomized by Herbert Packer's influential *Two Models of the Criminal Process.* As denoted by its label, the prodefendant Due Process Model is concerned primarily with protecting the defendant's right to a fair procedure. Packer, H. L. (1968). *The limits of the criminal sanction.* Stanford, CA: Stanford University Press.

9. See Uviller, H. R. (1999). *The tilted playing field: Is criminal justice unfair?* New Haven, CT: Yale University Press.

10. This approach contrasts starkly with the law in the United Kingdom. Section 76 of the Police and Criminal Evidence Act (1984) instructs that a confession should not be admitted when it "was or may have been obtained" under

circumstances that were "likely . . . to render [the confession] unreliable." This presumptive inadmissibility can be overcome only if the prosecution proves to the court beyond reasonable doubt that the confession was not obtained in such a manner.

11. See Mnookin, J. (2010). The courts, the National Academy of Science, and the future of forensic science. *Brooklyn Law Review, 75,* 1209–1275; Garrett, B. L., & Neufeld, P. J. (2009). Invalid forensic science testimony and wrongful convictions. *Virginia Law Review, 95,* 1–97; Giannelli, P. C. (1997). The abuse of scientific evidence in criminal cases: The need for independent crime laboratories. *Virginia Journal of Social Policy & Law, 4,* 439–478; Risinger, D. M. (2010). The NAS/NRC report on forensic science: A path forward fraught with pitfalls. *Utah Law Review, 2,* 225–246.

12. A notorious memo circulated in the District Attorney's Office of Dallas County, Texas, in 1963 instructed prosecutors how to exercise their peremptory strikes during jury selection: "Do not take Jews, Negroes, Dagos, Mexicans or a member of any minority race on a jury, no matter how rich or how well educated." Quoted in *Miller-El v. Cockrell,* 537 U.S. 322, 335 (2003). Bigotry aside, this memo punctuates how the adversarial nature of the process overwhelms the search for factual truth.

13. As observed by Judge Marvin E. Frankel, witness preparation is a "major item in battle planning, not a step toward revelation of objective truth." Frankel, M. E. (1978). *Partisan justice,* p. 16. New York: Hill & Wang.

14. See Fuller, L. L. (1961). *The adversary system: Talks on American law,* ed. Harold J. Berman. New York: Vintage Books; Freedman, M. H. (1998). Our constitutional adversary system. *Chapman Law Review, 1,* 57–90; Burns, R. P. (1999). *A theory of the trial,* p. 153. Princeton, NJ: Princeton University Press. For critiques of this approach, see Frank, J. (1949). *Courts on trial.* Princeton, NJ: Princeton University Press; Weinreb, L. L. (1977). *Denial of justice.* New York: Free Press.

15. See, e.g., Lind, E. A., Thibaut, J., & Walker, L. (1973). Discovery and presentation of evidence in adversary and nonadversary proceedings. *Michigan Law Review, 71,* 1129–1144; Simon, D., Stenstrom, D., & Read, S. J. (2008). On the objectivity of investigations: An experiment. Paper delivered at the Conference on Empirical Legal Studies, Cornell University, September; Glöckner, A., & Engel, C. (under review). Role induced bias in court: An experimental analysis. MPI Collective Goods Preprint, No. 2010/37. Available at SSRN: http://ssrn.com/abstract=1676142.

16. Research shows that people's biases are exacerbated by their perception that their opponents are biased, a phenomenon that can spiral into an escalating conflict. Kennedy, K. A., & Pronin, E. (2008). When disagreement gets ugly: Perceptions of bias and the escalation of conflict. *Personality and Social Psychology Bulletin, 34,* 833. A study that simulated investigations in an adversarial setting

found that participants believed that they were objective. At the same time, they believed that their (fictitious) adversary was biased, and that she felt the same about them. Simon, Stenstrom, & Read (2008), *supra* note 15.

17. See Medwed, D. S. (2010). Brady's bunch of flaws. *Washington & Lee Law Review, 67*, 1533–1567; Sundby, S. E. (2002). Fallen superheroes and constitutional mirages: The tale of *Brady v. Maryland. McGeorge Law Review, 33,* 643–663.

18. Sklansky, D. A., & Yeazell, S. (2006). Comparative law without leaving home: What civil procedure can teach criminal procedure, and vice versa. *Georgetown Law Review, 94,* 683–738.

The right to disclosure of exculpatory evidence is even weaker in the widespread domain of plea negotiations. The Court has yet to establish a general duty to disclose exculpatory evidence during plea negotiations. The Court has ruled that the prosecution has no pre-plea agreement duty to disclose evidence that could impeach its witness. *United States v. Ruiz,* 536 U.S. 622, 633 (2002).

19. Research finds that when comparing people's judgments of a certain object, holistic judgments lead to higher variance than do judgments that are disaggregated into the task's constitutive elements. See Arkes, H. R., Shafferi, V. A., & Dawes, R. M. (2006). Comparing holistic and disaggregated ratings in the evaluation of scientific presentations. *Journal of Behavioral Decision Making, 19,* 429–439; Arkes, H. R., González-Vallejo, C., Bonham, A. J., Kung, Y., & Bailey, N. (2010). Assessing the merits and faults of holistic and disaggregated judgments. *Journal of Behavioral Decision Making, 23,* 250–270. These findings indicate that general verdicts mask the more nuanced judgments of each of the elements that constitute the criminal charge. It follows that requiring jurors to vote separately on each of the elements of the charge would increase the accuracy of the verdicts.

20. As discussed in Chapter 2, the lack of accountability results in less critical and more superficial patterns of thinking. See Tetlock, P. E., Skitka, L., & Boettger, R. (1989). Social and cognitive strategies for coping with accountability: Conformity, complexity, and bolstering. *Journal of Personality and Social Psychology, 57,* 632–640; Tetlock, P. E. (2002). Social functionalist frameworks for judgment and choice: Intuitive politicians, theologians, and prosecutors. *Psychological Review, 109,* 451–471.

21. For example, the Court has upheld an order refusing an evidentiary hearing to explore a jurors' allegations that other jurors had consumed large amounts of alcohol, marijuana, and cocaine during the trial and slept through part of the hearings. *Tanner v. United States,* 483 U.S. 107 (1987).

22. The Court recently stated: "The Federal Constitution's jury-trial guarantee assigns the determination of certain facts to the jury's exclusive province." *Oregon v. Ice,* 129 S. Ct. 711, 716 (2009). As the Court conceives its role, once

"a jury is convinced beyond a reasonable doubt, we can require no more." *Holland v. United States,* 348 U.S. 121, 140 (1954).

23. Santos, F. (2007). Vindicated by DNA, but lost on the outside. *New York Times,* November 25, p. A1. http://www.nytimes.com/2007/11/25/us/25jeffrey .html?pagewanted=1&_r=1&hp. Jeff Deskovic was exonerated by a DNA test, after having served fifteen years of a possible life sentence. Innocence Project, profile, Jeff Deskovic. http://www.innocenceproject.org/Content/Jeff_Deskovic .php.

24. Many of the exonerees had five or more hearings. Alan Newton, for example, had no fewer than fifteen proceedings. Garrett, B. L. (2011). Appendix: Appeals and post-conviction litigation by DNA exonerees and case characteristics. http://www.law.virginia.edu/pdf/faculty/garrett/convicting_the_innocent /garrett_ch7_appendix.pdf.

25. See, e.g., 28 U.S.C. §§2241–2266; Hertz, R., & Liebman, J. S. (2005). *Federal habeas corpus practice and procedure.* Newark, NJ: Mathew Bender.

26. The study examined almost 2,400 *habeas corpus* proceedings conducted in 2003 and 2004. King, N. J., Cheesman, F., & Ostrom, B. J. (2007). *Habeas litigation in the U.S. district courts: An empirical study of habeas corpus cases filed by state prisoners under the Antiterrorism and Effective Death Penalty Act of 1996.* Washington, DC: U.S. Department of Justice, National Institute of Justice.

27. In *habeas* proceedings, this deference is imposed by statute. Section 28 U.S.C. §2254(d) requires courts to defer to reasonable factual determinations by state courts. As the Court has stated, "Federal courts are not forums in which to relitigate state trials." *Barefoot v. Estelle,* 463 U.S. 880, 887 (1983). See also *Sumner v. Mata,* 449 U.S. 539, 544 (1981).

28. *Jackson v. Virginia,* 443 U.S. at 318–319 (1979).

29. *Hernandez v. New York,* 500 U.S. 352, 369 (1991). See also LaFave et al. (2007), *supra* note 5, pp. 97–98. A commonly used standard is whether "*any* rational trier of fact could have found the essential elements of the crime beyond a reasonable doubt." *Jackson v. Virginia, supra* note 28, at 318–319.

30. *Wright v. West,* 505 U.S. 277, 296 (1992). As pointed out by William Stuntz, the preeminence of proceduralism results in a diversion of defense claims from factual to procedural issues. See Stuntz (1997), *supra* note 8, pp. 37–45. Paradoxically, while defense attorneys are all but precluded from challenging the factual foundation of guilty verdicts, they are regularly derided for insisting on procedural exactness, or "technicalities."

31. See *State v. Conway,* 816 So.2d. 290 (2002).

32. *District Attorney's Office v. Osborne,* 129 S. Ct. 2308 (2009). A limited right to access biological evidence was recognized by the Court in *Skinner v. Switzer,* 562 U.S. ___ (2011).

33. "Clemency is deeply rooted in our Anglo-American tradition of law, and is the historic remedy for preventing miscarriages of justice where judicial process has been exhausted." *Herrera v. Collins,* 506 U.S. 390, 411–412 (1993).

34. For illustrations of gubernatorial reticence, see the cases of Earl Washington and "The Norfolk Four": http://www.innocenceproject.org/Content/Earl_Washington.php; Wells, T., & Leo, R. (2008). *The wrong guys: Murder, false confessions, and the Norfolk Four.* New York: New Press.

35. *Manson v. Brathwaite,* 432 U.S. 98, 113 (1977).

36. *United States v. Ruiz, supra* note 18, at 633.

37. *Tanner v. United States, supra* note 21, at 120–121.

38. See, e.g., discussion in Chapter 5 (pp. 134–139), and Wells & Quinlivan (2009), *supra* note 7.

39. *Herrera v. Collins, supra* note 33, at 417.

40. Ibid.

41. *In re Davis,* 130 S. Ct. 1 (2009).

42. See Stuntz (1997), *supra* note 8; Pizzi, W. T. (1999). *Trials without truth: Why our system of criminal trials has become an expensive failure and what we need to do to rebuild it.* New York: NYU Press.

43. On occasion, the Court utters fleeting and abstract admissions that the system cannot be perfect. E.g., *District Attorney's Office v. Osborne, supra* note 32, at 2323 n. 10. This truism, however, rarely affects the manner in which cases are decided.

44. Fuller, L. L. (1961). *The adversary system: Talks on American law,* ed. Harold J. Berman. New York: Vintage Books; Freedman (1998), *supra* note 14. Our constitutional adversary system. *Chapman Law Review, 1,* 57–90; Burns, R. P. (1999). *A theory of the trial,* p. 153. Princeton, NJ: Princeton University Press. For disparaging critiques of this approach, see Frank (1949), *supra* note 14; Weinreb (1977), *supra* note 14.

45. Statement by George Treby, the recorder of London, sentencing Lord Russell to death for treason. *R. v. William Russell,* 9 St. Tr. 677, 666 (1683). Cited in Langbein, J. H. (2003). *The origins of adversary criminal trial,* p. 332. New York: Oxford University Press.

46. *Herrera v. Collins, supra* note 33, at 419.

47. *United States v. Garrison,* 291 F. 646, 649 (S.D.N.Y. 1923).

48. *Kansas v. Marsh,* 548 U.S. 163, 200 (2006).

49. Ibid., p. 193.

50. On prosecutorial intransigence in the face of exculpating DNA evidence, see Medwed, D. S. (2004). The zeal deal: Prosecutorial resistance to post-conviction claims of innocence. *Boston University Law Review, 84,* 125–183.

51. A survey of 798 Ohio law enforcement officials found that some 30 percent of police chiefs and prosecutors and 15 percent of judges believed that the

incidence of false convictions in their jurisdiction was zero, and a large number (77, 78, and 46) maintained that the incidence was less than 0.5 percent. This trust in the system was weaker when respondents were asked about the rate of false convictions in other jurisdictions in the United States, with a large majority of responses above 0.5 percent. Notably, the national estimates failed to meet the respondents' normative beliefs, as a majority (79, 78, and 78 percent, respectively) maintained that the acceptable level ought to be below 0.5 percent. Ramsey, R. J., & Frank, J. (2007). Wrongful conviction: Perceptions of criminal justice professionals regarding the frequency of wrongful conviction and the extent of system errors. *Crime & Delinquency, 53,* 436–470. Similar findings were made in a survey of Michigan law enforcement officials. Zalman, M., Smith, B., & Kiger, A. (2008). Officials' estimates of the incidence of "actual innocence" convictions. *Justice Quarterly, 25,* 72–100.

52. For notable critiques of the adversarial system, see Weinreb (1977), *supra* note 14; Frankel (1978), *supra* note 13; Langbein, J. H. (1979). Land without plea bargaining: How the Germans do it. *Michigan Law Review, 78,* 204–225; Langbein, J. H., & Weinreb, L. L. (1978). Continental criminal procedure: "Myth" and reality. *Yale Law Journal, 87,* 1549–1568; Thomas (2008), *supra* note 8.

53. See Goldstein, A. S., & Marcus, M. (1977). The myth of judicial supervision in three "inquisitorial" systems: France, Italy, and Germany. *Yale Law Journal, 87,* 240–283; Goldstein, A. S., & Marcus, M. (1978). Comment on continental criminal procedure. *Yale Law Journal, 87,* 1570–1576; Allen, R. J., Kock, S., Riecherberg, K., & Rosen, D. T. (1988). The German advantage in civil procedure: A plea for more details and fewer generalities in comparative scholarship. *Northwestern Law Review, 82,* 705–762; Freedman (1998), *supra* note 14.

54. Summers, S. J. (2007). *Fair trials: The European criminal procedural tradition and the European Court of Human Rights.* Oxford: Hart Publishing. Legal nationalism also has popular manifestations. In a 1999 survey conducted by the American Bar Association, only 30 percent of respondents were either extremely or very confident in the American justice system. Yet 80 percent agreed or strongly agreed that "the American justice system is still the best in the world." American Bar Association (1999). Perceptions of the U.S. justice system, pp. 58–59. http://www.abanow.org/wordpress/wp-content/files_flutter /1269460858_20_1_1_7_Upload_File.pdf.

55. *Kansas v. Marsh, supra* note 48, at 188. In passing, Justice Scalia also portrayed these European states as being antidemocratic (noting that they abolished the death penalty "in spite of public opinion rather than because of it") and hypocritical ("Abolishing the death penalty has been made a condition of joining the Council of Europe, which is in turn a condition of obtaining the economic benefits of joining the European Union").

56. See Sklansky, D. A. (2009). Anti-inquisitorialism. *Harvard Law Review, 122,* 1634–1704.

57. *Manson v. Brathwaite, supra* note 35. Elsewhere the Court all but concedes that it has no choice but to trust juries: "the proper evaluation of evidence under the instructions of the trial judge is the very task our system must assume juries can perform." *Watkins v. Sowders,* 449 U.S. 341, 347 (1981).

58. Hoffman, M. B. (2007). The myth of factual innocence. *Chicago-Kent Law Review, 82,* 663–690.

59. *Manson v. Brathwaite, supra* note 35, at 113; *Watkins v. Sowders, supra* note 57, at 348.

60. *Manson v. Brathwaite, supra* note 35, at 116.

61. *Lego v. Twomey,* 404 U.S. 477, 484–485 (1972).

62. *Manson v. Brathwaite, supra* note 35, at 113; *Watkins v. Sowders, supra* note 57, at 348.

63. On the psychological construct of *system justification,* see Jost, J. T., & Hunyady, O. (2002). The psychology of system justification and the palliative function of ideology. In W. Stroebe & M. Hewstone, eds., *European review of social psychology,* vol. 13, pp. 111–153. Hove, UK: Psychology Press/Taylor & Francis (UK). In this regard, system justification theory overlaps with cognitive dissonance theory. See Festinger, L. (1957). *A theory of cognitive dissonance.* Evanston, IL: Row, Peterson.

64. Perceiving oneself as competent and fair is a ubiquitous and powerful personal need. See Pronin, E., Gilovich, T., & Ross, L. (2004). Objectivity in the eye of the beholder: Divergent perceptions of bias in self versus others. *Psychological Review, 111,* 781–799; Frantz, C. M. (2006). I AM being fair: The bias blind spot as a stumbling block to seeing both sides. *Basic and Applied Social Psychology, 28,* 157–167; Schlenker, B. R. (2003). Self-presentation. In M. R. Leary & J. P. Tangney, eds., *Handbook of self and identity,* pp. 492–518. New York: Guilford Press.

65. See, e.g., Baumeister, R. F., Dale, K., & Sommer, K. L. (1998). Freudian defense mechanisms and empirical findings in modern social psychology: Reaction formation, projection, displacement, undoing, isolation, sublimation, and denial. *Journal of Personality, 66,* 1081–1124.

66. In *Brown v. Allen,* Justice Jackson explained the power of the Court: "We are not final because we are infallible, but we are infallible only because we are final." 344 U.S. 443, 540 (1953) (Jackson, J., concurring).

67. See Justice Scalia's opinion in *Kansas v. Marsh, supra* note 48; Allen, R. J., & Laudan, L. (2008). Deadly dilemmas. *Texas Tech Law Review, 41,* 65–92.

68. Frank (1949), *supra* note 14, p. 35. When all else fails, mistaken convictions can be corrected at the very end of the process, via innocence commissions, such as those established in England, Scotland, and Norway, as well in North Carolina. In general terms, these quasi-judicial agencies are designed to review possible false convictions and refer valid cases back to the court

system. On the English commission, see Criminal Cases Review Commission (2009). *Annual report and accounts, 2008/2009*. London. On the North Carolina Innocence Inquiry Commission, see http://www.innocencecommission -nc.gov/index.htm. Although relying on innocence commissions is hardly a just or effective way to sort out criminal guilt, belated justice is far superior to injustice.

69. For a notable critique of rights, see Kennedy, D. (2002). The critique of rights in critical legal studies. In W. Brown & J. Halley, eds., *Left legalism/Left critique*, pp. 178–227. Durham, NC: Duke University Press.

70. See references to *Manson v. Brathwaite, supra* note 35, and *Watkins v. Sowders, supra* note 57.

71. In principle, this rule can be applied to evidence obtained by flawed procedures, and it should extend also to cases where the jury is likely to give undue weight to evidence that is otherwise admissible. Mueller, C. B., & Kirkpatrick, L. C. (2009). *Evidence*, p. 175. New York: Aspen Publishers.

72. For example, 94 percent of the 160 surveyed judges responded (correctly) that "An eyewitness' perception and memory for an event may be affected by his or her attitudes and expectation," but only 31 percent were familiar with the steepness of the forgetting curve. Wise, R. A., & Safer, M. A. (2004). What US judges know and believe about eyewitness testimony. *Applied Cognitive Psychology, 18*, 427–443.

73. Wise, R. A., & Safer, M. A. (2010). A comparison of what U.S. judges and students know and believe about eyewitness testimony. *Journal of Applied Social Psychology, 40*, 1400–1422.

74. This survey included 42 judges. Benton, T. R., Ross, D. F., Bradshaw, E., Thomas, W. N., & Bradshaw, G. S. (2006). Eyewitness memory is still not common sense: Comparing jurors, judges and law enforcement to eyewitness experts. *Applied Cognitive Psychology, 20*, 115–129. These judges' responses were more accurate than lay people, but no better than law enforcement agents.

75. Although the following recommendations focus on enhancing the integrity of human testimony, there is much to be gained also by improving the science, methods, and expertise involved in analyzing and testifying about forensic evidence. See National Academy of Science (2009). *Strengthening forensic science in the United States: A path forward*. Washington, DC: National Academies Press; Mnookin, J. L., Cole, S. A., Dror, I. E., Fisher, B. A., Houck, M. M., Inman, K., Kaye, D. H., Koehler, J. J., Langenburg, G., Risinger, D. M., Rudin, N., Siegel, J., & Stoney, D. A. (2011). The need for a research culture in the forensic sciences. *UCLA Law Review, 58*, 725–779.

76. Sullivan, T. P., Vail, A. W., & Anderson, H. W. (2008). The case for recording police interrogations. *Litigation, 34*, 1–8.

77. Notably, the study revealed greater circumspection in trusting inaccurate witnesses, as exposing the simulated jurors to videotapes of inaccurate wit-

nesses reduced the conviction rate from 49 percent to 33 percent. The rate was hardly affected when the witnesses were accurate (50 vs. 46 percent). Reardon, M. C., & Fisher, R. P. (2011). Effect of viewing the interview and identification process on juror perceptions of eyewitness accuracy. *Applied Cognitive Psychology, 25,* 68–77.

78. Although recall from Chapter 5 that the creation of an electronic record can itself introduce bias. In particular, focusing the video camera exclusively on the suspect during interrogations inflates the perceived voluntariness of the suspect's statements and results in unwarranted trust in coerced confessions.

79. For an illuminating view of the development of the English criminal process, see Langbein (2003), *supra* note 45.

80. As Jeremy Bentham stated, "oral testimony has a great superiority over written testimony." Bentham, J. (by Dumont, M.) (1825). *Treatise on judicial evidence: Extracted from the manuscripts of Jeremy Bentham, Esq.* London: J. W. Paget.

81. Federal Bureau of Investigation (2006). Memorandum on electronic recording of confessions and witness interviews. March 23.

82. See discussion in Federal Rules of Criminal Procedure, Notes of Committee on the Judiciary, House Report 94-247 (1975 Amendment). http://www.cap defnet.org/codes/18_usc_appendix_16.htm.

83. See discussion in Thomas, G. C., III (2010). Two windows into innocence. *Ohio State Journal of Criminal Law, 7,* 575–601 (pp. 591–592).

84. See LaFave et al. (2007), *supra* note 5, §20(1).

85. See The Justice Project (2007). Expanded discovery in criminal cases: A policy review. http://www.pewtrusts.org/uploadedFiles/wwwpewtrustsorg/Reports /Death_penalty_reform/Expanded%20discovery%20policy%20brief.pdf.

86. The deposition of witnesses in criminal proceedings is permitted in some form also in Indiana, Iowa, Missouri, and North Dakota. See discussion in Thomas (2010), *supra* note 83.

87. For a critique of the FBI's objections, see Sullivan, T. P. (2008). Recording federal custodial interviews. *American Criminal Law Review, 45,* 1297–1345. Critics might oppose this proposed measure also on the grounds that it alters the principle of orality. However, as mentioned, the proposition should not be seen as a challenge to the principle of orality, as the recorded testimony should supplement, rather than replace, oral testimony.

88. For example, section 136.2 of the California Penal Code authorizes the trial court in a criminal case to issue a protective order when "upon a good cause belief that harm to, or intimidation or dissuasion of, a victim or witness has occurred or is reasonably likely to occur."

89. As the Court stated in *Crawford v. Washington* (*supra* note 7), a witness's statements will be admissible when the defendant is responsible for her unavailability for testifying in court. See also *Reynolds v. United States,* 98 U.S. 145, 158–159 (1879); *Giles v. California,* 554 U.S. 353 (2008).

90. Personal use of helmet cameras has been implemented in a number of jurisdictions, including San Jose, California, and in the United Kingdom. See Cowan, C. (2009). Helmet cams for cops. *Foxnews,* November 3. http://live shots.blogs.foxnews.com/2009/11/03/helmet-cams-for-cops/; Travis, A. (2007). Police to use helmet cams to record public order incidents. *The Guardian,* July 12. http://www.guardian.co.uk/uk/2007/jul/12/humanrights.ukcrime.

91. Nor should the policy be blocked by concerns over failures to record. See Sullivan, T. P., & Vail, A. W. (2009). The consequences of law enforcement officials' failure to record custodial interviews as required by law. *Journal of Criminal Law & Criminology, 99,* 215–234.

92. For a strong argument in favor of recording interrogations, see Sullivan (2008), *supra* note 87.

93. Statement of Alan K. Harris, Deputy Prosecutor, Hennepin County, quoted in Sullivan, T. P. (2005). Electronic recordings of custodial interrogations: Everybody wins. *Journal of Criminal Law & Criminology, 95,* 1127.

94. Bereiter, B. (2007). Lawmakers approve lineup changes. July 24. http://news14.com/content/top_stories/585227/lawmakers-approve-lineup-changes/Default.aspx.

95. On the freestanding concept of due process, see Israel, J. H. (2001). Freestanding Due Process and criminal procedure: The Supreme Court's search for interpretive guidelines. *Saint Louis University Law Journal, 45,* 303–432; Taslitz, A. (2005). What remains of reliability: Hearsay and freestanding Due Process after Crawford v. Washington. *Criminal Justice Magazine, 20(2);* Dripps, D. A. (2003). *About guilt and innocence: The origins, development, and future of constitutional criminal procedure.* Westport, CT: Praeger.

96. At the oral arguments in *Perry v. New Hampshire* (No. 10-8974, November 2, 2011), the justices seemed resolutely averse to the concept of freestanding due process rights. See Lithwick, D. (2011). See no evil: Eyewitness testimony may be unreliable, but the Supreme Court doesn't want to be the one to say so. *Slate,* November 2. http://www.slate.com/articles/news_and_politics/supreme_court_dispatches/2011/11/perry_v_new_hampshire_the_supreme_court_looks_at_eyewitness_evid.single.html. The case dealt with a suggestive lineup, which is the most notable application of a freestanding due process right. See *Manson v. Brathwaite, supra* note 35.

97. Reforms of lineup procedures have been put into effect in some ten states, including North Carolina, New Jersey, Rhode Island, Vermont, and Delaware. Mandatory taping of interrogations has been implemented by Alaska, Minnesota, North Carolina, Illinois, Wisconsin, and numerous other states. See http://www.innocenceproject.org/news/LawView5.php. For notable state court decisions, see *Stephan v. State,* 711 P.2d 1156, 1162 (Alaska, 1985); *State v. Scales,* 518 N.W.2d 587, 591 (Minnesota, 1994); *Commonwealth v. DiGiambattista,* 813 N.E.2d

516, 533–534 (Massachusetts, 2004); *State v. Larry R. Henderson* (A-8-08) (New Jersey, 062218).

98. On Dallas Count's Conviction Integrity Unit, see http://www.dallasda .com/conviction-integrity.html.

99. Suffolk County District Attorney's Office. Report of the task Force on Eyewitness Evidence. http://www.innocenceproject.org/docs/Suffolk_eyewitness .pdf.

100. See Fisher, S. Z. (2009). Eyewitness identification reform in Massachusetts. *Massachusetts Law Review, 91, 52–66.*

101. Police Chiefs' Association of Santa Clara County. Line-Up Protocol for Law Enforcement. http://www.ccfaj.org/documents/reports/eyewitness/expert/Santa %20Clara%20County%20Eyewitness%20Identification%20Protocols.pdf.

ACKNOWLEDGMENTS

I am deeply indebted to the following colleagues for reading, and very much improving, the manuscript: Scott Altman, Keith Findley, Richard Leo, Daniel Markovits, Anne Simon, Chris Slobogin, and George Thomas III. For beneficial contributions, I thank Bruce Ackerman, Albert Alschuler, Akhil Amar, Jack Balkin, Rebecca Brown, Steve Clark, Mirjan Damaška, Shari Diamond, John Donohue, Phoebe Ellsworth, Neal Feigenson, Ron Fisher, Brandon Garrett, Jon Gould, Philip Heymann, Sam Gross, Dan Kahan, Saul Kassin, Dan Klerman, Jay Koehler, John Langbein, Rob MacCoun, Richard McAdams, Tracey Meares, Charles Ogletree, Steven Penrod, Robert Post, David Sklansky, Carol Steiker, Kate Stith, Alan Stone, Lloyd Weinreb, Gary Wells, Rich Wiener, and Jim Whitman.

The book has benefited from the comments and critiques received at faculty workshops at Harvard Law School, Northwestern Law School, The University of Chicago Law School, USC Gould School of Law, and Yale Law School.

I thank my colleagues at USC's Gould School of Law for their friendship, support, and collegiality. For his generous support I thank my dean, Bob Rasmussen. Tom Lyon has been a terrific mentor and friend.

Over the years, my thinking has been enriched in numerous and imperceptible ways by teachers, colleagues, and students. I thank the many students who took an interest in this topic at Harvard Law School, USC Dornsife College of Letters, Arts and Sciences, USC Gould School of Law, and Yale Law School.

For their wonderful assistance, I thank the staff of the library at USC Gould School of Law: Luis Alas, Pauline Aranas, Judy Davis, Cindy Guyer, Diana Jaque, Rosanne Krikorian, Paul Moorman, Wendy Nobunaga, Anahit Petrosyan, Brian Raphael, Claudia Raphael, Karen Skinner, Leonette Williams, and Jessica Wimer. Thanks are due also to my research assistants, Matt Bennett, Philip Gutierez, Chistopher Hasbrouck, and Kyle Kinkead.

I am indebted to Keith Holyoak for chaperoning me into the world of experimental psychology, and to Steve Read for the sustained collaboration. Doug Stenstrom has been helpful in many ways.

Much gratitude is owed to Elizabeth Knoll of Harvard University Press for captaining the manuscript from conception to completion. Thanks also to the folks at Westchester Book Services for their fine editorial work.

I owe deep gratitude and respect to Jennifer Thompson-Cannino—a victim and a hero—for opening the eyes of many, mine included.

Finally, and most fondly, I thank my children, Alexandra, Ellie, and Noah, for being so cool and understanding of their father, who seemed at times incapable of completing this manuscript.

INDEX

Abductive reasoning, 21–22, 24, 238n15

Accountability, 39–40, 377n20; ameliorative effects, 39, 48, 220; bias increased by, 39, 258n200; and institutional oversight, 39; via transparency, 48

Accuracy, 2–4, 206–222; and denial of error, 213–215, 379n43, 379–380n51, 380n54, 381nn57,64,66; and deposition of witnesses, 219–220, 383n86; of event memories, 92–95, 287nn16,17, 287–288n18 (see also under Fact-finding at trial); exonerations' implications for, 4 (see also Exonerations); factors affecting, overview, 3; factors in eyewitness identification, 57; factual, marginalization of, 209–213, 375nn2,7,8, 375–376n10, 376nn12,13, 376–377n16, 377nn18,19,20,21, 377–378n22, 378nn27,29,30,32; limited diagnosticity of adjudication, 204, 373nn205,206, 374nn207,208; and plea bargaining, 16, 210; and protection of witnesses, 220, 383n88; rate in eyewitness identification, overview, 53–55, 262nn5,6, 263nn8,9, 264nn12,13; of raw vs. synthesized testimony, 15, 146, 219, 236n74; as reform goal, 14–16, 208–209;

shortfall, 3–4, 206–209; shortfall, narrowing, 215–221, 381–382n68, 382nn71,72,74,75, 382–383n77, 383nn78,80,86,87,88,89, 384nn90,91. *See also under* Fact-finding at trial

Adjudication breakdowns, 7–8, 207–208, 232nn40,42

Adjudicative process, limited diagnosticity of, 3, 204, 373nn205,206, 374nn207,208. *See also* Fact-finding at trial; Fact-finding mechanisms

Adversarial process, 26, 208, 210–211, 214, 218, 235n65, 261n241, 376n16, 380n52. *See also* Informational disadvantage

Adversarial pull, 31–33, 48–49, 251n138, 252nn145,146, 252–253n147, 253n148

Aggravating factors, 189–191, 357n72

Alibi testimony, 163–165, 178, 338nn133,135,136, 339nn138,139, 141,143

Alicke, M. D., 248n110

Allport, Gordon, 100, 294n62

Al Qaeda, 40–42, 252n145

American Bar Association, 380n54

American Society of Trial Consultants, 170

Amygdala activity, 300n107

Catalan, Juan, 338n135, 339n138
Ceballos, Richard, 150n131
Central Park Jogger case, 121, 161, 252n145, 310n5
Chatman, Charles, 339n141
Circuitous influences. *See* Coherence effect
Clark, Robert, 372n185
Clark, S. E., 277n114
Clemency, 379n33
Cognition/metacognition (metamemory), 58, 60, 104
Cognitive dissonance theory, 248n112, 255n172, 381n63
Cognitive Interview, 118, 141, 287n16, 309–310n204, 310n205
Cognitive psychology, 2
Cognitive Reflection Task, 326n21
Coherence effect, 33–36, 75, 174–177, 186, 254nn159,161,163, 255n165, 354n50, 370n170. *See also under* Fact-finding at trial
Cole, Timothy, 165, 339n143
Coleman v. Alabama, 257n196
Collaborative inhibition, 369n158
Columbo, Detective (fictional character), 141–142
Commitment effect, 67–68, 155–156, 272n82
Commitment escalation, 29–31, 248nn112,113,114, 249nn115,117, 250nn131,132,133, 250–251n135
Common law, 373n206
Competence and self-concept, 30, 247n107
Confessions: admissibility, 161, 178, 310n2, 335n112, 336n121, 350n234, 375–376n10; as basis for false convictions, 7, 118–122; as evidence, 160–162, 335nn111,112, 336nn113,121, 337nn122,123,124, 128,130; as evidence of last resort, 120; regularity of, 120; Supreme Court on, 134–135, 139, 143, 310n2; third-degree methods used, 132; true vs. false, 121. *See also* Interrogating suspects

Confidence/confidence inflation, 115, 308nn181,183,188,191
Congruence heuristic, 255n169
Conversation Management, 141
Conviction Integrity Unit (Dallas County District Attorney's Office), 46–47, 221, 261n239
Cotton (Ronald) case: alibi testimony, 165; conviction/sentencing, 18; defense attorney, 236n2; evidence, 18–20; evidence transformations, 6–7; exoneration, 18, 229n22; Gauldin's role, 19, 57, 69, 113, 229n22, 236n2; inflation of victim's confidence, 76, 78; Poole as true perpetrator, 18–19, 65, 68; previous convictions of Cotton, 17–18; victims'/witness's identification, 18–20, 57, 65, 67–69, 80, 90–91, 156, 231n37; victims'/witness's motivation, 146–147. *See also* Thompson, Jennifer
Court-appointed attorneys, 233n53
Crawford v. Washington, 383n89
Crimes: arrest-to-adjudication period, 15, 236n73; cleared by arrest, 4, 26–27, 226n8, 243n70; failure to punish, 4, 226n9; as underreported, 4, 27, 225n7. *See also* Murder cases; Rape cases
Criminal Interrogation and Confessions (Reid & Associates), 122, 127–130, 139, 316nn70,72,73, 318n90, 318–319n91, 320n108. *See also* BAI
Criminal investigations. *See* Investigations, psychological aspects; Investigations in criminal cases
Crombag, H. M., 295n68
Cross-examination, 180–183, 209–210, 350nn1,5,8, 351nn12,17
Crowe, Michael, 132
Culpability cases, 9, 90, 108, 117, 228n19
Curative instructions, 186–188, 353n36, 354nn40,44,49,50, 355nn52,53, 355–356n57, 356nn65,66

348n217; reform recommendations, 177–179, 349nn230,231,233, 350n234; reliance on witness confidence, 153–154, 158, 330nn63,64, 331nn67,68, 334n95; seeing is believing, 154; sensitivity to accuracy factors, 152–153, 329nn51,52,53,55, 330nn56,59,60; story model of persuasion, 169–170, 177, 341n163, 341–342n164; substandard investigations, 145–146, 217; synthesized testimony, 146, 159–160, 167, 219, 236n74; System I vs. II cognitive processing, 342n165; and trust in accuracy of identifications, 55; valence judgments (goodness vs. badness), 173, 346n203; witness preparation, 147, 182, 210, 376n13

Fact-finding mechanisms, 180–205; appellate and post-conviction review, 202–203, 205, 211–212, 372nn193, 194, 373nn197,202; comprehending/complying with jury instructions, 199, 369n160, 369–370n165, 370nn166,167; conclusion and reform recommendations, 203–205, 373nn205,206, 374nn207,208,210; cross-examination, 180–183, 209–210, 350nn1,5,8, 351nn12,17; deterring false testimony, 181–182; drawing inferences, 199–200, 370n169, 370–371n170; exposing false testimony, 182–183, 350nn5,8, 351nn12,17; improving memory of trial evidence, 198–199, 369nn156,158,159; informational persuasion, 198–200, 369nn156, 158,159,160, 369–370n165, 370nn166,167,169, 370–371n170; jurors' assurance of impartiality, 192–193, 360nn92,94,95, 361nn96,98,99, 362n105; jury deliberation, overview, 197–202, 366nn143,144, 367nn145,146,147, 367–368n148, 368nn149,151, 152,153, 372nn185,191,192; jury polarization, 201–202,

372nn191,192; jury selection, 171, 192, 210, 360n92, 376n12; limited diagnosticity of adjudication, 204, 373nn205,206, 374nn207,208; overview, 180, 207–208; preponderance of evidence standard, 196, 365n139, 365–366n140; presumption of innocence, 193–195, 362nn108,109,111, 363nn115, 116,117; prosecutor's burden of production, 194, 363nn115,116,117; reasonable doubt standard, 193, 195–197, 363nn119,121,122, 363–364n124, 364nn127,128, 130,131,132, 365nn138,139, 365–366n140, 366n141; social influence, 198, 200–201, 371nn173,174,175,177; strength of the inculpating evidence, 204, 374n210. *See also* Jury instructions

False acquittals, 4, 13–14, 90, 193, 196, 365n138

False convictions: adjudication breakdowns, 7–8, 232nn40,42; aversion to, 193; denial of incidence of, 379–380n51; innocence commissions for correcting, 381–382n68; investigation breakdowns, 5–7, 230nn27,29,31, 231nn37,38, 231–232n39; legitimacy, 215; via misidentification, 55, 150, 264n12; nonevidential factors, 231–232n39; pseudo-corroboration's role, 148; rate, 4, 227n15, 379–380n51; reasons for reducing incidence of, 13–14, 235n69; Supreme Court on, 213–214

False memories. *See under* Memory

Familiarity effect, 67, 155

FBI (Federal Bureau of Investigation): Mayfield case, 40–43, 46, 258n203, 259nn207,209,211,217,221; Murrah Federal Building bombing, 268n49; on sharing interrogation tapes with the defense, 219

Federal Judicial Center, 364n127

CPSIA information can be obtained
at www.ICGtesting.com
Printed in the USA
JSHW041045141222
34210JS00007BA/51/J

9 780674 046153